S0-BEP-657

BEST PRACTICES IN LITERACY INSTRUCTION

BEST PRACTICES IN LITERACY INSTRUCTION

Third Edition

Linda B. Gambrell
Lesley Mandel Morrow
Michael Pressley
Editors

Foreword by John T. Guthrie

THE GUILFORD PRESS
New York London

A Division of Guilford Publications, Inc.
72 Spring Street, New York, NY 10012
www.guilford.com

Printed in the United States of America

This book is printed on acid-free paper.

Last digit is print number: 9 8 7 6 5 4 3 2 1

Library of Congress Cataloging-in-Publication Data

Best practices in literacy instruction / edited by Linda B. Gambrell, Lesley Mandel Morrow, Michael Pressley ; foreword by John T. Guthrie.— 3rd ed.

p. cm.

Includes bibliographical references and index.

ISBN-13: 978-1-59385-391-4 (pbk. : alk. paper)

ISBN-10: 1-59385-391-2 (pbk. : alk. paper)

ISBN-13: 978-1-59385-392-1 (hardcover : alk. paper)

ISBN-10: 1-59385-392-0 (hardcover : alk. paper)

1. Language arts—United States. 2. Reading comprehension—United States. 3. Literacy—United States. I. Gambrell, Linda B. II. Morrow, Lesley Mandel. III. Pressley, Michael.

LB1576.B486 2007

372.6—dc22 2006028659

ABOUT THE EDITORS

Linda B. Gambrell, PhD, is a Professor in the Eugene T. Moore School of Education at Clemson University. Prior to coming to Clemson University, she was Associate Dean for Research at the University of Maryland. From 1992 to 1997, she was principal investigator at the National Reading Research Center, where she directed the Literacy Motivation Project. Dr. Gambrell began her career as an elementary classroom teacher and reading specialist in the public schools. She has written books on reading instruction and has published in such journals as the *Reading Research Quarterly, The Reading Teacher, Educational Psychologist,* and *Journal of Educational Research.* She has served as President of the National Reading Conference and the College Reading Association and was recently elected to serve as President of the International Reading Association (2007–2008). In 2004 she was elected to the Reading Hall of Fame. Prior awards include the 1998 International Reading Association's Outstanding Teacher Educator in Reading Award, the 2001 National Reading Conference's Albert J. Kingston Award, and the 2002 College Reading Associate Laureate Award. Dr. Gambrell's current interests are in the areas of reading comprehension strategy instruction, literacy motivation, and the role of discussion in teaching and learning.

Lesley Mandel Morrow, PhD, holds the rank of Professor II at Rutgers University's Graduate School of Education, where she is Chair of the Department of Learning and Teaching. She began her career as a classroom teacher, then became a reading specialist, and later received her PhD from

Fordham University. Her area of research deals with early literacy development and the organization and management of language arts programs. Her research is carried out with children and families from diverse backgrounds. Dr. Morrow has produced more than 250 publications, including journal articles, chapters in books, monographs, and books. She has received numerous grants from the federal government for her research and has served as a principal research investigator for several research centers. She received Excellence in Research, Teaching, and Service Awards from Rutgers University, as well as the International Reading Association's Outstanding Teacher Educator in Reading Award and Fordham University's Alumni Award for Outstanding Achievement. Dr. Morrow was an elected member of the Board of Directors of the International Reading Association and served as president of the organization in 2003–2004. She is an elected member of the Reading Hall of Fame.

Michael Pressley, PhD, who passed away in May 2006, was University Distinguished Professor at Michigan State University, as well as Director of the Doctoral Program in Teacher Education and Director of the Literacy Achievement Research Center, with both roles part of his professorship in the Department of Teacher Education and the Department of Counseling, Educational Psychology, and Special Education. He was an expert on effective elementary literacy instruction, with his research appearing in more than 350 journal articles, chapters, and books. Dr. Pressley served a 6-year term as editor of *Journal of Educational Psychology*. He was honored with awards from the National Reading Conference, the International Reading Association, the American Educational Research Association, and the American Psychological Association, among others. Dr. Pressley received the 2004 E. L. Thorndike Award from Division 15 of the American Psychological Association, which is the highest award given for career research accomplishment in educational psychology. Previous awardees include Jean Piaget, B. F. Skinner, and Jerome Bruner. For many teachers and K–6 students, he was best known as the coauthor of Open Court Reading and Writing, the reading series widely regarded as the most scientifically evidence-based instructional program currently available. Recent calls across the United States for balanced literacy instruction were anticipated in the conception developed by Dr. Pressley in *Reading Instruction That Works: The Case for Balanced Teaching*, now in its third edition.

CONTRIBUTORS

Peter Afflerbach is Professor at the Reading Center, Department of Curriculum and Instruction, at the University of Maryland, College Park. Dr. Afflerbach's interests include reading assessment, reading comprehension, and the use of the verbal reporting methodology. His work appears in theoretical and practical journals, including *Reading Research Quarterly*, *Journal of Literacy Research*, *Cognition and Instruction*, *Elementary School Journal*, *Journal of Adolescent and Adult Literacy*, and *The Reading Teacher*. Dr. Afflerbach serves on the Reading Committee of the National Assessment of Educational Progress (NAEP), the 2009 Reading Framework Committee of NAEP, and the Reading Committee of the National Assessment of Adult Literacy. He is an editor of the forthcoming *Handbook of Reading Research* (fourth edition) and serves on the editorial advisory boards of *Journal of Educational Psychology* and *Reading Research Quarterly*.

Richard L. Allington is Professor of Education at the University of Tennessee. He has served as President of the International Reading Association and the National Reading Conference and has been named to the Reading Hall of Fame. He has written extensively on the topics of struggling readers and exemplary classroom reading instruction. Dr. Allington's books include *Classrooms That Work* and *Schools That Work*, both coauthored with Patricia M. Cunningham; *What Really Matters for Struggling Readers*; and most recently *Big Brother and the National Reading Curriculum: How Ideology Trumped Evidence.*

Kim Baker is Associate Professor in the School of Education at the Sage Colleges in Troy, New York. She is Program Director of Literacy/Special Education and Special Education at the graduate level. In addition to teaching undergraduate- and graduate-level language arts courses, she also works closely with an after-school enrichment and literacy program in the inner city. She has been an elementary school teacher in Missouri and New York. An active member of many professional organizations, Dr. Baker was Chair of the Teacher as Researcher Committee for the International Reading Association, encouraging teachers to be active participants as they reflect on and research their classroom practice.

Rita M. Bean is Professor of Education at the University of Pittsburgh, where she teaches graduate reading courses. She also serves as Co-Director of the LEADERS Project, a multiyear professional development initiative for teachers, kindergarten to third grade. Dr. Bean recently completed a 4-year term as a member of the Board of Directors of the International Reading Association. She has been a classroom teacher and a reading specialist for kindergarten through grade 12. She is active in reading organizations on the state and national levels. Her interests include the role of the reading specialist, reading instruction, and reading teacher preparation. Dr. Bean has published articles in *The Reading Teacher, Reading Research and Instruction, Reading and Writing Quarterly, Journal of Research in Education,* and numerous other journals.

Vicki L. Benson is currently studying mild and moderate reading disabilities in the Special Education doctoral program at the University of California, Berkeley. Prior to entering the program, she taught at the elementary level, earned her MA as a Reading Specialist, and conducted educational research. As a doctoral student, her research interests are examining the underpinnings of reading difficulties, refining instructional methods, and developing teacher education.

Camille L. Z. Blachowicz is Professor of Education at the National College of Education of National-Louis University, where she directs the Reading Program and teaches courses related to diagnosis and remediation of reading difficulties and reading research. Her books include *Teaching Vocabulary in All Classrooms* (with Peter J. Fisher) and *Reading Comprehension: Strategies for Independent Learners.* Along with her research, writing, and staff development, she is Co-Director of Literacy Partners, a literacy improvement project funded by the Chicago Community Trust and the Chicago Public Schools, and Director of the Early Literacy Technology Project, funded by the Spencer Foundation.

Cathy Collins Block is Professor of Education at Texas Christian University (TCU) in Fort Worth, Texas. She has served on the Board of Directors of the International Reading Association and the National Reading Conference. Dr. Block has written extensively in the fields of comprehension and vocabulary development, exemplary teaching practices, and the effects of curricular initiatives. Recently published books include *Metacognition in Literacy and Learning, Comprehension Process Instruction: Creating Reading Success in Grades K–3, Powerful Vocabulary for Reading Success* (curricula for grades 3–6), *The Vocabulary Enriched Classroom,* and *Reading First and Beyond: The Complete Guide for Teachers and Literacy Coaches.* She received the TCU Chancellor's Award for Distinguished Achievement as a Creative Teacher and Scholar and has written more than 80 research articles for *Reading Research Quarterly, The Reading Teacher, Journal of Adolescent and Adult Literacy,* and *The Elementary School Journal.*

Karen Bromley is Distinguished Professor in the School of Education at Binghamton University, State University of New York (SUNY), where she teaches courses in literacy, language arts, and children's literature. She is the recipient of the SUNY Chancellor's Award for Excellence in Teaching and the New York State Reading Educator Award. Before coming to Binghamton, she was a third-grade teacher and reading specialist in New York and Maryland. Dr. Bromley has written several books for classroom teachers on topics related to comprehension, vocabulary, and writing, and has contributed many chapters and articles to professional books and journals.

María S. Carlo is a psychologist studying bilingualism in children and adults. Her research focuses on the cognitive processes that underlie reading in a second language and understanding the differences in the reading processes of bilinguals and monolinguals. Dr. Carlo is Assistant Professor of Teaching and Learning in the School of Education at the University of Miami. She is coprincipal investigator on three federally funded research projects that study the Spanish and English literacy development of Latino/a children in grades K–5. From 2004 to 2006 she was a member of the National Academies Board on Testing and Assessment Committee on the U.S. Naturalization Test Redesign.

Patricia M. Cunningham is Professor at Wake Forest University. Her research interests include finding alternative ways to teach children for whom learning to read is difficult. She is the author of *Reading and Writing in Elementary Classrooms* and *Phonics They Use: Words for Reading and Writing.* She is also coauthor, with Richard L. Allington, of *Classrooms That*

Work and *Schools That Work.* Along with Dorothy Hall, Dr. Cunningham developed the Four Blocks literacy framework, which is currently used as the balanced literacy framework in thousands of classrooms throughout the United States. She and Dorothy Hall are also Co-Directors of the Four Blocks Literacy Center, which is housed at Wake Forest University.

Douglas Fisher is Professor of Language and Literacy Education in the Department of Teacher Education at San Diego State University (SDSU) and the Director of Professional Development for the City Heights Educational Collaborative. He is the recipient of an International Reading Association Celebrate Literacy Award, as well as a Christa McAuliffe Award for excellence in teacher education. Dr. Fisher has published numerous articles on reading and literacy, differentiated instruction, and curriculum design, as well as books, such as *Improving Adolescent Literacy: Strategies at Work* and *Language Arts Workshop: Purposeful Reading and Writing Instruction.* He has taught a variety of courses in SDSU's teacher-credentialing program, as well as graduate-level courses on English language development and literacy. He has also taught classes in English, writing, and literacy development to public school students.

Peter J. Fisher is Professor of Education at the National College of Education of National-Louis University. Dr. Fisher taught in elementary and high schools in England prior to coming to the United States to pursue doctoral studies at the State University of New York at Buffalo. His research interests include vocabulary development and instruction and the role of storytelling in education, and his work has been supported by grants from the Spencer Foundation and the Illinois State Board of Higher Education. In 1997 he was inducted into the Illinois Reading Hall of Fame. Dr. Fisher is coauthor (with Camille L. Z. Blachowicz) of *Teaching Vocabulary in All Classrooms* and the author of numerous articles and book chapters. He has been a featured speaker at state and local conferences.

James Flood, Distinguished Professor of Education at San Diego State University (SDSU), has taught in preschool, elementary, and secondary schools, and has served as a language arts supervisor and vice principal. He has also been a Fulbright Scholar at the University of Lisbon in Portugal and President of the National Reading Conference. Dr. Flood has chaired and co-chaired many International Reading Association, National Council of Teachers of English, National Council on Rehabilitation Education, and National Reading Council committees, and has coauthored and edited many articles, columns, texts, handbooks, and children's materials on reading and language arts issues. Included are those that were codeveloped with Diane Lapp: *Content Area Reading and Learning,* which is in its second edition, and *The Handbook of Research on Teaching Literacy through the Communicative and Visual Arts*. His many educational awards include being named as the Outstanding Teacher Educator in the Department of Teacher Education at SDSU, the Distinguished Research Lecturer from SDSU's Graduate Division of Research, and a member of both California's and the International Reading Association's Hall of Fame. Dr. Flood is a coeditor of *The California Reader* and a member of the Board of Directors of the International Reading Association.

Linda B. Gambrell (*see* About the Editors).

Linda Kucan is Assistant Professor in the Department of Instruction and Learning at the University of Pittsburgh. Her research interests include multitext/multigenre contexts for learning, as well as comprehension, vocabulary, and teacher discourse.

Melanie R. Kuhn is Assistant Professor in Literacy Education at the Rutgers Graduate School of Education, where she teaches courses on assessment and instruction for struggling readers. She has a broad range of teaching experience, from a bilingual public school in Boston to work with struggling readers at an international school in London. Dr. Kuhn has been engaged in research grants on fluency, assistive technology, and, most recently, as part of the Mid-Atlantic Collaborative for Applied Research in Education. She was selected as the recipient of the National Reading Conference's Early Career Achievement Award for 2005. She is also the author or coauthor of several chapters and articles, with Steven Stahl, including "Fluency: A Review of Developmental and Remedial Practices" in the *Journal of Educational Psychology*. Her research interests include literacy instruction for struggling readers, comprehension development, and vocabulary instruction.

Linda D. Labbo is Professor of Language and Literacy Education at the University of Georgia. Her early career included teaching kindergarten through fifth grade. She conducts research on early literacy development, focusing on computer-related literacy instruction and preservice teacher preparation. Dr. Labbo has coauthored, written, and edited handbooks, columns, books, and articles in such journals as *Reading Research Quarterly*, *Language Arts*, *Journal of Literacy Research*, and *The Reading Teacher*. Her coedited book, with David Reinking, Michael McKenna, and Ronald Kieffer, *Handbook of Literacy and Technology: Transformations in a Post-Typographic Word* (currently in its second edition), won an American Library Association Award and the Edward Fry Book Award from the National Reading Conference. Her educational awards include the Computers in Reading Research

Award from the International Reading Association's Technology in Literacy Education Special Interest Group and a Phi Delta Kappa Faculty Research Award. Dr. Labbo currently serves as a co-primary investigator on a grant funded by the National Science Foundation to develop and examine the effectiveness of interactive multimedia anchor cases on preservice teachers' professional development.

Laura Lang is a reading specialist, English teacher, and Academic Assistance Coordinator at New Trier High School's freshman campus in Northfield, Illinois. She spearheaded the development of New Trier's Literacy Team, an ongoing collaboration of content-area teachers from the freshman campus. Ms. Lang also serves as a literacy consultant to the American history grant "Creating a Community of Scholars." She earned a BS in English Education from Northwestern University in 1996 and in 2000 received an MSEd with a concentration in reading from National-Louis University.

Diane Lapp, Distinguished Professor of Education in the Department of Teacher Education at San Diego State University, has taught in elementary and middle schools. Her major areas of research and instruction are related to struggling readers and their families who live in urban settings. Dr. Lapp serves as a director and instructor of field-based preservice and graduate programs and continues to team teach in public school classrooms. She has coauthored and edited many articles, columns, texts, handbooks, and children's materials on reading and language arts issues. These include *Teaching Reading to Every Child*, a reading methods textbook in its fourth edition; *Content Reading Instruction, Third Edition*; and *The Handbook of Research in Teaching the English Language Arts, Second Edition.* She has chaired and co-chaired several International Reading Association (IRA) and National Reading Conference committees and is currently the Co-Chair of IRA's Early Literacy Commission. Her educational awards include the California Reading Hall of Fame, the International Reading Association Hall of Fame, and IRA's 1996 Outstanding Teacher Educator of the Year. Dr. Lapp is the coeditor of California's literacy journal *The California Reader.*

Christina L. Madda is a doctoral student in Literacy, Language, and Culture at the University of Illinois, Chicago. She formerly taught English as a Second Language before earning an MA in Learning Sciences at Northwestern University, where she also went on to work as a research analyst. Her current research interests include family literacy and issues related to biliteracy.

Jacquelynn A. Malloy is a doctoral candidate at Clemson University's Eugene T. Moore School of Education. She is a member of Clemson's Internet Reading Research Group and is involved in a 3-year Institute of Education Sciences grant (in collaboration with the University of Connecticut) to investigate the Internet reading comprehension skills of middle-school students at risk of dropping out. Ms. Malloy is an assistant editor of *Reading Research Quarterly* and associate editor of *Reading Matters*, a journal of the South Carolina Reading Association. Her research interests include literacy motivation, the use of technology in the classroom, and metacognition.

Susan Anders Mazzoni is a literacy coach for public school systems and teaches in the Department of Curriculum and Instruction at the University of Maryland, College Park. She has worked as a research assistant at the national Reading Research Center. Her work has been published in *The Reading Teacher*, *Reading Psychology*, and *Educational Psychology Review*, as well as in a number of edited books. Ms. Mazzoni has teaching experience in Baltimore County and Baltimore city public schools and also has extensive experience teaching adult literacy. Her research interests are in the areas of metacognition, comprehension, and motivation.

Michael C. McKenna is Thomas G. Jewell Professor of Reading at the University of Virginia. He has authored, coauthored, or edited 15 books and more than 80 articles, chapters, and technical reports on a range of literacy topics. His books include *The Literacy Coach's Handbook*, *Assessment for Reading Instruction*, *Help for Struggling Readers*, *Teaching through Text*, and *Issues and Trends in Literacy Education*. Dr. McKenna's research has been sponsored by the National Reading Research Center and the Center for the Improvement of Early Reading Achievement. He is the co-winner of the National Reading Conference's Edward Fry Book Award and American Library Association's Award for Outstanding Academic Books. He serves on the editorial board of *Reading Research Quarterly*, and his articles have appeared in that journal as well as the *Journal of Educational Psychology*, *Educational Researcher*, *The Reading Teacher*, and others. He has co-edited themed issues of the *Peabody Journal of Education* and *Reading and Writing Quarterly*. His research interests include comprehension in content settings, reading attitudes, technology applications, and beginning reading.

Aimee Morewood is currently a doctoral candidate in Reading Education at the University of Pittsburgh. She has worked for 2 years on Pennsylvania's External Evaluation Team for Reading First and is the Reading Supervisor for the University of Pittsburgh's Reading Clinic. She has presented at conferences at both the local and national levels. Ms. Morewood's interests include the impact of professional development on teacher change and student achievement, as well as clinical experiences included in reading specialist programs.

Lesley Mandel Morrow (*see* About the Editors).

Donna Ogle is Professor of Reading and Language at the National College of Education, National-Louis University, in Chicago. She is past president of the International Reading Association and former board member of the National Reading Conference. Dr. Ogle is currently directing two grants in Chicago schools: Project ALL (Advancing Literacy for Learning in Grades 4–8) and the McDougal Foundation Transitional Literacy Project (linking middle and high school teachers with students and families), and is senior consultant to the Chicago Striving Readers Grant. Her coauthored books include *Reading Comprehension: Strategies for Independent Learners, Integrating Instruction: Science and Literacy,* and *Literacy for a Democratic Society.*

P. David Pearson serves as Dean of the Graduate School of Education at the University of California, Berkeley, and as a faculty member in its Language and Literacy program. His current research focuses on issues of reading instruction and reading assessment policies and practices at all levels—local, state, and national.

Michael Pressley (*see* About the Editors).

Taffy E. Raphael is a member of the Literacy, Language and Culture faculty in Literacy Education at the University of Illinois, Chicago (UIC). Prior to joining the UIC faculty, Dr. Raphael taught intermediate-grade students in Illinois and North Carolina. In addition, she has taught and conducted research at the University of Utah (1980–1982), Michigan State University (1982–1997), and Oakland University (1997–2001). Dr. Raphael's work was recognized by her receiving the 1997 Outstanding Teacher Educator in Reading Award from the International Reading Association. Her research has focused on question–answer relationships and strategy instruction in writing and, for the past decade, Book Club, a literature-based reading program. She has published in the leading research journals and has coauthored and edited several books on literacy instruction. She is currently Director of Partnership READ, a school–university partnership to improve literacy instruction through professional development, funded through the Searle Funds of the Chicago

Community Trust and recognized by the American Association of Colleges for Teacher Education's 2006 Best Practices Award for Effective Partnerships. She was selected for the International Reading Association Reading Hall of Fame in 2002.

Timothy Rasinski is Professor of Literacy Education at Kent State University. He has written over 150 articles and authored, coauthored, or edited many books and curriculum programs on reading education. He is coauthor of the award-winning fluency program Fluency First (Wright Group). His interests include reading fluency, word study, and teaching struggling readers in the elementary and middle grades. His research on reading has been cited by the National Reading Panel and has been published in such journals as *Reading Research Quarterly*, *The Reading Teacher*, *Reading Psychology*, and the *Journal of Educational Research*. Dr. Rasinski served on the Board of Directors of the International Reading Association and was coeditor of *The Reading Teacher*, the world's most widely read journal of literacy education. He currently serves as coeditor of the *Journal of Literacy Research*. Dr. Rasinski served as President of the College Reading Association and won the A. B. Herr Award from the College Reading Association for his scholarly contributions to literacy education. Prior to coming to Kent State University, he taught as an elementary classroom and Title I teacher in rural Nebraska.

David Reinking is the Eugene T. Moore Endowed Professor of Teacher Education at Clemson University. He is currently coeditor of *Reading Research Quarterly*, one of the leading research journals in the field of education. Previously, he was editor of the *Journal of Literacy Research*, published by the National Reading Conference. For more than 20 years Dr. Reinking's published research and scholarship have focused on how digital technologies affect reading and writing and how those technologies might be integrated into literacy instruction. He served as the lead editor for the first volume of the *Handbook of Literacy and Technology*, which won two awards, and he is coeditor of the recently published second volume. Currently, he is coprincipal investigator for a major project funded by the U.S. Office of Education investigating Internet comprehension among middle school students at risk of dropping out of school.

D. Ray Reutzel is the Emma Eccles Jones Endowed Professor of Early Childhood Education at Utah State University, where he directs the Center for Early Childhood Education and is a member of the Department of Elementary Education. He began his career as a kindergarten teacher and later taught grades 1, 3, and 6. His area of research includes early literacy, fluency, and teacher knowledge for reading instruction. Dr. Reutzel has produced more than 150 publications, including articles in *Early Childhood Research Quarterly, Reading Research Quarterly, Journal of Educational Research, Journal of Literacy Research, Reading Psychology, Language Arts,* and *The Reading Teacher.* His recent books include *The Essentials of Teaching Children to Read* and *Strategies for Reading Assessment and Instruction: Helping Every Child Succeed.* He received the College Reading Association's A. B. Herr Award for Published Contributions to Reading Education and Utah State University's Alumni Award for Outstanding Professional Achievement and Researcher of the Year in the College of Education and Human Service. He is a coeditor of *The Reading Teacher* and was recently elected Vice President of the College Reading Association.

Diane H. Tracey is Associate Professor of Education at Kean University, where she teaches graduate classes to students pursuing their master's degrees as reading specialists. She has written widely on topics related to literacy achievement, is a recipient of state and federal grant awards, and is an active presenter at national conferences. Her most recent publication is *Lenses on Reading: An Introduction to Theories and Models,* written with Lesley Mandel Morrow. She has served on editorial review boards for the *Journal of Literacy Research, The Reading Teacher,* and the *National Conference Yearbook,* and is past chair of the International Reading Association's Technology Committee. In addition to university teaching, Dr. Tracey is a literacy consultant for school districts and educational software companies.

Tricia A. Zucker is a doctoral student in Reading Education at the University of Virginia's Curry School of Education. Her research interests include emergent and beginning readers, literacy and technology, and differentiated instruction. She is currently exploring how tutors and parent volunteers can support students' literacy development with technology and effective methods for differentiating instruction at independent literacy centers.

A TRIBUTE TO MICHAEL PRESSLEY (1951–2006)

The publication of the third edition of *Best Practices in Literacy Instruction* is occasion for both joy and sadness. The joy is that we have had the opportunity to work closely with noted scholars to develop a collection of research-based readings on topics that are both current and significant in the field of literacy. The sadness is the loss of Michael Pressley, our dear friend, colleague, and coeditor. Michael passed away in May 2006, having worked on this third edition up until shortly before his passing. We dedicate this edition to Michael with deep love and appreciation.

Michael's career was prodigious and exemplary. He began his career as a cognitive psychologist and then turned to research in classrooms to learn as much as he could about creating the very best reading teachers. He held positions at the University of Wisconsin (postdoctoral), California State University–Fullerton, the University of Western Ontario, the University of Maryland, the State University of New York–Albany, and the University of Notre Dame, and completed his career in the College of Education in the Department of Teacher Education/Educational Psychology at Michigan State University. His more than 350 publications in journals, books, and book chapters have made a huge contribution to comprehension strategy instruction, the development of cognitive monitoring skills, and exemplary teaching. He served as coeditor of *Journal of Reading Behavior* and *Applied Cognitive Psychology*, and editor of *Journal of Educational Psychology*. He was the recipient of many awards and recognitions, including the American Psychological Society Early Contribution Award, the American Educational Research Association Sylvia Scribner Award, the International Reading Association Albert B. Harris Award, the National Reading Conference Oscar Causey Award, the American Psychological Society Thorndike Award, and election to the Reading Hall of Fame.

In addition to his tremendous contributions to the field of literacy, he was a personality that will never be forgotten. He was a devoted husband to Donna and father to Tim. He always talked about his family to his colleagues with great pride, love, and affection. Michael was honest and passionate about his work. He said and wrote what he believed to be right and just, without concern for ramifications. You didn't have to worry about what Michael was thinking—he said it all. You always knew where you stood with him. Occasionally, Michael seemed like a lion, but this man was truly a kind and gentle lamb who cared deeply about his students and colleagues. He was also an eccentric. On any given day you might see him dressed in a baseball jacket, tee shirt, and cap, then the next day he would look like an ad for *Gentlemen's Quarterly*.

All of us who knew Michael or read his work have been moved by his passion for literacy. His impact in the field of literacy has been phenomenal. He was exceptionally intelligent and insightful, and he understood the art and the science of teaching. He also had the capacity to figure out the science of reading, and he knew what could be done in schools to improve literacy instruction. He definitively was an original—quite a character—which was part of his attraction and charm. Michael will be greatly missed, but there is no doubt that his legacy in literacy instruction will live on for years to come.

FOREWORD

The title *Best Practices in Literacy Instruction* promises a lot, but the contents of the volume deliver even more. These pages can accurately be described as "must" reading for reading teachers and aspiring classroom educators.

TARGETING TEACHER EXPERTISE

Deep inside each author in this book is a faith in teachers. This faith affirms that teachers count and their professionalism is a necessity. In today's politicized climate of school accountability and "teaching to the test," the expertise of educators becomes vital. A script cannot teach children—only a teacher can teach children. This volume conveys the understanding of literacy and its learning that all educators need. This knowledge includes what reading is, how children learn, and how expert teachers orchestrate a classroom into a productive hum of literacy learning.

NEW ACTORS ON STAGE

It is sensible to ask what the third edition of this book contains that the second one did not provide. For one thing, new authors were invited to this stage. While the best chapters from the preceding edition have been retained, new and crucial ones have been added. With each chapter written by a nationally known author, the leaders in the field have radically updated the previous edition. Newly minted ideas and recent refinements on older ones run through these pages. In these chapters the voices of experience speak loudly and clearly. They ring with an urgent and action-oriented tone. These authors are persuasive about their perspectives for how best to move children toward higher literacy.

BRIMMING WITH BEST PRACTICE

New themes in this book include direct portraits of professional development in reading. Based on successful programs in education generally and detailed descriptions of preservice and inservice reading education, you will find excellent guidelines for the most complex of qualities—teacher expertise. There are two completely new chapters on topics of current interest—English-language learners and the professional development of literacy teachers. An expanded treatment of helping students navigate nonfiction text is provided. A sweeping portrait of comprehensive literacy instruction is offered, with principle number one being "fostering literacy motivation." Chapter 1 illustrates the vital roles of authentic reading, collaborative learning, and the power of children's choice. A new treatment is provided for multitexts, multimedia, and their integration in compelling contexts for learning. Adolescent literacy, which may be the most rapidly rising new topic in the field, is treated with the depth that it demands. The importance of helping adolescents become aware of their reading, to take charge of their literacy through metacognition, and to grow in engagement are all treated eloquently.

AHEAD OF ITS TIME

At its core, this book showcases the thinking of national literacy leaders. Many of their ideas seem so sensible that one wonders why they were not presented in previous volumes. But the fact is that many of their suggestions for best practice did not exist previously, or did not exist in this nuanced form of expression. Many thoughts and recommendations for instruction that you encounter here are ahead of their time in the sense that they have not been proven experimentally. At some points in history—and this is one of them—the urgency of improving reading becomes too compelling to wait for researchers to catch up in every respect. So, in many cases, practice must lead research, and some of the recommendations presented here represent those potential nuggets of possibility.

Teachers will find many needs met here. The ideas packed into these pages are easy to absorb. They attempt to respond to pressing questions and to satisfy our quest for connections. Painted in practical terms, let us hope these concepts will now find their way from the classroom context in which they are presented in this volume to the classroom context of the teacher who reads about them.

What is left out of this book? I could name many topics. I could list quite a few people. The reading field is large and expanding. But, despite these omissions, there is no grander survey available now. No more inclusive collection exists for the seasoned teacher and the specialist seeking to be better informed. There is no broader tool kit to equip the professional educator for tomorrow in school.

JOHN T. GUTHRIE, PHD
University of Maryland, College Park

ACKNOWLEDGMENTS

We would like to especially thank all of the chapter authors for their outstanding contributions. They represent some of the most highly regarded scholars in the field of reading. Their unbridled enthusiasm for literacy teaching and learning is reflected throughout this volume.

Joy is the word that comes to mind when we think about working with Chris Jennison, Senior Editor at The Guilford Press. Chris, you are a great friend and colleague. Thank you for having the confidence and patience to guide the publication of this third edition. Thank you as well to Anna Nelson, Senior Production Editor, for helping us meet all those deadlines. And finally, we extend our deep appreciation to Jacquelynn Malloy for the intellectual exuberance and hard work she provided in helping us bring this book to fruition.

CONTENTS

Introduction 1
Linda B. Gambrell, Lesley Mandel Morrow, and Michael Pressley

PART I: PERSPECTIVES ON BEST PRACTICES

1. Evidence-Based Best Practices for Comprehensive Literacy Instruction 11
Linda B. Gambrell, Jacquelynn A. Malloy, and Susan Anders Mazzoni

2. Balance in Comprehensive Literacy Instruction: Then and Now 30
P. David Pearson, Taffy E. Raphael, Vicki L. Benson, and Christina L. Madda

PART II: BEST PRACTICES FOR ALL STUDENTS

3. Best Practices in Early Literacy Development in Preschool, Kindergarten, and First Grade 57
Lesley Mandel Morrow and Diane H. Tracey

4. Best Practices for Struggling Readers 83
Richard L. Allington and Kim Baker

5. Best Practices for Literacy Instruction for English-Language Learners 104
María S. Carlo

6. Best Practices in Adolescent Literacy Instruction 127
Donna Ogle with Laura Lang

PART III: EVIDENCE-BASED STRATEGIES FOR LITERACY LEARNING AND TEACHING

7. Best Practices in Teaching Phonological Awareness and Phonics 159
Patricia M. Cunningham

8. Best Practices in Vocabulary Instruction 178
Camille L. Z. Blachowicz and Peter J. Fisher

9. Best Practices in Fluency Instruction 204
Melanie R. Kuhn and Timothy Rasinski

10. Best Practices in Teaching Comprehension 220
Cathy Collins Block and Michael Pressley

11. Best Practices in Teaching Writing 243
Karen Bromley

12. Best Practices in Literacy Assessment 264
Peter Afflerbach

PART IV: PERSPECTIVES ON SPECIAL ISSUES

13. Instructional Resources in the Classroom: Deepening Understanding through Interactions with Multiple Texts and Multiple Media 285
Linda Kucan, Diane Lapp, James Flood, and Douglas Fisher

14. Organizing Effective Literacy Instruction: Differentiating Instruction to Meet the Needs of All Children 313
D. Ray Reutzel

15. Effective Use of Technology in Literacy Instruction 344
Michael C. McKenna, Linda D. Labbo, David Reinking, and Tricia A. Zucker

16. Best Practices in Professional Development for Improving Literacy Instruction 373
Rita M. Bean and Aimee Morewood

PART V: FUTURE DIRECTIONS

17. Achieving Best Practices 397
Michael Pressley

Index 405

BEST PRACTICES IN LITERACY INSTRUCTION

INTRODUCTION

Linda B. Gambrell
Lesley Mandel Morrow
Michael Pressley

The third edition of *Best Practices in Literacy Instruction* contains the latest insights and research on literacy instruction that have direct implications for classroom instruction. The contributors to this practitioner-oriented guide are well aware of the pressures and difficulties incumbent in teaching a diverse classroom of learners in a society where mandates from federal and district authorities often make it difficult for teachers to independently implement well-reasoned decisions that they feel will best suit the needs of their students. In the second edition, the authors encouraged teachers to be active decision makers in designing literacy instruction for their students. In this updated third edition, we encourage preservice and practicing teachers alike to develop a *vision* of what they hope to achieve with regard to literacy development for their unique set of students, particular classroom context, and school- or district-level constraints. By keeping a clear vision in mind, we hope this volume will encourage and empower teachers to evaluate, choose, and orchestrate those practices that will aid in fulfilling that vision for their students—and, with it, sufficient evidence-based support to justify their practices. Although this book is designed with the practicing teacher in mind, we hope that it will also be used in teacher training and professional development, for graduate students and reading specialists, and for administrators who seek to improve the level of reading instruction in their schools.

As literacy researchers seek answers to specific questions about the efficacy of instructional techniques and procedures, they take into account various influences such as classroom context, motivation, teaching methods, social interaction, and teacher–student interactions. The contributors to this volume have been active in conducting classroom-based research and program innovations that focus on literacy development. They believe that teachers can be most effective when they are informed decision makers with a vision that will guide them in incorporating the newest research-based information as well as valid traditional ideas about literacy instruction. Thus, the chapters in this book provide practical classroom-based strategies and techniques as well as principles to assist in evaluating and orchestrating best practices for effective instructional decision making.

This book is organized into five parts: Perspectives on Best Practices, Best Practices for All Students, Evidence-Based Strategies for Literacy Learning and Teaching, Perspectives on Special Issues, and Future Directions. In Part I, the authors explore the core beliefs and philosophies of classroom literacy that will serve them in creating their vision and choosing instructional strategies and methods to fulfill that vision. Traditional and evolving ideas regarding balance in designing and implementing classroom instruction are discussed, as is the overarching concept of comprehensive literacy instruction. Part II addresses the perspectives relevant to designing instruction to suit the needs of all students. In particular, the unique needs of early learners, English-language learners, struggling readers, and adolescents are discussed. Part III presents the latest research-based information about classroom literacy practices. Topics include current practices in phonological awareness and phonics, vocabulary, fluency, and comprehension instruction, as well as writing development and assessment of literacy skills. Part IV provides an overview of many of the current issues in the field of literacy instruction, including a discussion of the best uses of multiple texts and multiple media, organizing differentiated literacy instruction, the use of technology in literacy programs, and professional development practices that support the propagation of best practices for comprehensive literacy instruction. The book concludes with a commentary by Michael Pressley reflecting on future directions for achieving best practices.

PART I. PERSPECTIVES ON BEST PRACTICES

In Chapter 1, Linda B. Gambrell, Jacquelynn A. Malloy, and Susan Anders Mazzoni present an overview of best practices for comprehensive literacy instruction. Encouraging teachers to be visionary decision makers, they present an overview of 10 evidence-based best practices for comprehensive literacy instruction. With a realization that ideas about what it means to be literate are evolving in response to technological and societal changes, the authors suggest an appropriate mindset for the thoughtful incorporation of best practices in the classroom.

In Chapter 2, P. David Pearson, Taffy E. Raphael, Vicki L. Benson, and Christina L. Madda present a historical viewpoint on how ideas regarding balanced literacy instruction began and how these have evolved in recent years. New research informs the current reconceptualization of balanced literacy instruction, which avoids the trappings of unidimensional views by clearly defining what is meant by balance in instruction and then reviews the research that supports the essential elements of this definition. In the current politicized climate of high-stakes accountability, the authors consider the radical changes that teachers face in implementing and maintaining comprehensive literacy-based instruction. They suggest an ecological approach to balanced literacy instruction that takes into account the multiple dimensions found along the content and contextual continua of individual classrooms and their teachers.

PART II: BEST PRACTICES FOR ALL STUDENTS

In Chapter 3, Lesley Mandel Morrow and Diane H. Tracey begin a discussion of best practices for all students by addressing the crucial early stages of literacy development. Based on the philosophical and theoretical findings relating to early development and various influential initiatives that focus on the unique needs of preschool, kindergarten, and first-grade learners, the authors discuss current research that encourages teachers to acknowledge and nurture the literacy potential of students while striving to address their oral language and social needs. Children come to us in these early grades with varying degrees of experience in a literate culture and need to be regarded as readers and writers with emerging skills that require our explicit and systematic attention. Best practices for instruction are presented in a clear and organized manner that will assist teachers in designing their classrooms and their instructional practices to encourage the literate lives of our youngest students.

Seeking to address the needs of struggling readers, Richard L. Allington and Kim Baker begin Chapter 4 with a discussion of the types of instructional programs that can accelerate the reading and writing development of students who experience special difficulties. In particular, instruction that is personalized, interactive, and contextually supported is highlighted, as is the need for requiring sufficient opportunities for reading and writing practice. The authors also address the essential components of prevention, acceleration, and long-term support that are required to address the needs of students who experience difficulties in reading and writing.

María S. Carlo begins Chapter 5 with a discussion of the various ways in which students who are English-language learners (ELL) differ from each other, as well as how they differ from students who are native English speakers. The present context of educational policy, having been influenced by demographic changes, highlights the need for teachers to become knowledgeable in ELL literacy instruction and practice. Differences between learning English as a first or second language are detailed as is the importance of oral language facility in reading and writing text. In particular, Carlo elaborates on the teaching of phonological awareness skills and alphabetics to ELL students and provides helpful instructional ideas and suggestions that will serve to assist the classroom teacher in framing and implementing literacy instruction that bridges the gap between oral and written language acquisition.

In Chapter 6, Donna Ogle and Laura Lang discuss the multifaceted literacy needs and concerns of middle and high school students. While reading is important to content-area learning at these levels, content-area teachers do not always feel comfortable or adequately prepared in addressing the literacy needs of their students. Unfortunately, a comprehensive approach to literacy support is often not encouraged by their administrators. Proposed solutions to these institutional concerns are addressed in the chapter, and a freshman high school program that focuses on thoughtful literacy development to better prepare students for the reading and writing requirements of secondary education is described at length. The authors conclude with a discussion of the current trends and needs in the field of adolescent literacy research.

PART III. EVIDENCE-BASED STRATEGIES FOR LITERACY LEARNING AND TEACHING

In discussing the importance of phonological awareness and phonics at crucial points in the development of decoding ability in Chapter 7, Patricia M. Cunningham presents research findings that support instructional practices for use by teachers in their classrooms. A multitude of ideas for incorporating these techniques and methods in classrooms to target specific elements of decoding skill are presented.

In Chapter 8, Camille L. Z. Blachowicz and Peter J. Fisher present evidence-based guidelines for vocabulary instruction. Considering the needs of diverse learners who present varying levels of background knowledge and literacy experience, Blachowicz and Fisher detail five evidence-based guidelines for nurturing independent word learners. The importance of wide reading, teacher modeling, and wordplay are discussed, as are the importance of literacy contexts and student use of resources and strategies to encourage independent word learning.

In Chapter 9, Melanie R. Kuhn and Timothy Rasinski reflect on current thinking in fluency instruction. After discussing the role that fluency plays in freeing up attentional resources for comprehension and metacognitive tasks, the authors present research that supports instructional techniques such as reading while listening, variations of repeated readings, and structured fluency development lessons and assessments.

Cathy Collins Block and Michael Pressley begin Chapter 10 with an uplifting update of research in reading comprehension, which informs their discussion of four new ways for teachers to group their comprehension instruction. Recent research on metacognition and strategies for reading comprehension are reviewed, and valuable insights are offered that should inform instruction. The authors then provide a comprehensive lesson plan that incorporates the newest research with the best of the traditional methods that will guide teachers in providing effective compression instruction to students at all levels of ability.

Karen Bromley begins Chapter 11 with a review of the theoretical constructs that support best practices in writing instruction. Research that details the interplay of writing and grammar, spelling, and the needs of special populations is discussed, and the implications for classroom instruction are detailed. Bromley stresses the importance of context, self-evaluation, and providing sufficient time for writing, as well as the value of establishing a writing community and developing reading/writing connections.

In Chapter 12, Peter Afflerbach addresses the issue of bringing balance to literacy assessment in a manner that will inform instruction and guide literacy acquisition. An overreliance on high-stakes testing moves us out of balance by providing a single type of information to one particular audience. Regular classroom assessments that can truly inform instruction for individual students will provide teachers with the tools they need to guide students to greater levels of achievement and engagement. A detailed account of how teachers can bring their assessments into greater balance is provided, along with insights for advocating for change in student assessment practices.

PART IV. PERSPECTIVES ON SPECIAL ISSUES

Part IV begins with a discussion by Linda Kucan, Diane Lapp, James Flood, and Douglas Fisher in Chapter 13 on the rich contexts for learning that are developed by teachers who are not constrained by curricular boundaries. Students are provided an opportunity to develop knowledge in several disciplines while gaining insight into reading and language arts through the use of multiple texts and media. Research on the strategies that have been successful when incorporating various types of texts in the classroom is presented to support the principles of the "best practices in action" portion of the chapter.

The complexities of providing instruction to students of diverse needs is discussed by D. Ray Reutzel in Chapter 14. Noting the crucial aspects of assessments that inform instruction, he presents an assortment of techniques for differentiating instruction to meet the needs of individual students. Advice on making the best use of available time for literacy instruction is followed by guidelines for addressing both whole-class and small-group lessons that are both efficient and effectual, according to recent research.

In Chapter 15, observing that our understanding of what constitutes literacy is constantly evolving, Michael C. McKenna, Linda D. Labbo, David Reinking, and Tricia A. Zucker discuss the ever-changing needs of literacy instruction that are driven by rapid changes in technology. Through a successful integration of technology in the classroom, learning that is socially constructed and collaborative can be enhanced. The support that digital media provide for struggling readers is an additional consideration for teachers of students with diverse learning needs, as are the inherently engaging aspects of using computer technologies in the classroom. Stories from the classroom serve to illustrate how teachers can best make use of the latest in technology to improve reading comprehension, reader response, and literacy engagement by students at all levels of learning and ability.

In Chapter 16, Rita M. Bean and Aimee Morewood address the importance of professional development to continued literacy achievement for students. While the educational system continues to expect much of its teachers, districts do not always provide adequate time and financial resources to provide for quality inservice training, especially with regard to teacher practices and beliefs. After presenting the six salient features of quality inservice programs, a review of studies addressing the needs of teachers for continued development is provided. Various options for addressing the ongoing needs of teachers include study groups, online coursework, teacher research, literacy coaching, involvement in curriculum development, and the establishment of a community of learners.

This book concludes with a commentary by Michael Pressley. In Chapter 17, he reflects on where we are today with respect to our knowledge about best practices for comprehensive literacy instruction, and he looks to the future by focusing on areas and topics that need to be more fully explored.

In sum, the chapters that follow are replete with the latest in theory, research, and best practices for comprehensive literacy instruction. With a focus on developing a vision for literacy instruction, teachers and administrators are provided with an array of instructional methods and techniques that are supported by the best research-based evidence in the literature. With these tools in hand, teachers are well prepared to meet the challenges of providing comprehensive literacy instruction for all students.

Part I

PERSPECTIVES ON BEST PRACTICES

Chapter 1

EVIDENCE-BASED BEST PRACTICES FOR COMPREHENSIVE LITERACY INSTRUCTION

Linda B. Gambrell
Jacquelynn A. Malloy
Susan Anders Mazzoni

This chapter will:

- Describe the features of evidence-based best practices for comprehensive literacy instruction.
- Discuss the important role of teachers as visionary decision makers.
- Present 10 evidence-based best practices for comprehensive literacy instruction.
- Propose a mindset for thoughtful incorporation of best practices for comprehensive literacy instruction.

Literacy instruction continues to be a hot topic in education, in the media, and with politicians at every level of government. One of the core issues driving today's concerns about reading instruction is the pressure for students to perform well on state assessments. The stakes are high, and the penalties for inadequate performance on these tests are great. Schools are directed to show Adequate Yearly Progress (ATP) on state assessments or face sanctions such as school takeover by the state or allowing parents to choose other schools, perhaps in other districts, for their children to attend. At the district level, state standards are imposed that seek to coordinate with federal programs, such as the Reading First Initiative under the No Child Left Behind Act (NCLB), as well as district-level proposals to improve instructional programs that are of concern. In each school, principals are called upon to meet federal, state, and district-level requirements while providing for teachers and students with varying needs and abilities. And in every classroom, it is the teacher who struggles to meet the challenge of providing appropriate literacy instruction for his or her students.

In a commentary in *Education Week*, Pressley (2005) describes how the federal quest for research-based reading instructional practices has led us to focus on five factors of instruction—phonemic awareness, phonics, fluency, vocabulary, and comprehension (National Reading Panel, 2000)—perhaps to the exclusion of others. Although these areas of skill development are essential to reading instruction, they are by no means a magic bullet that will lead to successful literacy attainment by all students, and they do not address areas of reading and writing that are seen by many states, districts, schools, and teachers as being just as important. In this book we argue for consideration of *evidence-based best practices within a comprehensive framework* of literacy instruction that includes attention to motivation, composition, oral language, and critical thinking.

There is universal agreement in our field that the foundation for all instructional practice, regardless of one's theoretical or pragmatic orientation to reading, is the goal of improving reading achievement for all students. Indeed, there are many points of agreement in the reading profession, even among individuals with diverse philosophies (Braunger & Lewis, 2006; Flippo, 2001; Rasinski, 2001). In a study designed to explore the contexts and practices on which literacy experts could agree, Flippo (1998, 2001) conducted a survey of experts representing a wide spectrum of beliefs and philosophies. She found that literacy experts are in agreement on the contexts and practices that both facilitate learning to read and make learning to read difficult. According to Rasinski (2001), the major finding from Flippo's study of literacy experts is that "the perceived gulf that exists between orientations to research and practice in literacy education by literacy researchers and scholars is not as large as it may seem" (p. 159).

Although we have learned a great deal about literacy and instruction over the past few decades, there remains significant controversy over what constitutes "best practices" in literacy instruction. Interestingly, our developing understanding of the literacy process appears to contribute to the ongoing debate. We have become increasingly aware of the complexity of reading development and instruction; consequently, many researchers have adopted broader perspectives regarding the nature of literacy and how literacy learning occurs (Brauger & Lewis, 2006). For example, since the 1970s, researchers have moved from performing laboratory controlled experiments, in which one aspect of learning was studied independent of context, to conducting research in naturalistic classroom settings where contextual variables such as affective environment, authenticity of tasks, social interaction, parental involvement, or types of materials can be considered and evaluated. Research has shown that, indeed, many contextual variables make a difference in literacy learning. Furthermore, as workplace demands have evolved due to changes in industry and technology, so has our definition of what it means to be literate. Simply being able to decode and answer low-level literal questions about a piece of text is no longer sufficient. Becoming fully literate has come to mean, among many things, using strategies independently to construct meaning from text, using text information to build conceptual understanding, effectively communicating ideas orally and in writing, and developing the intrinsic desire to read and write (Braunger & Lewis, 2006; Biancarose & Snow, 2004).

EVIDENCE-BASED BEST PRACTICES

While no single instructional program, approach, or method has been found to be effective in teaching all children to read, *evidence-based best practices* that promote high rates of achievement have been documented. An evidence-based best practice refers to an instructional practice that has a record of success that is both trustworthy and valid. There is evidence that when this practice is used with a particular group of children, the children can be expected to make gains in reading achievement (International Reading Association, 2002a, 2002b).

What counts as evidence of reliable and trustworthy practice? A position paper published by the International Reading Association (2002b) asserts that such evidence provides:

- *Objective* data that any evaluator would identify and interpret similarly.
- *Valid* data that adequately represent the tasks that children need to accomplish to be successful readers.
- *Reliable* data that will remain essentially unchanged if collected on a different day or by a different person.

- *Systematic* data that were collected according to a rigorous design of either experimentation or observation.
- *Refereed* data that have been approved for publication by a panel of independent reviewers.

Allington (2005) has raised the question "What counts as evidence in evidence-based education?" In our view, evidence-based instruction involves teachers making decisions using "professional wisdom integrated with the best available empirical evidence" (Allington, 2005, p. 16). According to Allington, such a definition honors the wisdom and evidence derived from professional experience while at the same time recognizing the important role of empirical research.

Furthermore, no single investigation or research study ever establishes a practice as effective. When evaluating claims of evidence for best practices, we must determine whether the research was data-based, rigorous, and systematic (Bogdan & Biklen, 1992; International Reading Association, 2002b). It is important to note that it is the *convergence of evidence* from an array of research studies, using a variety of research designs and methodologies, that allows us to determine best practices.

In order to provide instruction using best practices as well as make appropriate instructional decisions, teachers need a strong knowledge of good evidence, drawn from both professional wisdom and the research. One of the most important questions a teacher can ask is "What evidence is available that suggests that using this practice in my classroom will support comprehensive literacy instruction and increase reading achievement for my students?"

COMPREHENSIVE LITERACY INSTRUCTION

The goal of comprehensive literacy instruction is to ensure that all students achieve their full literacy potential. Students need to be able to read and write with competence, ease, and joy. Comprehensive literacy instruction emphasizes the personal, intellectual, and social nature of literacy learning, and supports the notion that students learn new meanings in response to new experiences rather than simply learning what others have created. Thus, comprehensive literacy instruction is in keeping with constructivist learning theory and social learning perspectives that emphasize the development of students' cognitive abilities, such as critical thinking and decision making. Our students need and deserve comprehensive literacy instruction that is well informed and based on a broad model of the reading process.

Comprehensive literacy instruction:

- Is a balanced approach.
- Incorporates evidence-based best practices.
- Builds on the knowledge that students bring to school.
- Acknowledges that reading and writing are reciprocal processes.
- Recognizes that comprehension is the ultimate goal of literacy instruction.
- Emphasizes meaning construction through literacy tasks and activities that require critical thinking.
- Offers opportunities for students to apply literacy strategies in the context of meaningful tasks.
- Provides for differentiated instruction in accordance with the diverse strengths and needs of students (i.e., struggling readers, second-language learners).

Teachers who provide comprehensive literacy instruction have a vision of literacy that is continually informed by evidence-based best practices. They understand literacy learning well enough to adapt the learning environment, materials, and methods to particular situations and students. In the final analysis, comprehensive literacy instruction rests on the shoulders of teachers who make informed decisions about the instructional approaches and practices that are most appropriate for a particular student.

TEACHERS AS VISIONARY DECISION MAKERS

Researchers who have entered classrooms in the past few years to observe and record the types of instruction that are occurring in high-achieving learning environments have found that, beyond a carefully orchestrated integration of skills and strategies, content, and literature, successful classrooms are led by teachers who motivate and support individual students in ways that cannot be prescribed by any one program, method, or practice (Pressley, 2003; Pressley, Allington, Wharton-McDonald, Block, & Morrow, 2001; Wharton-McDonald, Pressley, & Hampston, 1998). What has become increasingly clear through research that probes more deeply into the inner workings of effective classrooms is that the teacher is the crucial factor in the classroom. In fact, study after study points to teacher expertise as the critical variable in effective reading instruction. The teacher who is knowledgeable and adept at combining and adjusting various methods, practices, and strategies to meet the needs of a particular set of students with a differentiated set of needs is most likely to lead students to higher levels of literacy achievement and engagement.

Effective teachers are able to differentiate and contextualize their instruction and to support the practices they choose through evidence provided by research and through discussions and collaborations with colleagues in their schools and districts. In particular, research on effective teachers reveals the following common themes:

- Effective teachers are supported within a context of strong school and faculty commitment to improving student achievement. Teachers work within and across grades to coordinate the curriculum in ways that will enhance student growth and development. Ongoing professional development is provided so that teachers can become apprised of research-based practices and share evidence from their classrooms (Taylor, Pearson, Peterson, & Rodriguez, 2003).
- Effective teachers are much like coaches. Instead of telling students what they must do to become better readers and writers, they use discussion and inquiry to guide students in constructing meaning from text (Taylor, Pearson, Clark, & Walpole, 2000; Allington & Johnston, 2002).
- Effective teachers incorporate higher-level responses to text, both oral and written, and emphasize cognitive engagement during literacy activities. They are explicit in tying strategy instruction to authentic literacy activities that are meaning-centered while teaching skills as needed to whole groups, small groups, and individual students (Taylor et al., 2003).
- Effective teachers provide access to a variety of books and time to engage with print in authentic ways in an effort to encourage students to be lifelong learners (Reutzel & Smith, 2004; Routman, 2003; Cunningham, Cunningham, & Allington, 2002; Baumann & Duffy, 1997; Gambrell, 1996).

Students who are taught in these classrooms are engaged, strategic, and see a clear path between instruction and real-life reading tasks. The instruction provided for students in these classrooms is both differentiated and contextualized to address all aspects of literacy required of students as they progress through the grades.

Teachers are ultimately the instructional designers who implement best practices in relevant, meaningful ways for their particular community of learners. In other words, best practices can be *described*—but not *prescribed*.

BEST PRACTICES IN ACTION

Literacy researchers have converged on a word to describe the driving force that guides teachers in coordinating and integrating practices effectively—*vision.* Although this is not a word you might expect to see in a discussion of evidence-based practices, the teachers' vision of literacy achievement has long been heralded as the crucial factor in ensuring that the goal of improving literacy instruction for all students is met. According to Calfee (2005), ensuring that "children have the opportunity to acquire the level of literacy that allows them full participation in our democratic society depends on a corps of teachers who possess extraordinary minds and hearts" (p. 67).

Calfee asserts that teachers not only must possess a domain of skills and knowledge to lead students to acquire this level of literacy success but also must acquire a sensitivity to student needs and be passionate in their willingness to make their vision work. Duffy (2003, 2005) describes the teachers' ultimate goal as that of *inspiring students to be readers and writers*—to engage students in "genuinely literate activities" where they are doing something important with literacy. This engagement should reflect the teachers' instructional vision—the reason they are passionate about teaching reading and writing.

Teachers who are visionary decision makers are empowered to identify and select evidence-based literacy practices to create an integrated instructional approach that adapts to the differentiated needs of students. Such teachers possess the following types of knowledge:

- *Declarative knowledge*—knowing "what works," the evidence-based best practices for comprehensive literacy instruction.
- *Procedural knowledge*—knowing how best practices are implemented.
- *Conditional knowledge*—knowing when a particular practice is preferable to another.
- *Reflective knowledge*—knowing when a practice is working effectively, or not.
- *Adaptive knowledge*—knowing how to combine or adapt practices or techniques to meet the needs of particular groups of students or individuals (i.e., struggling readers, second-language learners).

A teacher's vision should clearly be knowledge-based and should encompass what he or she wishes to achieve for each student. How detailed one's vision becomes is certainly an individual matter and subject to personal experiences and situations, but without a vision the teacher is left to sway and sputter as a candle facing the winds of curricular change and federal, district, and school-level impositions. It is the teacher with vision who is able to stand firm in the belief that with knowledge and heart, evidence-based best practices can be selected and adapted to meet the needs of each individual student encountered each day.

TEN EVIDENCE-BASED BEST PRACTICES FOR COMPREHENSIVE LITERACY INSTRUCTION

In keeping with the characterization of teachers as visionary decision makers, we present 10 evidence-based best practices for comprehensive literacy instruction that are generally accepted by experts in the field and are worthy of consideration (Table 1.1). These practices are based on a broad view of the reading process, one that incorporates the full range of experiences that children need in order to reach their literacy potential. We believe that best practices are characterized by meaningful literacy activities that provide children with both the *skill* and the *will* they need to become motivated and proficient literacy learners.

The authors of the chapters in this book have moved well beyond traditional low-level conceptions of literacy. Clearly, each author describes best practices that promote critical thinking and strategic, versatile reading and writing. For example, ideas are presented on how evidence-based literacy instruction can help students:

- Become independent users of comprehension strategies to gain meaning from text relevant to their goals.
- Acquire word-recognition, vocabulary, and fluency skills and strategies, so that they will have "thinking power" left for meaning.
- Read and write in different genres and for a variety of purposes and audiences.
- Use texts and computers in high-level literacy activities such as searching for information and making intertextual links.

We are clearly in the process of redefining what it means to be "literate" in today's world. Print, in various forms, is playing an increasingly important role in our society, and jobs are requiring a level of literacy that is unsurpassed in history (Biancarosa & Snow, 2004). Best practices, then, must include instruction that will help our students meet these demands.

The chapter authors throughout this book have addressed and expanded on the broad research consensus that supports the following 10 evidence-based best practices.

TABLE 1.1. Ten Evidence-Based Best Practices for Comprehensive Literacy Instruction

1. Create a classroom culture that fosters literacy motivation.
2. Teach reading for authentic meaning-making literacy experiences: for pleasure, to be informed, and to perform a task.
3. Provide students with scaffolded instruction in phonemic awareness, phonics, vocabulary, fluency, and comprehension to promote independent reading.
4. Give students plenty of time to read in class.
5. Provide children with high-quality literature across a wide range of genres.
6. Use multiple texts to link and expand vocabulary and concepts.
7. Build a whole-class community that emphasizes important concepts and builds upon prior knowledge.
8. Balance teacher- and student-led discussions of texts.
9. Use technologies to link and expand concepts.
10. Use a variety of assessment techniques to inform instruction.

1. *Create a classroom culture that fosters literacy motivation.* Motivation exerts a tremendous force on what is learned and how and when it will be learned. Motivation often makes the difference between superficial and shallow learning and learning that is deep and internalized (Gambrell, 1996). Clearly, students need both the *skill* and the *will* to become competent and motivated readers (Guthrie & Wigfield, 2000; Paris, Lipson, & Wixson, 1983). Best practices include ways that teachers support students in their reading development by creating classroom cultures that foster reading motivation, such as providing a book-rich classroom environment, opportunities for choice, and opportunities to interact socially with others. The most basic goal of any literacy program should be the development of readers who *can read* and who *choose to read.* Teachers can provide instruction in the most essential literacy skills, but if our students are not motivated to read, they will never reach their full literacy potential.

2. *Teach reading for authentic meaning-making literacy experiences: for pleasure, to be informed, and to perform a task.* Authentic literacy activities are reading and writing events that are like those that occur in people's lives, as opposed to reading and writing solely to learn (Purcell-Gates, 2002, 2005). We know that as young children learn and use their developing oral language, they do so for real reasons and purposes (Halliday, 1975). Therefore, in order for literacy learning to be meaningful to students, teachers need to be mindful of the reasons and purposes they establish for reading and writing tasks.

Authentic literacy activities are often designed to focus on communicating ideas for shared understanding rather than simply to complete assignments or answer teacher-posed questions. Authentic literacy events include activities such as reading to share stories and information, reading to find out how to do or make something, and writing a letter to a pen pal. It is more likely that children will transfer their classroom literacy learning to real life when they engage in authentic literacy learning in the classroom (Teale & Gambrell, in press; Teale & Sulzby, 1986).

3. *Provide students with scaffolded instruction in phonemic awareness, phonics, vocabulary, fluency, and comprehension to promote independent reading.* The report of the National Reading Panel (NRP) (National Institute of Child Health and Human Development, 2000) identified phonemic awareness, phonics, vocabulary, fluency, and comprehension as critical to the development of the reading process and provided research support for instruction in these areas (see Pressley et al., 2001, for a discussion of the NRP report). Children often need concentrated instructional support in these areas in order to learn important skills and strategies that they might have difficulty discovering on their own. The gradual-release-of-responsibility model provides such scaffolded instruction.

In general, the gradual-release model describes a process in which students gradually assume a greater degree of responsibility for a particular aspect of learning. During the first stage, the teacher assumes most of the responsibility by modeling and describing a particular skill or strategy. In the second stage, the teacher and students assume joint responsibility; children practice applying a particular skill or strategy, and the teacher offers assistance and feedback as needed. Once students are ready, instruction moves into the third stage, in which students assume all, or almost all, of the responsibility by working in situations where they independently apply newly learned skills and strategies. This gradual withdrawal of instructional support is also known as scaffolded instruction, because "supports" or "scaffolds" are gradually removed as students demonstrate greater degrees of proficiency.

We view the gradual-release-of-responsibility and scaffolded instruction as consistent with constructivist principles when they are used within meaningful, authentic contexts (Graham & Harris, 1996; Harris & Graham, 1994). Indeed, many authors in this book provide examples of how to integrate these models within meaningful reading and writing programs that include use of literature, technology, authentic writing experiences, choice, and collaborative learning.

4. *Give students plenty of time to read in class.* There is clear evidence from reading research that the amount of time spent reading (reading volume) is the major contributor to increased vocabulary and comprehension (Allington, 1983; Hayes & Ahrens, 1988; Nagy & Anderson, 1984;

Stanovich, 1986). In a classic study, Anderson, Wilson, and Fielding (1988) found a significant relationship between the amount of reading school children do and their reading achievement. In this study of 155 fifth graders, the amount of book reading that students reported was the best predictor of performance on several measures of reading achievement.

In addition, other studies have supported the inclusion of time to read during the school day. Research by Reutzel and Hollingsworth (1991) found that sustained reading of trade books was as effective as comprehension skills instruction in increasing reading comprehension. Linehart, Zigmond, and Cooley (1981) reported that time spent in silent reading was positively related to gains in reading achievement.

According to Cunningham and Stanovich (1998), lack of reading practice delays the development of fluency and word recognition skills. Thus, for struggling readers comprehension is hindered, frustrating reading experiences increase, and further practice is avoided. Time for reading is important for all readers, but it is especially important for struggling readers. Good readers tend to have more practice in reading, and consequently they become more and more proficient, while poor readers spend less time reading and have fewer experiences with appropriate-level reading materials.

During independent reading time students get the practice needed to consolidate the skills and strategies they have been taught, and they thereby come to "own" them. According to Allington (2005), such practice provides students with the opportunity to develop the autonomous, automatic, and appropriate application of reading skills and strategies *while actually reading.* Adequate time for reading is essential so that students have the experience that is needed to increase reading proficiency.

5. *Provide children with high-quality literature across a wide range of genres.* While early readers benefit from the support of decodable texts, the effective teacher makes use of high-quality literature during teacher read-alouds and as independent reading texts for students as their reading skills improve. Pressley et al. (2001) reviewed research on exemplary first-grade classrooms and found that direct teaching, supported by immersion in high-quality literature, promotes reading engagement and growth. Duke (2000) reported on the scarcity of information texts in first-grade classrooms, raising concern about the lack of experience young children have with respect to informational text. As content-heavy expository texts become more prevalent in the later elementary years, we are remiss if we do not provide exposure to, and explicit instruction in comprehending, the full range of genres our students are expected to read. Our classrooms must have a wide variety of genres and styles of high quality literature.

6. *Use multiple texts that link and expand vocabulary and concepts.* Using a variety of texts on common topics promotes concept and vocabulary

development as well as critical thinking. Hartman found in his 1995 research that good readers are able to construct meanings from text that are then interconnected with those derived from other texts as well as cultural and social-experiential knowledge. These meanings are indeterminate in nature—open to change and adaptation as new meanings are acquired. Lenski (2001) extends this work to include intertextual connections that are enhanced by teacher questioning and student discussion. Students who have authentic purposes for reading and a variety of quality literature, both narrative and expository, are able to construct meanings and develop concepts through the reading of multiple texts (Moje & Sutherland, 2003; Soalt, 2005).

7. *Build a whole-class community that emphasizes important concepts and builds upon prior knowledge.* The best predictor of what students will learn is what they already know. Prior knowledge is the foundation upon which new meaning (or learning) is built. Effective teachers assess students' conceptual understanding, beliefs, and values and link new ideas, skills, and competencies to prior understandings. They also provide experiences that equip each child with sufficient background knowledge to succeed with literacy tasks. Such practices are also consistent with Vygotsky's (1978) notion of "zone of proximal development," which suggests that optimal learning occurs when teachers determine children's current level of understanding and teach new ideas, skills, and strategies that are at an appropriate level of challenge.

In her ongoing research into the literacy practices and values that are situated in learning communities and cultures, Purcell-Gates (2005) suggests that educators should become aware of the differences between the types of texts and purposes for literacy that are found in students' home environments and those presented at school. By incorporating culturally meaningful teaching methods in literacy instruction, teachers can build classroom communities that view literacy as a valuable means of getting information and pleasure from reading text and for communicating students' knowledge through writing.

8. *Balance teacher- and student-led discussions of texts.* From a social-constructivist perspective, literacy is a social act. Readers and writers develop meanings as a result of co-constructed understandings within particular sociocultural contexts. This means, among many things, that text interpretation and level of participation are influenced by the size and social makeup of a group, the cultural conventions of literacy (e.g., What are reading and writing for? What are the literacy goals of the community?), as well as the different perspectives others convey about text. The term *collaborative learning* is often used to refer to the exchange of ideas that results in co-constructed understanding. Collaborative learning and the social perspective have brought to the fore the importance of peer

talk. Interest in the positive benefits of the role of discussion in learning has resulted in new classroom participation structures, such as book talk discussion groups, literacy clubs, and small-group investigations of specific topics related to a content area and communication of findings to others.

We know, however, that discussion does not just "happen." Children need assistance in developing interpersonal skills. They also need a degree of teacher assistance and influence in order to stimulate new learning. However, research has shown that the rewards are great. Collaborative learning contexts have been found to result in greater student achievement and more positive social, motivational, and attitudinal outcomes for all age levels, genders, ethnicities, and social classes than individualized or competitive learning structures (Johnson & Johnson, 1983; Johnson, Johnson, & Maruyama, 1983; Johnson, Maruyama, Johnson, Nelson, & Skon, 1981; Sharan, 1980; Slavin, 1983, 1990).

Several studies provide evidence that discussions of text promote reading comprehension, motivation to read, and higher-order thinking skills (Almasi, McKeown & Beck, 1996; Almasi, O'Flahavan, & Arya, 2001; see the review of research by Gambrell, 1996). Discussions that are teacher-led and student-led are enhanced when students can share ideas and build upon their prior knowledge (Kucan & Beck, 2003; Gambrell, 2004), question the author or challenge the text (Almasi, 1995), and read books that are engaging and that promote discussion (Evans, 2002).

9. *Use technologies to link and expand concepts.* The integration of Internet use and other computer mediated instruction in the K–12 classroom is increasing. However, the empirical evidence to support instructional strategies for using these technologies is just beginning to emerge (Coiro & Schmar-Dobler, 2005; Azevedo & Cromley, 2004). Recommendations from teachers and researchers who focus on these "new literacies" are available for teachers to adapt to their classrooms (Karchmer, Mallette, Kara-Soteriou, & Leu, 2005; Leu, Castek, Henry, Coiro, & McMullan, 2004). What we are coming to understand is that reading on the Internet requires different skills than reading traditional text, and that it is important that we understand these differences in order to provide appropriate instruction for our students (Coiro, 2003). It is incumbent on teachers, therefore, to acquaint themselves with new research as it emerges and to incorporate this new knowledge into their classrooms as suits their particular instructional needs. Our students are entering an age when knowledge of technology is a requirement and not a luxury. As educators, we are obligated to prepare them for that reality.

10. *Use a variety of assessment techniques to inform instruction.* Johnston and Costello (2005) situate their discussion of literacy assessment within current understandings of literacy as a complex construct and the need

to view assessment as a social practice. Whether assessments are formal or informal, summative or formative, they influence the amount and type of support provided the teacher in tailoring instruction to specific students, whole classrooms, and district-level needs (Harlen & Crick, 2003; McDonald & Boud, 2003).

Once teachers are empowered by their vision and have at their disposal a plethora of practices and instructional methods from which to choose, they are free to orchestrate an integration of evidence-based practices to provide comprehensive literacy instruction to their students. No matter how well a particular practice is shown to be effective by research, *optimal literacy teaching and learning can only be achieved when skillful, knowledgeable, and dedicated teachers are given the freedom and latitude to use their professional judgment to make instructional decisions that enable children to achieve their full literacy potential.*

As we increase our understanding of effective literacy instruction, our conceptions of best practices will continue to broaden and deepen. Our students need and deserve instruction that embraces the richness and complexity of the reading process as well as instruction that is both evidence-based and comprehensive. This is no easy task. It requires commitment, time, and knowledge. It begins with a teacher who is a visionary decision maker, one who can identify the strengths and needs of each individual child and plan instruction accordingly. While the challenge is daunting, the rewards are great as we help children become engaged lifelong readers and writers.

ENGAGEMENT ACTIVITIES

1. Observe a language arts block in a classroom. Which observable contextual variables, such as the affective environment, types of social interactions, authenticity of tasks, or class materials and organization seem to best support student engagement with literacy learning? Which aspects of the classroom context would you alter to better support the literacy instruction offered?
2. Richard Allington defines evidence-based instruction as "professional wisdom integrated with the best available empirical evidence" (2005, p. 16). Identify a literacy instruction method or practice that you have observed or used in the classroom and discuss the ways in which it meets Dr. Allington's definition of an evidence-based practice.
3. In this chapter, the authors list 10 evidence-based best practices for comprehensive literacy instruction (pp. 19–24); however, this list is not meant to be exclusive or exhaustive. Consider the literacy instructional practices that you think should be added to this list and give reasons why you, as a

literacy professional, think they should be included. Provide evidence to support your decision.

4. Try to articulate your vision for literacy teaching and learning. Commit to writing what you wish to accomplish as a literacy instructor as well as what you wish for each of your students to achieve. Refer to this vision statement often as you teach or as you learn more about teaching. Be certain to adjust and enhance your vision statement as new knowledge and expertise dictate.

REFERENCES

Allington, R. (1983). Fluency: The neglected reading goal. *The Reading Teacher, 36,* 556–561.

Allington, R. L. (2005). What counts as evidence in evidence-based education. *Reading Today, 23*(3), 16.

Allington, R. L., & Johnston, P. H. (2002). *Reading to learn: Lessons from exemplary fourth-grade classrooms.* New York: Guilford Press.

Almasi, J. (1995). The nature of fourth graders' sociocognitive conflicts in peer-led and teacher-led discussions of literature. *Reading Research Quarterly, 30,* 314–351.

Almasi, J. F., McKeown, M. G., & Beck, I. L. (1996). The nature of engaged reading in classroom discussions of literature. *Journal of Literacy Research, 28*(1), 107–146.

Almasi, J. F., O'Flahavan, J. F., & Arya, P. (2001). A comparative analysis of student and teacher development in more proficient and less proficient peer discussions of literature. *Reading Research Quarterly, 36*(2), 96–120.

Anderson, R. C., Wilson, P. T., & Fielding, L. G. (1988). Growth in reading and how children spend their time outside of school. *Reading Research Quarterly, 23*(3), 285–303.

Azevedo, R., & Cromley, J. G. (2004). Does training on self-regulated learning facilitate students' learning with hypermedia? *Journal of Educational Psychology, 96*(3), 523–535.

Baumann, J. F., & Duffy, A. M. (1997). *Engaged reading for pleasure and learning: A report from the National Reading Research Center.* Athens, GA: National Reading Research Center.

Biancarosa, G., & Snow, C. E. (2004). *Reading Next—a vision for action and research in middle and high school literacy: A report to Carnegie Corporation of New York.* Washington, DC: Alliance for Excellent Education.

Bogdan, R. C., & Biklen, S. K. (1992). *Qualitative research for education: An introduction to theory and methods* (2nd ed.). Boston: Allyn & Bacon.

Braunger, J., & Lewis, J. P. (2006). *Building a knowledge base in reading* (2nd ed.). Newark, DE: International Reading Association.

Calfee, R. (2005). The mind (and heart) of the reading teacher. In B. Maloch, J. V. Hoffman, D. L. Schallert, C. M. Fairbanks, & J. Worthy (Eds.), *54th yearbook of the National Reading Conference* (pp. 63–79). Oak Creek, WI: National Reading Conference.

Coiro, J. (2003). Exloring literacy on the Internet. *The Reading Teacher, 56*, 458–464.

Coiro, J., & Schmar-Dobler, B. (2005). *Reading comprehension on the Internet: Exploring the comprehension strategies used by sixth-grade skilled readers as they search for and locate information on the Internet.* Unpublished manuscript, University of Connecticut. Available at: *ctell1.uconn.edu/coiro/research.html.*

Cunningham, P. M., Cunningham, J. W., & Allington, R. L. (2002). *Research on the components of a comprehensive reading and writing instructional program.* Draft: September 11, 2002. Retrieved March 28, 2001, from *www.wfu.edu/academics/fourblocks/research.html.*

Cunningham, A. E., & Stanovich, K. E. (1998). What reading does for the mind. *American Educator, 22*(1), 8–15.

Duffy, G. G. (2003). *Explaining reading: A resource for teaching concepts, skills, and strategies.* New York: Guilford Press.

Duffy, G. G. (2005). Developing metacognitive teachers: Visioning and the expert's changing role in teacher education and professional development. In S. E. Isreal, C. C. Block, K. L. Bauserman, & K. Kinnucan-Welsch. *Metacognition in literacy learning: Theory, assessment, instruction and professional development* (pp. 299–314). Mahwah, NJ: Erlbaum.

Duke, N. K. (2000). 3.6 minutes a day: The scarcity of informational texts in first grade. *Reading Research Quarterly,35*(2), 202–224.

Evans, K. S. (2002). Fifth-grade student's perceptions of how they experience literature discussion groups. *Reading Research Quarterly, 37*(1), 46–68.

Flippo, R. F. (1998). Points of agreement: A display of professional unity in our field. *The Reading Teacher, 52*, 30–40.

Flippo, R. F. (Ed.). (2001). *Reading researchers in search of common ground.* Newark, DE: International Reading Association.

Gambrell, L. B. (1996). Motivating contexts for literacy learning. In L. Baker, P. Afflerbach, & D. Reinking (Eds.), *Developing engaged readers in school and home communities.* Mahwah, NJ: Erlbaum.

Gambrell, L. B. (2004). Exploring the connection between oral language and early reading. *The Reading Teacher, 57*(5), 490–492.

Graham, S., & Harris, K. R. (1996). *Making the writing process work: Strategies for composition and self-regulation.* Cambridge, MA: Brookline Books.

Guthrie, J. T., & Wigfield, A. (2000). Engagement and motivation in reading. In M. L. Kamil, P. B. Mosenthal, P. D. Pearson, & R. Barr (Eds.), *Handbook of reading research, Vol. 3* (pp. 403–422). Mahwah, NJ: Erlbaum.

Halliday, M. A. K. (1975). *Learning how to mean.* London: Arnold.

Harris, K. R., & Graham, S. (1994). Constructivism: Principles, paradigms, and integration. *Journal of Special Education, 28*(3), 233–247.

Harlen, W., & Crick, R. D. (2003). Testing and motivation for learning. *Assessment in Education: Principles, Policy and Practice, 10*(2), 169–207.

Hartman, D. K. (1995). Eight readers reading: The intertextual links of proficient readers reading multiple passages. *Reading Research Quarterly, 30*(3), 520–561.

Hayes, D. P., & Ahrens, M. (1988). Vocabulary simplification for children: A special case of "Motherese"? *Journal of Child Language, 15*, 395–410.

International Reading Association. (2002a). *Evidence-based reading instruction: Putting the National Reading Panel report into practice.* Newark, DE: Author.

International Reading Association. (2002b). *What is evidence-based reading instruction?* (Position Statement). Newark, DE: Author.

Johnson, D. W., & Johnson, R. T. (1983). The socialization and achievement crisis: Are cooperative learning experiences the solution? In L. Bickman (Ed.), *Applied social psychology* (Annual 4). Beverly Hills, CA: Sage.

Johnson, D., Johnson, R., & Maruyama, G. (1983). Interdependence and interpersonal attraction among heterogeneous and homogeneous individuals: A theoretical formulation and a meta-analysis of the research. *Review of Educational Research, 533,* 5–54.

Johnson, D., Maruyama, G., Johnson, R., Nelson, D., & Skon, L. (1981). Effects of cooperative, competitive, and individualistic goal structures on achievement: A meta-analysis. *Psychological Bulletin, 89,* 47–62.

Johnston, P., & Costello, P. (2005). Theory and research into practice: Principles for literacy assessment. *Reading Research Quarterly, 40*(2), 256–267.

Karchmer, R. A., Mallette, M. H., Kara-Soteriou, J., & Leu, D. (Eds.). (2005). *Innovative approaches to literacy education: Using the Internet to support new literacies.* Newark, DE: International Reading Association.

Kucan, L., & Beck, I. L. (2003). Inviting students to talk about expository texts: A comparison of two discourse environments and their effects on comprehension. *Reading Research and Instruction, 42,* 1–29.

Lenski, S. D. (2001). Intertextual connections during discussions about literature. *Reading Psychology*(*22*). 313–335.

Leu, D. J., Jr., Castek, J., Henry, L. A., Coiro, J., & McMullan, M. (2004). The lessons that children teach us: Integrating children's literature and the new literacies of the Internet. *The Reading Teacher, 57,* 486–503.

Linehart, G., Zigmond, N., & Cooley, W. (1981). Reading instruction and its effects. *American Educational Research Journal, 18,* 343–361.

McDonald, B., & Boud, D. (2003). The impact of self-assessment on achievement: The effects of self-assessment training on performance in external examinations. *Assessment in Education: Principles, Policy and Practice, 10*(2), 209–220.

Moje, E. B., & Sutherland, L. M. (2003). The future of middle school literacy education. *English Education,* 149–164.

Nagy, W. E., & Anderson, R. C. (1984). How many words are there in printed school English? *Reading Research Quarterly, 19*(3), 304–330.

National Institute of Child Health and Human Development (2000). *Report of the National Reading Panel. Teaching children to read: An evidence-based assessment of the scientific research literature on reading and its implications for reading instruction* (NIH Publication No. 00-4769). Washington, DC: U.S. Government Printing Office.

National Reading Panel (2001). *Report of the National Reading Panel: Teaching Children to Read.* Retrieved July 10, 2005, from *www.nichd.nih.gov/publications/nrp/smallbook.htm.*

Paris, S., Lipson, M., & Wixson, K. (1983). Becoming a strategic reader. *Contemporary Educational Psychology, 8,* 293–316.

Pressley, M. (2003). Balanced elementary literacy instruction in the United States. Presented to the International Literacy Conference, Ontario, Canada. Retrieved November 20, 2005, from *literacyconference.oise.utoronto.ca/papers/pressley.pdf.*

Pressley, M. (2005, December 14). The rocky year of Reading First. *Education Week.* Retrieved June 17, 2006, from *www.edweek.org.*

Pressley, M., Allington, R. L., Wharton-McDonald, R., Block, C. C., & Morrow, L. M. (2001). *Learning to read: Lessons from exemplary first-grade classrooms.* New York: Guilford Press.

Purcell-Gates, V. (2002). Authentic literacy in class yields increase in literacy practices. *Literacy Update, 11*(1), 9.

Purcell-Gates, V. (2005, December). *What does culture have to do with it?* Oscar S. Causey Research Award address, National Reading Conference, Miami Beach.

Rasinski, T. V. (2001). A focus on communication with parents and families. In R. F. Flippo (Ed.). *Reading researchers in search of common ground* (pp. 159–166). Newark, DE: International Reading Association.

Reutzel, D. R., & Hollingsworth, P. M. (1991). Investigating topic-related attitude: Effect on reading and remembering text. *Journal of Educational Research, 84*(6), 334–344.

Reutzel, D. R., & Smith, J. A. (2004). Accelerating struggling readers' progress: A comparative analysis of expert opinion and current research recommendations. *Reading and Writing Quarterly, 20,* 63–89.

Routman, R. (2003). *Reading essentials: The specifics you need to teach reading well.* Portsmouth, NH: Heinemann.

Sharan, S. (1980). Cooperative learning in small groups: Recent methods and effects on achievement, attitudes, and ethnic relations. *Review of Educational Research, 50,* 241–271.

Slavin, R. E. (1983). *Cooperative learning.* New York: Longman.

Slavin, R. E. (1990). *Cooperative learning: Theory, research, and practice.* Englewood Cliffs, NJ: Prentice Hall.

Soalt, J. (2005). Bringing together fictional and informational texts to improve comprehension. *Reading Teacher, 58*(7), 680–683.

Stanovich, K. E. (1986). Matthew effects in reading: Some consequences of individual differences in the acquisition of literacy. *Reading Research Quarterly, 21*(4), 360–406.

Taylor, B. M., Pearson, P. D., Clark, K., & Walpole, S. (2000). Effective schools and accomplished teachers: Lessons about primary grade reading instruction in low-income schools. *Elementary School Journal, 101,* 121–166.

Taylor, B. M., Pearson, P. D., Peterson, D. S., & Rodriguez, M. C. (2003). Reading growth in high-poverty classrooms. The influence of teacher practices that encourage cognitive engagement in literacy learning. *Elementary School Journal, 104,* 3–28.

Teale, W. H., & Gambrell, L. B. (in press). Raising urban students' literacy achievement by engaging in authentic, challenging work. *The Reading Teacher.*

Teale, W. H., & Sulzby, E. (1986). Emergent literacy: Writing and reading. Norwood, NJ: Ablex.

Vygotsky, L. S. (1978). *Mind in society.* Cambridge, MA: Harvard University Press.

Wharton-McDonald, R., Pressley, M., & Hampston, J. M. (1998). Literacy instruction in nine first grade classrooms: Teacher characteristics and student achievement. *Elementary School Journal, 99,* 101–128.

Chapter 2

BALANCE IN COMPREHENSIVE LITERACY INSTRUCTION: THEN AND NOW

P. David Pearson
Taffy E. Raphael
Vicki L. Benson
Christina L. Madda

This chapter will:

- Consider how conceptions of balance have changed over time.
- Revisit the research base that supports the importance of balance in the literacy curriculum.
- Offer our reconceptualization of balance in light of new research, new insights, and today's changing context.
- Consider the implications of external forces and the challenges they present to ensuring balance in comprehensive literacy instruction.

DEFINING BALANCE IN THE LITERACY CURRICULUM

Balance, a key term of the late 1990s, was born out of what the popular press (e.g., Levine, 1994; Lemann, 1997) and the research community (e.g.,

Pearson, 2004) have termed the "Reading Wars." The idea of balance has drawn advocates from both sides of the aisle—some taking a whole-language perspective as the balanced approach (e.g., McIntyre & Pressley, 1996) and others viewing an early code emphasis as the cornerstone of a balanced framework (e.g., Lyon, 1997). Each side claimed to be the balanced parties in this debate. However, as we have argued in previous editions of this volume, the unidimensional views of balance that often emerged from these debates fail to capture its true complexity. The political context of the debate has placed curricular decisions, such as how much or how little phonics, at center stage—thus watering down the notion of balance by minimizing the importance of many other facets of literacy instruction. At stake then, and what continues to be at stake as we struggle to reconceptualize balance in light of our new research and insights, is the experience we provide students as they enter schooling and begin the process of learning to read, write, and talk about all kinds of texts.

As we reflect on balance roughly a decade after our first entry into this space, not only is it important to remind ourselves of where we've been, but also we must consider what is unique about where we currently stand. The presence of new and changing literacy demands of the 21st century, as well as today's political climate with its high-stakes accountability, holds implications for what it means to achieve balance in literacy instruction and how it is we can get there. The contributors to this volume want the literacy experience to be what research suggests, and we believe to be, is "fully" balanced: to focus on a range of texts, to build strategies for working with today's texts and other media, and to prepare students to manage the variety of informational sources they encounter daily in a range of settings and for many purposes. We begin this chapter by revisiting past conceptions of balance and the forces that have shaped them. Second, we consider what we've learned from research about the core elements that constitute a balanced literacy program and why they are crucial. We then extend the discussion as we consider today's educational context and the ways in which it calls for a more progressive and reconceptualized notion of balance.

Evolving Conceptions of Balance

Determining the evidence for best practices for a balanced literacy curriculum requires the fundamental step of defining the construct—balance—and the components to which the research base applies. Two questions frame this section:

1. How have conceptions of balance evolved over time?
2. What research base supports the need for balance in the literacy curriculum?

Our initial conceptions of balance—as described in earlier editions of this book (Pearson & Raphael, 1999, 2003) grew out of the antagonistic "Reading Wars" debate (Pearson, 2004). In these renditions, the debate positioned skills (i.e., phonics) against holistic (i.e., whole-language) approaches to teaching reading, or—in its more current framing—literacy as a set of cognitive skills (Snow, Burns, & Griffin, 1998) versus a set of cultural practices that, in turn, shape and influence cognition and identities (Gee, 2000). The content of the debate has played out in issues involving curricular content, the nature of texts, teacher preparation and professional development, and, particularly, who controls the decisions within these areas.

These debates are not new or unique. A century ago, the reading debates pitted ABCs (synthetic phonics) against analytic phonics (words first, then the letters) (Mathews, 1966). Right after World War II, the debate focused on look–say (exemplified by the classic Dick and Jane readers) versus phonics (see Chall, 1967; Mathews, 1966). In one form or another, the debate has always been about the *emphasis* during earliest stages of formal reading instruction—whether to focus on *breaking the code* (i.e. code-emphasis) or *understanding what we read* (i.e., meaning-emphasis) (see Chall, 1967, 1997, for a historical treatment of the debate).

The code-emphasis side takes a "simple view of reading" (Gough & Hillinger, 1980): reading comprehension = decoding × listening comprehension. Those who advocate the simple view argue that since the code (the cipher that maps letters onto sounds) is what students do not know, the sooner they learn it, the better they will be able to read. Get phonics and decoding out of the way early so that students can begin to engage in regular reading—by translating letters into the sounds of oral language and then using the same cognitive processes that facilitate listening comprehension to understand what they read.

The meaning-emphasis side argues that since making meaning is the ultimate goal of reading, it is best to start students off with that very same expectation. If teachers provide relevant "scaffolding" to help students determine textual meaning(s), learners will, as a natural by-product, acquire the cipher for mapping sounds onto letters. Moreover, in their emphasis on meaning, advocates argue for beginning on many fronts simultaneously such as the following three: oral reading activities; shared reading (where teachers and students together read and study a book); and writing through pictures and temporary spellings. Ultimately, the code-emphasis side argued that we should teach students what they do not directly know, while the meaning-emphasis side argues that we should bootstrap what they do not know by relying on what they do know (see Pearson, 1976, for a full treatment of these issues).

In addition to the early debates about emphasis, literacy educators debated about the *instructional focus.* The concern was whether the growth of each individual *child* or the sanctity of the *curriculum* should dominate the teachers' decision-making processes. One camp wanted to make sure that each child experienced the optimal curriculum for his or her development. For example, Harste, Woodward, and Burke (1984) wrote about approaches that made the child the primary curriculum informant. The individual-child camp argued that there are many paths to reading acquisition, while the curricular-sanctity camp argued that there are many variations in the way the single path is traversed. The question was how to balance curricular-driven instructional decisions (i.e., all my students must learn X) with child-driven instructional decisions (i.e., Jason will learn X when he is ready).

Over the past decade, the context for debates about balance has broadened. As painful and enduring as the Reading Wars have been in the past, they have helped educators and researchers see the problems of a single-dimension either–or approach (Pearson, 2004). We currently argue in favor of a conception of balance that responds to the complex and challenging settings that characterize today's literacy teaching and learning. We have become more sophisticated as a field about what and how we teach, while we continue to struggle to ensure that all students are able to participate in a full range of meaningful literacy practices. Today, we must recognize that balance is not an external construct achieved by coordinating phonics and whole-language components. Rather, achieving balance is a complex process that requires flexibility and artful orchestration of literacy's various contextual and conceptual aspects. Reconceptualizing balance requires attention to the wide array of the components at work, to their interconnectedness and to the contextual elements that influence how balance manifests itself in today's classroom.

Balance Today

Three sources of evidence point to the importance of a balanced literacy curriculum today. First, a look at U.S. students' achievement levels, as reflected in standardized norm-referenced tests (e.g., the National Assessment of Educational Progress [NAEP], indicates that there is work to be done to ensure that all students are achieving the highest levels of literacy. Second, research syntheses, as well as large-scale studies of effective literacy instruction, suggest that there is a broad range of skills, strategies, genres, and contexts that must be considered in a complete literacy curriculum—and a finite amount of time in which teachers have to teach it. Third, a critical analysis of "balanced literacy" as a historical construct worthy of our attention divulges some limitations of long-standing models and the need to reconsider the construct.

Current State of Achievement

Results from large-scale assessments of students' literacy achievement in U.S. schools are cause for concern about current practices. The diversity of our student population is steadily increasing, and performance levels on national assessments show a widening achievement gap between students of diverse backgrounds (i.e., from ethnic and racial minority groups, speaking a first language other than English, living in poverty) and mainstream (i.e., white, middle-class, native English-speaking) students. For example, the achievement data in Figure 2.1 reflects students' performance levels on the 2002 NAEP (Grigg, Daane, Jin, & Campbell, 2003). Using Figure 2.1, compare the scores of black and Hispanic students in 12th grade to those of white and Asian–Pacific Islander students in grade 8. You'll notice that by 12th grade, as a group, students from diverse backgrounds have fallen 4 years behind their mainstream peers. The average 12th-grade black student's score (267) is at the same level as the average eighth-grade Asian–Pacific Islander student (267), and slightly below that of the average eighth-grade white student (272). An average 12th-grade Hispanic student's score (273) is only 1 point above that of an average eighth-grade white student. Such a large disparity in average scores suggests that a variety of means will be required to address the problem.

Effective Literacy Instruction

There are many reasons that can explain the achievement gap reflected in tests such as the NAEP. These explanations include such factors as economic disparities and related differences in experiential background before entering school, high mobility rates, and so forth—factors that are

Ethnicity	Grade 4	Grade 8	Grade 12
White	229	272	292
Black	199	245	267
Hispanic	201	247	273
Asian–Pacific Islander	224	267	286

FIGURE 2.1. Achievement gap.

well beyond the control of a classroom teacher or school staff. Yet, we know from research that there are important factors that we can control within schools and classrooms that influence student achievement levels—those of curriculum that frame instruction (i.e., *what* to teach) and the quality of teaching in implementing the curriculum (i.e., *how* it is taught). For example, a review of research that led to the National Reading Panel Report (National Reading Panel, 2000) suggests that a complete reading program must include instruction in comprehension and fluency as well as basic understanding of the symbol system at the word level (phonics and phonemic awareness).

Others have demonstrated the centrality of concept knowledge or vocabulary learning in general and particularly for students who do not speak English as their native language (Carlo et al., 2004). Taylor, Pearson, Peterson, and Rodriguez (2003, 2005) identified a set of classroom practices, dubbed "teaching for cognitive engagement," that support higher levels of achievement; the set includes teacher coaching rather than telling, students' active participation in activities that require high levels of thinking (e.g., book club discussions, inquiry groups), high levels of questioning, and time for students' sustained engagement in reading and writing.

How do these findings connect with the achievement gap? Research documents the limited opportunities diverse students have for high-quality instruction, even within what teachers believe to be a balanced curriculum. Researchers such as Darling-Hammond (1995) and Fitzgerald (1995) have documented that, when compared to mainstream peers, students of diverse backgrounds tend to receive a great deal of instruction in lower-level skills and little instruction in reading comprehension and higher-level thinking about text. It is a conspiracy of good intentions—one that might be labeled "first things first," where the logic is something like "Let's get the words right and the facts straight before we get to the 'what ifs' and 'I wonders' of classroom instruction." And, of course, the conspiracy is that many lower-performing students spend their entire school careers getting the words right and the facts straight, never reaching that higher-level thinking. One reason for this disparity and conspiracy—lowered expectations for the achievement of students of diverse backgrounds and related limited instructional focus areas—is something we can, and should, change.

Unpacking the Components of Balanced Literacy

As we described above, historically different proponents have excluded or privileged certain literacy components (e.g., pitting instruction in basic skills *against* use of authentic, meaningful literature and literacy experiences).

Thus, for many years the term *balance* as appropriated by either side in the Reading Wars debate led to an oversimplified notion—one that applies only to balance within literacy instructional elements. In the remainder of this chapter, we unpack the construct of *balance* with an eye toward what it might become. In doing so, we argue for the need for a comprehensive literacy curriculum that gets at all components of literacy (Pearson & Raphael, 1999; Au & Raphael, 1998) while avoiding the potential problem of literacy's becoming the curricular bully, driving out and overshadowing other important school subjects.

BEST PRACTICES IN ACTION

By deconstructing and then reassembling the phenomenon known as balance, we believe we can build a case for the rich knowledge bases teachers need to implement comprehensive literacy instruction that is truly balanced. In so doing, we "complexify" balance by moving beyond the code versus meaning debate (i.e., balance in the past) to argue that there are many independent elements of literacy that must be simultaneously balanced (i.e., balance today). As a beginning, we find it useful to consider a series of continua that reflect multiple dimensions of literacy instruction. These include (1) contextual continua and (2) content continua.

Contextual Continua

While there are many contextual aspects that literacy educators attempt to balance in their daily teaching activities, we have chosen to focus here on four: authenticity, classroom discourse, teachers' roles, and curricular control (see Figure 2.2). Illustrations of these four concepts exemplify why a mere meeting in the middle between code- and meaning-emphasized instruction is not enough to achieve that balance we seek in literacy instruction.

First, the notion of *authenticity* has been identified as important to students' literacy learning (Florio-Ruane & Raphael, 2004). The argument underlying the promotion of authenticity is that too many school tasks are unauthentic, unrealistic, and, by implication, not useful for engaging in real-world literacy activities; that is, instead of teaching kids how to "do school," we should be teaching them how to "do life." The content students read, write, and talk about and the activity settings in which students work should be grounded in authentic tasks and goals. These include writing for real audiences and purposes (e.g., Flint & Cappelo, 2003), writing to make sense of their lives (Dyson, 2003; Schultz, 2002), and reading to engage in book club or other discussions with teachers

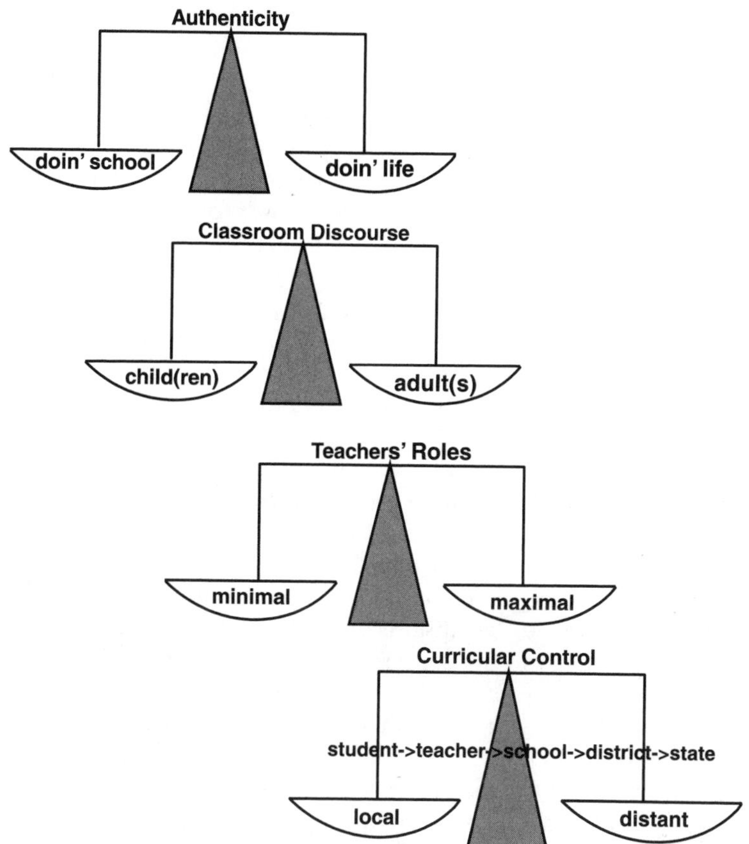

FIGURE 2.2. Balancing contextual factors.

and peers (e.g., Raphael, Florio-Ruane, George, Hasty, & Highfield, 2004). To be downplayed are activities such as writing solely to demonstrate knowledge of conventions or reading to successfully answer a set of comprehension questions. On the face of it, it might seem hard to disagree with an emphasis on authenticity. However, if authenticity were pursued too singlemindedly, some useful skills might never be acquired. If all instruction were held to the authenticity criterion, there might be no occasion for treating formal features of language (e.g., its structure, sound–symbol system, punctuation) as objects of study. For example, children arguably need to understand the "code"—how sounds are captured in written language, conventions for conveying stress and intonation—for engaging in lifelong literacy; yet, the practice activities associated with becoming fluent in such areas may be limited to school practice tasks or reading practice readers. One way of labeling what might be lost under a regime of hyperauthenticity is knowledge "about language" and how it works in different contexts. Clearly, balance is important across the continuum bounded by "doing school" and "doing life."

A second contextual aspect is the type of *classroom discourse* that students experience. Sociolinguists such as Cazden (2001) and Philips (1972) note the importance of control, specifically over topics and turn taking. Teachers may control topics and turns, topics but not turns, turns but not topics, or neither topic nor turn. Students can exert similar control. Depending on the goal of the literacy event, activity, or lesson, different patterns of classroom talk are appropriate. Moreover, many scholars today underscore the variations in children's experiences with the discourse of the classroom or school setting more generally. Gee (2000) and others point out how inextricably linked literacy development is to oral language and its use. Thus, the discourse patterns and related identities students bring to school may align differentially with the way in which language is used in schools. Students' primary language practices directly influence the degree to which they can participate in the literacy practices of schooling. Balance, then, must take into account not only who is controlling the topics and turns under discussion, but which language(s) and discourses are practiced in the context of schooling.

The *teachers' roles* within a classroom are closely related to the type of classroom discourse. Au and Raphael (1998) characterize variations in teachers' roles in terms of the amount of teacher control and student activity. They define five teacher roles: (1) explicit instructing, (2) modeling, (3) scaffolding, (4) facilitating, and (5) participating. These reflect decreasing control by the teacher and increased activity on the part of the student (see Figure 2.3). Thus, students are most passive when teachers are engaged in direct instruction and most active when they assume more conversational control. Au and Raphael's description implies that it is just as mistaken to assume that literacy learning is limited to situations in which the teacher is engaged in explicit instruction as it is to assume that learning is meaningful only when the teacher is out of the picture. Maloch (2002) found that just because the teacher shares her thinking does not mean that students are taking on the language they are hearing for their own uses and purposes. It is important to have variability in support levels if students are to take up learning. Further, researchers such as Rodgers (2004) have demonstrated how teachers' roles vary even within these different discourse settings. Rodgers's observations of teaching and learning over time illustrated the lack of an apparent scope or sequence to the teaching contexts and related teacher and student roles. That is, teachers did not start out with greater control and move steadily to lesser. Rather, teachers varied the amount of support

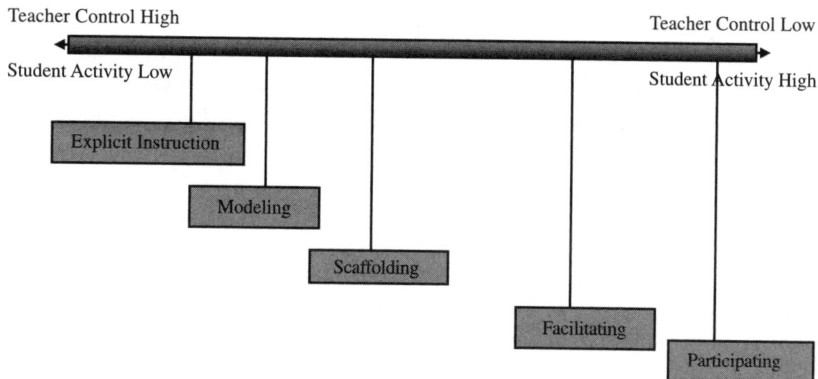

FIGURE 2.3. Teachers' roles.

they provided and the related degree of teacher control and student activity levels according to their perceptions of what students needed, thus demonstrating that the delicate element of balance is one partially crafted by the teacher.

A fourth aspect is *curricular control*—who, or what, "calls the shots" in terms of how teachers and students spend their time in classrooms. At one extreme, control is most distant from the classroom (e.g., at the national or state levels) where curriculum is controlled by those least familiar with the specific students who study the curriculum. Such control may be exerted through mandating of the textbooks to be used, specifying standards or benchmarks of performance, or (as appears to be increasingly dominant) the tests that students, teachers, and schools are held accountable to. At the other extreme, control is in the hands of those most intimately involved with the students, specifically classroom teachers or grade-level teams. And, in some classrooms, teachers cede curricular control to their students—in terms of the books they read, the pieces they write, and the artifacts they choose to bring forward to represent their learning.

Balancing across these two extremes is crucial. On the one hand, all educators must make clear those standards to which they would hold students accountable as these students move through the curriculum. Fourth-grade teachers have the right to assume that certain curriculum content was covered and mastered prior to the students' entering grade 4. Similarly, the fourth-grade teacher has a right to know what information these students will be held accountable for when they matriculate to their next grade level. However, perhaps only the parents of these fourth graders know them better than their classroom teachers. Thus, to dictate specific instructional methods and even specific curriculum materials for reaching benchmarks and standards is to deny students the right to have those decisions made by the individuals who know them best—their teachers. In short, when curricular control is too distant from the classroom, it is difficult for schools and teachers to adhere to their basic professional responsibility to adapt to individual differences.

Content Continua

Balancing the contextual aspects of literacy instruction sets the stage for balance within the content of what is taught. We highlight several aspects of the curricular content, some of which have been central to debates about literacy instruction and some of which have been implicit or understated in the debates. All, we think, are essential to a complete view of balance. They are (1) skill contextualization, (2) text genres, (3) text difficulty, (4) response to literature, (5) subject-matter emphasis, (6) balance within the language arts, and (7) balance within reading instruction (see Figure 2.4).

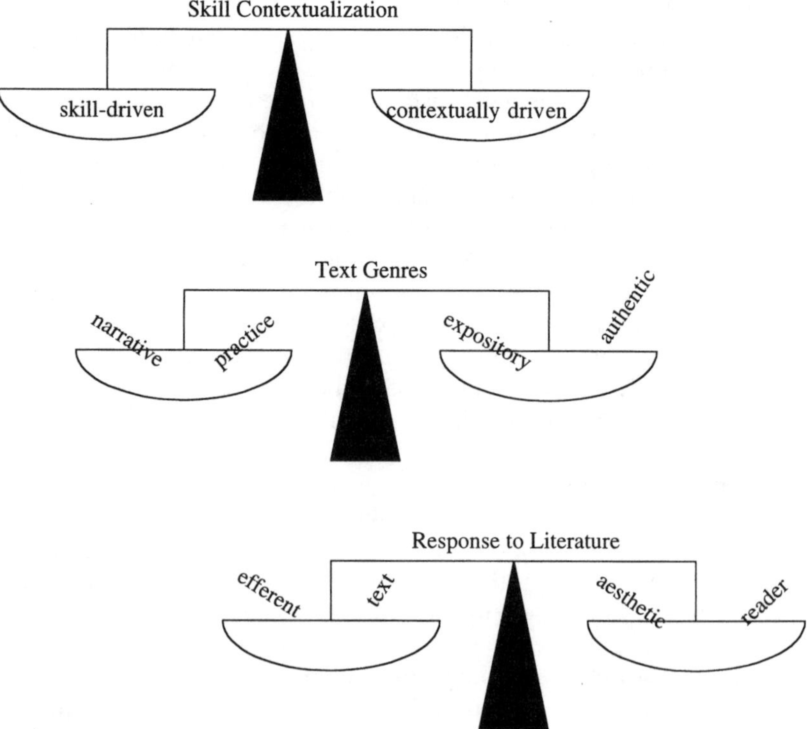

FIGURE 2.4. Balancing curricular content.

Skill contextualization (Pearson & Raphael, 1990) refers to the primary "context" from which the instruction of a particular skill or strategy arises. At the one extreme, teachers may rely on a predetermined curriculum of skill instruction, often tied to a curricular scope and sequence that operates within and across grade levels. At the other extreme, the texts and the tasks that arise in the course of instruction, or, even more common, the needs that a given student or set of students demonstrate, are the determining force behind what is taught. In the latter view, the curriculum is unveiled as teachable moments occur, with the text, the tasks, and the students functioning as springboards to skill or strategy instruction.

We suggest the need for teachers to operate flexibly between these two extremes. It makes a great deal of sense, for example, to teach about point of view as students read historical fiction related to the American Civil War, even if point of view happens to be scheduled at some other point in the academic year's guide to curriculum. Conversely, it makes little sense, in the context of reading Bunting and Diaz's (1994) *Smoky Night* to a group of second graders, to highlight the /fl/ blend in *flames*, simply because it appeared in the text at the same time that the /fl/ blend popped up in an instructional scope and sequence plan. However, strict reliance on emerging questions, issues, or teachable moments as the standard by which teachers determine the content of the literacy curriculum creates problems or uncertainties since, at some point, aspects of the literacy curriculum really do have to be covered.

A second area of content balance is *genre* (e.g., Hicks, 1998; Nodelman, 1992; Pappas & Pettegrew, 1998). Genre refers to the types of texts that form the basis of the literacy curriculum—stories, personal narratives, poems, essays, descriptions, a range of specific expository structures. However, literacy can no longer be defined simply as the reading and writing of printed text. Instead, we need to consider the multiple and overlapping forms of literacy, including digital, visual, spoken, and printed forms, that constitute the act of constructing and expressing meaning today (New London Group, 1996). For example, multimedia formats such as the Internet combine elements such as text, sound, color, images, and layout to convey meaning. It is critical that we help students develop literate competencies within such forms of "new literacies" (see Kress, 2001; Lankshear & Knobel, 2003; Gee, 2000).

Further, new literacies include weblogs, console games, instant messaging, looking up "cheats" on the Internet for game playing, and chatting online (Pahl & Rowsell, 2005). Thus, students today engage in multiple genres that transcend traditional notions contrasting informational with narrative texts. Related literate actions are complex, varied, sophisticated, and extend beyond school-based literate activities (Moje, Young, Readance, & Moore, 2000). These new technologies raise questions about what it means to balance teaching across genres and what new genres students need to learn to control to achieve different purposes. They raise questions of how new genres can support students' learning within more traditional genres.

The debate about genre isn't limited to defining text forms. It also involves questions of balancing authentic and instructional texts. Some literacy educators argue that young readers learn best when reading and responding to authentic literature, which reflects purposeful use of language, complex natural language, and compelling story lines (e.g., Dyson, 2003). Others have argued that such literary criteria make little sense in selecting books that young readers need to become fluent readers (e.g., Hiebert, 1998). Teachers need the flexibility to travel the full range of positions on this axis as well. Even our youngest students must be able to handle, read (even if it's "pretend-read"), and respond to high-quality literary texts—texts written by authors to inform, persuade, entertain, and inspire. However, when it comes to acquiring the skills that enable authentic reading, relying on traditional literature to promote skill development may serve neither the literature nor the skills well. Factors ranging from word placement on a page to relationships between words and pictures may actually make wonderful literary texts though poor materials for practicing and fine-tuning skills. Also, the sheer amount of practice reading that early readers need to engage in calls for a host of easy-to-read books students can read at their independent level. As engaging as these books may be to young and enthusiastic readers, many, perhaps most, may never qualify as quality literature. Neither high-quality trade books nor practice books can serve as the sole diet of books for young readers to become proficient in literacy activities.

The third dimension of content balance relates to *text difficulty*, regardless of the genre of the text. For students to gain the literacy skills and strategies they need, teachers today have two responsibilities (see Raphael et al., 2004). First, they must ensure that excellent diagnostic decisions are made about where to place students instructionally—to make sure that students are taught what they need using texts written for their instructional reading level. But, today, that means realistically that many students will be taught to read using texts that are below or far below what is appropriate to their age level. So, the second responsibility teachers have is one of access. They must ensure that all students are given access to age-appropriate texts and held accountable for writing in response to the text and talking about the issues with their peers and the teacher—in settings such as "Book Club" (Raphael, Pardo, & Highfield, 2002). Thus, teachers must balance students' exposure to texts of high quality that requires engagement in high levels of reading, writing, and talk with students' opportunity to improve their independent reading abilities through focused teaching using texts written at their instructional level.

The fourth dimension of content balance is *response to literature* (Beach & Hynds, 1991). The debate here stems from complex issues related to readers' individual interpretations of text and the tensions concerning social and cultural values that almost inevitably arise in literature discussions. This debate has been traveled along two axes—reader-driven versus text-driven understandings, and conventional (i.e., culturally sanctioned) versus personal interpretations. As our field has moved toward authentic literature as the basis for our reading programs, teachers find themselves face to face with students' response to the content of literature: the enduring themes of the human experience (love, hate, prejudice, friendship, religious values, human rights, and so forth). Fourth and fifth graders reading Taylor's (1990) *Mississippi Bridge* will undoubtedly initiate conversations about how African Americans were treated by southern whites in the 1930s, which can lead to conversations about racial relations today. Third graders reading and responding to McLerran's book (1991) *Roxaboxen* unpack their own family stories and memories and consider the relationships they have with family members across generations.

Debates about response are deeply rooted in beliefs about the functions of schooling, the separation of church and state, and the roles of parents and teachers. Further, they are rooted in beliefs about the development of students' interpretive dispositions—whether we privilege each reader's interpretation of the story's meaning or author's message, or whether there is a "correct" (official or conventional) meaning that teachers are obligated to help students learn for later demonstration that they have acquired that conventional meaning. Balancing response to literature actually involves balancing the tension between the two goals of schooling—connecting to the past and preparing to meet an uncertain future. On the one hand, schools are obligated to teach students the cultural lore of our society, our history, our cultural and linguistic tools, our norms for interaction, and so forth. On the other hand, schools must build our future citizenry, helping students become adults who can live in a world that will undoubtedly differ significantly from the world we live in today. This tension between convention and invention must be addressed through a curriculum that balances the individual with the culture.

A fifth dimension of content balance turns on the relationship between literacy and other *subject-matter domains*, such as mathematics, science, social studies, art, music, and the like. The point here is simple but important: As much as we might like to see literacy assume a central role in the school curriculum and as much as we might be grateful for the recent No Child Left Behind (NCLB; 2002)-induced focus on reading, we are keenly aware of the dangers we will face if the elementary or secondary curriculum becomes too literacy-centric. There are at least three reasons for all literacy educators to press for greater balance across subject-matter areas: (1) to assure a steady source of knowledge to fuel the comprehension and composition processes; (2) to find contexts in which students can authentically apply their literacy strategies; and (3) to ensure the integrity of disciplinary knowledge as a goal in its own right.

It is foolhardy for those who care about reading and writing acquisition to press for its emphasis at the cost of disciplinary knowledge. Reading and writing are not abstract processes. When we read, when we write, we read and write about something in particular—a text lies in front of us in reading or just behind the mind's eye in writing. We create or understand texts that are grounded in knowledge and experience. If we deny access to the knowledge that comes from rich curricular experiences in the disciplines, we ultimately deny progress to students' reading and writing accomplishments. The second reason is, in a sense, the logical complement of the first. Earlier, in discussing the contextual continuum of authenticity, we made an implicit argument for spplying reading and writing skills and strategies to contexts in which reading and writing were put to service in "real" reading and writing tasks. Nowhere in the school curriculum is this authenticity better portrayed than in the acquisition of disciplinary knowledge and processes.

The benefits of reading and writing are rendered transparent when they are viewed as tools for the acquisition of knowledge and insight typically found in subject-matter learning. Indeed, much has been written recently (e.g., Cervetti, Pearson, Bravo, & Barber, 2006; Romance & Vitale, 1992; Palincsar & Magnusson, 2001) about the efficacy of reading and writing as tools to support inquiry-based science learning. In fact, we believe that if one regards literature (with its inherent emphasis on the stuff of human experience—love and hate, friendship and betrayal, humankind and nature) as a discipline—on a par with science and social studies and mathematics for example—then we can view reading and writing (and we would add oral language) as tools for learning across all of these domains. The third reason is moral in nature: students need a fair shot at all of these subject matters because they are part of the human experience and our particular cultural heritage. To deny their place in the curriculum or to delay their curricular emphasis until after the basics of reading, writing, and language are acquired is to do harm to both their integrity and to the efficacy of good literacy instruction. The literacy curriculum is the better for strong and complementary disciplinary emphases. As Cervetti et al. (2006) put it, reading needs to be transformed from being a curricular "bully" (which it pretty much is in the wake of NCLB and the Reading First Act of 2002) into serving as a curricular "buddy" to enhance both the learning of disciplinary knowledge and its own application in that learning.

In considering the sixth content aspect, *balance within the language arts*, one of the great virtues of the language arts (traditionally thought of as reading, writing, listening, and speaking) is that, while they are surely distinct from one another in function, they are mutually synergistic. What we learn in and through oral language can be put to work in reading and writing, and vice versa. For example, we learn new vocabulary through oral language that allows us to call up the meaning of a specific word when we encounter it in print and later use it in an essay. Conversely, a word we first encounter in a story or an article, such as *glorious* or *misanthrope*, might well make it into our oral language and later our writing. And the new knowledge that we acquire when we listen to a teacher read a book or a story that is beyond our reading level can become the prior knowledge we will use to understand a new text on our own tomorrow. The point? Just because you as a teacher love reading and view it as the nucleus of early schooling does not mean that you will want to privilege it over the other language arts for the very reason that reading is enhanced by progress in listening, speaking, and writing. Hence, the need for balance within the language arts.

Finally, in considering *balance within reading instruction*, we earlier touched on this most salient issue in the debate by emphasizing the code versus meaning distinction. But we are now armed with strong evidence to ensure this sort of balance, for we know—by virtue of the work of the National Reading Panel (NRP; 2000) and a long tradition of research curriculum and pedagogy stemming back into the 1980s (e.g., Anderson, Hiebert, Scott, & Wilkinson, 1984), the 1960s (e.g., Chall, 1967), and even earlier (e.g., Gray, 1948)—that the research confirms the importance of mastering lower-level processes such as phonics and phonemic awareness, as well as thoroughgoing instruction in comprehension and vocabulary. We would add, to go one level deeper into curriculum, that the research also supports balance within each of these important areas of reading instruction—phonemic awareness, phonics, comprehension, and vocabulary (we combine these last two in our discussion as a pair of meaning-emphasis approaches).

Phonemic Awareness

Here the research (National Reading Panel, 2000) suggests that explicit instruction in various elements of phonemic awareness, such as rhyming, phonemic segmentation (breaking a word into its phonemic units—*bat* →/buh/aa/tuh/), and phonemic blending (putting the parts together—

/buh/ /aa/ /tuh/→ *bat*) pays dividends in the long run in terms of its transference to beginning-reading achievement. But we also know that the instruction can include many engaging oral language games (see Snow et al., 1998) and even invented spelling (see Adams, 1990; Clarke, 1988). There is no need to privilege dense skill-oriented programs over engaging language activities.

Phonics

If we recast phonics as word-reading strategies (Ehri, Nunes, Stahl, & Willows, 2001), we find the need for balance here too. We know that the NRP report, its narrow sample of subject populations notwithstanding, concluded that what mattered was early emphasis on the code, not an emphasis on any particular approach to phonics. We know from other work (e.g., Ehri et al., 2001; Gaskins, Ehri, Cress, O'Hara, & Donnelly, 1997a, 1997b) that approaches to word reading are complementary and that students need a full repertoire of tools to do justice to the challenge of pronouncing unknown words encountered in text.

Ehri (1995) talks about four strategies that we find particularly useful as ways of conceptualizing the curricular goals of teachers and the learning needs of students. Ehri suggests that students need to learn to read words using these four approaches—sequential decoding, analogy, contextual analysis, and sight word recognition. Sequential decoding, or letter-by-letter decoding, is the stuff of which the time-honored ABC approach is made. And students can indeed sound out words in this way. Analogy should be focused on word families or phonograms—words that are spelled and pronounced similarly, such as *cat, fat, sat, bat,* and the like. Gaskins et al. (1997a, 1997b) found, in building the Benchmark School curriculum, that analogy instruction was much more effective after sequential decoding has been established among readers. Contextual analysis is an ad hoc form of problem solving—what you do when you come to a word you cannot pronounce, and it involves both intraword (morphological analysis) and extraword (the surrounding context) analysis in order to work. Finally, there is immediate sight word recognition, and it plays two roles in word reading. First, some words, such as *give, have, the,* and *get,* must be learned as sight words because they violate the principles one learns from instruction in sequential decoding and analogy. Second—and this is the really important face of sight word reading—the goal of the other three approaches is to move words from students' repertoire of "arduously analyzable" (I can figure these out if I work at it) to "immediately recognizable" (I know that word; it's *irrefutable*). In short, the goal of phonics and context instruction is to get to the point where readers need them only minimally, freeing up their thinking skills for higher-level processes. Balanced phonics instruction—or, more accurately, balanced word reading instruction—is essential to skilled reading.

Balanced Comprehension Instruction

We know from the National Reading Panel that comprehension can be improved by explicit strategy instruction and by a variety of approaches to vocabulary instruction. And we also know from previous work (see Pearson & Fielding, 1991; Murphy & Wilkinson, 2005) that rich conversations about text can improve comprehension of both the texts within which the instruction is embedded and new texts that students subsequently read on their own. Hence, we are prepared to conclude that all three of these approaches—strategy instruction, rich talk about text (of the sort described in the earlier section on students' responses to literature), and semantically rich conversations about word meanings (see Beck, McKeown, & Kucan, 2002; Blachowicz & Fisher, 2002) should all be a part of a balanced curriculum. At this point in our research history, there seems to be no basis for privileging any one of the three over the other two, and they do seem to relate well to one another as a complementary set.

RETHINKING BALANCE

In thinking about balance then and now, it has become clear that we need to avoid overemphasizing any one particular dimension of literacy instruction. Instead, balance today requires attention toward multiple dimensions that fall along the context and content continua. We borrow from environmental science the concept of "ecological balance," which suggests a system that works together to support each individual component—a comprehensive literacy curriculum that doesn't pit one aspect against another. In doing so, we hope to suggest that we must shift the debates about balance *away* from single-dimension discussions of what to teach and what not to teach, and *toward* the notion that achieving a balanced literacy curriculum is a logical goal of all literacy educators. The ecologically balanced curriculum that follows is based on research focused on a literature-based program, Book Club, for upper elementary reading instruction (Raphael et al., 2002) and a K–5 literacy curriculum designed for the Kamehameha Early Education Program (Au & Carrol, 1997). Both programs are grounded in the belief that ownership of literacy is central to students' lifelong success (see Au & Raphael, 1998). The literacy instructional content that forms the ecological system consists of four areas: (1) comprehension, (2) composition, (3) literary aspects, and (4) language conventions (see Figure 2.5).

Comprehension	Composition	Literary Aspects	Language Conventions
Background Knowledge: prediction Text Processing: summarizing sequencing identifying importance Monitoring: clarifying planning	Process planning drafting revising Writing as a Tool Writing from Sources On-Demand Writing	Literary Elements: theme plot character setting Response to Literature: personal creative critical	Sound/Symbol Grammar Syntax Interaction

FIGURE 2.5. An ecologically balanced curriculum.

Each of these four areas is supported by extensive bodies of research using a range of rigorous research methods (see Raphael & Brock, 1997). We must be conscious not to weigh in too heavily against any particular curriculum aspect, such as downplaying the role of phonics, as depicted in Figure 2.6. Nor should we be overly optimistic about teaching only a small part of the curriculum and hoping the rest will follow, as depicted in Figure 2.7. And, if we take seriously the idea that instruction must be

Comprehension	Composition	Literary Aspects	Language Conventions
Background Knowledge: prediction Text Processing: summarizing sequencing identifying importance Monitoring: clarifying planning	Process: planning drafting revising Writing as a Tool Writing from Sources On-Demand Writing	Literary Elements: theme plot character setting Response to Literature: personal creative critical	Sound/Symbol Grammar Syntax Interaction

FIGURE 2.6. Balance askew when curriculum is ignored.

balanced within the language arts and between the language arts and other subject areas, then we need an even more complex picture, as in Figure 2.8.

So, now we want to wed these two driving metaphors—of ecological balance and orchestrating balance on multiple balance beams simultaneously to create a truly complex but, we think, apt model of good teaching. Unpacking the cluster of dimensions in our balance beam metaphor, focusing on the specifics of content and contextual facets that constitute reading instruction demonstrates some of the complexities in that debate. If we allow teachers the prerogative, for particular situations and students, of positioning themselves on each of these scales independently of the others, then we avoid the overemphasis of any one single dimension and move toward the balance we need to achieve today.

Effective teachers cannot be easily pigeonholed into curricular boxes. If they are good at what they do—orchestrating a complex curriculum in the face of an enormous range of individual differences among students—then they learn to slide along each of these dozen or so contextual and content continua we have identified. At any given moment, they might be at different points along each of the continua, and then, with the slightest change in the instructional ecology of the classroom, change their position on half of them, knowing that in the very next minute they might make another four or five minor shifts in emphasis. Call it orchestration, call it a curricular dance (more like a ballet), call it responsive teaching—no matter the label, it is the essence of professional practice. We believe there is merit in the metaphor of multiple balance beams, each with at least one

Comprehension	Composition	Literary Aspects	Language Conventions
Background Knowledge: prediction Text Processing summarizing sequencing identifying importance Monitoring: clarifying planning	Process: planning drafting revising Writing as a Tool Writing from Sources On-Demand Writing	Literary Elements: theme plot character setting Response to Literature: personal creative critical	Sound/Symbol Grammar Syntax Interaction

FIGURE 2.7. Balance askew when curriculum is overemphasized.

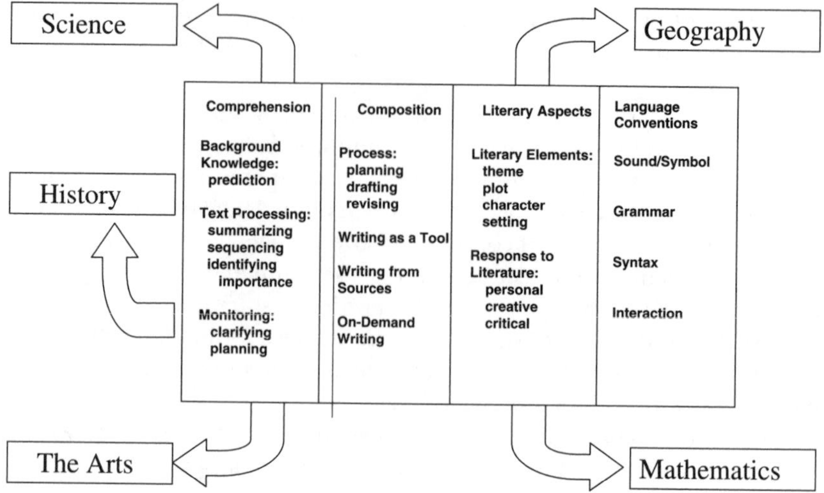

FIGURE 2.8. Balancing within the language arts and between the language arts and other subjects.

and sometimes two axes that must be traversed thoughtfully and independently. It makes balance a more elusive construct, but also a more powerful one—one that we hope we can all strive to achieve in our teaching.

ENGAGEMENT ACTIVITIES

1. Obtain your school, district, or state's standards and/or curriculum related to literacy. Given the ecologically balanced system proposed here, discuss the degree to which these materials reflect or obscure balance within and across contextual factors (i.e., authenticity, classroom discourse, teachers' roles, and curricular control) and curricular content (i.e., skills contextualization, genre, text difficulty, response to literature, subject-matter emphasis, balance within language arts, and balance across reading instruction). Consider the question "What can I do?" based on your findings.
2. The argument for balance in this chapter places much of the responsibility in the hands of the classroom teacher. This teacher must make professional decisions about how to teach particular students with specific needs, use specific curriculum to achieve particular goals, and so forth. How can the profession best support those teachers who lack the professional experiences that may be important to making wise decisions and creating balance?
3. Given your professional experiences, where do you think the challenges to providing or creating a balanced curriculum emerge? What can you

do, as an individual as well as a member of a particular professional community, to infuse balance throughout the literacy curriculum and general classrooms for which you share responsibilities?

REFERENCES

Adams, M. J. (1990). *Beginning to read: Thinking and learning about print.* Cambridge, MA: MIT Press.

Anderson, R. C., Hiebert, E. H., Scott, J. A., & Wilkinson, I. A. G. (1984). *Becoming a nation of readers: The report of the commission on reading.* Washington, DC: U.S. Department of Education.

Au, K. H., & Carrol, J. H. (1997). Improving literacy achievement through a constructivist approach: A KEEP demonstration classroom project. *Elementary School Journal, 97,* 203–221.

Au, K. H., & Raphael, T. E. (1998). Curriculum and teaching in literature-based programs. In T. E. Raphael & K. H. Au (Eds.), *Literature-based instruction: Reshaping the curriculum* (pp. 123–148). Norwood, MA: Christopher-Gordon Publishers.

Beach, R., & Hynds, S. (1991). Research on response to literature. In R. Barr, M. L. Kamil, P. B. Mosenthal, & P. D. Pearson (Eds.), *Handbook of reading research* (Vol. 2, pp. 453–489). New York: Longman.

Beck, I. L., McKeown, M. G., & Kucan, L. (2002). *Bringing words to life: Robust vocabulary instruction.* New York: Guilford Press.

Blachowicz, C., & Fisher, P. (2002). *Teaching vocabulary in all classrooms* (2nd ed.). Columbus, OH: Prentice-Hall.

Bunting, E., & Diaz, D. (1994). *Smoky night.* San Diego, CA: Harcourt.

Carlo, M. S., August, D., McLaughlin, B., Snow, C. E., Dressler, C., Lippman, D. N., et al. (2004). Closing the gap: Addressing the vocabulary needs of English-language learners in bilingual and mainstream classrooms. *Reading Research Quarterly, 39*(2), 188–215.

Cazden, C. B. (2001). *Classroom discourse: The language of teaching and learning.* Portsmouth, NH: Heinemann.

Cervetti, G., Pearson, P. D., Bravo, M. A., & Barber, J. (2006). Reading and writing in the service of inquiry-based science. In R. Douglas, M. Klentschy, & K. Worth (Eds.), *Linking science and literacy in the K–8 classroom* (pp. 221–244). Arlington, VA: National Science Teachers Association Press.

Chall, J. S. (1967). *Learning to read: The great debate.* New York: McGraw-Hill.

Chall, J. S. (1997). *Learning to read: The great debate* (3rd ed.). New York: McGraw-Hill.

Clarke, L. K. (1988). Invented versus traditional spelling in first graders' writings: Effects on learning to spell and read. *Research in the Teaching of English, 22*(3), 281–309.

Darling-Hammond, L. (1995). Inequality and access to knowledge. In J. A. Banks & C. A. M. Banks (Eds.), *Handbook for research on multicultural education* (pp. 465–483). New York: Macmillan.

Dyson, A. H. (2003). *The brothers and sisters learn to write: Popular literacies in childhood and school culture.* New York: Teachers College Press.

Ehri, L. C. (1995). Phases of development in reading words. *Journal of Research in Reading, 18,* 116–125.

Ehri, L., Nunes, S., Stahl, S., & Willows, D. (2001). Systematic phonics instruction helps students learn to read: Evidence from the National Reading Panel's meta-analysis. *Review of Educational Research, 71*(3), 393–447.

Fitzgerald, J. (1995). English-as-a-second-language reading instruction in the United States: A research base. *Journal of Reading Behavior* (now *Journal of Literacy Research*), *27,* 115–152.

Flint, A. S., & Cappello, M. (2003). Negotiating voice and identity in classroom writing events. *National Reading Conference Yearbook, 52,* 181–193.

Florio-Ruane, S., & Raphael, T. E. (2004). Reconsidering our research: Collaboration, complexity, design, and the problem of "scaling up what works." *National Reading Conference Yearbook, 54,* 170–188.

Gaskins, I. W., Ehri, L. C., Cress, C., O'Hara, C., & Donnelly, K. (1997a). Procedures for word learning: Making discoveries about words. *The Reading Teacher, 50,* 312–327.

Gaskins, I. W., Ehri, L. C., Cress, C., O'Hara, C., & Donnelly, K. (1997b). Analyzing words and making discoveries about the alphabetic system: Activities for beginning readers. *Language Arts, 74*(3), 172–174.

Gee, J. P. (2000). The limits of reframing: A response to Professor Snow. *Journal of Literacy Research, 31,* 355–374.

Gough, P. B., & Hillinger, M. L. (1980). Learning to read: An unnatural act. *Bulletin of the Orton Society, 30,* 171–176.

Gray, W. (1948). *On their own in reading: How to give children independence in attacking new words.* Chicago: Scott Foresman.

Grigg, W. S., Daane, M., Jin, Y., & Campbell, J. R. (2003). *The nation's report card: Reading 2002* (No. NCES 2003-521). Washington, DC: U.S. Department of Education, Institute of Education Sciences.

Harste, J. C., Woodward, V. A., & Burke, C. L. (1984). *Language stories and literacy lessons.* Portsmouth, NH: Heinemann.

Hicks, D. (1998). Narrative discourses as inner and outer word. *Language Arts, 75*(1), 28–34.

Hiebert, E. H. (1998). Selecting texts for beginning reading instruction. In T. E. Raphael & K. H. Au (Eds.), *Literature-based instruction: Reshaping the curriculum* (pp. 195–218). Norwood, MA: Christopher-Gordon.

Kress, G. (2001). *The modes and media of contemporary communication.* New York: Oxford University Press.

Lankshear, C., & Knobel, M. (2003). *New literacies and changing knowledge in the classroom.* Buckingham: Open University Press.

Lemann, N. (1997, November). The reading wars. *The Atlantic Monthly, 280,* 128–134.

Levine, A. (1994, December). The great debate revisited. *The Atlantic Monthly.* Available at *www.theatlantic.com/politics/educatio/levine.htm.*

Lyon, G. R. (1997). *Report on learning disabilities research.* (Adapted from testimony by Dr. Reid Lyon before the Committee on Education and the Workforce in the U.S. House of Representatives on July 10, 1997.) Retrieved January 2, 2002, from *http://www.ldonline.org/ld_indepth/reading/nih_report.html*

Maloch, B. (2002). Scaffolding student talk: One teacher's role in literature discussion groups. *Reading Research Quarterly, 37,* 94–112.

Mathews, M. M. (1966). *Teaching to read: Historically considered.* Chicago: University of Chicago Press.

McIntyre, E., & Pressley, M. (1996). *Balanced instruction: Strategies and skills in whole language.* Boston: Christopher-Gordon.

McLerran, A. (2004). *Roxaboxen.* HarperTrophy.

Moje, E. B., Young, J. P., Readence, J. E., & Moore, D. W. (2000). Reinventing adolescent literacy for new times: Perennial and millennial issues. *Journal of Adolescent and Adult Literacy,* 43, 400–410.

Murphy, P. K., & Wilkinson, I. (2005, April). *Making sense of group discussions: What the studies tell us: A meta-analysis.* Paper presented at the annual conference of the American Educational Research Association, Montreal.

National Reading Panel (2000). *Teaching children to read: An evidence-based assessment of the scientific research literature on reading and its implications for reading instruction* (National Institute of Health Pub. No. 00-4769). Washington, DC: National Institute of Child Health and Human Development.

New London Group. (1996). A pedagogy of multiliteracies: Designing social futures. *Harvard Educational Review, 66,* 60–92.

No Child Left Behind Act of 2001, Public Law No. 107-110 (2002). Available at *www.ed.gov/policy/elsec/leg/esea02/index.html.*

Nodelman, P. (1992). *The pleasures of children's literature.* New York: Longman.

Pahl, K., & Rowsell, J. (2005). *Literacy and education: Understanding the new literacy studies in the classroom.* London: Chapman.

Palincsar, A. S., & Magnusson, S. J. (2001). The interplay of firsthand and text-based investigations to model and support the development of scientific knowledge and reasoning. In S. Carver & D. Klahr (Eds.), *Cognition and instruction: Twenty five years of progress* (151–194). Mahwah, NJ: Erlbaum.

Pappas, C., & Pettegrew, B. S. (1998). The role of genre in the psycholinguistic guessing game of reading. *Language Arts, 75*(1), 36–44.

Pearson, P. D. (1976). A psycholinguistic model of reading. *Language Arts, 53*(3), 309–314.

Pearson, P. D. (2004). The reading wars: The politics of reading research and policy—1988 through 2003. *Educational Policy,18*(1), 216–252.

Pearson, P. D., & Fielding, L. (1991). Comprehension instruction. In R. Barr, M. L. Kamil, P. Mosenthal, & P. D. Pearson (Eds.), *Handbook of reading research* (Vol. 2, pp. 819–860). New York: Longman.

Pearson, P. D., & Raphael, T. (1990). Reading comprehension as a dimension of thinking. In B. F. Jones & L. I. Idol, *Dimensions of thinking and cognitive instruction: Implications for reform, Vol. 1* (pp. 209–240). Hillsdale, NJ: Erlbaum.

Pearson, P. D., & Raphael, T. E. (1999). Toward an ecologically balanced literacy curriculum. In L. B. Gambrell, L. M. Morrow, S. B. Newman, & M. Pressley (Eds.), *Best practices in literacy instruction* (pp. 22–33). New York: Guilford Press.

Pearson, P. D., & Raphael, T. E. (2003). Toward a more complex view of balance in the literacy curriculum. In L. M. Morrow, L. B. Gambrell, & M. Pressley (Eds.), *Best practices in literacy instruction* (2nd ed., pp. 23–39). New York: Guilford Press.

Philips, S. U. (1972). Participant structures and communicative competence: Warm Springs children in community and classroom. In C. Cazden, V. P. John, & D. Hymes (Eds.), *Functions of language in the classroom* (pp. 370–394). New York: Teachers College Press.

Raphael, T. E., & Brock, C. H. (1997). Instructional research in literacy: Changing paradigms. In C. Kinzer, D. Leu, & K. Hinchman (Eds.), *Inquiries in literacy theory and practice* (pp. 13–36). Chicago: National Reading Conference.

Raphael, T. E., Florio-Ruane, S., George, M., Hasty, N. L., & Highfield, K. (2004). *Book Club Plus: A literacy framework for primary grades.* Littleton, MA: Small Planet Communications.

Raphael, T. E., Pardo, L. S., & Highfield, K. (2002). *Book Club: A literature-based curriculum* (2nd ed.). Lawrence, MA: Small Planet Communications.

Rodgers, E. (2004). Interactions that scaffold reading performance. *Journal of Literacy Research, 36,* 501–532.

Romance, N. R., & Vitale, M. R. (1992). A curriculum strategy that expands time for in-depth elementary science instruction by using science-based reading strategies: Effects of a year-long study in grade four. *Journal of Research in Science Teaching, 29*(6), 545–554.

Schultz, K. (2002). Looking across space and time: Reconceptualizing literacy learning in and out of school. *Research in the Teaching of English, 36,* 356–390.

Snow, C. E., Burns, M. S., & Griffin, P. (Eds.). (1998). *Preventing reading difficulties in young children.* Washington, DC: National Academy Press.

Taylor, B. M., Pearson, P. D., Peterson, D. P., & Rodriguez, M. C. (2003). Reading growth in high-poverty classrooms: The influence of teacher practices that encourage cognitive engagement in literacy learning. *The Elementary School Journal, 104,* 3–28.

Taylor, B. M., Pearson, P. D., Peterson, D. P., & Rodriguez, M. C. (2005). The CIERA School Change Framework: An evidenced-based approach to professional development and school reading improvement. *Reading Research Quarterly, 40*(1), 40–69.

Taylor, M. (1990). *Mississippi bridge.* New York: Skylark.

Part II

BEST PRACTICES FOR ALL STUDENTS

Chapter 3

BEST PRACTICES IN EARLY LITERACY DEVELOPMENT IN PRESCHOOL, KINDERGARTEN, AND FIRST GRADE

Lesley Mandel Morrow
Diane H. Tracey

This chapter will:

- Discuss theory, philosophy, and research that has had an impact on early-childhood education and early literacy instruction.
- Discuss federal initiatives that have influenced early literacy development in grades pre-K, K, and 1.
- Discuss exemplary early literacy instruction by describing a kindergarten day.
- Discuss an agenda for future research and practice in early literacy instruction.

EVIDENCE-BASED BEST PRACTICES

Babies begin to acquire information about literacy from the moment they are born. They continue to build on their knowledge of oral language, reading, and writing as they go through early childhood and beyond based on the experiences they have at home and in school. A great deal of attention is now being focused on literacy development in early childhood and especially preschool, an area somewhat neglected in the past. Teachers, parents, and administrators have not perceived preschoolers as readers or writers. Their emphasis was on oral language development and social and emotional development. Because of increased research very young children are now viewed as individuals with literacy skills. Although the literacy activities that preschool, kindergarten, and some first-grade children demonstrate and participate in are not conventional, they must be acknowledged and encouraged because they have implications for future success in reading. Like a child's first words and first steps, learning to read and write should be an exciting, fulfilling, and rewarding experience. This chapter draws on current research and blends it with theory and practice that have proved successful in developing literacy in the past. It presents a program for developing literacy in children from birth through first grade. It is influenced by the joint position statement of the International Reading Association and the National Association for the Education of Young Children entitled *Learning to Read and Write: Developmentally Appropriate Practices for Young Children* (1998). It also takes into account the *National Reading Panel Report* (2000); *Put Reading First* (2001), developed by the Center for the Improvement of Early Reading Achievement; the *National Early Literacy Panel Report* (2004); as well as the International Reading Association position paper about *Reading in Preschool* (2006). Other pertinent research dealing with this topic will be documented throughout. The chapter is based on the following rationale:

1. Literacy learning begins in infancy.
2. Families need to provide a literacy-rich environment and literacy experiences at home to help children acquire skills. Families need to be actively involved in their children's literacy learning when they enter school.
3. Teachers need to be aware that children come to school with prior knowledge about reading and writing and that this knowledge is different from one child to the next.
4. Literacy learning requires a supportive environment that builds positive feelings about self and literacy activities.
5. Learning requires a rich literacy environment with accessible materials and varied experiences.
6. Teachers and parents must serve as models for literacy by scaffolding and demonstrating strategies that need to be learned.
7. During literacy experiences children should interact within a social context to share information, which motivates them to learn from one another.

8. Early reading and writing experiences should be meaningful and concrete and should actively engage children.
9. Early reading and writing experiences need to provide systematic, intentional, explicit instruction of skills.
10. A literacy development program should focus on experiences that include reading, writing, listening, speaking, and viewing.
11. Diversity in cultural and language backgrounds must be acknowledged and addressed in early literacy development.
12. Differences in literacy achievement from one child to the next in the same grade will vary and must be addressed with small-group instruction, early intervention, or inclusive classroom programs.
13. Assessment of achievement should be frequent, match instructional strategies, and use multiple formats for evaluating student behavior.
14. Standards for early literacy grade-level benchmarks should be tied to instruction and assessment and used as a means for reaching goals for all children to read fluently by third grade.
15. We must work toward having universal preschool in the public sector for three- and four-year-olds, and all-day kindergarten.
16. Programs should be research-based. For example, we know from the results of the National Reading Panel Report (2000) that certain components in reading instruction are necessary to ensure student success.

Historical Influences on Early Literacy Instruction

Philosophers have influenced early literacy instruction, and theorists have focused on child development, early childhood education, and literacy development. Philosophers such as Pestalozzi and Froebel (Rusk & Scotland, 1979) talked about natural environments in which children would unfold through sensory experiences involving learning through touch, smell, taste, size, and shape. Play was crucial, as was the social, emotional, and physical development of the child. Intellectual development was important; however, it was no more of a priority than social, emotional, and physical development. John Dewey's (1916/1966) progressive education philosophy had a strong influence on preschool and kindergarten practices from the 1920s throughout the rest of the 20th century. Dewey led us to themed units of study that connect learning to meaning and purpose. He influenced the environments in preschool and kindergarten, with classrooms set up with different content-area activity centers. The block corner, music and art centers, dramatic-play area, science and social studies displays, and the library corner were the result of Dewey's ideas. A typical day included the following:

1. Circle time to talk about the weather and the calendar and to focus discussion on a science or social studies theme. If the theme were "good health," for example, the class would listen to a story and sing a song in keeping with this theme.
2. Free play allowed children to paint at easels, build with blocks, engage in dramatic play with dress-up clothing, and work in a pretend kitchen. Children explored and experimented with materials in social settings, with little direction other than safety precautions.
3. Snack and rest time were included because of the emphasis on good health and learning about good nutrition.
4. Children had outdoor play for large-motor development.
5. The day ended with a storybook reading.

There was no attempt at formal lessons; in fact, they were frowned on as inappropriate for the developmental stage of the child; however, teachable moments were used to advantage. There was no place in this program for formal reading instruction.

Montessori (1965) had a strong effect on early childhood and literacy instruction, believing that materials for children needed to serve a purpose for learning. She created manipulative activities to develop skills that focused on getting the right answer. Very few group lessons occur in this program, except to introduce new materials into the classroom. Children work independently at their own pace and level. According to Montessori, young children needed to use their senses to learn; therefore, she created many materials that involved the senses, such as tactile letters and wooden letters with different colors for long and short vowels.

Learning theorists Piaget (Piaget & Inhelder, 1969) and Vygotsky (1981) also had a strong impact on early childhood and literacy instruction. Both suggested social settings for learning. Those who interpret Piaget's theory of cognitive development for instruction describe a curriculum that encourages exploration of natural environments and learning rather than direct or explicit teaching. Vygotsky described learning in a similar manner to that of Piaget; however, he proposed that adults should scaffold and model behaviors they wanted children to learn. These theories and philosophies that influenced early childhood education were concerned with the following:

- Prepared and natural environments for learning.
- Equal emphasis on social, emotional, physical, and intellectual development.
- Supportive adults who encourage social interaction for learning to occur.

- A focus on learning rather than teaching.
- Awareness that children must be actively involved to learn.

Reading Readiness and Early Literacy

Morphett and Washburne (1931) believed in postponing formal reading instruction until the child was developmentally "old enough." Their research concluded that children with a mental age of 6 years 6 months made better progress on a test of reading achievement than younger children. Although many educators believed that natural maturation was the precursor to literacy, others grew uncomfortable with simply waiting for children to become ready to read. They did not advocate formal reading instruction in early childhood but did begin to provide experiences that they believed would help children become ready for reading. Instead of waiting for a child's natural maturation to unfold, educators focused on nurturing that maturation by teaching children what they believed to be a set of prerequisite skills for reading, focusing on *auditory discrimination* of familiar sounds, similar sounds, rhyming words, and the sounds of letters; *visual discrimination*, including color recognition, shape, and letter identification; left-to-right eye progression; *visual-motor* skills, such as cutting on a line with scissors and coloring within the lines; and *large-motor* abilities, such as skipping, hopping, and walking in a straight line. While the practice of many of these skills can still be seen in today's classrooms, new research has extended our understanding of the ways in which young children's literacy abilities develop, and, subsequently, have impacted our classroom practices.

Literacy Research for the Past 35 Years

Research from the 1960s through the 1990s brought to life new information about the importance of children's oral language development, early writing development, emergent reading behaviors, and family literacy experiences. With this new information and the whole-language movement, educators moved away from the abstract reading readiness activities thought to be the precursors to reading, toward more natural ways of developing reading, as in the past. Although the explicit teaching of skills was seen as not appropriate for young children, "emergent literacy behaviors" were being recognized and encouraged. Marie Clay (1966) promoted this term and the reading of good literature to children. Emergent literacy recognized scribble writing and invented spelling as the beginning of conventional writing and encouraged these behaviors. Children engaged in pretend reading, often using pictures or props to help them read the story. Emergent literacy saw a dynamic relationship between the communication skills (reading, writing, oral language, and listening), because each influences the other in the course of development. Development occurs in everyday contexts of the home, community, and school through meaningful and functional experiences that require the use of literacy in natural settings. For example, when studying a theme such as dinosaurs from a whole-language and emergent literacy perspective, the teacher may focus on some letters and sounds in the initial consonants found in the names of dinosaurs. Including a child's family in the development of his or her emergent literacy skills is encouraged.

Comprehensive and Balanced Literacy Instruction

A position statement by the International Reading Association, entitled *Using Multiple Methods of Beginning Reading Instruction* (1999), suggests that there is no one single method or single combination of methods that can successfully teach all children to read. "Therefore, teachers must have a strong knowledge of multiple methods for teaching reading and a strong knowledge of the children in their care so they can create the appropriate balance of methods needed for the children they teach." A comprehensive balanced perspective in reading instruction means the careful selection of the best theories available and the use of learning strategies to match the learning styles of individual children. This might mean the use of more skill-based explicit instruction for some and problem-solving strategies for others (Morrow & Tracey, 1997). According to Pressley (1998), explicit teaching of skills is a good start for constructivist problem-solving activities, and constructivist activities permit consolidation and elaboration of skills. One method does not preclude or exclude the other. A balanced perspective is not simply a combination of random strategies. A teacher may select strategies from different learning theories to provide balance. One child, for example, may be a visual learner and benefit from sight word instruction. Another child's strength may be auditory learning, and he or she will learn best from phonics instruction. The balanced approach focuses more on what is important for each individual child than the latest fad in literacy instruction.

Balanced instruction is grounded in a rich model of literacy learning that encompasses both the elegance and complexity of the reading and language arts processes. Such a model acknowledges the importance of both form (phonics, mechanics, etc.) and function (comprehension, purpose, meaning) of the literacy processes and recognizes that learning occurs most effectively in a whole–part–whole context.

Current Influences on Early Literacy

Publications from the federal government and professional associations, such as *Preventing Reading Difficulties in Young Children* (Snow, Burns, &

Griffin, 1998), *Learning to Read and Write: Developmentally Appropriate Practices* (International Reading Association and National Association for the Education of Young Children, 1998), and the National Reading Panel Report (2000), all deal with concerns about early literacy instruction and how to improve it. In the spring of 2002, the Elementary and Secondary Education Act that includes the No Child Left Behind bill was passed. Although early literacy development has been a focus throughout the years, it is presently in the spotlight more than ever because of these documents.

The National Reading Panel Report (2000) suggests that instruction in early literacy needs to be organized and systematic. It also identifies areas on which to concentrate during instruction. The elements identified are (1) phonemic awareness, (2) phonics, (3) comprehension, (4) vocabulary, and (5) fluency. It is important to know that the panel selected only some areas related to reading instruction to review. Members of the National Reading Panel (NRP) did not study writing and its connections to reading success, nor did they study motivation. According to the NRP, some areas were omitted because there was not enough available quality research to determine their importance. In addition, they could not study everything related to reading instruction; instead, they reviewed only studies considered to be scientifically based reading research with a quantitative experimental design.

Research studies and syntheses conducted over the past decade have helped us understand the importance of young children's experiences with oral and written language. The preschool years, ages 3 and 4, are extremely important for social, emotional, physical, and cognitive development. High-quality preschool experiences can translate into academic and social competence (Barnett, 1995; Neuman & Dickinson, 2001). The preschool years are especially important for oral language development and initial experiences with reading and writing that link to later school achievement (Snow et al., 1998). Awareness must be heightened and administrators, educators, families, and policy makers need to be informed about the importance of preschool and in particular preschool literacy development.

Support for Developing Language and Literacy Development in Preschool

All preschool-age children need rich language and literacy experiences so that they are prepared to benefit from reading and writing instruction in school. Currently, only a small proportion of 3- and 4-year-olds benefit from literacy experiences as a result of family involvement and/or access to quality preschool programs (IRA/NAEYC, 1998).

Children who have high-quality preschool experiences with an emphasis on language and literacy are more likely to acquire strong language and literacy skills that translate into achievement in the early grades and throughout their schooling. Children who attend high-quality preschool are less likely to be retained in kindergarten through grade 3, have higher graduation rates from high school, and have fewer behavior problems (Barnett, 1995; Campbell & Raney, 1995; Cunningham & Stanovich, 1997; Peisner-Feinberg & Burchinal, 1997). If a child does not have the appropriate language development by age 3, he or she is not likely to succeed in school. With quality preschool, a child can catch up and go on to be successful. The benefits of having a preschool education are found across economic backgrounds, although children from families with the least formal education and the lowest incomes appear to benefit the most (Barnett, 1995; Fuerst & Fuerst, 1993; Schweinhart, Barnes, Weikart, Barnett, & Epstein, 1993). For these reasons we must have universal preschool in the public sector.

The National Early Literacy Panel (2004) studied research to identify abilities of children from birth through five that predict later achievement in literacy. The abilities identified were:

1. Oral language development: expressive and receptive vocabulary.
2. Alphabetic code: alphabet knowledge, phonological/phonemic awareness, invented spelling.
3. Print knowledge: environmental print, concepts about print.
4. Rapid naming of letters and numbers.
5. Visual memory and visual perceptual abilities.

Involving children in appropriate activities that will help them to develop these areas is important. Researchers demonstrates that experiences with storybook reading, discussions about books, listening comprehension, and writing are crucial in early literacy development (Bus,Van IJzendoorn, & Pellegrini, 1995; Wells, 1985).

Based on the evidence provided, access to many language and literacy experiences will enhance young children's development. Thus, preschools need to focus on a wide range of language and literacy experiences organized into the curriculum.

BEST PRACTICES IN ACTION

Language and Literacy Experiences to Focus on in Preschool Programs

Content analyses of preschool standards for language and literacy development are being prepared and provide guidelines for learning. The following content guidelines for language and literacy in preschool were created from a review of 15 state standards documents for preschool language and literacy programs:

- *Oral language development*: gestural expression, verbal expression, vocabulary and background knowledge, listening (attention to and comprehension of talk), phonological development including phonemic awareness.
- *Literacy development*: Print awareness, print conventions and book handling knowledge, letter name knowledge, alphabetic principle, knowledge of text structures, comprehension of stories, interest in books, beginning writing (Schickedanz, 2004).

Implications for the guidelines as they translate into practice are described in the following section.

Quality preschools include oral language experiences that focus on gestural expression, verbal expression, vocabulary development, building background knowledge and listening to others talk to understand and comprehend what they say (Dickinson, Cote, & Smith, 1993). Children learn phonological awareness, that is, words are made up of individual sounds. They learn this in oral language experiences such as chanting poems, singing songs, and clapping the sounds they hear in words (Adams, 1990, 2001; Carroll, Snowling, Hulme, & Stevenson, 2003; Strickland & Schikedanz, 2004).

Quality preschools include experiences for literacy development as they expose children to print conventions and book handling. This means that children have experiences learning that there is a front, back, top, and bottom to books. They learn that there is a left-to-right sequence in books, and there is a difference between the print and pictures. There are experiences to learn letter names, to identify letters visually, and to learn letter sounds. For example, it is educational when children's names are used to learn that words contain sounds, to identify letters and letter sounds. Children are not expected to master all of the above when they are in preschool; however, it is essential to introduce them to all of these areas of knowledge (Strickland & Schickedanz, 2004).

Good preschools help children learn about different types of text such as stories, informational books, menus, signs, and newspapers. Such programs help children to be aware of and read print in the environment. They also help children learn to comprehend stories and develop an interest in books. Research demonstrates that one of the most important activities for building success in literacy is reading aloud to children. The experience is most valuable when accompanied by interactive discussions with adults and children to introduce new vocabulary and language structures. Such conversation leads to understanding or comprehension of the story read

(Morrow & Gambrell, 2004; Storch & Whitehurst, 2002; Bus et al., 1995; Wells, 1985). Finally, experiences with beginning writing are important. As children make their first writing attempts by scribbling, making letter-like forms, using invented spelling, and also writing in a conventional manner, their literacy development grows. Writing teaches children about letters, sounds, and the meaning of text (Schickedanz & Casbergue, 2004).

Daily routines in a quality preschool program include whole-group morning meetings as children gather on a rug and discuss and write a morning message about the theme being studied. Children work individually and in small groups at centers where they engage in reading and writing. For example, they partner-read in the literacy center, write in their journal at the writing center, or work in the literacy-enriched themed play setting. While children are independently engaged the teacher meets with small groups and works on literacy activities suited to their individualized needs. At another time there is a story read aloud, related to a theme, with discussion before and after reading to develop comprehension. There are mini-lessons for developing phonological awareness as songs and poems are sung and chanted. There are mini-lessons on letter identification in meaningful contexts. Children explore in playful content area centers during a time set aside for this. The whole group meets again for a conversation that summarizes activities of the day and predicts what might happen tomorrow (Roskos, Tabors, & Lenuart, 2004; Dickinson, McCabe, Anastasopoulos, Peisner-Feinberg, & Poe, 2003). Throughout the day literacy instruction is integrated into all the content areas as the teacher helps the children become aware of the literacy skills they are learning (Morrow, 2005).

Every child is entitled to high-quality early literacy instruction. With that in mind, we describe an exemplary kindergarten day. The description is based on the findings of a study when several teachers were observed for a year to determine exemplary literacy instruction (Morrow, Tracey, Woo, & Pressley, 1999). This investigation took place in five states in which supervisors nominated exemplary teachers. Teacher selection was based on supervisory observations, achievement of the teachers' students over a 5-year period, and the teachers' reputations with colleagues, parents, and children. We present a composite of the teachers' methods, highlighting the physical environment of the classroom and the content and management of the language arts block. The classroom is an all-day kindergarten program, which is a necessity for children to learn what they need to in order to be ready for first grade.

Family Involvement

Family members are children's first teachers. They are the teachers children have for the longest period of time. Quality early childhood programs engage family members as an integral part of the language and literacy programs in school and at home. All children are likely to become more successful readers and writers when teachers have a strong family involvement component in their literacy program (Tabors, Snow, & Dickinson, 2001; Wasik, 2004). In addition to back-to-school nights, programs, and bringing cupcakes for birthday parties, parents must be informed by teachers about the literacy program and how they can help at home and in school. Equally important, teachers need to be informed about children's at-home life and literacy experiences from parents. Parents need to come to school during the day to observe the program, to read to children, to share their cultural backgrounds, to help make center materials, and to supervise during center time. We know that parents work, but they can spend an hour twice a year if teachers provide many different times for them to come to school. Families must feel welcome in school and as partners in the education of their children.

A DAY IN A LITERACY-RICH KINDERGARTEN

The time of the year is March, and the kindergarten children in Ms. Fazi's room are familiar with the classroom routines. They have already acquired many skills that are expected in kindergarten. This classroom description is to introduce many of the critical components, materials, and routines in pre-K, kindergarten, and first-grade classrooms.

Introduction to the Kindergarten Teacher and Students

Michelle Fazi has been teaching kindergarten for the past 7 years. Recently she completed a master's degree and now is eligible for a reading specialist certification. She teaches in a middle-income community. She has 22 students in her all-day kindergarten, including 9 European American, 6 Asian American, 5 African American, and 2 Hispanic children. Twenty percent of Michelle's class speaks one of four languages at home: Spanish, Japanese, Hindi, and Mandarin Chinese. Thirteen students are boys, and nine are girls. There is a full-time aide assigned to a physically disabled student in a wheelchair.

Michelle's Teaching Philosophy

Michelle's philosophy of teaching includes integration of the curriculum so that students can build connections between content areas. She purposefully integrates her literacy skill development in reading, writing, listening, speaking, and viewing with her social studies and science themes as much as possible. Her small-group literacy instruction is explicit by emphasizing specific skill development. Her approach to teaching reading, in which she attends to individual differences, requires her to have dozens of books that range in difficulty from a single word or two on each page to books with one or two sentences per page.

Ms. Fazi has a special interest in using informational texts with her children. She recognizes that background knowledge and vocabulary are enhanced by using expository material and that students need to read informational text in a variety of forms such as reading how-to manuals, applications, instructions, and websites. She has also found that at-risk students and boys are particularly drawn to expository or informational text.

Setting the Stage for Instruction: Michelle's Classroom Environment

Michelle's classroom is inviting, with well-defined centers around the room. The displays on the walls clearly reflect the theme being studied and show evidence of the children's growing literacy development. Nearly all of the displays include charts that Michelle has written with samples of children's writing, or artwork. In the whole-group area (a large carpeted space), Michelle has an easel with chart paper for the morning message, a calendar, weather chart, helper chart, a daily schedule, classroom rules, a hundreds chart used to count the days in school, a pocket chart, and a word wall.

Michelle's literacy center has a rug for independent reading and is also used for whole-class meetings. The area includes lots of space for storing books. There are baskets of books grouped by level of difficulty that coordinate with Michelle's small-group reading instruction. For example, students reading in the green basket during small-group instruction know that books in the green basket are ones they can read independently. Other shelves hold baskets organized by topics and authors, such as dinosaurs, sports, alphabet books, and books by Dr. Seuss or Eric Carle. Michelle rotates the books monthly. Colored stickers on the books and baskets assist students in returning them to the correct spot. Student-made books are displayed in another basket. Books about the current theme are on a special open-faced shelf.

The literacy center has flannel board characters and a flannel board, puppets, and props for storytelling. There is a rocking chair for the teacher and other adults to read to the class. The children use the rocking chair to read independently and to read to one another. The listening area in the center has a CD or tape player for listening to stories. There is a selection of manipulatives for learning about print. These include magnetic letters, puzzle rhyme cards, and letter chunks on small tiles for making words.

The writing center is an extension of the literacy center. There is a round table for small groups of children to meet with the teacher. There are shelves with many types of paper, lined and unlined, a stapler, markers, crayons, colored pencils, dictionaries, alphabet stamps, and ink stamp pads. A word wall in the writing center has each of the letters of the alphabet taped on horizontally. When the children learn a new word, it is taped under the letter it begins with on the word wall. Children use the words when they need a spelling or to practice reading. During instruction children may be asked to think of words that begin with the same letter and sound as a word on the word wall or to think of words that rhyme with a word wall word. Michelle places her students' names on the word wall and high-frequency kindergarten sight words the children are expected to learn.

Michelle's *Science Center* includes the class guinea pig, rabbit, and hermit crab. Equipment includes magnets, objects that sink and float, and plants. Materials are added to match the themes being studied, and there are always new hands-on experiments.

The *Dramatic Play Center* includes kitchen furniture such as a stove, table and chairs, refrigerator, with empty food boxes that display print. Changes are made to the area to reflect the themes being studied during the year. This center is often converted into a restaurant where children can take orders, read menus, and check their bills. The restaurant helps with learning about multicultural food and customs. This year the class has had an Italian, Chinese, Mexican, Portuguese, Jewish deli, and Japanese restaurant.

The *Block Center* includes wooden blocks of all sizes and shapes and other toys for construction such as LEGO®. There are toy trucks, cars, trains, buses, people, and animals in this area. There are labels that designate where the different toys go, such as trucks, cars, people, and so on. There are large index cards and tape for labeling structures created by the children. Children's writing in invented spellings (e.g., Plz Sav) is visible on block buildings under construction. Children sign their names on the labels.

Located near the sink is the *Art Center*, which contains an easel, table, chairs, and shelves. Michelle has her easels opened three times each week. On the shelves are scissors, markers, crayons, and paper of many colors, types, and sizes. There is paste as well as collage materials such as cotton balls, doilies, foil paper, and wallpaper samples.

The *Math Center* contains math manipulative materials for counting, adding, measuring, weighing, graphing, and distinguishing shapes. There are felt numbers to use on the felt board, magnetic numbers for magnetic boards, numbers to sequence in a pocket chart, and geometric shapes such as squares, triangles, cylinders, rectangles, etc.

The children sit at circular tables; there are five tables with four to five children at each table. In a quiet corner of the room there is a horseshoe-shaped table, which Michelle uses for small-group instruction. Shelves located next to the table have materials needed for small groups such as letters of the alphabet, rhyming cards, leveled books, sentence strips, index cards, white boards, markers, and word study games.

Center Management

Michelle uses her centers daily—5-year-olds learn best when they are manipulating materials such as those found in centers. To ensure that students visit two specific centers a day, Michelle has designed a contract on which she indicates the centers where children are expected to work daily. The contract has the name of each center and an icon representing the center. These same labels and icons are at the actual centers. When children complete work in a center, they check it off on their contracts. The completed work from a center is placed in the basket labeled "Finished Work." At the end of each day, Michelle discusses and reviews with the children completed work from the centers and assigns centers for the next day. Any incomplete work, or work that indicates a child needs help with a concept, is placed in the "Unfinished" folder. There is a time during the day for completing unfinished work. When children complete their two assigned centers, they can work at any center they choose. Thus, children have required activities in centers assigned by Michelle and activities in centers of their own choice.

Assessing Students to Determine Instructional Needs

In order to provide instruction to meet the varied levels of reading and writing of her students, Michelle spends considerable time assessing them with formal and informal measures. In September, January, March, and June, she assesses students' knowledge about concepts of print and books, phonological and phonemic awareness, ability to recognize and write letters of the alphabet, knowledge of letter–sound relationships, ability to read sight words, listening comprehension, and writing ability. Michelle plans instruction based on the needs she identifies. As children begin to read conventionally, she takes monthly running records for each child. This system of recording children's reading behavior assesses the types of errors or miscues that children make, the decoding strategies they use, and their progress. Michelle also takes anecdotal notes about students' behaviors that indicate both progress and points of difficulty. She collects samples of children's writing four times a year, analyzes them, and places them in student portfolios. Michelle also observes students' social, emotional, and physical development.

Small-Group Reading Instruction

Michelle has developed a schedule that allows her to work with small groups of children for reading instruction. With the assessment information she collects, she places students with similar needs together for small-group instruction. As she works with students, she takes careful notes regarding progress in literacy and adjusts the members of her various groups as needed. While in small groups, Michelle provides instruction in phonological awareness, letter identification, letter–sound relationships, knowledge about books and print concepts, vocabulary, listening comprehension, oral language, and writing. She presently has four small groups and meets with each group three times a week. On Fridays she attends to any special needs that come up during the week. Michelle finds that she needs to meet with her students who are struggling more often than with other groups, and frequently does this on Friday.

Michelle's Daily Schedule

8:45 When children arrive at school, they do the following:
- Carry out their jobs.
- Make entries into their journals.
- Complete unfinished work, practice skills needing extra attention.

9:00 The group meets as a whole for the morning meeting.
- Morning greetings are shared.
- Choral reading of poems.
- The calendar and weather are discussed.
- The number of days left until school ends is counted.
- The schedule for the day is reviewed.
- The morning message is read and added to.
- There are singing and movement activities.
- The teacher reads a book using shared reading techniques.

9:30 Small-group reading instruction and center activities.

10:30 Snack and play.

10:50 Writing block (interactive writing, mini-lesson, and writing workshop).

11:45 Play/lunch/rest.

1:00 Math lesson.

1:30 Theme-related activities, centers, and reading aloud.
2:15 Creative arts, music, gym.
2:50 Closing circle.
- Reading aloud.
- Sharing and reviewing activities of the day and what was learned.
- Planning for tomorrow.

A Typical Day in Michelle's Classroom

During this week Michelle and her children are studying dinosaurs. In Michelle's classroom, reading, writing, listening, speaking, and math activities are integrated throughout the dinosaur theme. However, Michelle also meets individual needs in small-group reading instruction. We describe the routine activities as they occur on Monday since they set the stage for the rest of the week.

When Children Arrive at School

It is 8:45 on Monday morning, and quiet chatter begins to fill Michelle's classroom as her students arrive. Classical music plays in the background as children complete their morning routines. Children move their nametags on the attendance board from the side labeled "Not Here" to "Here" and place their name stickers into the "Buy Lunch" or "Milk" can. Several children cluster around the easel, where they work together to read the morning message Michelle has written and discuss the question of the day. The morning message is predictable to help children who do not yet conventionally read decipher its meaning. Today's message says: "Good Morning Kindergarteners. Today is Monday, March 6, 2006. We will have Art today. Do you like dinosaurs? Yes No."

Michelle placed a picture of a dinosaur above the question to assist students with reading the word. She also wrote each sentence in a different color to represent different ideas to think about. Students are used to having "yes" or "no" questions asked and respond with tally marks, under the words *yes* and *no.* The students check the helper chart for their jobs such as feeding the animals, watering plants, and recording the temperature and day's weather on the weather graph. The Zoo Keeper reads the list posted by the animal cages to make sure he has completed all his tasks. The pictures placed next to each step help him read the chart and to remember what to do.

Students know it is time for writing their Weekend News in their journals. Michelle greets each student as she circulates among the writers, gently reminding some children to use spaces between words, suggesting others use classroom tools such as the word wall to spell needed words. As she listens to completed entries, she has the opportunity to chat with the children about their weekend. When the 2-minute warning bell rings, several children are already in the meeting area on the rug in the literacy center, reading books, alone or with a partner. Those still writing begin to put away their materials and place their unfinished work in the Not Finished basket. They will be able to complete their entries later during center time. Once the student shakes the tambourine announcing morning meeting, everyone gathers and forms a circle on the carpet.

The Morning Meeting

"Good morning, Emily," Michelle begins as they shake hands around the circle. Because they are beginning a new month, March, they echo-read a poem called "March" from *Chicken Soup with Rice* (Sendak, 1962). Michelle has written the poem on chart paper. At the end of the month the children will illustrate personal copies of this poem, and it will be placed in their Poem Books, along with other poems used throughout the year. As the calendar person, weather reporter, and schedule person lead the class in these activities, Michelle records the attendance and lunch count, which the messenger takes to the office.

Michelle leads the class in reading the morning message together. The children discuss the results of the tally of the day's question on the message "Do you like dinosaurs?" For those who said "no," they tell why they don't like dinosaurs. For those who said "yes," they discuss why they like them. Michelle leads a discussion related to the morning message about the end marks or punctuation marks at the end of each sentence. The period and question marks are named, explained, and circled.

Michelle has a new poem for the theme being studied that is hanging on another chart called "I'm a Mean Old Dinosaur" (Pruett, 1991). Michelle reads the poem to the class and tracks the print with a pointer. After the first reading, the children echo-read the poem with their teacher. Michelle covers a different word in each sentence of the poem with a post-it. She discusses with the children what they think the word might be.

MICHELLE: When I get all "blank," I just roar. What word could be placed in the blank space? Think what might make a dinosaur roar.

STUDENT 1: When he gets all mad.

MICHELLE: When I get all mad, I just growl. Does that make sense?

CLASS: Yes.

MICHELLE: Does it match what you know about dinosaurs?

STUDENT 2: Well, some dinosaurs get mad, but maybe not all of them.

MICHELLE: So, it does make sense.

Student 3: Yes, it makes sense, but it could be hungry too.

Michelle writes the words *mad* and *hungry* on separate 5 × 8 index cards and proceeds in the same manner until the class has four words on cards that could fit into that sentence. The words they come up with are *mad, tired, hungry,* and *sad.*

MICHELLE: Words need to make sense in the sentence, and they need to match the letters in the words we are reading.

STUDENT 3: You have to look at the letters.

MICHELLE: Right. Let's check the first letter and see which word matches.

They check *mad,* but none of the letters matches; they check *tired,* but again none of the letters matches; then, they check *hungry,* and all the letters match. The class continues with filling in the words left out on the chart. When all the words are figured out, the teacher echo-reads it with the children again. Before center time, Michelle puts on some music for the children to walk around the room acting like dinosaurs.

Center Time

Michelle spends a few minutes reviewing the center activities and describing new activities placed in the centers for the exploration of dinosaurs. Centers have materials that are in place over a period of time, and they are enriched with activities that reflect the current theme. A description of what has been added to each center relating to the dinosaur theme follows.

- *Writing Center:* Dinosaur-bordered writing paper, dinosaur books, dinosaur stickers, a dinosaur dictionary, a dinosaur-shaped poster with words about dinosaurs.
- *Literacy Center:* Fiction and nonfiction dinosaur books, dinosaur books with accompanying CDs, a dinosaur vocabulary puzzle, a dinosaur concentration memory game, a teacher-made dinosaur lotto game.
- *Computer Center:* A virtual reality multimedia program for printing dinosaur stationery, postcards, posters, and masks, and for visiting a virtual museum exhibit about dinosaurs.
- *Science:* Small skulls and old animal bones are displayed, along with a magnifying glass and rubber gloves to examine the bones; materials to draw what the children think the entire animal may have

looked like; dinosaur pictures to sort into "walked on two feet" and "walked on four feet" categories. There are recording sheets for all activities.

- *Math*: Measuring tools in a basket and sheets to record the measurement of various plaster bones of dinosaurs; dinosaur counters; little plastic dinosaurs in an estimation jar; a basket containing 50 little dinosaurs numbered from 1 to 50, the aim being to put the dinosaurs into sequential order.
- *Blocks*: Toy dinosaurs, trees, bushes, and some dinosaur books are placed into the block center.
- *Art Center*: Dinosaur stencils and dinosaur stamps are added to the art center. There are clay models of dinosaurs and many pictures of dinosaurs to help students make their own sculptures.

Dramatic Play

The dramatic play area is transformed into a paleontologist's office: Chicken bones are embedded in plaster of paris blocks; students use wood-carving tools and small hammers to remove the bones while wearing safety goggles; paper and pencil are used for labeling the bones, and trays for displaying findings; dinosaur books and posters of fossils and dinosaurs abound.

After Michelle reviews center activities, her students look at their contracts and proceed to their "have to" activities. The activities that must be done are often skills in which the students need practice such as matching pictures with letters to reinforce letter–sound knowledge. When they complete their required activities, children may select any center such as blocks or dramatic play. Children check off the center they have worked in on their contract.

Small-Group Reading Instruction

The first group that Michelle sees is reviewing a book they have read before, *We Went to the Zoo* (Sloan & Sloan, 1994). It is a simple patterned text with repeated words and phrases with some slight variations in the pattern. Michelle provides a guided book introduction as children look through the book stopping to talk about each page. During the book introduction, the students are asked to find the words *saw* and *many*, since these words caused some difficulty during the first reading. They also discuss the names of the animals in the book. As the group reads, Michelle notices that one student makes no errors in reading, and he finishes quickly. Michelle makes a note to think about moving him to a more advanced guided-reading group. After the children finish reading, Michelle asks everyone to turn to page 7. "I noticed that James read, 'we saw the . . .' and started to read *po-* for *polar bear,* but then he used the first letter, *b,* and read *bear* instead. He remembered that the words have to match the letters." During guided reading Michelle was able to complete a running record on one child. She noted that this student read *seals* instead of *otters* and said "pander bears" instead of "bears." Michelle decides that tomorrow she will help this child to pay more attention to the print in the words as he reads.

Michelle's next group will be reading the book *Who Can Run Fast?* (Stuart, 2001). The group has worked with this book before. To review, they echo-read the book with the teacher. In the lesson that follows, Michelle will help the children become more independent readers. She will teach them how to figure out unknown words by using the meaning of a sentence and by looking at the letters in the words. They begin with a game called "Guess the Covered Word," an activity they used while reading *I'm a Mean Old Dinosaur* (Pruett, 1991) during the morning meeting. This time the covered word in the sentence "I can blank fast" is the word *run.* The children are encouraged to select a word that makes sense in the sentence and then to look at the letters in the word to see which is the correct word. Possible words that were considered included *walk, eat, hop, sleep,* and *run.* After successfully determining the correct word, the children are reminded that, when we read, the word must make sense and the printed letters must match the sounds of the words that we say. Michelle explains that this is what good readers do when they are reading alone and trying to figure out words. The activity is repeated in other sentences throughout their book.

The next group is composed of emergent readers. Michelle is working on building a sight vocabulary with them made up of thematic words in which the students are interested such as *dinosaur, big, extinct,* and *T-Rex.* She writes the words on 5 × 8 cards for the students' very own word boxes and gives them the words *I like* so they can create sentences with the cards, such as *I Like Dinosaurs.* They say the letters in the words and think of the letters in their own names that are in the words.

Snack and Play

By mid-morning everyone needs a break. The snack is dinosaur animal crackers and what Michelle is calling dinosaur juice. When snack time is over, children look at books or play with some quiet table toys if time permits.

Writing Workshop

The children gather for writing in the whole-class meeting area. Michelle introduces the writing activity for the week. The children will be writing informational texts about dinosaurs. They are to select one dinosaur they like the most and mention as many facts about that dinosaur as they can. They brainstorm what dinosaur they want to write about and discuss facts they already know. Tuesday they will begin to browse through dinosaur books for information and start to write. Children will write facts and draw pictures. There are many levels of writing—from scribble writing to letter strings, invented spelling, and some conventional writing. When the activity is completed at the end of the week, Michelle will take everyone's work and fashion it into a class book. At the end of the week one of the dinosaur books reads as follows:

Dinosaur Facts
T-Rex yz 35 fet tl. (T-Rex was 35 feet tall.)
HE yx a met etr. (He was a meat eater.)
HE yz men. (He was mean.)

Play, Lunch, and Nap

Children play either outside or in the gym, depending on the weather. Lunch is in the cafeteria, and children have a rest time on rugs in the classroom after lunch. Many of the children do sleep. At the beginning of nap time, Michelle plays an audiotape of the story *Dinosaurs before Dark* (Osbourne,1992).

Math

There is a specific math curriculum followed in Michelle's kindergarten. We describe here only the theme-related literacy activities that Michelle added. Today the class brainstorms a list of as many dinosaurs as they can name. Using the index of a dinosaur encyclopedia, they locate pictures of various dinosaurs; the names are copied onto a chart. After making a list of 10 dinosaurs, the children are asked to vote for their favorite ones, while a student records the votes, using tally marks for counting. Five dinosaurs receive the most votes, and their names are circled with a red marker: Iguanodon, Spinosaurus, Stegasaurus, Triceratops, and Tyrannosaurus.

Art, Music, Gym

At this time of day the class goes to a special teacher for art, music, or gym. Michelle has coordinated with these teachers about the theme being studied, so the art teacher is working on paper mache dinosaur sculptures with the children, the music teacher has found some great dinosaur songs, and the gym teacher has thought of some movement activities to help the students walk and run like dinosaurs.

Closing Circle with Read-Aloud

At closing time students clean up and gather in the meeting area for their closing circle and a read-aloud. Today Michelle has chosen an informational big book titled *Discovering Dinosaurs* (Sokoloff, 1997). This book provides children with more facts about dinosaurs that they may use in their writing and for the mural habitat they will create. Before she reads, she points out some of the features of this informational book. For example, there are labels on figures, captions describing pictures, headings introducing new topics, and vocabulary written in a bolder and bigger size than the rest of the words. This book will introduce children to a topic not yet discussed in class—differences between dinosaurs that were plant eaters, versus meat eaters. After reading, Michelle helps children list the characteristics of plant-eating and meat-eating dinosaurs on a shared writing chart. Finally, she and the children review the activities of the day, discuss those they liked best, and plan for tomorrow.

Family Involvement

Before the dinosaur unit began, Michelle—as done with all units throughout the year—sent home a short note about the activities that would be done in school, the skills being taught, and suggestions for activities for parents to do at home. During the unit she reminded parents about the activities. She asked for volunteers to come and read dinosaur books during storybook time. She also asked for artifacts or books about dinosaurs that parents might share with the class. She asked for help during writing workshop to assist students with words they needed help in spelling, and she asked for help during center time to assist children with activities while she worked with small groups of children. She offered multiple options and multiple time periods for participation. At the end of the unit parents were invited to school to see all the work done about dinosaurs. Michelle found that parent participation helped her run her program with more efficiency and helped her students carry out their work with a higher level of achievement. Parents respected the work she was doing, and the more they helped, the more they wanted to help. Parents who hadn't volunteered in the past began to ask about coming to school and getting involved.

REFLECTIONS AND FUTURE DIRECTIONS

Although we know much about early literacy growth, we need to continue research in this important area. We need to place a great deal of emphasis on preschool literacy instruction. Most of the research already completed has been done with children in first grade; not nearly as much has been implemented in kindergarten and preschool classrooms. While we know a lot about early literacy development, further research on organizing and managing language arts instruction during the school day is needed. We especially need more research on how to deliver instruction—for example, comparing explicit approaches to more open-ended spontaneous teaching approaches. We also need further study of exemplary teachers to determine how they became exemplary. We need to be advocates for universal preschool and all-day kindergarten. With working parents and those who cannot afford to send their children to private preschool, this is an absolute necessity. The children who come to kindergarten without a preschool experience, as compared to those who have been to preschool, are at an extreme disadvantage. Finally, an emphasis on incorporating parent involvement into the pre-K through grade 1 reading program is necessary as well. Parental involvement should include not only coming to back-to-school night, parent–teacher conferences, and bringing cupcakes for birthdays, more importantly it should also include having parents practice the work done in school at home with their children and spend time in the classroom a few times a year to share information with the class, read to children, help at center time, and learn what their children's day is like in preschool, kindergarten, or first grade.

CONCLUDING COMMENTS

The children in this early-childhood classroom experience literacy in many different forms. They are involved in an environment that incorporates literacy as a part of the entire day. The literacy experiences are planned to be appropriate, because there is concern for individual needs and learning styles. Michelle is enthusiastic about her teaching, and her excitement is contagious. As a result, her students assume a positive attitude toward literacy learning, toward one another, and toward themselves.

The children in Michelle's classroom have extensive exposure to children's literature through the use of shared read-alouds, independent reading, buddy reading with a peer, and guided reading for skills development. Writing experiences include journal writing, writing workshop, and language experience activities. Both reading and writing include meaningful, intentional systematic development of skills

Michelle's room was rich with materials for children to experience choice, challenge, social interaction, and success. Her day was structured to include varied experiences that were developmentally appropriate and yet still retained an emphasis on the acquisition of skills. Children learned rules and routines for using the classroom materials whenever they were engaged in self-directed roles. Michelle was consistent in her management techniques. Therefore, the children knew what was expected of them and, consequently, carried out the work that needed to be done. Consistent routines helped the day to flow smoothly.

The affective quality in the room was exemplary. Michelle speaks to the children with respect. She does not raise her voice, nor does she use punitive remarks, inapt facial expressions, or negative intonations. In this atmosphere, and from Michelle's modeling, children learn to understand appropriate ways of interacting with others.

Michelle allowed time for children to mature at their natural pace, with concern for social, emotional, and intellectual development. She also was aware of the need to foster development, making appropriate materials available for exploration, and undertaking specific skill instruction for individual needs. She integrated the language arts curriculum and content-area teaching by reinforcing listening, speaking, reading, writing, and viewing skills as she taught science, math, and social studies. She utilized content-area texts to teach literacy skills.

ENGAGEMENT ACTIVITIES

1. Select one of the National Reading Panel's skills to develop, such as phonemic awareness, phonics, vocabulary, comprehension, or fluency, in a theoretical classroom setting.
2. Create an experience for an early-childhood classroom that reflects the doctrines of both Piaget and Vygotsky in teaching the skill you selected. Create three more experiences for the same skill, using the theories of Montessori, Dewey, and Skinner, respectively.
3. Observe an early-childhood classroom (preschool through second grade). Decide which theoretical influences have determined the types of practices carried out. Document your findings with specific anecdotes illustrating the theory.

REFERENCES

Professional Literature

Adams, M. J. (1990). *Beginning to read: Thinking and learning about print.* Urbana: University of Illinois Center for the Study of Reading.

Adams, M. J. (2001). Alphabetic anxiety and explicit systematic phonics instruction: A cognitive science perspective. In S. B. Neuman & D. K. Dickinson (Eds.), *Handbook of early literacy research* (pp. 66–80). New York: Guilford Press.

Barnett, W. S. (1995). Long-term effects of early childhood programs on cognitive and school outcomes. *The Future of Children, 5*(3), 25–50.

Bus, A., Van IJendoorn, M., & Pellegrini, A. (1995). Joint book reading makes for success in learning to read: A meta-analysis on intergenerational transmission of literacy. *Review of Educational Research, 65,* 1–21.

Campbell, F. A., & Raney, T. L. (1995). Cognitive and school outcomes for high-risk African-American students in middle adolescence: Positive effects of early intervention. *American Educational Research Journal, 32*(4), 743–772.

Carroll, J. M., Snowling, M. J., Hulme, C., & Stevenson, J. (2003). The development of phonological awareness in preschool children. *Developmental Psychology, 39*(5), 913–923.

Center for the Improvement of Early Reading Achievement. (2001). *Put reading first.* Washington, DC: U.S. Department of Education.

Clay, M. M. (1966). *Emergent reading behavior.* Doctoral dissertation. University of Auckland, New Zealand.

Cunningham, A. E., & Stanovich, K. E. (1997). Early reading acquisition and its relation to reading experience and ability 10 years later. *Developmental Psychology, 33*(6), 934–945.

Dewey, J. (1966). *Democracy and education.* New York: Free Press. (Original work published 1916)

Dickinson, D. K., Cote, L., & Smith, M. W. (1993). Learning vocabulary I preschool: Social and discourse contexts affecting vocabulary growth. In C. Daiute (Ed.), *The development of literacy through social interaction: New directions in child development* (pp. 67–78). San Francisco: Jossey-Bass.

Dickinson, D. K., McCabe, A., Anastasopoulos, L., Peisner-Feinberg, E., & Poe, M. (2003). The comprehensive language approach to early literacy: The interrelationships among vocabulary, phonological sensitivity, and print knowledge among preschool-aged children. *Journal of Educational Psychology, 95*(3), 465–481.

Fuerst, J., & Fuerst, D. (1993). Chicago experience with an early childhood program: The special case of the child parent program. *Urban Education, 28*(1), 69–96.

International Reading Association. (1999). *Using multiple methods of beginning reading instruction.* Newark, DE: International Reading Association.

International Reading Association. (2006). *Reading in preschool.* Newark, DE: International Reading Association.

International Reading Association and National Association for the Education of Young Children. (1998). *Learning to read and write: Developmentally appropriate practices for young children.* Newark, DE: International Reading Association.

Montessori, M. (1965). *Spontaneous activity in education.* New York: Schocken.

Morphett, M. V., & Washburne, C. (1931). When should children begin to read? *Elementary School Journal, 31,* 496–508.

Morrow, L. M. (2005). *Literacy development in the early years: Helping children read and write* (5th ed.). Boston: Allyn & Bacon.

Morrow, L. M., & Gambrell, L. B. (2004). *Using children's literature in preschool: Comprehending and enjoying books.* Newark, DE: International Reading Association.

Morrow, L. M., & Tracey, D. H. (1997). Strategies used for phonics instruction in early childhood classrooms, *Reading Teacher, 50*(8), 664–651.

Morrow, L. M., Tracey, D. H., Woo, D. G., & Pressley, M. (1999). Characteristics of exemplary first grade literacy instruction. *Reading Teacher, 52,* 462–476.

National Early Literacy Panel Report. (2004). Washington, DC: National Institute for Literacy, National Family Literacy Association.

National Reading Panel Report. (2000). *Teaching children to read.* Washington, DC: National Institute of Child Health and Human Development.

Neuman, S. B., & Dickinson, D. K. (Eds.). (2001). *Handbook of early literacy research.* New York: Guilford Press.

Peisner-Feinberg, E. S., & Burchinal, M. R. (1997). Relations between preschool children's child-care experiences and concurrent development: The cost, quality, and outcomes study. *Merrill-Palmer Quarterly, 43,* 451–477.

Piaget, J., & Inhelder, B. (1969). *The psychology of the child.* New York: Basic Books.

Pressley, M. (1998). *Reading instruction that works: The case for balanced teaching.* New York: Guilford Press.

Roskos, C., Tabors, P. O., & Lenuart, L. A. (2004). *Oral language and early literacy in preschool: Talking, reading, and writing.* Newark, DE: International Reading Association.

Rusk, R., & Scotland, J. (1979). *Doctrines of the great educators.* New York: St. Martin's Press.

Schickedanz, J. (2004). Content standards for preschool literacy: A summary of guidelines from 15 states. *The Reading Teacher, 58,* 45–47.

Schickedanz, J., & Casbergue, R. (2004). *Writing in preschool: Learning to orchestrate meaning and marks.* Newark, DE: International Reading Association.

Snow, C. E., Burns, M. S., & Griffin, P. (1998). *Preventing reading difficulties in young children.* Washington, DC: National Academy Press.

Storch, S. A., & Whitehurst, G. J. (2002). Oral language and code-related precursors to reading: Evidence from a longitudinal structural model. *Developmental Psychology, 38,* 934–947.

Strickland, D., & Schickedanz, J., (2004). *Learning about print in preschool: Working with letters, words, and beginning links with phonemic awareness.* Newark, DE: International Reading Association.

Tabors, P. O., Snow, C. E., & Dickinson, D. K. (2001). Homes and schools together: Supporting language and literacy development. In D. K. Dickinson & P. O. Tabors (Eds.), *Beginning literacy with language: Young children learning at home and school* (pp. 313–334). Baltimore, MD: Brookes Publishing.

Vygotsky, L. S. (1981). The genesis of higher mental functions. In J. J. Wertsh (Ed.), *The concept of activity.* White Plains, NY: Sharpe.

Wasik, B. H. (Ed.). (2004). *Handbook on family literacy.* Mahwah, NJ: Erlbaum.

Wells, G. (1985). *The meaning makers.* Portsmouth, NH: Heinemann.

Children's Literature

Osbourne, M. P. (2000). *Dinosaurs before dark.* New York: Random House Listening Library.

Pruett, D. (1991). *I'm a mean old dinosaur.* Monterey, CA: Evan Moor.

Sendak, M. (1962). *Chicken soup with rice.* New York: Scholastic.

Sloan, P., & Sloan, S. (1994). *We went to the zoo.* Boston: Sundance.

Sokoloff, M. (1997). *Discovering dinosaurs.* New York: Sadlier.

Stuart, M. (2001). *Who can run fast?* New York: Sadlier-Oxford.

Chapter 4

BEST PRACTICES FOR STRUGGLING READERS

Richard L. Allington
Kim Baker

This chapter will:

- Discuss how most children experiencing reading difficulties can have their literacy development accelerated when they have access to sufficient appropriate instruction.
- Discuss how teachers who provide personalized interactive lessons, skills instruction within context, and substantial reading and writing opportunities are most effective.
- Discuss how a comprehensive system with three components—prevention, acceleration, and long-term support—is needed in schools to meet the needs of students experiencing literacy difficulties.

EVIDENCE-BASED BEST PRACTICES

Not all children, unfortunately, acquire literacy easily. Although there has always been much debate as to just why some children struggle to become readers and writers, in this chapter we focus on how exemplary instructional support might be provided to such children and leave the issue of the etiology of learning difficulties for others to consider. In our view, children who find learning to read and write more difficult are best served not by identifying some label for them, but by designing and delivering sufficient and appropriate instruction and substantial opportunities to actually engage in high-success reading and writing activities. Thus, we draw on our experiences in two long-term school-based research projects to offer detailed descriptions of interventions that we consider exemplary in nature and outcomes.

The Critical Role of Classroom Reading Lessons

Providing all children with exemplary classroom literacy instruction is an essential first step in addressing the needs of children who find learning to read and write more difficult. In our studies of exemplary first-grade teachers (Pressley, Allington, Wharton-McDonald, Block, & Morrow, 2001), for instance, we found that the greatest impact of the exemplary teachers we studied was on the development of reading and writing proficiency in the lowest-achieving children. In other words, in the classrooms of the exemplary first-grade teachers, there were far fewer children who ended first grade still struggling with reading and writing. Likewise, Mendro, Jordan, and Bembry (1998) studied the effects of 3 consecutive years of high-quality teaching on student reading development. They compared the achievement of children placed in high-quality classrooms with that of students who were unfortunate enough to have attended lower-quality classrooms over the same period. Although the children's average standing on national norms rose consistently year after year in the high-quality classrooms, the standing of children in the lower-quality classrooms dropped each year. After 3 years, the achievement of children who had similar initial achievement now differed by almost 40 percentile ranks! The results of this large-scale study have been replicated with respect to the impact of quality classroom instruction on reading development (Allington & Johnston, 2002; Pressley et al., 2001; Snow, Barnes, Chandler, Goodman, & Hemphill, 1991; Taylor, Pearson, Peterson, & Rodriguez, 2003), especially the reading development of struggling readers.

Now, it would not have seemed necessary, in some senses, actually to conduct studies showing that access to high-quality teaching is important —essential, in fact. Who would argue against providing high-quality classroom instruction? But then, who argues for it? How often are resources allocated to improving classroom instruction from funding provided by the Title 1 program of the No Child Left Behind Act (NCLB) or special education under the Individuals with Disabilities Education Act (IDEA)? How often are such funds allocated for the purchase of needed classroom instructional materials, for instance, to purchase a classroom supply of texts of an appropriate level of complexity for use by students with learning disabilities? Or how often are funds allocated to provide professional development opportunities for classroom teachers to learn how to better document the development of children who are struggling with literacy learning?

Instead, these programs more often fund additional personnel, including specialist support teachers (reading teachers, learning disabilities teachers, speech and language teachers), school psychologists, social workers, or paraprofessional personnel. There may be a role for any and all of these extra personnel, but in our view a necessary first step is ensuring that children have access to high-quality classroom instruction regardless of their label or participation in a special program.

One question that we now routinely pose is whether there is evidence that specialized personnel enhance the quality of classroom instruction. In other words, what evidence is available that points to the ways that the school psychologist has improved classroom teaching? The same question might be asked about the roles of the social worker, the learning disability specialist, the reading teacher, or the paraprofessional. If the presence of specialized personnel is not improving classroom instruction, at the very least we should reconsider the role demands for such positions so that improving the quality of classroom teaching becomes a central attribute of each specialist's role (Walmsley & Allington, 1995).

One unintended effect of federal education programs targeted at improving the education of struggling learners may be a reduced professional responsibility that many general education teachers have for the reading instruction and outcomes of struggling readers served by specialized teachers in special programs. In other words, teaching struggling readers to read is seen as primarily the responsibility of the specialized teachers. But struggling readers spend, perhaps, 15–20% of their school day in special programs. The rest of the day they sit in the general education classroom. In order to adequately address the problems faced by struggling readers, we must also be concerned with the quality of instruction encountered in the other 80–85% of the day—the time spent in his general education classroom. We like to think of this as a plan that extends the notion of intervention as necessary all day long.

Intervention all day long means, simply, that struggling readers have books they can read in their hands all day long. Lessons that address their learning needs all day long. This would mean not only reorganizing classroom reading instruction so that it matched struggling readers' needs but also assuring that science and social studies lessons would require texts that struggling readers could read accurately, fluently, and with understanding and that address the requisite content. Such is rarely the case now, but the use of such multilevel curriculum materials was one feature of the exemplary fourth-grade classrooms we studied (Allington & Johnston, 2002).

Supplemental Support for Struggling Readers

However, even exemplary classroom teachers cannot do it all. Although such teachers dramatically reduce the incidence of reading difficulties, a few children typically continue to struggle even in these exemplary classrooms. Some children have enormous instructional needs that simply cannot be met in the day-to-day bustle of the classroom. Their needs for close and personalized teaching simply exceed the capacity of even exemplary teachers. It seems to be both a quantity and quality problem.

Most of these children simply need closer and more explicit teaching than can be accomplished by a teacher with the responsibility for a classroom filled with 25 children. These children need, for instance, more guided reading opportunities and more high-success independent reading. As Guthrie (2004) notes, because good readers typically spend 500% more time reading than struggling readers, "Educators should attempt to increase engaged reading time [for struggling readers] by 200%–500%. This may require substantial reconfigurations of curriculum" (p. 1).

Most classrooms will need a substantially expanded supply of books and textbooks at appropriate levels of difficulty for those struggling readers—typically, levels different from those used in the daily classroom lessons and activities. Some struggling readers will need particularized instruction—an emphasis on hearing sounds in words, for instance—that may require not only more time to provide than the classroom teacher has available but also a particular instructional expertise that classroom teachers do not routinely acquire, even exemplary classroom teachers (Allington, 2006). Thus, another feature of exemplary intervention efforts is the useful and targeted deployment of special support teachers and personnel who provide the intensive and personalized instruction that those few children need in order to thrive in school.

Unfortunately, it is common today also to find that a school employs a large number of paraprofessionals in attempting to meet the instructional needs of children who find learning to read difficult, usually funding such personnel with disbursements allocated by Title 1 or IDEA. In other words, huge numbers of paraprofessionals are employed in remedial and special education programs (Howes, 2003; International Reading Association, 1994). However, there is substantial evidence that students gain little academic benefit when paraprofessionals deliver intervention instruction (Achilles, 1999; Anderson & Pellicier, 1990; International Reading Association, 1994). In fact, the use of paraprofessionals in classrooms of any kind has been shown to have no positive effect on student achievement (Boyd-Zaharias & Pate-Bain, 1998; Gerber, Finn, Achilles, & Boyd-Zaharias, 2001). The key to understanding these findings is located in the need children have for access to expert instruction. Too often, it seems, school programs are designed such that children who find learning to read difficult are paired with inexpert paraprofessional staff for instruction and practice.

Paraprofessionals might provide supportive practice opportunities, but such activities seem more successful when the lessons are planned and the materials selected by the teacher or reading teacher. Paraprofessionals can be provided with professional development that allows them to successfully use one or more lesson routines (Allington & Cunningham, 2007), but unfortunately many paraprofessionals receive little, if any, such professional development.

So, what might an exemplary program for addressing the needs of struggling readers look like? It would, of course, begin with exemplary classroom teaching. Support for exemplary classroom teachers would be available in the form of expert specialists, who provide appropriate and intensive services for children in need of such added attention. This support might be offered during the school day, after school, or during the summer. It might be offered in the classroom or in another location. There might be paraprofessional support for either the classroom teacher or the specialist teacher, or for both. But the efforts of the paraprofessional would be to focus on providing supportive reading and writing practice, organized and closely monitored by the classroom or reading teacher.

A grand scheme, you say, but what exactly would it look like? In the following sections, you will meet (1) an exemplary first-grade teacher and spend a day in her classroom, and (2) an exemplary support teacher—certified and experienced in both reading and special education—and spend a day with her as she goes about supporting teachers and children as they learn to read and write.

BEST PRACTICES IN ACTION

Exemplary Classroom Instruction for Children Who Find Learning to Read and Write Difficult

Georgia teaches in a small rural district in northern California. Nearly two-thirds of the children come from low-income families, and one-sixth of them are members of ethnic minority groups. Seasonal employment in agriculture supports a mobile low-wage workforce in this community. Because of the transient nature of agricultural work, Georgia's class membership had a 50% changeover during the latest school year.

However, when you walk into Georgia's first-grade classroom, the mood is one of a community that is actively engaged and interested in what it is doing. Students are working in groups and alone, reading and writing, sharing and exchanging ideas and information. Georgia integrates reading and writing throughout the day and across subjects. Print surrounds the students on all four walls, including students' stories, students' artwork with labels, charts of songs and poems, and a pocket board for sentences about the basal story from guided reading.

Georgia's language arts program involves a weekly schedule of varied reading and writing activities, not the more common daily schedule. At least three times a week, the students have independent reading time while Georgia holds individual reading conferences. A literature-based core reading program is used twice weekly for guided reading, supplemented with appropriately leveled little books for additional guided reading lessons. The class is divided by reading ability into four groups for the twice-weekly guided reading sessions, but it is heterogeneously grouped for daily independent reading time and often for the small-group guided reading lessons drawn from a large supply of leveled books. While Georgia meets with guided reading groups, the other students have center activities. Friday is an independent reading day for all groups. Each day after lunch, the students have independent reading time.

Georgia also reads aloud daily, offering a chance for predictions, sharing of personal knowledge and experiences, and vocabulary building. Often, she chooses books that enhance a math, science, or social studies concept on which the class is working.

Writers' Workshop is a vital component in the planned weekly literacy program. Twice a week, students are composing for at least 45 minutes and engaged in small-group and individual writing lessons. Other writing assignments, responses to their reading, personal journals, and whole-class generated big books offer diverse writing opportunities. The students have cubbies and are encouraged to write notes to one another.

A *Day in First Grade*

Students enter school at 8:20 A.M., quickly hang up their jackets, put away lunches, and group on the rug. On Mondays, there is oral sharing time, when students have the opportunity to participate in telling an experience or not. Georgia quickly takes lunch count, attendance, and has two helpers who write the day of the week and the date. (At the beginning of the school year, she modeled this and, by January, handed it over to students to do on their own.) While this is going on she engages the rest of the class in "reading the room"—reading words from the Word Wall and from the poems and songs around the room. When the students finish their calendar information, the class reads it silently and then in unison. Then the pledge is said and a patriotic song is sung, with a student pointing to the large printed words on a chart. Again, an activity that Georgia did at first has been taken over by the students. This usually takes 10–15 minutes, and by 8:35 A.M. the class is engaged in guided reading and centers, independent reading, or Writers' Workshop. Georgia has organized a time block of 90 minutes for literacy activities. Over two-thirds of this period involves students daily in individual reading and writing. Writers' Workshop, guided reading and centers, independent reading, and conferences are included throughout the week.

Guided reading revolves around both a basal selection and books drawn from Georgia's large collection of leveled little books. Georgia has all the students gather on the rug as she performs a prereading activity. With this week's basal story, *Over in the Meadow* (Keats, 1993), she has the children close their eyes and think about animals and plants in a meadow. She tells them, "There is a creek, not as big as our local creek, and a tree trunk nearby, with ants crawling on it. Up in the blue sky are clouds. If you were sitting back in this meadow, you would be smelling things, seeing things, and hearing things."

Georgia then directs the students to the story, illustrated by Ezra Jack Keats. A discussion ensues about the fact that this is an old story—Keats did not write it—and how they have read other retold stories. Georgia reads it aloud from a big book edition, and the students comment that it is a counting book, a rhyming book, and a repeating book. *Muskrat, snug,* and *chirp* are discussed as vocabulary as she reads, because they are hard words to determine from the pictures. Georgia asks questions about the muskrat; she has just elaborated on *snug* by saying "I like snug. It reminds me of being warm and comfortable." She demonstrates "chirping" when asked "What is *chirp*?" by a student.

Georgia had the written numbers *one* through *ten* on cards and arranged them, using a pocket board, in a column and placed blank cards across from them in another column. As the students worked on remembering which animal matched which number in the *Over in the Meadow* story, they flipped the cards to reveal the correct names. Georgia also used this exercise to stress sounds and words. She used the word numbers *one* and *eight* to talk about how *one* starts with the *w* sound, not *o*, and how *e* and *i* says /ay/ in eight. As students matched the animals to the number from the story, they silently—in their heads—read. Then in unison they read the story again, with all the students appearing to be able to read. At their seats, using the table of contents, they all found the story in individual books and read chorally.

Then Georgia directed her students to write in their journals about their favorite baby animal and why it was their favorite. During this time, Georgia and her aide circulated, helping students sound out words. With *cheetah,* Georgia directed a student to look at her mouth as she said the word, stretching it out. The student said, and then wrote *ch- -ee- -ta.* This sound stretching was a common feature in the classroom during writing. Both Georgia and her aide linked the students' sound spelling to developing phonemic segmentation by modeling word stretching and encouraging the students to do this on their own. This, in and of itself, has been shown to be a powerful activity for fostering growth in phonemic awareness (Scanlon & Vellutino, 1997).

The next day, in the students' smaller guided reading groups, Georgia worked with the pocket board, using sentences from the story but leaving blank the animals and their activities. The students filled in these missing words by reading the sentence in their head, talking with one another, and deciding what should fit. Afterward, they read it silently or whisper-read, then read aloud together. Finally, Georgia directed the students to read from individual books, loud enough for her to hear when she moved around but not loud enough to disturb their neighbors.

The reading teacher, who provides instruction to five students in a pullout program, now arrives and takes those students to her room for an added small-group lesson. The reading teacher coordinates what she is working on with Georgia. Later, she pulls one student for a lesson geared toward the specific phonological difficulties that child is having. She has trained Georgia's aide and supervises the aide's work with another student. In this case the aide implements the pause–prompt–praise strategy for fostering fluency and growth of self-regulation while reading (Allington, 2006), having the child read and reread books selected by the reading teacher as appropriate.

The aide is in the classroom all morning and spends most of her time working in a similar manner, providing extended high-success reading practice, with a focus on self-monitoring, with other students while Georgia oversees her interactions and offers bits of advice about each student. Next, the students who have been with the reading teacher move up to work with Georgia. She shares pages from several books about bees. Then she introduces the Storybox book *The Bee*, by Joy Cowley (1990), preparing the students by activating their background information about bees, previewing the cover and the following pages, and setting the readers up to whisper-read successfully on the first try. She then has them reread it two times, stressing that the sentences make sense. Next, she does a minilesson on the double *ee* sound, starting with *bee* and making a list with *see, meet, beet, cheetah,* and *bees,* all words from this story and a recently read book. The students think of sentences about what bees can do: *Bees can sting. Bees can collect nectar. Bees can drink.* Although they know only the beginning letter of *collect,* the students spell everything else as Georgia writes. As Georgia writes *collect,* she models stretching out the sounds of the word to better be able to hear and spell them. Students whisper-read the chart, read all the sentences together, and then each student picks a sentence to read alone. This high-success minilesson lasts about 20 minutes, and then these children return to their seats to engage in independent reading.

Guided reading is alternated with independent reading of books chosen from the baskets. The baskets are filled with teacher-selected books that the students have encountered during previous lessons. This is a quiet reading time, but students share with one another or sometimes read with partners, taking turns. With the groups heterogeneously mixed and a variety of leveled books available, students model good reading strategies and fluency for one another.

During this time, Georgia has individual reading conferences, takes running records, jots down notes, and offers personal instruction in reading strategies to encourage self-monitoring, multiple strategy use, and independence. In one reading conference with a struggling emergent reader, Georgia encourages his use of multiple strategies: self-monitoring, decoding, and—most importantly—meaning making. *Apples and Pumpkins* by Anne Rockwell (1994) is a new book for this reader, so Georgia encourages talking about it a little bit, looking at the title and discussing the opening illustration and what he thinks is going on. When the student reads "country farm" instead of "Comstock Farm," Georgia praises the attempt, saying it was a really good word that made sense. She then claps out the syllables in *Comstock*, directing the student to look closely at the letters, and he is able to sound it out by syllables. Early in the story the student reads "greens and chickens" for "geese and chickens." Georgia draws attention to the mistake, asking, "Does that make sense?" The student quickly rereads the phrase correctly. She then encourages the use of multiple strategies, using picture cues, making sense, use of letter–sound relationships, and reading on to find out what happens.

The student slowly but successfully reads "The geese and chickens and a big fat turkey walked with us on our way to the . . . where the apples grow." The word skipped is *orchard*. Georgia builds upon the student's knowledge, asking "Where do apples grow? What do we call a lot of trees? What parts of the word look familiar?" until the student uses existing prior knowledge and the word part *or-* to correctly pronounce "orchard."

As the student reads on, he becomes more fluent. Another mistake, "for me vine"/ "for the vine"/ "from the vine" is a quick succession of readings. The student is self-correcting as Georgia asks, "Does that make sense?" Another self-correction leads Georgia to ask, "How did you figure out that it was 'carry'?" The student does not know how to verbalize what strategies he used, so Georgia suggests some: "Did you look at all the letters? Did you look at the pictures? Did you go on?" For a final mistake, "fake" for "face," Georgia again stresses making sense: "Read it again and see if that makes more sense to you, from the beginning." Thus, she encourages another strategy, rereading along with meaning making, in cross-checking. The student successfully reads "At home we carve a jack-o-lantern face on our big orange pumpkin." Georgia praises him for his use of multiple strategies and for sticking to the reading even though the book has many hard words.

The days that students have reading from the literature baskets are also Writers' Workshop days. The teacher and the aide give individual attention and encouragement to the writers. Checklist cards for editing encourage correct final punctuation, capitals, and spelling. Most of the students spell phonemically, sounding out words and stretching the sounds. Back in January, Georgia created a priority word list of 25 nonphonemic and high-frequency words. The students have a list of them on their tables and are expected to refer to it whenever they need to use these words in writing. After 3 months, students were spelling them correctly without looking at the lists. Today, there is much use of the Word Wall (Cunningham & Allington, 2007) for spelling other words.

A typical example is a boy adding to a story on giant sea turtles. He is reading from a book about sea turtles to gather new information. He has already written two drafts that have been revised and edited. As he writes, he uses the Word Wall and the information and spelling from the book he is using as a resource. Another student is working on a chapter book about animals, because she has decided to combine two works in progress, one on horses and one on dogs.

After recess, Georgia has a math lesson on telling time on the hour and on the half-hour. It begins as a whole-class discussion on the rug as Georgia models the time for reading, for recess, and for leisure reading, using a large yellow clock with movable hands. Again literacy is stressed. To tie in with this unit on telling time, she reads aloud *The Bear Child's Book of Hours* by Anne Rockwell (1987). Students then proceed to more individualized work back at the tables, each writing his or her own *My Book of Hours and Half-Hours.* Each student fills in clocks and composes sentences that match personal experiences with the assistance of Georgia and her aide, scaffolding when necessary. Lunchtime and another recess end this busy morning.

When students return from lunch, they settle down for independent leisure reading time. Crates of books of different reading levels are available, including many easy ones, as well as magazines and student-published books. Students share responses with one another, partner-read, or read segments to one another from the books they have chosen. There is a very low hum to this reading time. Twenty-five minutes later, students go to the gym. When Georgia picks them up from the gym, she comes prepared with clipboards, paper, and pencils. They discuss the various sights and smells they envisioned earlier on the rug, before reading *Over in the Meadow* (Keats, 1993). Then, Georgia directs them to write down anything they observe as they go on their 10-minute playground/ meadow walk. Students are busy talking, smelling, looking, and sharing ideas as they gather data and write their own observations.

This day, the students have written in response journals, in their individual "book of hours," and now on clipboards about their trip to the meadow, writing in their own words everything they have seen, smelled, or heard. Georgia teaches both reading and writing skills explicitly, typically in the context of a reading or writing activity. She is opportunistic, selecting multiple occasions daily to provide explicit skills information, during whole-group, small-group, and individual meetings. But Georgia is also systematic, incorporating much of her strategy and skills instruction into her guided reading lessons, Writers' Workshop conferences, and reading conferences. All of these activities offer students instruction on a personalized basis.

Before the children leave for the day, Georgia makes sure each student has selected a well-practiced little book to take home to read that night to his or her parents.

Exemplary Instructional Support for Children Who Find Learning to Read and Write Difficult

Joyce is a reading teacher in an old mill town on a river in the Northeast. The school serves a significant number of at-risk students, with 40% of the children eligible for free or reduced-price lunch. Joyce starts her day at 8:00 A.M., snatching small conferences with the various teachers whose rooms she pushes into, getting plastic baskets ready with books for the various first-grade rooms she enters, and setting up her small, cozy room for the two pullout sessions she does each day. At 9:00, she enters the first of five first-grade classrooms she visits on a daily basis.

The "warm-up" involves 10 students who come over immediately as Joyce spreads out multiple copies of eight little books. These are all rereads in which students quickly engage, with comments such as "I can read this one" (e.g., *The Ghost*; Cowley, 1990) or "Let's read this one together" (e.g., *In a Dark, Dark Wood*; Ross, 1990). Joyce works with and listens to each student read in a whisper, their version of silent reading. As they finish one book, students take or trade for another. After 10 minutes, Joyce collects those texts and gives each child a copy of *Where's the Halloween Treat?* (Ziefert, 1985), first introduced the preceding day.

Joyce starts the guided reading with "Where are your eyes going to be?" The students chime in: "On the words." Working on the title, one student knows the word *the*, another, *Halloween*; still another guesses *trick*. Noting that *trick* makes sense, Joyce asks, "Is that *trick* or *treat*?" The student answers, "*Treat* because of the *t* at the end." Students read the text together, misreading *us* for *me*. When asked, "Is that *us*?" they reread, saying that the word starts with an *m*, and self-correcting to *me*. Joyce points out, "I hear a rhyme. Listen for two words," and rereads the pages. Students quickly suggest *eat/treat*. "Detective ears" are used to find more rhyming words as the story progresses. Joyce picks up the pace; so does the group, self-correcting individually as they go along. When they finish the story, Joyce has them turn back to page 6, finding the words *good*, *eat*, and *six*. She cues each word with "What's it going to start with?" This reread with a minilesson on rhymes takes about 10 minutes.

For the final 10 minutes, Joyce introduces a new book, *Going Up?: The Elevator Counting Book* (Cummins, 1995). Finger-pointing to the first word, she asks, "What does it say?" As she covers the *ing*, students quickly chant "go"; then they chant "going" as she uncovers the whole word. From the title, students predict where the character is—in an elevator. Joyce asks the students, "Why is this a good name for a book about an elevator, and how does it know when to stop?" Students have various responses, which are all accepted positively. Then they begin to read as Joyce finger-points to each word. The elevator stops at floor number five. She then asks them to predict what will happen next: The numbers go down as the elevator goes down. Then they all read the rest of the text together. Before leaving, Joyce tells the students that they will work on writing books tomorrow.

Joyce quickly goes back to her small room, where she picks up the next basket of books and hurries on to her second first-grade class. In this class, students start their warm-up with *Jack-O'-Lantern* (Frost, 1990). Each student has his or her own copy. Joyce has extra copies for those children who took the book home and forgot to bring it back. Joyce spreads out other books for warm-up, with the instruction "Everyone find one page to read to me. When I have heard you read your page, take a different book." Joyce encourages rereading, thinking of a word that makes sense, and starts with the beginning sound and voice-print match. One student, who picked the first page of *Scarecrow* (Bacon, 1993), reads. Joyce asks him how the book ends, which he does not know. She tells him to find the end of the book, and together they read the last pages, working on self-correcting and understanding. After the 10-minute warm-up, the students are directed to put the books in the middle and are told they can keep *Jack-O'-Lantern* and take it home again.

In this group, she introduces *Where's the Halloween Treat?* (Ziefert, 1985). Looking at the title, students are directed to the *H* and asked "What sound does it make?" Students all say /h/ and start thinking of a word that makes sense with the cover picture. They offer *haunt*, *house*, *Halloween*. Another student reads "Where's the," and everyone choruses "Halloween." Joyce begins the book, finger-pointing to the words as she goes along. By the second page, students are chiming in and predicting a good thing to eat behind the door. *Sandwich* and *apple* are accepted; the word *skeleton* prompts "Is that something good to eat?" By the third page, the students are using the repetition and their knowledge of numbers to read with no assistance. When asked how they know it is *seven*, students say it starts with an *s*, and another adds that it ends with *n*. Near the end of the book, Joyce asks the students to predict: "What do you think they did when the ghost said 'Boo'?" Answers vary from "They stayed," to "They ran," to "They were afraid." The children finish the story to see what would happen and revise their predictions as needed.

With 5 minutes left, Joyce has the students begin writing their own book, modeled after the book they just read. The classroom teacher allows them to continue writing as Joyce leaves.

Joyce's third first-grade class does a warm-up reading time for 10 minutes. Then *Where's the Halloween Treat?* is read chorally, a reread for three students and new to two others. With this group, Joyce takes from her basket of *My Journal* books, with each child's name at the bottom of the cover. In the book, they are working on patterns and words they can make from them to use in writing. The students are directed to make a box, then a *u* in the box, then a vertical line, and then an *s*. Joyce asks, "What's that word?" Students respond, "Us." After writing it under the box, Joyce asks, "What would rhyme with *us*?" Students think of *bus*. Joyce models on a pad, writing *us* and putting a *b* in front of it, while she thinks aloud, "If we can write *us*, we can write *bus*. We need to put the *b* first, then *us*." Students are now directed to write *Give* on the bottom of their page; the students and Joyce spell it. Next they are asked to write *us* from above, read the two words, and add a number: *Give us 7*. Then, together they spell *good things to eat*, with the students spelling the beginning and ending sounds and the *ing*. Joyce ends her half-hour by telling the students, "When I come back tomorrow, we will cut up these sentences and do a new book."

It is now 10:30 A.M. and time for Joyce's fourth first-grade class. Six students in this group quickly dive into the warm-up books Joyce brought in a plastic basket. As she comments positively to one student, "I like the way you are finger-pointing," other students start finger-pointing. Joyce works individually with each student. Then, a new book for this group is introduced, *Jack-O'-Lantern* (Frost, 1990). The end of the lesson revolves around the word *made*. "We are going to write the word *made*. Think about it. How big a box?" Joyce asks. She uses a small easel blackboard to model a box with three spaces, the last divided with a dotted line. The students fill in *m, a, d*, as Joyce ends by saying, "There is a letter we don't hear at the end." Students predict *n* or *t*, and Joyce tells them *e*. They add the *e*, commenting that there are three sounds but four letters. This leads to students writing in their journals about the kind of face they would make on a pumpkin. Joyce has each student say the sentence he or she wants to write, concentrating on adjectives. Students quickly write "I made a," and then Joyce helps them stretch the words *vampire, scary, wolf, happy,* or *mad.* She then directs them to the word *face* in their book. On a blank piece of paper, she writes each sentence, cuts it up, and puts it and a copy of *Jack-O'-Lantern* in a zip-loc bag for each student to take home.

Joyce is a little behind schedule, arriving in the fifth classroom at 11:10. The children do warm-up reading and then Joyce holds up the new book, *Jack-O'-Lantern,* saying, "Look at the cover. What do you see?" The students say, "Pumpkin." Joyce responds, "Do you think that word says *pumpkin*?" The students reply, "No." Her "Why?" is answered with "Because it starts with a *j*." Joyce prompts them: "What is another name that starts with *j*?" They answer "jack-o'-lantern." Different students take turns finger pointing and reading with Joyce. Then the students read in pairs from their own copies of the book. Joyce then has each student pick one page to read out loud to her after first practicing it in pairs.

Joyce now has a prep time and lunch, which she spends preparing the different baskets for the five first-grade lessons tomorrow. Over lunch, she talks with the fourth-grade teacher in whose room she will work for an hour.

Joyce is giving daily intensive tutoring to the two first graders who are struggling most with reading. At 12:30 she provides a one-on-one pullout session with one of the first graders. She picks up the student, quickly walking with her to her small tutoring room. Out of a packet kept in the reading room, the student picks a copy of *The Monster's Party* (Cowley, 1990) with her name on it. She reads it, finger pointing as Joyce listens. Then Joyce picks *Sing a Song* (Melser, 1990) out of her packet. As the student reads it, she takes a running record. When she gets stuck on the word *about,* Joyce prompts, "What can you do if you don't know it?" The student says, "Read on," and she does. Although she does not self-correct here, she does so later on when reading *together* for *bed* and *tuck* for *us.* In both cases, she appears to use both letters and meaning to help self-correct. As the student completes the book, Joyce asks, "Can you tell me one thing in this story you liked?" The girl likes the splashing. Joyce continues: "What else happened in the story?" The student replies, "They got out." Joyce asks, "How did they get out?" The student answers, "Jump." She is asked to find the word and does.

The next book they read is *Hairy Bear* (Cowley, 1990). They discuss that *we* and *together* mean more than one tiger. Up on the blackboard Joyce and the student work on the word *out,* making a box with one wall and one segment divided with a dotted line. The student fills in the *t,* Joyce the *o* and *u.* They then work on a box for *about,* the word the student missed in her reread for the running record. The student hears and writes each sound, then practices writing *about*. Then, she writes *out* and *about* on 3" × 5" cards that will be added to her word box, a recipe box. For 2 minutes, they practice words from the box. Then, while the student picks another story to read, Joyce writes a sentence on jumping from *Sing a Song* (Melser, 1990): "Out, Out, Out we jump." The student reads the sentence. Joyce cuts it up, has her assemble it, and read again. Into a bag go the cut-up sentence, the book, and the 3" × 5" cards *out* and *about* to go home for practice.

In the last 3 minutes, they discuss real and make-believe as a new book, *Dan the Flying Man* (Cowley, 1990), is introduced. Joyce begins reading, with the book in front of the student, and has the student finger-point to the words. Joyce leaves blanks at the end of the sentence, and the student correctly supplies *trees* and *train*. Halfway through, the student takes over. Joyce joins in again at the ending, which has a change of wording. The student goes back to her room as Joyce goes on to the fourth-grade class.

The fourth-grade teacher has requested that Joyce work with her to enhance her writing instruction. In September, Joyce had modeled the writing process, brainstorming, rough drafts, revising, conferencing, editing, and publishing. She and the teacher worked on modeling peer conferences that sensitively gave feedback, constructive criticism, and specific ideas to the writer. With the writing process smoothly working in late October, Joyce continued to help with writing conferences but also was available for reading conferences and small heterogeneously grouped work. Language arts time was structured so that remedial assistance included students with special needs who were working on reading and writing material at their independent and instructional levels. More frequent conferences in reading and writing were provided for them.

Joyce enters the room as the teacher is reading the beginning of *The Eerie Canal* (Reber, 1991). The introduction to the book had taken place earlier. Joyce points out at the end of the chapter, "I met a lot of characters. They keep mentioning Tom. I think he will be important." A student adds that another character, Sandy, is being described in detail and must be important too. As the teacher reads, Joyce and the children discuss the opening chapters, and inferences and predictions flow. Questions such as "I'm getting a funny feeling," "What do you think right now?," "What do you feel?," "Can you picture that?," and "What made you think it?" all encourage responses, the sharing of ideas, and predictions.

Both teachers then lead the discussion to important characters and significant events that happen to them. In groups of two or three, they discuss, share ideas, and write about the two main characters and important events they experienced in the opening chapters. Joyce and the teacher circulate among the students, listening, prompting, and asking questions to expand ideas and encourage examples. In the return to whole-class discussion and a composite list of events, the conversation also includes the author's style and how he pulled the reader right into the story. They contrast it to Cynthia DeFelice's style in *The Light on Hogback Hill* (1992), the current read-aloud, which has a much slower beginning and draws the reader in slowly. As this discussion continues, Joyce leaves.

It is now 2:00 P.M. and time to pick up the other first grader for intensive one-on-one tutoring. After this, Joyce visits a third-grade classroom. This third-grade teacher worked with Joyce for several weeks earlier this year, and now Joyce stops in to observe and then discuss her observations with the teacher about once a month. This is an extension of the coaching role that provides teachers with long-term support and professional conversation about the successes and concerns they are experiencing. After this debriefing session it is time for Joyce to be ready to respond to any number of queries or requests from teachers in her school. Sometimes the requests are easy, sometimes not, but supporting classroom teachers in their attempts to offer higher-quality reading instruction is central to Joyce's vision of her role.

How Joyce Developed Her Role

Joyce and her school have participated in a variety of studies with a nearby university for 10 years. Organizational support from a former administration allowed and even encouraged change involving teachers and their ideas. Earlier, some 12 years ago, when Joyce was a special education teacher, she started pushing into the classrooms. She started with one teacher:

> "It was contagious. People were upset I couldn't come into their room. Part of it was that they were getting something back. They were learning how to teach with literature, and they really wanted to have their special education kids with them more of the time. We were learning together how to best do this."

When she earned her reading specialist credential and shifted from special education to reading teacher several years ago, both the remedial reading and special education programs were completely pullout. At that time, an administrator wanted to start a brand-new kindergarten and first-grade reading program that incorporated a push-in model for supplemental instructional support.

> "The K–1 teachers never had exposure to working with someone in their rooms before. They might not have invited me in, but I just couldn't feasibly do a pullout in K–1. Plus it was really successful with the way my special ed program was operating. . . . I don't think people

like to see you come in with a halo of authority. I would always say we should sit and talk. First, we had discussion time. I would say to them, 'I need to know what I'm doing, when I'm in the room, so let's decide what your goals are and what you want to accomplish, and I'll talk about some of my goals and what I want to accomplish. Then let's figure out how we can do this together in the room at the same time.' Every person was different."

One teacher and Joyce worked on flexible grouping, with students rolling in and out between them. For another teacher, she modeled read-alouds and having the children respond to stories. "I had to give her something concrete, something predictable, something she could do every day by herself."

In subsequent years Joyce's role changed:

> "The teachers have gotten comfortable with providing reading instruction from leveled book collections. I don't have to spend much time giving whole-class lessons. I'm spending more time with students, individualizing more. I try to do a lot more things quickly—quicker than I used to. I make sure they read lots of books when I'm with them. I'm seeing the kids more often. The real secret has to be that the classroom teachers really know how to do instruction, and that we figure out a plan, where some days I'm integrated in everything and other days maybe I'm not integrated. I'm working with my kids, but also I'm pulling out other kids that have that same problem."

Joyce and the teachers she works with feel "that we are both responsible for all of the kids in that room," yet she works primarily with the kids that really need the additional instruction.

The remedial program has become very collaborative. Several days, throughout the year, substitutes come in, rotate, and relieve the classroom teachers so that they can attend roughly hour-long conferences with Joyce. Planning focuses on the very specific needs of certain children and how those needs will be addressed. Joyce has changed from a complete push-in model to primarily a push-in model, with two periods a day in which she pulls out students for one-on-one tutoring. One positive outcome of all these changes has been a large reduction in the number of children being labeled and placed in special education.

REFLECTIONS AND FUTURE DIRECTIONS

Certainly more studies that continue the research into exemplary classroom and reading teachers and their instructional practices are needed.

Another area in which there is little or no research involves looking at comprehensive intervention programs that include long-term support. This crucial component needs to be better understood so that schools can offer professional development, create budgets, and coordinate instructional support that will provide exemplary support programs for children throughout their schooling.

Exemplary early literacy interventions begin with an emphasis on ensuring that all children have access to high-quality classroom instruction. But classroom teaching is complex, and classroom teachers will likely never to be able to meet the substantial demands on time and expertise that some children pose. This suggests, then, two roles for special program personnel. The first involves working with classroom teachers to enhance the quality of literacy instruction offered as part of the general education experience (often labeled coaching). This might occur in any number of ways, but in the cases that we observed the specialists offered training, advice, information, and appropriate materials to classroom teachers in order to enhance classroom instruction. The second role is to provide direct instruction to children who find learning to read difficult—but instruction that extends classroom lessons and is offered in a more intensive and personalized manner. Delivering such instruction requires working with classroom teachers over a period of time, but the benefits suggest that the effort pays substantial dividends.

CONCLUDING COMMENTS

What have we learned about addressing the needs of struggling readers? First, high-quality classroom reading instruction is absolutely essential. Struggling readers need high-quality instruction all day long. That means texts they can read not just in reading/language arts lessons but in science and social studies as well. One reason struggling readers read so much less than better readers is that they are, too often, sitting all day in classrooms where there are few books they can read accurately, fluently, and with understanding. Second, struggling readers need a steady supply of essential strategy lessons accompanied by extensive opportunities to independently practice and apply those strategies in high-success reading materials (Swanson & Hoskyn, 1998). Finally, even when high-quality classroom reading instruction is available, some struggling readers will need more expert and more intensive reading instruction than classroom teachers will be able to provide—thus, the critical role of reading specialists. In the most effective supplemental support programs, care is taken to link the supplementary lessons to classroom instruction while still attending to the specific needs of individual students.

ENGAGEMENT ACTIVITIES

1. Track the volume of reading that struggling readers in your classroom (or school) do over a 1-week period. Compare this to the volume of reading better readers do. Are struggling readers doing at least as much reading as better readers? If not, what can be done to expand the reading volume of struggling readers?
2. Examine the texts you find in any struggling reader's desk. How many of the texts can that child read accurately, fluently, and with comprehension? Is the desk filled with books that are too difficult?
3. Interview an elementary school principal and ask about the school's literacy program. How does it meet the needs of all students? What components are in place for preventing reading and writing difficulties? What support is there for intervening and accelerating the progress of students who struggle with reading and writing?
4. Research how many fourth-grade students in your district will need additional support in middle school.
5. Find out about preventive, accelerated, and longer-term support plans in place in your school district. Are there clear links between preschool and elementary school programs, and elementary and middle-school programs?

ACKNOWLEDGMENTS

The development of the case studies reported in this chapter was supported in part under the Educational Research and Development Program (Grant Nos. Rll7GIOO15 and R305A60005) and the National Research Center on English Learning and Achievement, as administered by the Office of Educational Research and Improvement, U.S. Department of Education. However, the contents of this chapter do not necessarily represent the positions or policies of the sponsoring agencies.

REFERENCES

Professional Literature

Achilles, C. M. (1999). *Let's put kids first, finally: Getting class size right.* Thousand Oaks, CA: Corwin Press.

Allington, R. L. (2006). *What really matters for struggling readers* (2nd ed.). Boston: Allyn & Bacon.

Allington, R. L., & Cunningham, P. M. (2007). *Schools that work* (3rd ed.). New York: Longman.

Allington, R. L., & Johnston, P. H. (2002). *Reading to learn: Lessons from exemplary fourth-grade classrooms.* New York: Guilford Press.

Anderson, L. W., & Pellicier, L. O. (1990). Synthesis of research on compensatory and remedial education. *Educational Leadership, 48*(1), 10–16.

Boyd-Zaharias, J., & Pate-Bain, H. (1998). *Teacher aides and student learning: Lessons from Project STAR.* Arlington, VA: Educational Research Service.

Cunningham, P. M., & Allington, R. L. (2007). *Classrooms that work: They can all read and write* (4th ed.). Boston: Allyn & Bacon.

Gerber, S. B., Finn, J. D., Achilles, C. M., & Boyd-Zaharias, J. (2001). Teacher aides and students' academic achievement. *Educational Evlauation and Policy Analysis, 23*(2), 123–143.

Guthrie, J. T. (2004). Teaching for literacy engagement. *Journal of Literary Research, 36*(1), 1–28.

Howes, A. (2003). Teaching reforms and the impact of paid adult support on participation and learning in mainstream schools. *Support for Learning, 18*(4), 147–153.

International Reading Association. (1994). Who is teaching our children? Implications of the use of aides in Chapter 1. *ERS Spectrum, 12,* 28–34.

Mendro, R. L., Jordan, H., & Bembry, K. L. (1998, April). *Longitudinal teacher effects on student achievement and their relation to school and project evaluation.* Paper presented at the annual meeting of the American Educational Research Association, San Diego, CA.

Pressley, M., Allington, R. L., Wharton-McDonald, R., Block, C. C., & Morrow, L. (2001). *Learning to read: Lessons from exemplary first-grade classrooms.* New York: Guilford Press.

Scanlon, D. M., & Vellutino, F. R. (1997). A comparison of the instructional backgrounds and cognitive profiles of poor, average, and good readers who were initially identified as at risk for reading failure. *Scientific Studies of Reading, 1*(3), 191–216.

Snow, C., Barnes, W., Chandler, J., Goodman, I. F., & Hemphill, L. (1991). *Unfulfilled expectations: Home and school influences on literacy.* Cambridge, MA: Harvard University Press.

Swanson, H. L., & Hoskyn, M. (1998). Experimental intervention research on students with learning disabilities: A meta-analysis of treatment outcomes. *Review of Educational Research, 68*(3), 277–321.

Taylor, B. M., Pearson, P. D., Peterson, D. S., & Rodriguez, M. C. (2003). Reading growth in high-poverty classrooms: The influences of teacher practices that encourage cognitive engagement in literacy learning. *Elementary School Journal, 104*(1), 4–28.

Walmsley, S. A., & Allington, R. L. (1995). Redefining and reforming instructional support programs for at-risk students. In R. L. Allington & S. A. Walmsley (Eds.), *No quick fix: Rethinking literacy programs in America's elementary schools* (pp. 19–41). New York: Teachers College Press.

Children's Literature

Bacon, R. (1993). *Scarecrow.* Crystal Lake, IL: Rigby.

Cowley, J. (1990). *The bee.* Bothell, WA: Wright Group.

Cowley, J. (1990). *Dan the flying man.* Bothell, WA: Wright Group.

Cowley, J. (1990). *The ghost.* Bothell, WA: Wright Group.

Cowley, J. (1990). *Hairy bear.* Bothell, WA: Wright Group.

Cowley, J. (1990). *The monster's party.* Bothell, WA: Wright Group.

Cummins, P. (1995). *Going up?: The elevator counting book.* Glenview, IL: Celebrations Press.
DeFelice, C. (1992). *The light on Hogback Hill.* New York: Scribner's.
Frost, M. 1990). *Jack-o'-lantern.* Bothell, WA: Wright Group.
Keats, E. J. (1993). *Over in the meadow.* New York: Scholastic.
Melser, J. (1990). *Sing a song.* Bothell, WA: Wright Group.
Reber, J. (1991). *The eerie canal.* Unionville, NY: Trillium Press.
Rockwell, A. (1994). *Apples and pumpkins.* New York: Aladdin Paperbacks.
Rockwell, A. (1987). *The bear child's book of hours.* New York: Crowell.
Ross, C. (1990). *In a dark, dark wood.* Bothell, WA: Wright Group.
Ziefert, H. (1985). *Where's the Halloween treat?* New York: Viking Press.

Chapter 5

BEST PRACTICES FOR LITERACY INSTRUCTION FOR ENGLISH-LANGUAGE LEARNERS

María S. Carlo

This chapter will:

- Provide background information relevant to understanding the demographic and policy context surrounding instruction for English-language learners (ELLs).
- Highlight the differences in learning to read a first versus a second language.
- Highlight the role of oral language proficiency in learning to read and discuss the implications for the teaching of English alphabetics to children not fully in command of the English language.

This chapter focuses on research and theory that can guide the design and delivery of instruction in English alphabetics for English-language learners (ELLs). In writing a review piece of this sort, one risks portraying ELLs as a homogeneous group of learners that stand to benefit uniformly from the instructional practices one happens to review. Such a portrayal of ELLs would be, of course, incorrect. The ELL designation applies to youngsters who vary by age, country of origin, mother tongue, socioeconomic status, degree of access and exposure to formal schooling, and so on. Variations among these factors influence the extent to which instructional practices can favorably impact learning to read in a second language. Indeed, strategies that may prove effective with 10-year-old ELLs who have already learned to read in their first language may have little applicability for teaching 15-year-old ELLs who have been denied access to formal schooling prior to entering the United States. Such vast differences in the social and educational conditions and learner attributes characterizing ELLs should not be taken as an indication that reading instruction for this population cannot follow a principled and systematic process. Rather, it should indicate that a first step in a principled approach to ELL reading instruction involves identifying the various ways in which ELLs differ from one another and from native English speakers. It should also indicate the need to examine the role that these differences may play in determining the success of an instructional intervention. Thus, a goal throughout this chapter will be to direct attention to the sources of differences in ELL reading development that may dictate the need to radically alter instruction or (more likely) to adapt instruction in English alphabetics to accommodate students' literacy needs better.

The influence of the report of the National Reading Panel (NRP; 2000) on the delivery of reading instruction to schoolchildren in the United States has prompted questions about the extent to which the findings of the NRP are applicable to children who are learning to read in a language that they do not speak natively. In this chapter the discussion is limited to highlighting ELL factors that are relevant to instruction in alphabetics (one of the three areas of concern to the NRP), with a particular focus on the interplay between oral language development and the development of knowledge of alphabetics.

This discussion on best practices for ELLs begins with a description of the demographic shifts in the U.S. school population and a brief discussion of the policy context surrounding ELL instruction in the United States. The focus on demographic and policy changes serves to highlight the fact that both are creating increased demand for expertise in ELL reading instruction from all literacy practitioners.

THE DEMOGRAPHIC AND EDUCATIONAL POLICY CONTEXT

The most recent estimates available from the National Clearinghouse for English Language Acquisition and Language Instruction Educational Programs (NCELA; 2006) indicate that there are approximately 4.7 million students who meet the criteria for ELL designation in US schools. This number represents a 95% increase in the ELL population since 1991, compared to 12% growth in the overall K–12 population in the United States. In as many as 16 states the growth in ELL population has exceeded 200% (NCELA, 2006). Across the United States, ELLs constitute approximately 19% of enrollments, but as many as 10 states have enrollments upward of 20% (Capps et al., 2005).

According to estimates available as of the year 2000, the majority of ELLs—about 79% or so—are Spanish-speaking. Vietnamese, Hmong, and Cantonese speakers are the next three largest groups, accounting for 1.95, 1.55, and 1.02% of the ELL population. The rest represent as many as 380 different language groups (Hopstock & Stephenson, 2003).

At the same time that the number of ELLs is increasing, the availability of varied pedagogical models for serving this population is decreasing despite the fact that every study that has compared English-only and bilingual models has failed to find evidence suggesting that bilingual programs are detrimental to ELL academic learning (August & Shanahan, 2006).

The passage of ballot initiatives in California, Arizona, and Massachusetts has resulted in the elimination or has limited the availability of instructional models that are based on bilingual instruction. In some cases this has also limited the availability of English as a second language (ESL) instruction for ELLs. In California, for example, Proposition 227 prescribes that "children who are English learners shall be educated through sheltered English immersion during a temporary transition period not normally intended to exceed one year" (Unz & Tuchman, 1998).

The demographic trends, coupled with reports of a disappointing level of success toward closing the educational achievement gap for ELLs (August & Shanahan, 2006), accentuate the urgent need for instructional approaches that attend to the linguistic and instructional needs of ELLs. The causes of the educational achievement gap are complex, and the solutions surely do not reside exclusively in the realm of literacy education. But, increasing the effectiveness of our efforts in literacy development for ELLs is an important part of the solution.

LEARNING TO READ IN A SECOND LANGUAGE

One way to gain appreciation of the challenges children encounter when learning to read a language they do not fully command is to reassess what a native English-speaking child knows about the English language when he or she begins formal instruction in reading and after at least 5 years of sustained exposure to the language. During this time, a child has acquired the ability to perceive (although not necessarily to isolate and manipulate) pretty much all the sounds of his or her language (Menn & Stoel-Gammon, 2000). He or she is able to recognize changes in the meanings of words in relation to changes in sound—for example, recognizing that the addition of a single sound /s/ to *cat* significantly alters its meaning. Not only does he or she understand how the phoneme /s/ works in cat, but also he or she implicitly knows its function as an inflectional morpheme that when added to other words signals "more than one" (Tager-Flusberg, 2000).

At the time a child begins formal reading instruction, his or her vocabulary will consist of several thousand words, and he or she will have command over most of the grammar used (Tager-Flusberg, 2000). In fact, in terms of the simplest grammatical forms, the child's usage will be comparable to that of adult native speakers (Tager-Flusberg, 2000). Additionally, the child will have acquired some fairly sophisticated knowledge of language pragmatics. It will be possible to understand, for example, that if mom asks whether it is time to do homework, mom is not really asking for a time check. The difference between intended meanings and stated meanings is in some cases already apparent (Bryant, 2000).

The books the native speaker will use to learn to read have been designed with his or her language abilities in mind. The words that appear in the books are words that he or she can use and that others in his or her linguistic community use on a daily basis. The child is learning that print is talk written down, and fortunately the books contain examples of how others in his or her world talk.

In this light, the challenges associated with learning to read in a language one does not speak or understand become more obvious. Learning to read builds on a child's capacity to communicate orally. Learning to read in a language one does not command orally can present multiple challenges for a child. A very basic example of such challenges involves recognizing what constitutes a word in the new language, something we assume most native speakers have mastered in relation to oral language when they are ready to learn to read. Yet, at the very early stages of learning, second-language learners must confront the challenge of figuring out a reliable way of recognizing boundaries for words in the new language (Saffran, Senghas, & Trueswell, 2001). Natural speech is a continuous blend of words; so, word boundaries are not clearly identifiable. The pauses one hears between words are not really present in the acoustic signal. In developing their first language, children are aided by multiple linguistic and social scaffolds that gradually build their skill to recognize the boundaries for words in speech.

The challenges are not confined to the emergent stages of second-language (L2) learning. Equally challenging is the task of constructing meaning from text when a high proportion of the words in the text are unknown or when the complexity in the grammatical structure of sentences in the texts surpasses the grammatical proficiency of the reader.

In issuing their recommendations about optimal conditions for learning to read in a second language, the experts on the National Research Council's Committee on Preventing Reading Difficulties in Young Children recognized the fundamental relationship between oral language proficiency and early reading achievement (Snow, Burns, & Griffin, 1998). They recommended that

> if language-minority children arrive at school with no proficiency in English but speaking a language for which there are instructional guides, learning materials, and locally available proficient teachers, these children should be taught how to read in their native language while acquiring proficiency in spoken English and then subsequently taught to extend their skills to reading in English.
>
> If language-minority children arrive at school with no proficiency in English but speak a language for which the above conditions cannot be met and for which there are insufficient numbers of children to justify the development of the local capacity to meet such conditions, the instructional priority should be to develop the children's proficiency in spoken English. Although print materials may be used to develop understanding of English speech sounds, vocabulary, and syntax, the postponement of formal reading instruction is appropriate until an adequate level of proficiency in spoken English has been achieved. (p. 11)

State educational policies have resulted in high-stakes testing affecting all children. Therefore, delaying reading instruction for ELLs, especially given the little guidance offered by the research community in answering questions related to either the appropriate lengths of such delays or effective methods for promoting and/or accelerating the acquisition of oral language skills for ELLs, is not a reasonable proposition for many if not most school districts. But, the theoretical and empirical evidence that points to the critical role of oral language in first-language literacy development, coupled with pressures for accountability in student literacy outcomes, demands that we think creatively about ways of designing reading instruction that explicitly attends to weaknesses in oral proficiency so that ELLs can benefit from the reading instruction they will receive. Properly scaffolded reading instruction can become an additional source of language input, and well-chosen print materials can, by virtue of the modality, afford opportunities to revisit, reexamine, and contrast that input in a manner that is conducive to language learning.

INSTRUCTION IN ALPHABETICS

Like all children, ELLs will benefit from opportunities to learn in an environment that is affirming of their individual and social identity and from instruction that builds upon their strengths and recognizes their instructional needs. The following sections review literature that can help inform decisions about how to adapt early reading instruction so that it builds on learners' strengths and addresses their language needs and their literacy needs in the areas of phonological awareness, alphabet knowledge, and phonics knowledge. As suggested by the National Reading Panel (2000) and the NRC (Snow et al., 1998) report, all three skills are foundational components for learning to read in English.

Phonological Awareness

Phonological awareness is often defined as awareness that words are made of smaller units of sound that can be manipulated and changed (Moats, 2000; Snow et al., 1998). This awareness is fundamental to learning to read in languages that employ an alphabetic writing system. The ability to isolate sounds and correlate them to the orthographic system is essential for grasping the alphabetic principle and is an essential step toward developing the ability to effortlessly retrieve the meaning of printed words from the oral lexicon.

In order to learn to read in English, ELLs, like native speakers, need to develop phonological awareness (PA). The review by the National Literacy Panel (August & Shanahan, 2006) on the development of reading readiness skills among ELLs concluded that there was a great deal of variation in the level of attainment of PA among ELLs and that this variation in levels of attainment was related to factors such as age, level of L2 proficiency, language and literacy experiences as well as the degree of mastery of each language relative to the other (Lesaux & Geva, 2006). However, the NLP also concluded that difficulties in PA are not placing ELLs at risk for reading difficulties at a higher rate than native speakers (Lesaux & Geva, 2006). The NLP also points out that achievement in PA does not appear to function in a purely language-specific manner. Rather, the evidence suggests that PA skills developed in the native language may be instrumental to the development of second-language PA, as evidenced by the fact that assessments of PA in the first language are predictive of reading outcomes in the L2 (Lesaux & Geva, 2006).

Given the variation in PA attainment among ELLs, it is important to understand the possible sources of variation. In particular, it is worth considering how differences in oral language proficiency might affect the development of PA in a second language.

Those who study the development of PA among native speakers often point to two properties of natural speech that make it difficult for children to grasp on their own the concept that words are made of smaller units of sound (Moats, 2000). In natural speech phonemes are unsegmented and coarticulated (Moats, 2000). That is, words are not uttered one sound at a time; rather, sounds blend into one another. Additionally phonemes are influenced by the phonemes that precede and follow them. To develop PA children need to be able to ignore what is most salient to them in a word, namely its meaning, and create discrete units out of a speech signal that is seamless (Moats, 2000). To complicate matters further, those discrete sounds that are extracted from speech are never identical to the sounds as they occur within a word. This is because in making the sounds discrete one strips them of the qualities they achieve when pronounced in a coarticulated manner in natural speech (Moats, 2000). Thus, when one asks a child to decide if the sound /p/ appears in the word *plant*, one is not exactly asking the child to compare two identical entities.

Now consider an additional characteristic of speech perception—the categorical perception of phonemes—that can differentially impact second-language speakers and native speakers (Bialystok & Hakuta, 1994). Even though phonemes are articulated as a continuous acoustic signal, the perception of phonemes is categorical. A classic illustration of this exists in the acoustic feature that allows one to contrast the phonemes /b/ and /p/; namely, voice-onset timing (VOT). These two phonemes differ in the time lapsing between the output of air on the lips and the vibration of the vocal cords. Technically speaking, /b/ fades into /p/ as VOT increases, but perceptually and thus experientially /b/ changes to /p/ at a particular time point in VOT (Bialystok & Hakuta, 1994; Moats, 2000). The time point at which this drastic change in perception occurs varies by language. Spanish speakers perceive the switch earlier than English speakers, for example (Bialystok & Hakuta, 1994). What is relevant to the present analysis is the fact that the boundaries for the perception of phonemes are set very early in development. Moreover, the boundaries that are set in one's first language are the same ones that apply when processing phonemes in a second language, at least during the initial stages of second-language development (Bialystok & Hakuta, 1994). Over time, and with exposure to the second language, the boundaries shift closer to those applied by native speakers, but they never quite correspond exactly to the boundaries of native speakers (Bialystok & Hakuta, 1994).

When applied to the previously described task of deciding whether the sound /p/ appears in *plant*, the second-language speaker is confronted with the following challenge. Just like the native speaker, he or she must compare the discrete phoneme /p/ articulated by the examiner to the coarticulated /p/ in *plant*. Unlike the native speaker, the second-language speaker must further analyze the sounds using the phonemic categories set by his or her first language.

The good news, as was reported earlier, is that ELLs are capable of mastering this seemingly complicated task. How they come to master it is not fully understood, and neither are the reasons why they fail to master it when they do. One might speculate that those who succeed are aided by the metalinguistic skills—including PA skills—they have developed in their first language, as evidence suggests that systematic exposure to more than one language can in fact enhance metalinguistic abilities in bilingual children (Bialystok, 1997). Additionally, one would expect that systematic instruction in PA also aids the process. Nevertheless, it is important to understand the complexity of the process in order to make instructional decisions that address differences in the rate of attainment of this skill among ELLs.

As one considers the effects of limited English proficiency on the acquisition of phonological awareness, it would seem appropriate to draw attention to the distinction between speech production and speech perception, partially because the presence of accented speech is often mistaken for PA difficulties. While speech perception and production are undeniably related to each other, they are by no means synonymous. The presence of accented speech, as evidenced for example in some Spanish speakers' highly similar pronunciation of *fit* and *feet*, does not necessarily indicate an inability to perceive the shift in meaning signaled by the vowel difference in these two words during speech perception. The development of phonological awareness is very much a process that hinges on the perception of sound differences and the ability to manipulate those sounds in one's head. If we are concerned about ELLs' phonological awareness development, we need to directly assess their ability to perceive and manipulate sounds. A reliance on samples of continuous natural speech production will not provide an accurate assessment of PA.

How should one train a child who is an emergent English learner to perceive the sounds of English? While it may appear that giving ELL students practice with sound discrimination activities may be one fruitful way to encourage the development of phonemic perception abilities, two arguments are offered against doing so or at least against doing so at the expense of opportunities for exposure to meaningful communication. The report on *Preventing Reading Difficulties in Young Children* (Snow et al., 1998) reviews evidence that links phonological awareness development to language proficiency among native speakers of English (see also Goswami, 2000). The report states, for example, that

> performance on phonological awareness tasks by preschoolers was highly correlated with general language ability. Moreover, it was measures of semantic and syntactic skills, rather than speech discrimination and articulation, that predicted phonological awareness differences. Correlations between metalinguistic and more basic language abilities have similarly been reported by others (e.g., Bryant, MacLean, Bradley, & Crossland, 1990;

> Bryant, 1974; Smith & Tager-Flusberg, 1982). These findings indicate that the development of phonological awareness (and other metalinguistic skills) is closely intertwined with growth in basic language proficiency during the preschool years. (p. 53)

If language proficiency differences among native speakers can impact the development of PA, it stands to reason that any investments in developing the language proficiency of ELLs could also have an effect on their ability to discriminate phonemes in the second language, and further down the line, when coupled with phonological awareness instruction, on their ability to reflect upon and manipulate phonemes in English (Rolla-San Francisco, Carlo, August, & Snow, 2006).

On theoretical grounds, it is also worth noting that, while phonemes are not in and of themselves a unit of meaning, they are the smallest unit of sound that makes a difference in meaning. The differences in meaning that are signaled by phoneme changes may, possibly, provide a stronger motivation to attend to the changes in sound than might be afforded by discrimination tasks in which semantic contrasts are reduced.

Learning the Alphabet

For many second-language learners, learning to read in a second language also involves learning a new script. The literature on children learning to read in their native language points to the importance of learning to discriminate among the letters in the alphabet in a rapid and reliable manner (Adams, 1990). Most children learn to differentiate these graphic symbols after many years of exposure to them, through language games, books, and access to print-rich environments (Adams, 1990). Research has shown that children's knowledge of the letters of the alphabet is a strong predictor of future reading achievement (Adams, 1990).

Despite the demonstrated importance of letter recognition skills to the development of reading ability in monolingual readers, little attention has been directed at understanding the development of these skills in the context of second-language reading, particularly among children whose early literacy experiences, whether via environmental print or formal instruction, involve use of a different script (e.g., Arabic) or even an entirely different writing system (e.g., Japanese).

To date, perhaps the most persuasive data suggesting that acquisition of letter knowledge could be an exacting and prolonged process for English learners lacking familiarity with the Roman alphabet was provided by Brooks (1977) in a study developed to demonstrate the superiority of grapheme–phoneme correspondence strategies over paired-associate learning for word recognition among adults. In this study English-speaking college students learned a set of six novel characters and learned to pair each with one of six known sounds. The subjects' fluency in recognizing the new alphabet developed over many trials and required approximately 200 trials before they were able to apply the sound–symbol correspondences efficiently enough to speed the recognition time of the words over what it took to recognize the words learned through paired association. As Brooks reports: "[The] comparisons between the paired-associate and orthographic conditions, however, do not quite get at the feeling of frustration so strongly expressed by many of our subjects. As they tell the story they often would have all the letters translated before they could put together a full word" (p. 167).

These skilled college readers expended a great deal of effort to learn a very small set of new symbols. It is probably safe to assume that young inexperienced readers attempting to master a larger set of symbols will need a great deal of practice to reliably distinguish letters of the alphabet if their first encounters with this alphabet occur at school. Qualitative differences in early print experiences may call for differentiation in alphabet instruction among ELLs.

Word Identification

In order to read with comprehension ELLs, like native speakers, need to be able to recognize printed words accurately and effortlessly (Birch, 2002; Perfetti, 1992). Research on the development of word recognition among young ELLs has generated some understanding about the degree of success ELLs experience in achieving accurate identification of printed words. In the NLP report Lesaux and Geva (2006) concluded that, as a group, second-language learners do not differ from native speakers in their attainment of the ability to accurately decode and apply grapheme–phoneme correspondences to words in print and in their spelling. However, caution in interpreting this finding is recommended, because, as Lesaux and Geva point out, the prevalence of differences in the efficiency of word identification skills has not been thoroughly studied. One risk associated with ignoring speed differences in word identification is that one may erroneously reach the conclusion that the well-documented gaps in ELLs' overall reading attainment (August & Shanahan, 2006) must be due to differences in higher-level skills such as knowledge of word meanings, syntactic processing, or background knowledge because they have mastered accurate word identification. While it is to be expected that differences in the attainment of higher-level skills will affect reading outcomes for ELLs, one must also keep in mind potential differences in the efficiency of processing of words because, as we know from research on monolinguals (Gough, 1972; Perfetti, 1992; Stanovich, 1986) these can significantly disrupt the reading process. Thus, both research on the development of word reading abilities among ELLs and instructional practices in reading must address processing speed issues, as these may in fact be more sensitive to differences in performance between ELLs and monolinguals (Ransdell & Fischler, 1987; Mägiste, 1979).

ELLs, like their native-speaking peers, need to develop what Perfetti (1992) refers to as impenetrable word recognition processes. This means that identification of the word via phonological and orthographic information occurs quickly and that it does so with little demand placed on attentional resources. It also means that the outcome of this process is activation of the word's *meaning* (not just pronunciation) without reliance on contextual or other higher-order information. Accurate word reading that does not result in activation of a word's meaning does not meet the conditions for impenetrability. Word reading that does not lead to automatic access of a word's meaning is likely to lead to the application of what Stanovich (1986) refers to as compensatory strategies when discussing the word reading difficulties of native speakers. If, upon encountering a word and perhaps even after accessing its correct pronunciation, ELLs need to rely on the surrounding context and prior knowledge to generate what would be nothing more than a guess as to what the word might mean, they too will be applying compensatory strategies.

If one aims to develop the autonomous word reading skills displayed by fluent monolingual readers among ELL readers, one must move beyond teaching practices that restrict performance to the achievement of accurate word pronunciation. Word identification instruction must be designed so as to enable students to pronounce the word *and* access its meaning or meanings. In a recent study of Spanish-speaking ELLs, Proctor, Carlo, August, and Snow (2005) reported evidence that suggests that "given adequate L2 decoding ability, L2 vocabulary knowledge is crucial for improved English reading comprehension outcomes for Spanish-speaking ELLs" (p. 246). For students to be able to access the meanings of words once they have activated the appropriate phonological codes, they need to develop a deep and broad oral vocabulary. With this in mind we turn to a discussion of vocabulary instruction for ELLs.

Vocabulary

The gap in English vocabulary knowledge between ELLs and their native-speaking counterparts is wide (Nation, 2001). Native speakers start school with the advantage of having accumulated several thousand English words in their oral vocabularies. Formal instruction will add words to that base at a rate of about 3,000 words every school year (Nagy, Herman, & Anderson, 1985). ELLs vary greatly from one another in both the breadth and quality of their vocabulary knowledge (Ordonez, Carlo, Snow, & McLaughlin, 2002), depending on the richness of the English input they have access to, the richness of the native language input they have access to, and among other factors their access to direct and systematic vocabulary instruction and other more general language instruction.

There is a wealth of research and theory that informs vocabulary instruction for native speakers (Beck, McKeown, & Kukan, 2002; Graves, 2005; Hiebert, 2005; Nagy, 1988; Stahl & Nagy, 2006). Direct and systematic vocabulary instruction for ELLs can follow the principles that guide best practices in vocabulary instruction for native speakers. However, in order to fully meet the needs of ELLs, some adjustments and modifications are necessary (Carlo et al., 2004).

Word Choice

One cannot provide effective vocabulary instruction for ELLs without thinking carefully about which words to teach. Moreover, the choice of words cannot be guided by the same principles we use to make word selections for native speakers, because their vocabulary needs are different. Indeed, vocabulary needs differ even among ELLs themselves, depending on their level of English proficiency. The most emergent ELLs will need to amass a large number of basic words that are part of the vocabulary of most 5-year-old native speakers. In many cases, the task of teaching these words is simplified by the fact that ELLs will already have the concepts indexed by those basic English words in their native language. Nevertheless, systematic opportunities for children to link their first-language words and concepts to English words need to be provided. Early and systematic introduction of these basic words is important, because they are used frequently in speech and in print, and instruction based on more sophisticated words builds on these more basic concepts (Beck et al., 2002). For example, instruction about the word *predicament* might rely on more basic words like *problem, mess,* or even *fix.* Of course, a word such as *predicament* could and should be taught by reference to synonyms in the child's first language if the language resources to do so are available. But, in the absence of bilingual teachers and/or bilingual materials, knowledge of the more frequent basic English words offers a bridge for teaching more sophisticated words that show up regularly in print.

First-Language Resources

A second modification recommended for ELLs involves making them aware of the resources for vocabulary learning that they already have in their first language. For children who read in their first language, access to a bilingual dictionary can be useful in supporting independent vocabulary learning strategies. Clearly, students need to be instructed on how to use this resource efficiently, emphasizing the importance of combining this resource with other vocabulary strategies such as using context to check the appropriateness of the meaning offered in the dictionary. Children who are not yet readers can also be encouraged to use bilingual dictionaries with the help of an adult speaker of the first language, thus facilitating the goal of legitimizing the language resources available within the family and community.

Another language resource that is available to children who speak languages that have common etymological roots with English are cognates. Cognates are words that have similar spelling and meaning in two languages. Often, cognates also have similar sounding pronunciations. Cognates can contain orthographic patterns that make the relationship between the words in the two languages highly transparent, as is the case with the word *doctor* in both Spanish and English. Sometimes the orthographic patterns make the relationship somewhat more opaque, as in *jardín–garden* or *frenesí–frenzy*. Children who can recognize these similarities in spelling and meaning and who can combine them with context-checking strategies can use cognate-recognition strategies as sources of information about unfamiliar words they encounter in text (Garcia & Nagy, 1993; Jimenez, Garcia, & Pearson, 1996; Nagy, Garcia, Durgunoglu, & Hancin-Bhatt, 1993).

The combination of cognate-recognition strategies with context-checking strategies is important, because some cognates can have multiple meanings. For example, the Spanish cognate for *mass* (*masa*) shares the English meaning relating to a quantity of matter but not the meaning relating to the religious ceremony. In Spanish, *masa* also refers to a type of dough.

The existence of words that share spellings but do not share meanings across the two languages also needs to be noted. These words are known as false cognates. An example of a false cognate is the word *pie*, which in Spanish means *foot*. The ratio of cognates to false cognates varies by language.

Oral Modality

Vocabulary instruction for ELLs needs to provide a way of accessing rich language. This is not easily done, because neither reading texts nor everyday oral language are good sources of rich language. Texts written at young students' reading levels (sensibly) avoid taxing young children's reading abilities with overly complex language (Beck et al., 2002). The language of everyday communication does not contain the sophisticated language that appears in high-quality children's literature. Thus, vocabulary instruction for ELLs needs to unlock the sophisticated language we want students to learn from most print sources. This can be achieved by seeking opportunities to enrich the language used in the classroom for everyday communication and also by incorporating read-alouds chosen for their rich vocabulary and language.

Frequency and Quality of Exposure

A final modification requires attention to issues of frequency of exposure and quality of the exposure to new words. Not all words require the same level of attention during instruction (Beck et al., 2002). As was noted earlier, ELLs are likely to have acquired many useful concepts in their first language. In those cases in which all that is needed is acquisition of a new label, it is not necessary to provide the more complex instruction that one would use to build new concepts. But, in those cases where the words one is targeting are more complex, then, one needs to ensure that there are repeated exposures to the word and that the experiences with the words are not superficial. This is no different from what one would recommend as exemplary vocabulary instruction for native speakers. However, the manner in which one designs the activities to promote deep processing of the words has to be modified so that information about a word's meaning is not provided only via language. It is important to keep in mind that ELLs are not only working from a smaller vocabulary set but also are working from a weaker grammatical knowledge base and possibly a different set of culturally based assumptions. While it may be sufficient for native speakers to work with linguistically contextualized explanations of word meanings, ELLs may require images and other extralinguistic sources of information about words in order to fully grasp their meaning.

Following this reasoning, it is also important to point out the limited value of context-analysis strategies, especially when used with less proficient ELLs. Students who lack the grammatical knowledge required to analyze the linguistic context surrounding a word may not gain sufficient information from the text to generate plausible hypotheses about a word's meaning. Moreover, if too many words in a passage are unknown, the chances of using context productively are greatly reduced (Carver, 1994).

BEST PRACTICES IN ACTION

Learning to read involves mastering a graphic representational system that must ultimately map onto a system of meanings that support oral comprehension (Gough, 1972). To read with comprehension, ELLs need to be able to link the phonological representation that has been accessed via decoding of the orthographic pattern to syntactic and semantic information about words reliably and efficiently. The explicit and systematic teaching of language to ELLs is a goal that extends beyond the realm of early reading instruction. But, early reading instruction can be designed in ways that maximize understanding of word meanings and grammatical functions and at the same time support the equally legitimate goal of helping students unlock the code. Highlighted here are three fairly simple activities and strategies that incorporate language scaffolds aimed at increasing the chances that ELLs will gain access to word meanings when reading.

Picture Walks

Illustrations play a very important role in scaffolding the reading experiences of beginning readers. Well-designed early readers often contain illustrations that carry the plot of a story accompanied by simple text denotive of concepts evident in the illustrations. The correlation between the text and the illustration supports students in noticing initial sounds and letters in words, common orthographic patterns across words that rhyme, etc. These scaffolds are very useful to native speakers who can easily access the words in English upon seeing the illustration and can then combine their knowledge of the word's sound with their knowledge of letter sounds. However, if the pictures do not serve to activate the English word because the object's label is not part of the child's oral vocabulary in English, then the pictures do little to support the acquisition and application of letter–sound correspondences.

In a research collaboration that includes the University of Houston, the Center for Applied Linguistics, and the University of Miami,[1] first-grade teachers are modifying the picture walks they do at the beginning of their guided reading lessons to provide the language the children will need to build associations among the pictures, the words in oral language, and the printed words in the text. In addition to helping the students build a narrative from the pictures, as is customarily done with picture walks, the teachers point to and provide the names in English for objects and actions depicted in the illustrations. This simple modification has the potential to increase the instructional value of illustrations contained in the early readers for the ELLs, because, in the absence of the image-to-language link, the desired language-to-print link cannot be easily established.

1. *Optimizing Educational Outcomes for English Language Learners.* Research grant awarded by the Institute for Educational Science to David Francis, Principal Investigator, University of Houston.

Teaching Sight Words and Orthographic Patterns with Picture Aids

The use of images for teaching word identification skills can be counterproductive if one allows students to use the image as a crutch for identifying the word instead of teaching them to use the word's orthography. But, it is equally counterproductive to teach ELLs to pronounce words for which they do not know the meaning. As stated earlier, the product of fluent word identification is activation of the correct lexical item. The following activity was adapted by Yania Aleman and Beatriz Iglesias, teachers in Miami–Dade County public schools, and tutors in a graduate course on clinical teaching taught by the author at the University of Miami. This activity using picture cards and words was designed to assist 8- to 10-year-old tutees who were ELLs and were experiencing difficulties in learning to read. The ELL adaptation consists of extending the use of the images beyond the use it is typically given with native speakers. The image is not used only to remind students of the orthographic contrast they are practicing, as is typically done with native speakers. Rather, it is used to remind ELLs of the meaning of every single word they work with during sight word practice and during instruction on orthographic patterns. The image does not need to represent the word perfectly. It only needs to serve as a reminder of the meaning that is discussed and agreed upon between the teacher and the student. Also, once the work with the orthographic pattern begins, the use of the image is restricted to trials in which the child is showing signs of giving up and only after having attempted to apply knowledge of the orthographic pattern. Ms. Alemán described the activity as follows.

> "*Preparations*: After introducing the blend/digraph, I used clip art to represent the words containing the pattern [see Figure 5.1 for /st/ and /sl/]. I tried to incorporate pictures that relate to the words' meaning. If the word was in the reading, I used a picture that relates to the story. I printed the picture and words on computer paper and cut them into individual word cards that can be easily folded."
>
> "*Introduction*: Once I introduced and taught the digraph/blend for the week, I presented each picture word card to the student. The student was able to see the word and the picture together. We practiced reading each word, using the pictures at least twice. Then I removed the illustration by folding the word card in half so that only the printed word is showing. If the student came across a word he had difficulty decoding he was able to flip the card and use the illustration to help him identify the word. The student practiced reading the words through sorting activities."

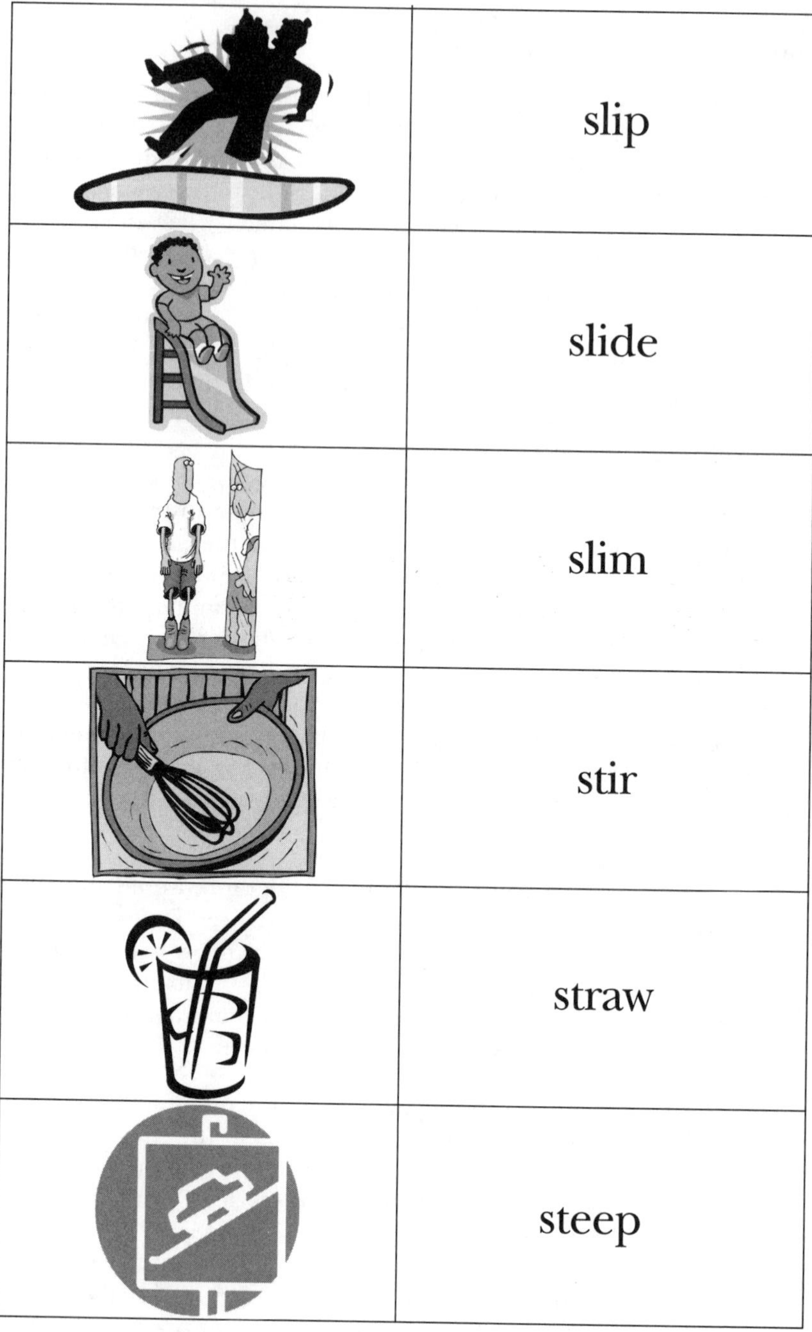

FIGURE 5.1. Picture representing words beginning with /st/ and /sl/.

Cognates

The following activity is intended for ELLs who are readers and speakers of Spanish. It formed part of a curriculum developed to increase ELLs' awareness of cognates in Spanish and English. The effectiveness of this curriculum is being tested in a joint study by researchers at the Center for Applied Linguistics and the University of Miami.[2] This particular activity was designed to increase learners' awareness of the variation in degree of orthographic and phonological similarity in Spanish–English cognates. It aims to encourage learners to look deeply into an English word's orthography to find similarities to words they may know in Spanish.

Sample Items: Identification of Letter Differences

Instructions to students: On the left-hand side, we have listed the Spanish cognates of the words from the passage. Write the English cognate for each Spanish cognate given. Once the English cognate has been written, indicate which letters are different between the cognates by circling the letters.

Spanish cognate	**English cognate**
astronaut	
momento	
planeta	
fotografía	

Sample Items: Identification of Sound Differences

Instructions to teacher: Show students the following Likert scale on the overhead projector. Explain that some of the cognates sound more alike than others. On the overhead projector, direct students to identify how alike or not alike the sets of cognates sound on a scale of 1 to 4. There are no right or wrong answers.

edifice / edificio

Sounds completely different	Sounds slightly different	Sounds similar	Sounds exactly alike
1	2	3	4

2. Transfer of Reading Skills in Bilingual Children. Research grant awarded by the National Institute of Child Health and Human Development and the Institute for Educational Sciences to Diane August, Principal Investigator, Center for Applied Linguistics, as part of the program project entitled Acquiring Literacy in English Crosslinguistic, Intralinguistic, and Developmental Factors.

mass / masa

Sounds completely different	Sounds slightly different	Sounds similar	Sounds exactly alike
1	2	3	4

infirm / enfermo

Sounds completely different	Sounds slightly different	Sounds similar	Sounds exactly alike
1	2	3	4

jocose / jocóso

Sounds completely different	Sounds slightly different	Sounds similar	Sounds exactly alike
1	2	3	4

REFLECTIONS AND FUTURE DIRECTIONS

In recent years we have witnessed the enormous effort involved in trying to ensure that every primary grade teacher develops the knowledge, skills, and disposition that are required to provide excellent reading instruction to young children. For these efforts to benefit ELLs, they must include appropriate attention to the role of language in the development of reading.

Teaching ELLs to read in English also requires a commitment to teaching English. To the extent that efforts toward preparing reading teachers have ignored the teaching of language, they have failed to address one of the greatest challenges ELLs face in becoming highly skilled readers of English. The NLP review (Lesaux & Geva, 2006) suggests that ELLs catch up to their native-speaking peers on low-level components of the reading process such as PA and word reading (at least with respect to word-reading accuracy). The NLP review also suggests that ELLs don't catch up to their native-speaking peers on aspects of text processing that make demands on syntactic and semantic language processes.

Closing the gap in reading comprehension of ELLs does not require abandoning the progress that has been achieved in improving the teaching of foundational reading skills to ELLs. Rather, it requires that the teaching of foundational skills such as PA and word identification be linked to an equally comprehensive, explicit, and systematic model for teaching oral English to ELLs.

CONCLUDING COMMENTS

Throughout this chapter research and theory on first-language reading development has been combined with research and theory on second-language learning to stress the importance of attending to the language–literacy link in designing reading instruction for ELLs. Research and theory speak directly to the involvement of oral language proficiency in the development of skills considered to be foundational to reading even among children who speak English natively. The language needs of ELLs cannot be comprehensively addressed through reading instruction alone. However, it is possible to capitalize on the many opportunities for language development that present themselves in the context of the reading lesson. The success of early reading instruction with native speakers of English depends in part on helping children establish a bridge between the orthography they need to learn and the language they already know. A step toward greater success in ELL reading instruction requires awareness of the fact that ELLs need to be supported as they build a bridge between the orthography they need to learn and a language they are still learning.

ENGAGEMENT ACTIVITIES

1. Find pictures depicting places or activities that one encounters routinely at home and places and activities one encounters routinely at school or in the larger community. Assess your ELL students by asking them to point to an object you name. Compare their identification of items (receptive vocabulary) to their production of the names of items you point to (productive vocabulary). Are there differences in their knowledge of English labels for the "at-home" words and the "out-of-home" words? If so, what might explain such differences?
2. Find a piece of expository text and a narrative text of roughly the same difficulty. Circle words that you believe would be most challenging to Spanish-speaking ELLs. Look them up in a Spanish–English dictionary, and note how many of the words in each text are cognates in Spanish. Are there differences in the prevalence of cognates across the two genres? If so, what might explain such differences?

REFERENCES

Adams, M. J. (1990). *Beginning to read: Thinking and learning about print.* Cambridge, MA: MIT Press.

August, D., & Shanahan, T. (2006). *Developing literacy in second-language learners.* Mahwah, NJ: Erlbaum.

Beck, I. L., McKeown, M. G., & Kukan, L. (2002). *Bringing words to life: Robust vocabulary instruction.* New York: Guilford Press.

Bialystok, E. (1997). Effects of bilingualism and biliteracy on children's emerging concepts of print. *Developmental Psychology, 33,* 429–440.

Bialystok, E., & Hakuta, K. (1994). *In other words: The science and psychology of second language acquisition.* New York: Basic Books.

Birch, B. (2002). *English L2 reading: Getting to the bottom.* Hillsdale, NJ: Erlbaum.

Brooks, L. (1977). Visual pattern in fluent word identification. In A. S. Reber & D. L. Scarborough (Eds.), *Toward a psychology of reading.* New York: Erlbaum.

Bryant J. B. (2000) Language in social contexts: Communicative competence in the preschool years. In J. B. Gleason (Ed.), *The development of language* (5th ed.). Needham Heights, MA: Allyn & Bacon.

Bryant, P. (1974). *Perception and understanding in young children: An experimental approach.* New York: Basic Books.

Bryant, P. E., MacLean, M., Bradley, L. L., & Crossland, J. (1990). Rhyme and alliteration, phoneme detection, and learning to read. *Developmental Psychology, 26*(3), 429–438.

Capps, R., Fix, M. E., Murray, J., Ost, J., Passel J. S., & Herwantoro S. (2005). *The new demography of America's schools: Immigration and the No Child Left Behind Act.* Retrieved May 1, 2006, from the National Clearinghouse for English Language Acquisition and Language Instruction Educational Programs, *www.ncela.gwu.edu/stats/2_nation.htm.*

Carlo, M., August, D., McLaughlin, B., Snow, C. E., Dressier, C., Lippman, D. N., Lively, T. J., & White, C. E. (2004). Closing the gap: Addressing the vocabulary needs of English-language learners in bilingual and mainstream classrooms. *Reading Research Quarterly, 39,* 188–215.

Carver, R. P. (1994). Percentage of unknown vocabulary words in text as a function of the relative difficulty of the text: Implications for instruction. *Journal of Reading Behavior, 26,* 413–437.

Garcia, G. E., & Nagy, W. E. (1993). Latino students' concept of cognates. In D. J. Leu & C. K. Kinzer (Eds.), *Examining central issues in literacy research, theory, and practice.* Chicago: National Reading Conference.

Goswami, U. (2000). Phonological and lexical processes. In M. Kamil, P. Mosenthal, P. D. Pearson, & R. Barr (Eds.), *Handbook of reading research* (vol. 3, pp. 251–267). Mahwah, NJ: Erlbaum.

Gough, P. (1972). One second of reading. In J. Kavanagh & I. Mattingly (Eds.), *Language by ear and by eye.* Cambridge, MA: MIT Press.

Graves, M. F. (2005). *The vocabulary book: Learning and instruction.* New York: Teachers College Press.

Hiebert, E. (2005). In pursuit of an effective, efficient vocabulary curriculum for elementary students. In E. Hiebert, H. Elfrieda, & M. Kamil. *Teaching and learning vocabulary: Bringing research to practice* (pp. 243–263). Mahwah, NJ: Erlbaum.

Hopstock P. J., & Stephenson T. G. (2003). Descriptive Study of Services to LEP Students and LEP Students with Disabilities. *Special Topic Report #1: Native languages of LEP students.* Retrieved May 1, 2006, from the National Clearinghouse for English Language Acquisition and Language Instruction Educational Programs, *www.ncela.gwu.edu/stats/2_nation.htm.*

Jimenez, R., Garcia, G. E., & Pearson, P. D. (1996). The reading strategies of bilingual Latina/o students who are successful English readers: Opportunities and obstacles. *Reading Research Quarterly, 31,* 90–112.

Lesaux, N., & Geva, E. (2006). Synthesis: Development of literacy in language-minority students. In D. August & T. Shanahan (Eds.), *Developing literacy in second-language learners.* Mahwah, NJ: Erlbaum.

Mägiste, E. (1979). The competing language systems of the multilingual: A developmental study of decoding and encoding processes. *Journal of Verbal Learning and Verbal Behavior, 18,* 79–89.

Menn, L., & Stoel-Gammon, C. (2000). Phonological development: Learning sounds and sound patterns. In J. B. Gleason (Ed.), *The development of language* (5th ed.). Needham Heights, MA: Allyn & Bacon.

Moats, L. C. (2000). *Speech to print: Language essentials for teachers.* Baltimore, MD: Brookes.

Nagy, W. E. (1988). *Teaching vocabulary to improve reading comprehension.* Newark, DE: International Reading Association.

Nagy, W. E., Garcia, G. E., Durgunoglu, A., & Hancin-Bhatt, B. (1993). Spanish–English bilingual students' use of cognates in English reading. *Journal of Reading Behavior, 25,* 241–259.

Nagy, W., Herman, P., & Anderson, R. C. (1985). Learning words from context. *Reading Research Quarterly, 20*(2), 233–253.

Nation, I. S. P. (2001). *Learning vocabulary in another language.* Cambridge, UK: Cambridge University Press.

National Clearinghouse for English Language Acquisition and Language Instruction Educational Programs. (2006). *National and Regional Numbers & Statistics.* Retrieved May 1, 2006, from *www.ncela.gwu.edu/stats/2_nation.htm.*

National Reading Panel. (2000). *Teaching children to read: An evidence-based assessment of the scientific research literature on reading and its implications for reading instruction: Reports of the subgroups* (NIH Publication No. 00-4754). Washington, DC: National Institute of Child Health and Human Development.

Ordonez, C. L., Carlo, M. S., Snow, C. E., & McLaughlin, B. (2002). Depth and breadth of vocabulary in two languages: Which vocabulary skills transfer? *Journal of Educational Psychology, 94*(4), 719–728.

Perfetti, C. (1992). The representation problem in reading acquisition. In P. Gough, L. Ehri, & R. Treiman (Eds.), *Reading acquisition* (pp. 145–174). Hillsdale, NJ: Erlbaum.

Proctor, C. P., Carlo, M. S., August, D., & Snow, C. E. (2005). Native Spanish-speaking children reading in English: Toward a model of comprehension. *Journal of Educational Psychology, 97,* 246–256.

Ransdell, S. E., & Fischler, I. (1987). Memory in a monolingual mode: When are bilinguals at a disadvantage? *Journal of Memory and Language, 26,* 392–405.

Rolla-San Francisco, A., Carlo, M., August, D., & Snow, C. (2006). The role of language of literacy instruction and vocabulary in the English phonological awareness of Spanish–English bilingual children. *Applied Psycholinguistics, 27*(2), 229–246.

Saffran, J. R., Senghas, A., & Trueswell, J. C. (2001). The acquisition of language by children. *Proceedings of the National Academy of Sciences, 98*(23), 12874–12875.

Smith, C. L., & Tager-Flusberg, H. (1982). Metalinguistic awareness and language development. *Journal of Experimental Child Psychology 34*(3), 449–468.

Snow, C., Burns, S., & Griffin, P. (1998). *Preventing reading difficulties in young children.* Washington, DC: National Academy Press.

Stahl, S., & Nagy, W. E. (2006). *Teaching word meanings.* Mahwah, NJ: Erlbaum.

Stanovich, K. E. (1986). Matthew effects in reading: Some consequences of individual differences in the acquisition of literacy. *Reading Research Quarterly, 21*, 301–406.

Tager-Flusberg, H. (2000). Putting words together: Morphology and syntax in the preschool years. In J. B. Gleason (Ed.), *The development of language* (5th ed.), Needham Heights, MA: Allyn & Bacon.

Unz, R. K., & Tuchman, G. M. (1998). *Proposition 227: English language education for children in public schools.* Retrieved May 1, 2006, from James Crawford's Language Policy Web Site & Emporium, *www.humnet.ucla.edu/humnet/linguistics/people/grads/macswan/unztext.htm.*

Chapter 6

BEST PRACTICES IN ADOLESCENT LITERACY INSTRUCTION

Donna Ogle

with Laura Lang

This chapter will:

- Describe the challenges of providing literacy instruction to adolescent readers in middle and high schools.
- Explain the importance of school-wide approaches to reading development.
- Outline key components of reading instruction.
- Provide supporting research that informs the focus on these components.
- Share an example from a ninth-grade high school campus that has established a school-wide literacy committee.
- Include resources for reading instruction.
- Suggest ways readers can apply some of these ideas in their own schools.

The challenges of teaching the reading strategies that middle and secondary students need are significant and multifaceted. Reading permeates the curriculum; yet, content-focused teachers generally don't feel responsible for developing the sophisticated reading strategies that students need to be successful. At upper levels there is no common pattern for instruction in content literacy. Schools struggle to find engaging and effective methods to build students' competence with the different skills and strategies they need to make sense of texts in science, mathematics, social studies, practical arts, and literature (Snow, 2002).

Most of the texts students need to read are expository and not necessarily user-friendly or "considerate." These informational texts and reports can be organized in a variety of ways, and the content-specific vocabulary is critical to their meaning. In addition to its own discourse, each discipline also offers its own unique way of representing information to readers. As a result students need to become flexible in developing strategies for engaging with varying text demands (Jetton & Alexander, 2004). They need to read primary-source documents, scientific reports, visual displays and charts, and mathematical representations. They also need to learn to analyze pieces of literature, evaluate the accuracy of information, determine authors' points of view, and use multiple sources in their inquiry and research.

Reading and learning from widely different types of texts is complicated by the fact that most students have not received much instruction in reading and learning with informational texts and textbooks in upper elementary school (Pressley, Wharton-McDonald, Hampson, & Echevarria, 1998). Therefore, content teachers with little experience in teaching reading must provide this instruction as they teach content. The reality is that content-area teachers have been reluctant to incorporate reading instruction into their teaching. Despite preservice preparation in literacy strategies, most studies have shown that young teachers do not maintain their attention to literacy teaching (Conley, 2005; Sturtevant, 1996; Bean, 1997). Therefore, both students and teachers often lack requisite confidence and commitment.

Complicating the situation is the increasingly wide range of competence and interests of the students. Many are good readers; however, the range of knowledge, interests, confidence, and abilities within one class is often great. Providing added challenge to middle and secondary teachers are adolescents who often appear disinterested in the demands of the content-area curriculum. Issues of motivation and perseverance in learning are significant at the upper levels (Reed, Schallert, Beth, & Woodruff, 2004; Guthrie, Alao, & Rinehart, 1997; Graves, 2004; Oldfather, 2002).

What can middle and high schools do? What approaches are being implemented? This chapter takes the perspective that continued literacy development for adolescents requires the cooperative efforts of whole-school teams of teachers and administrators. Literacy instruction needs to occur across the school (Moore, Bean, Birdyshaw, & Rycik, 2000; Ogle & Hunter, 2000). In addition, students requiring particular support should also have those opportunities provided in literacy labs or added reading courses. These courses alone won't make the difference, however. Since each content has its own types of texts and resource materials, students need and deserve guidance in knowing how to use them successfully. Therefore, coordinated efforts across school departments are needed to support students' literacy development. (Cooper, 2005; Schoenbach, Greenleaf, Cziko, & Hurwitz, 1999; Santa, Havens, & Maycumber, 2005).

This chapter begins by describing key components of successful reading instruction in middle and secondary schools. The information is grounded in school-based projects, both our own and those described in the literature. This section is followed by an example from a freshman high school where teachers are working together as a campus literacy team to enhance their effectiveness in promoting thoughtful literacy. The chapter concludes with a section describing a new energy that is emerging for adolescent literacy research.

For those readers who are reading teachers in middle and high schools, we hope this chapter will provide support for your goals as part of a team in a school. We believe that reading teachers working alone are not likely to be highly effective. Literacy needs to be conceived of as a school-wide commitment, and particular attention must be given to informational literacy development.

EVIDENCE-BASED BEST PRACTICES: HOW SCHOOLS ARE ABLE TO CREATE THIS SCHOOL-WIDE MODEL OF LITERACY

This section describes five keys to successful adolescent literacy programs. The essential foundation is that teachers together build a knowledge base about the complex and varied strategies readers need to be successful with challenging texts, the kinds that teachers regularly assign but too seldom scaffold for students. From this common understanding teachers can build frameworks that help them identify good teaching strategies or activities that lead to student independence in strategy use. A third key is involving students in understanding the active nature of reading and helping them participate in evaluating their own reading progress. This metacognitive control and monitoring is a hallmark of maturing readers. For students to be successful it is also important that they have texts available that are within their instructional range as readers. Providing a range of texts with varied text features can be essential in getting students to the point of engagement with content. Finally, utilizing the energy and motivation that come from students learning together, with, and from their peers is important.

Building Common Understanding of the Reading Process

Teachers need to know what good reading entails. This is the first step. Many middle and secondary teachers initially avoid thinking about reading, considering it a primary-level set of decoding tasks. In fact, the current national focus on beginning reading has contributed to this misperception. To raise secondary content teachers' awareness of the complexity of reading, many secondary staff development efforts have involved teachers in reading difficult, unfamiliar expository texts. This lets them experience reading as their students do—as novices in content. Modeling and thinking aloud about their own reading processes during such experiences, teachers can then better identify the supports needed to help their students develop thoughtful reading in difficult materials.

From these experiences teachers can build a language to talk about the kinds of strategies and "moves" good readers utilize as they engage with informative and technical texts. When teachers reflect on what they do to make sense of the text (or when an activity is done with a text on an overhead and group thinking aloud), they generate a list of activities, such as predicting, inferring, questioning, visualizing, rereading and revising, problem solving, and summarizing. This can be a foundation for further discussion of what is involved in reading, and it can lead to consideration of a variety of forms of texts and the kinds of strategies needed to read them successfully.

A great deal is known about the basic processes needed for readers to make sense of individual texts. Studies of mature readers engaged in thinking aloud while reading have been very helpful in identifying the ways readers actively construct meaning and monitor their engagement with texts before, during, and after reading. From their review of over 40 studies involving readers thinking aloud, Pressley and Afflerbach (1995) concluded that mature readers use a variety of processes flexibly as they read, including being aware of their purpose, previewing the material, reading selectively, connecting ideas to their prior knowledge, revisiting and revising ideas, interpreting and evaluating the text, and thinking about how to apply ideas and information.

Two of the most important considerations for teachers are the heavy use by students of unedited texts on the Internet and the importance of visual information in mathematics and social studies documents and textbooks (Moore & Scevak, 1997). Comparing the types of reading needed in various content materials can help teachers build their understanding that the term *reading* is a broad one that encompasses many different kinds of engagement with texts. In some of our school-based projects (Ogle & Hunter, 2000; Ogle, 2000; Ogle, Newman, & Spirou, 2005) these reflections have led teachers to focus on visual literacy and strategies to help students use their visual skills in learning. Issues of reading with multiple sources and thinking deeply about authors' perspectives and purposes are also the subject of much discussion.

Creating middle and high school teams of teachers who work together for literacy goals has been shown to be effective. Project CRISS (CReating Independence through Student-owned Strategies), a major research-validated staff development program (Santa et al., 2005), and the Strategic Literacy Initiative (Greenleaf, Schoenbach, Cziko, & Mueller, 2001; Greenleaf & Schoenbach, 2004) have both demonstrated that students benefit when groups of teachers commit over time to learn more about teaching literacy in their content areas. In the CRISS program (Santa et al., 2005) teachers engage in research in their own classrooms as a central component of the project. The Strategic Literacy Initiative is focused on helping teachers support struggling readers in the content classrooms rather than providing reading support in a separate pullout setting.

Langer's Partnership for Literacy (Close, Hull, & Langer, 2005) is an extension of her work on effective literacy programs. It is focused in helping teachers engage as "active investigators into the effects of their teaching on their students' learning and familiarizes them with many of the features that we have found to be characteristic of effective literacy instruction" (p. 5). Central to the project is teachers meeting in small professional communities in their schools, reading articles, examining taped lessons and reflecting on their own teaching. This focus on teacher collaborative reflection is another example of the seriousness with which educators are engaging as learners. Our own work in a Goals 2000 Project (Ogle & Hunter, 2000) in Chicago schools, where we brought together literacy teams representing all of the content departments to focus on learning strategies, and most recently with the Middle Level Literacy Project in Chicago and the New Trier Literacy Committee also confirm the importance of school-wide reflective collaborations.

Creating a Framework for Teaching and Student Strategy Control

Translating the information about reading into ways teachers can work together to provide instructional support for students and monitor their reading is important. For adolescent readers who move from teacher to teacher during the day, the importance of their being able to know how to be successful with a variety of school literacy tasks is clear. Too often students do not internalize the strategies or routines teachers use, and they fail to maintain an active approach to learning across their content subjects. When teachers work together in establishing particular strategies

and shared vocabulary for those strategies, more students develop the habits of strategic reading and learning (Ogle & Hunter, 2000).

Using a framework that describes the reading process as occurring before, during, and after reading texts provides a clear way for teachers to think of their role in modeling and encouraging active reading. Students need to learn to approach texts actively, thinking of their purposes, surveying the organization and presentation of content, and activating what they already know. Then, as they read, they employ strategies of monitoring their comprehension, connecting ideas, using the author's organization, and discerning the author's point of view. After reading, consolidating and connecting ideas and critically assessing the author's argument and relation to other texts are important. Teachers need to provide and model instructional activities that build their students' active reading behaviors. Table 6.1 provides a framework with which teachers can think about the processes involved in reading from both the perspective of what they can do and what they should expect to translate to independent student reading and learning strategies.

It is important to think about the variety of instructional tools teachers can use to help students make sense of individual texts and about what teachers do to empower students to take control of their own reading. The focus needs to be on ways to turn control of reading over to students. Therefore, teaching activities and strategies are best considered in light of how they can further students' understanding of active reading.

Teachers may use a graphic organizer, for example, to help students understand the underlying structure of a difficult piece of text. The example in Figure 6.1 is a graphic organizer that was developed to help students make their way through James Madison's *The Federalist Papers, No. 10.* Students who use this will be better able to understand the argument Madison makes in this essay; however, it won't necessarily help students learn to think about text organization and preview texts looking for structure unless teachers also explain to students the importance of structure and give them opportunities to identify text structures with many different easier texts.

A middle-level team at Cole Middle School in Rhode Island does just that. Students are introduced to the basic expository text structures early in the year and given experiences identifying each. Then, as part of their social studies activities, this knowledge is applied as each week students are asked to locate and share one current events story coming from a current newspaper or magazine that is appropriate for their social studies classroom. The teachers give students a guide they can use in reading and summarizing their selections (see Figure 6.2). The evaluation is explicitly laid out for the students (see Figure 6.3). In this way students apply what they learn about text structure and content as they read and share

TABLE 6.1. Reading and Learning Processes

Learning process	Teaching activities	Independent student application
Anticipation		
Preview text	Identify organizational structure Study graphics, pose questions Create a PLAN	Survey before reading Use graphic aids Identify needs/reading and focus Create a PLAN
Activate knowledge	Anticipation guide Group brainstorming KWL process Vocabulary categorization Knowledge rating	Preview text questions Brainstorm
Focus interest and set purpose	People search	KWL Generate questions Connect to other experiences and readings
Building knowledge		
Construct meaning	Make notes (Y or 3-column) Create group semantic maps Paired reading Use text frames to guide questions Read study guides	Make notes Create semantic maps or graphic organizers Visualize ideas, think of analogies Keep a journal Use SQ3R
Clarify ideas	Use INSERT notes Question the author Identify analogies	Read multiple sources Monitor confusion Make marginal notes
Consolidation of learning		
Construct	Write group summaries Create map of text Discuss key ideas Identify author's perspectives and point of view	Write personal summary Rehearse and reconstruct orally

(*continued*)

TABLE 6.1. *(continued)*

Learning process	Teaching activities	Independent student application
Consolidate	Keep dialogue journals Review notes (KWL+) Debate issues	Create mnemonics Compare to other texts Ask and answer questions Connect to other texts and experiences
Assess achievement	Discuss outcomes, value of study Identify unanswered questions Evaluate process and outcome	Evaluate ideas and outcomes Compare entry knowledge to that gained

current events articles. This continuing experience using text structures to summarize and share what has been read exemplifies how teachers can help students learn to independently look for the underlying organization of ideas in texts and to use that knowledge to make sense of what they read. And, when teachers across the content disciplines engage in using the same language as they help students identify and use text structures in their learning, students gain confidence in this important key to reading expository texts.

The research on developing learning strategies makes clear that students need extended opportunities to develop strategic approaches to their learning (Bransford, Brown, & Cocking, 1999). Simply introducing a strategy, like previewing and identifying highlighted vocabulary, is not enough (Deshler et al., 2001; Pearson & Gallagher, 1983). Teachers need to model the strategy several times with the course content they have assigned students to use. They need to check to see that students are able to preview actively and identify important terms. Students need opportunities to compare their efforts with those of other classmates. Then, the same approach to previewing and focusing on vocabulary needs to be reinforced in other content courses. The science and social studies teachers need to model using the strategy, think through with students the issues that confront them as they try to implement the strategy, and provide diagnostic help and support. All the content areas need to hold students accountable for using the previewing approach, collect sample pages on which students indicate their thinking as they preview a text page and give feedback, create rubrics so students can see what is required of good previewing, and continue to

TEXT ANALYSIS FRAME
The Federalist Papers, No. 10

Major argument:

The union needs to control the violence of faction . . .

First option:

Remove the causes by

1.

results are . . .

2.

results are . . .

Second option:

Control the effects by

1.

2.

Conclusion:

Advantage of a republic over a democracy and large over small republic because . . .

FIGURE 6.1. Text structure analysis of *The Federalist Papers, No. 10.*

use the system over time until students make notes in this format automatically. Students learn and internalize a systematic approach to reading that can serve them well when strategies are taught carefully and students are monitored on their use of the same strategies across various content areas and different years in school (Pressley et al., 1994).

To help teachers consider how to prioritize their use of time most effectively, it is valuable to differentiate what teachers and students do during instruction. There are several useful teaching strategies or routines that model active engaged reading, such as doing think-alouds (Bereiter & Bird, 1985), questioning the author (Beck, McKeown, Hamilton,

Name ______________________________

Steps When Reading a News Article

Title of article:

____

News source:

____

Date of publication:

____

What is your purpose for reading? What do you want to learn from this article? (Use the article's heading to form a question.)

As you read, think about the important facts. Record them below.

Think about the article you just read. What questions are you left with? Is there anything that you don't understand?

Think about the article you read. What happened? Record all effects below.

Why did it happen? Record all causes below.

FIGURE 6.2. Causes and effects in news articles.

Using at least one cause and effect signal word (list below), write the cause and effect sequence.

Signal words:

Cause	Effect
Because	As a result
The reason for	Outcome
On account of	Finally
Bring about	Consequently
Give rise to	Therefore
Created by	For this reason
Contributed by	Hence
Led to	Effect
Due to	Then
Since	So

FIGURE 6.2. (*continued*)

& Kucan, 1997), and having students work in small groups (Raphael & McMahon, 1994; Unrau & Ruddell, 1995). As teachers use these approaches for helping students learn, they also need to explain their purpose and value and show students how to translate them beyond the classroom into independent reading and study practices.

Engaging Students Metacognitively

Students need to understand what it means to be strategic readers. The term *strategy* is widely used to refer to specific processes or strategies like prediction and visualizing. However, when engaged in reading, we generally use many different "strategies," depending on the text and our purposes. The extensive strategy research that has been done includes both studies on individual strategies and on more extensive routines that involve more than one strategy. Pressley et al. (1994) and others have

Current Events Assignment

Purple Team Social Studies

Cole M.S. East Greenwich, RI

Ms. Bethany Friel

THE ASSIGNMENT:

Social studies students are required to complete one current events assignment each week. Current events assignments are due in class each Monday.

- News articles must be current and come from credible nontabloid news sources (examples: *Providence Journal, New York Times, cnn.com,* etc.).
- Articles must be appropriate for the social studies classroom. Therefore, articles involving death, crime, and entertainment news will not receive full credit. (Articles about death resulting from war *are* permitted, as well as the death of major public figures such as a former U.S. President.)

CONTENT AND GRADING:

Each current events assignment can earn a maximum of 10 points. The criteria and grading policy for the current events assignments are listed below.

- *List three facts.* You are retelling the story with three facts, so it is important to choose three very important main ideas. To receive full credit, your facts must be written in your own words and in complete sentences.—*3 points*
- *List two questions* about the article. Questions may be a phrase you do not understand, a concept that you do not understand, something you still wonder about, etc.—*2 points*
- *Identify a major example of problem and solution* from your news story. In one paragraph, you must describe the problem from the story, the solution described in the article, AND explain your own idea(s) for solving the problem. If your article doesn't describe a solution that has taken place, you can only state the problem and offer your own solution.—*3 points*
- *Attach a map of the location* in which the story takes place (maps can be easily found on *mapquest.com*)—2 points

Additional Requirements:

All current events assignments should also include the following format requirements:

- Heading: Student's name at top, title of article, news source (*Providence Journal, cnn.com*) and article's date of publication.
- News article should be stapled to the *back* of your written work.

FIGURE 6.3. Current events assignment.

called this more fluid use of strategies "transactional strategies." Readers who possess a set of strategies or processes use them as needed to construct meaning when texts are challenging. Therefore, the goal of instruction needs to be that students know or internalize a variety of strategies they can use when they encounter challenging texts. This involves metacognitive control—knowing what the task involves, considering possible ways of approaching it, and then selecting and implementing an approach and monitoring its success. These aspects of knowledge about strategies define what is called the reader's executive function or metacognition.

The research on strategy instruction supports the value of students learning to make their own determinations of which strategies to implement. Studies (Paris, Cross, & Lipson, 1984; El-Dinary, 2002; Pressley et al., 1994) confirm that students, even in elementary grades, can learn to be in control in these ways. By the time students are in middle school and high school, assessment of their knowledge and involving them in thinking about their own reading and learning are both important keys to improving literacy. Students who know what they can do to be successful in reading texts are much more likely to engage than are those without such understanding (Anderson & Roit, 1993). Therefore, giving students a language to talk about their reading and learning strategies and opportunities to monitor their own use of strategies is important.

One of the easiest ways we have found to begin this process is to teach students to read with a pencil in hand and make regular notations in the margins of the texts they are reading The INSERT notemaking system developed by Vaughan and Estes (1986) works well and is especially effective with students who argue that annotating a text takes too much time and disrupts the flow of their reading. Students learn to use a common notation system (+ for important ideas; ? for items that are unclear; – for things the reader disagrees with; ! for surprising ideas). After reading a portion of a text or an article, students gather in small groups of three to four to discuss their annotations. The items for which they have questions are often the first to be discussed. It is often helpful for the group to have a sheet of paper with a matrix on which they can record their responses to the text reading. In this way there is a shared record of their thinking, and it can also be saved for later assessment by both the teacher and students (see Figure 6.4).

In helping ninth graders become more self-reflective about how they annotate a fictional text, reading specialist Laura Lang has created a rubric for students to use after they have completed an assigned reading. As a class the freshman had already discussed the goals of notetaking, and Laura had modeled the process with a short passage. Each student then used the rubric to evaluate how successful he or she was in using this form of active reading independently (see Figure 6.5). Students were

Name ______________________________

Name ______________________________

Name ______________________________

?	−	✓	+

FIGURE 6.4. Insert notes group chart.

encouraged to use this form of notemaking in other content areas, too. The Spanish teacher included it on the guidelines for reading the selection "Pobre Ana"; the science teacher included it on directions for reading the chapter on the circulatory system. It is this process of teaching students to use active processing strategies as they read and then to turn the process over to them that creates better readers. This is a real shared example of formative assessment; both the teacher and students participate in determining how well they are learning to use the targeted strategies. The more students take ownership of their reading and learning, the more likely they are to participate fully in school.

Annotation Rubric: How Did I Do?

Name ______________________________
Chapter Title/Number ________________
Pages Nos. __________________________

Directions: For each category below, place an *X* on the line above the word that best describes your annotations.

N.A. = This category was not applicable on these pages.

I circled the names of all new characters who were introduced.

Always	Sometimes	Never	N.A.

I underlined any words or phrases that revealed the setting (time, place, weather, etc.).

Always	Sometimes	Never	N.A.

I wrote a summary at the top of every page.

Always	Sometimes	Never	N.A.

I put a question mark in the margin if there was something I didn't understand.

Always	Sometimes	Never	N.A.

I wrote an exclamation point in the margin if something crazy or unexpected happened.

Always	Sometimes	Never	N.A.

The grade I would give myself on my annotations: ________
Why?

FIGURE 6.5. Annotation rubric, Laura Lang.

In a recent book on formative assessment Clarke (2005) summarizes the concept:

> Doing formative assessment is about changing the way in which a lesson is constructed and managed, the culture and ethos of the classroom and the quality of questioning and feedback. Most of all, it is about the involvement of students in the learning process, beyond anything traditional teaching has previously allowed. The proven effect of teaching in this way, is that students do better at tests than before and become life-long independent learners. (p. 3)

Students are often unaware of what is involved in learning successfully. Teachers can do a great deal to make explicit the components of reading and learning and engage students in their own self-monitoring and assessment. Having students work with others as partners at the same level or tutoring younger students also put students in powerful roles. When students teach others, they often develop more understanding of the reading process and more confidence in their own abilities. M. Duderstead developed a program called Tall Friends in which struggling middle-grade readers tutored elementary students in basic reading strategies. Before each tutoring session Duderstead provided instruction to the older students, reviewing skills they also needed. As these middle graders worked with younger students, they built their own understanding and gained confidence in themselves as readers.

Ensuring That Students Have Materials Available That They Can Read

Teachers are increasingly aware that many students in their classes lack some of the basic reading abilities needed for success with their texts. Finding appropriate materials that students can read is another key to their being willing and able to learn from text. Schools that have tried to circumvent having students read by developing totally hands-on science classes or providing all materials on audiotapes are shortchanging students. It is much better that schools use the full resources of the librarians and the reading teachers and specialists to create environments full of interesting and accessible materials. Such are generally available with some effort, especially now that so many resources are on databases and accessible through Internet-based services.

One of our current middle-school projects in Chicago is developing content support materials for units in the science and social studies curricula (Chicago Mid-Tier Reading Project, 2004–2006). This project responds to the reality that too many students are reading substantially below their grade placement and struggle with designated textbooks. Central to these units are sets of short topical books at varied reading levels—from second grade to appropriate grade level. Teachers receive one to three copies of each of the books in the set. They do 1-minute fluency assessments on the students to get a general idea of their reading levels. From this they partner students with someone reading at approximately the same level so that each pair of students can share a book and read together. Students learn to use the Question–Answer–Relations framework (Raphael & Au, 2005) to write questions for each other on their first silent reading of each page of text. Teachers have developed different ways to help students monitor their reading; in some classrooms students write their questions on post-it notes. In others students work from a graphic organizer sheet to record their questions, answers, and pages read during each 20-minute session. Teachers involved in the project have reported that many students eagerly await their partner reading time and are asking to read these content books when they have choice times or when they can self-select activities.

Some of the power inhering in this project is that students are able to engage in learning about important curricular topics from materials that are not overly challenging. The new small texts are generally full of visual and graphic information and help all students, particularly the struggling readers and English-language learners, develop an understanding of content through pictures and diagrams. The size of the books also is inviting; most students feel they can read these skinny books!

As we follow the classrooms in this project we are also aware that students in urban schools often lack self-confidence as learners. The partner reading routine that puts them in the role of teacher for each other in materials in which they can have success has increased the interest and engagement of many of the students. It may be that these opportunities for increased self-control and successful collaboration may have a sustaining impact on students who are struggling in content learning.

Creating Contexts for Students to Learn Together

A final consideration is that students do well when they can learn together (Bransford et al., 1999). In both the example from Laura's lesson using a modified form of INSERT notemaking and in partner reading, students learn from each other. Teachers can create more engaged learning in classrooms by establishing settings that involve students working together in partnerships and teams rather than isolated as individuals. Much of the current work with adolescents has affirmed the importance of situating instruction in the social and shared context of classrooms and school (Guthrie & Davis, 2003; Oldfather, 2002).

Students like to work together and learn from one another. In Laura's class students became much more involved with the text as they listened to one another describe what they had marked in the text and why than they had just reading independently. They began to see new questions and ways to interpret what they had read. One student remarked, "I had no idea you could read that much into it!" Approaches that encourage shared exploration, study, and reflection by students deepen those students' interest and understanding. They help students understand the constructive nature of comprehension and how tenuous the connection between authors and readers can be. Perhaps most importantly, they give students opportunities to take on the roles of experts and teachers, fully participating in the learning possibilities created in stimulating classrooms.

Their friends and significant others are powerful forces in motivating adolescents and in determining what and how they read. Many students become more deeply engaged when they are given opportunities to engage socially in discussing reading material. As Schallert and Reed (1997) explain:

> Under ideal circumstances and for many students, talking with peers to negotiate an understanding of what was read is highly motivating. Not only are students likely to become involved in the active interaction often associated with peer-led discussion groups, they may be more interested in what they are reading as they anticipate what will happen when they meet in groups to discuss what they have read. (p. 81)

Student-to-student discussions are particularly helpful with English language learners. A growing and important area of research involves minority and English-language learners in middle and high schools. These students face particular challenges, since they may have acquired conversational English but lack familiarity with the academic routines and norms of American schools. They often encounter challenges with academic content vocabulary and disciplinary structures needed for success.

With the increasing diversity of our population, learning about and being interested in students' lives is important. This includes being more conscious of the varied cultural and social values and experiences of students and learning about students' lives outside of school—in their families and communities. Some research has shown that when teachers intentionally connect students' culture to instruction students are more likely to engage and learn. Lee (2005), for example, has used signifying, a black cultural communication tool, as a cultural bridge to high school students' learning Shakespeare.

As more researchers examine the social contexts for learning and the sociocultural dimensions of literacy development in schools (Hinchman & Zalewski, 1996; Bean, 2000; Oldfather, 2002), several questions emerge. These relate to how well schools know and respond to adolescents' interests and sense of well-being (Oldfather & McLaughlin, 1993), foster students' own inquiry and engaged learning (Ivey, 2004; Guthrie et al., 1997), and accommodate to the differences among adolescent students—in gender-related interests and needs (Smith & Wilhelm, 2004; Ivey, 2004; Cole, 1997), learning abilities (Boudah, Deshler, Schumaker, Lenz, & Cook, 1997), and culture (Ball, 2005; Gutierez, 2005)—in providing literacy instruction.

BEST PRACTICES IN ACTION: HOW SCHOOLS CAN DEVELOP STRONG INSTRUCTIONAL PROGRAMS— AN EXAMPLE FROM A FRESHMAN CAMPUS

Laura Lang, a reading specialist at the freshman campus of New Trier High School, has been working with the faculty and administration to develop a comprehensive program to support students' literacy learning needs. Part of her day is in the Literacy Lab, where students can come for individual help in reading and writing. She also works with teachers in their regular classrooms adapting content, team teaching, and coaching. Most exciting of all has been creating a literacy team so that the whole school can work together to provide support to all students in meeting the varied reading demands in this academically challenging school. Laura explains this process in the following section.

Identify the Need

During the summer of 2004, six department coordinators from New Trier High School's freshman campus joined forces to explore the role of literacy in content-area classes. The school's reading specialists had spent the preceding 2 years collaborating with individual teachers in these departments on an as-needed basis, and these collaborations revealed that teachers across disciplines were confronting common frustrations. These were exceptional teachers who were experts in their content areas and who were passionate about conveying their excitement about their subject to students. However, some recognized that they could no longer make assumptions about their students' literacy skills.

Students were not reading as carefully or critically as they had in years past, and this was hindering their ability to learn the course content or, in some cases, even to follow simple written directions. Their teachers wanted to become more comfortable offering direct reading skills instruction to the students. Other teachers wanted to incorporate more literacy-rich experiences into their classrooms. Most significantly, we all recognized that the reinforcement and repetition of strategy use and instruction are essential to developing lifelong critical literacy skills, but at that point there was no uniform school-wide approach to teaching those strategies.

Although the school offered a variety of professional development opportunities for its teachers, at that time there were no sustained programs designed specifically to encourage interdisciplinary exploration of literacy and its role in the classroom. With the support of our building principal and a stipend from our assistant superintendent for curriculum, a summer grant materialized.

Establish Team Goals and a Team Structure That Respects the School Culture

After some illuminating discussions about the role literacy plays in each of our disciplines, the summer grant collaborators proposed the creation of a literacy team on the freshman, or Northfield, campus. The team would have two primary goals.

1. Raise teachers' awareness of the components of successful literacy education by:
   - Establishing a school-wide shared vocabulary for teachers to use in their classrooms and with one another.
   - Supporting and developing literacy staff development opportunities for teachers.
   - Examining current curriculum to identify existing connections to our literacy goals.
   - Helping teachers choose the most appropriate activities to achieve a specific instructional objective.
   - Disseminating research findings regarding best practices.
2. Identify a set of literacy skills that all freshmen students should use by the end of freshman year and develop assessments that determine whether the skills have been learned.

As one of the campus reading specialists, I would coordinate the team, and ideally we would recruit representatives from every department in the school. Because our school operates through a shared leadership model, we knew that in order to promote this program we would have to demonstrate its relevance to every discipline in the school and that every discipline would have to be involved in determining the direction that our literacy work would take. We would meet once monthly during the school day.

Get the Right People on Board

At this point, I would be remiss if I didn't explain why we felt confident proceeding with our proposal—how we knew that a Literacy Team was a viable approach at New Trier's freshman campus. First, our building principal was our most vocal advocate. She encouraged us to "dream big," and she was particularly savvy to the politics of bringing a new program to fruition. When we first presented the Literacy Team to the faculty, the principal wanted to publicly explain why she supported this initiative. She consistently attended the Literacy Team meetings once they got under way, and, most importantly, she gave us the gift of time.

She provided substitutes for our classes, if needed, and purchased food for each meeting.

The second factor that was key to our success was the support of most of the department coordinators. They were excited about the future of the Literacy Team and agreed that it could address a genuine need in their individual departments. In addition, the coordinators were able to identify one or two teachers in their respective departments who they knew would be interested in pursuing this kind of work. In many cases, these were the teachers who had already worked with the reading specialists over the past few years. We knew how passionate these teachers felt about becoming better teachers of content-area reading.

Advertise, Advertise, Advertise

At the end of September, the summer grant team of department coordinators presented the idea of a Literacy Team to the freshman teachers at a Northfield campus staff meeting. As promised, the principal introduced our proposal and expressed her genuine support of our goals. After the meeting, interested teachers had an opportunity to sign up and be part of the inaugural literacy team. As the reading specialist who would be heading this group, I also sent out a follow-up email to the entire staff the next day. By the end of that day, about 20 teachers had expressed interest in the program. There were two departments that were not yet represented, and I contacted their leaders to ask for names of teachers we could personally recruit. In both of those cases, the coordinators themselves wanted to join us to find out more about how their departments could participate.

By the time our inaugural meeting arrived in October, we had amassed a wonderful group of teachers, administrators, and department coordinators who spanned a wide range of content offerings: French, Spanish, practical arts, performance arts, English, social studies, science, special education, mathematics, and health.

Give the Participants the Opportunity to Shape the Team's Work

The Literacy Team volunteers all share a common passion: to help every student in the school become a more confident and competent reader of diverse texts. During our first year of meetings, we came together to identify teacher and student literacy needs, and we explored some very basic research about best-practice literacy instruction. Although we accomplished a lot, we were trying to cover a lot of ground. We wanted to address all facets of literacy instruction, but we realized that we needed to focus our efforts a bit more during the upcoming year. To my delight, reading would be our focus.

At this point, I realized that I needed to make some recommendations about how we could proceed. I reflected on the conversations that had already taken place, and it became clear that the participants valued most the opportunity to share—and ultimately tackle—the frustrations that emerged in their individual classrooms. They had shared an incredible amount during those first few meetings, including lessons that they and their colleagues were using to address their students' reading problems. They were interested in the reading research, but they were even more excited about learning from their colleagues' efforts. Those sharing and collaborative learning sessions drew the most positive reviews. It was after these sessions that literacy team participants approached me, unsolicited, to tell me how much they had enjoyed and benefited from the preceding day's collaboration. The echoes of our conversations had lingered, one teacher said, and had woven their way into her daily lesson planning.

Our challenge, then, was to share our discoveries with the rest of the school. Best-practice reading instruction was occurring in every discipline, but often teachers did not have the opportunity to see it firsthand. The literacy team members agreed that all teachers should be able to view the wonderful lessons that were occurring in classrooms throughout the school, but classroom observations were not an immediately practical alternative.

I knew that a number of districts had created reading strategy guides for their faculties. These guides, often a collection of photocopied pages from reading textbooks and workbooks, typically included strategy descriptions and samples. When I brought a few samples into our spring Literacy Team meetings, we agreed that we too would set out to create a guide of our own. Before long, we started discussing logistics. The literacy guide had to look professional, and it had to be personalized to our faculty's needs. We also agreed that, once created, these guides could not be imposed upon—or simply handed to—our faculty. Literacy Team participants reminisced about all of the instructional guides and packets that they had received over the years, many of which now sat untouched on their desks.

We also knew that we wanted to try to get the guide out in the fall. Realistically we knew it would require far more time than remained in the first school year. We set short-term and long-term goals. Every Literacy Team participant was to scour his or her department for best-practices lessons that could be included in the guide. A small group of teachers volunteered to continue the work during the summer. As expected, our work continued long into the fall, longer than we had anticipated.

Those many hours of collecting resources, writing, typing, editing, formatting, and checking the printer's proofs eventually resulted in the *Northfield Literacy Guide*, which offers not only basic reading research and strategies but also specific examples of the way that New Trier teachers use reading strategies in their own classrooms. The *Literacy Guide* was published on November 23, 2005, and it has helped propel the work that we are currently doing during our second year together.

Offer Training in Reading Research and Strategies: Make It as Easy as Possible for Interested Teachers and Administrators to Be Involved

Members of the Literacy Team know that one of their chief aims this year is to distribute the Literacy Guide—with appropriate introduction and instruction—to the other members of their departments. This goal requires that we make a new commitment to our own learning. Now we must all consider ourselves teachers of reading.

Subsequently, this fall each Literacy Team member was given a copy of Cris Tovani's *Do I Really Have to Teach Reading?* (2004) and a tentative agenda for future meetings. The meetings topics range from choosing the most accessible texts for our students to establishing a clear purpose for reading to making our content-specific comprehension strategies visible to students. Each meeting begins with lunch and time for teachers to read a short section of Tovani's book and the *Literacy Guide* pages that correspond with that day's topic. Surprisingly, teachers have told us that they relish being given time to actually sit and read during a meeting! The second half of the meeting runs much like an informal book club meeting—participants are free to share their reactions to Tovani's ideas and are prompted to consider how to incorporate some of her ideas into their own classroom practice. We laugh, share frustrations, and question what we are currently doing in our classrooms. Finally, we share strategies for bringing the substance of these discussions back to each teacher's department.

The Literacy Team continues to be concerned primarily with helping teachers feel more comfortable helping students access their content texts. However, it is the relationship and collaboration among teachers of disparate disciplines that truly fuels our excitement and engagement in this important work. Every student benefits when teachers share a common language and a common passion.

REFLECTIONS AND FUTURE DIRECTIONS

Secondary students spend most of their school reading time engaged with content-area texts. The work done on establishing strategies readers can use to make sense of text has consistently shown that the use of thoughtful approaches to reading produces gains in comprehension. Most of these studies, however, have involved students reading single texts. There is little research on how students read and use multiple texts and sources. How do students make sense of primary-source documents in history? How do they compare different presentations of graphic data? Are students able to read and think analytically and critically when they are engaged in more extensive research and when they use Internet sources for this research (Robnolt, Rhodes, & Richardson, 2005; Snow, 2002)? Reading amidst electronic sources, among the most frequent types of reading done by adolescents, has barely been studied. Research is also needed to explore ways that teachers can help students use multiple texts and text types in their learning. The potential for much more self-guided learning using a variety of resources exists. Both pilot programs and research on these programs are needed; perhaps new relationships among learners (teachers, students, and the community) can evolve.

A major component of reading in middle and high schools involves attending to academic and technical vocabulary. It is a major issue in comprehension for English-language learners, but certainly transcends this population and affects all students in secondary schools. Vocabulary researchers differentiate general vocabulary from academic vocabulary specific to content areas (Blachowicz & Fisher, Chapter 8, this volume). Students continue to expand both types of vocabulary during the adolescent years. How to assist this growth is a major challenge. Secondary school content, in particular, consists largely of technical terms that are unfamiliar to students. How can students build their understanding of the enormous amount of content-specific terminology they are expected to learn across their subjects?

Attention has been so focused on primary-level literacy that what instruction students should receive later and how to make it effective have received little research attention. In fact, when the U.S. government's Office of Educational Research and Improvement (OERI) funded a group of 14 researchers to develop a research agenda for the most pressing issues in literacy for the 21st century, it determined that reading comprehension was the most crucial. This study (Snow, 2002) was funded through the RAND Corporation and was directed by Catherine Snow of Harvard University. Part of the group's rationale for choosing to focus on comprehension was the recognition that, while society requires higher levels of literacy from high school graduates than in the past, students in the United States are not showing achievement growth comparable to the growth students are achieving in other countries. On the recent international comparison of 15-year-olds (Progress in Student Achievement, or PISA), U.S. students emerged in the middle of the rankings, about 16th—well below the top countries.

More recently, the Alliance for Excellent Education, a group formed with the explicit purpose of getting more resources and programs for adolescent literacy, convened a small research group to develop an action paper. That report, *Reading Next: A Vision for Action and Research in Middle and High School Literacy* (Alliance for Excellent Education, 2004), established 15 key elements of effective adolescent literacy programs, 9 related to instruction and 6 to structural conditions necessary for the instructional recommendations to be well implemented. Several other national groups have also begun to focus attention on the literacy needs of adolescents. In 2005 the Secondary School Principals Association published a report on what schools need to do to develop higher levels of reading. The National Governors Association has also funded state-level grants to help governors develop state literacy plans and policies to improve adolescent literacy achievement. This initiative as well as the Alliance for Excellent Education effort (Reading Next) have been funded by the Carnegie Corporation, a major sponsor of upper-grade literacy projects.

The Striving Readers Grant Program of the U.S. Department of Education (2006), which has allocated up to $25 million to school districts for research-based programs, promises to provide good data *after* the 5 years of development and research are concluded. This large-scale effort focuses on three key elements: cross-school team efforts for literacy instruction, support for struggling readers (defined as 2 years or more below their grade level in reading), and ongoing assessment to guide instruction. Finally, the grants require extensive research on the designs and their implementation.

These calls for action in adolescent literacy build on the growing recognition of the need to extend reading instruction into secondary schooling. The International Reading Association's Commission on Adolescent Literacy in 2001 published the important Adolescent Literacy Position Statement, and more recently the National Reading Conference commissioned Donna Alvermann (2004) to write a position paper on adolescent literacy. Both of these papers identify the need for quality instruction at the secondary level and the importance of involving students actively and personally in their learning.

More intervention programs for struggling secondary readers have been developed recently. Alvermann and Rush's (2004) recent review of these programs indicates that we can expect more support for adolescent readers in the coming years. The successes schools have had in using CRISS and the Strategic Reading Initiative programs also make clear that models do exist for whole-school staff development.

Another recent wave of interest in literacy has been inspired by the New London Group's call for critical literacy and their attention to out-of-school literacies and the uses of technology (Luke & Elkins, 2000; Alvermann, 2004) This research is important and provides a lens through which teachers and schools can assess their own approaches to literacy; it also challenges the rigid focus on achieving knowledge "standards" and "authorial" reading of texts. These researchers remind us of the ever-expanding nature of literacy; the immediacy with which students can be in contact with others and the need for a "critical stance" with regard to any position or theoretical orientation are important.

CONCLUDING COMMENTS

With these new efforts and perspectives on literacy for the 21st century, we can certainly expect to know much more about adolescent literacy instruction and practices within the next several years. Our students clearly deserve this support. In a global community we can all gain from understanding what it means to be literate in this digital age. We can learn to select texts that are most useful in meeting our needs from the wide variety that are available. We can help students think more deeply by challenging interpretations and engaging in real-time dialogues with learners and experts around the world. We need to support students as they develop the habits of checking the perspective and authority of texts read and consulting a variety of sources. Teachers and larger community groups must also advocate so that *all* students have access to this new digital environment, not just those in more affluent districts. The potential is great for a global learning community replete with motivated and engaged learners, but it won't happen automatically. School-wide shared commitments and articulated instructional practices are needed. It takes teachers and administrators with vision who are willing to develop knowledge and to experiment with more collaborative teaching, as well as with an openness to including all students and the wider community in these efforts.

ENGAGEMENT ACTIVITIES

1. Reflect on the reading and learning processes in Table 6.1. Add to the middle column teaching activities you use to support students before, during, and after reading. If you find yourself short in one area, make a plan including more modeling. Then talk with your students about how they, too, can be more engaged with greater teacher support.
2. Review for students the various expository text structures widely used in English texts and create a graphic organizer for a text you will use with your students. The organizer included in Figure 6.1 can serve as a guide. After using it, discuss with your students how it did or didn't increase their attention to the author's main ideas and argument.
3. If you are not part of a team effort to help students apply active reading strategies across their school subjects, make a copy of the section detailing the example of the ninth-grade literacy team and find teachers with whom you can begin a dialogue about a more cooperative effort to improve students' reading.

RESOURCES FOR FURTHER LEARNING

Books for Reflection

Jetton, T. L., & Dole, J. A. (Eds.). (2004). *Adolescent literacy research and practice.* New York: Guilford Press.

Schoenbach, R., Greenfield, C., Cziko, C., & Hurwitz, L. (1999). *Reading for understanding: A guide to improving reading in middle and high school classrooms.* San Francisco: Jossey-Bass.

Tovani, C. (2004). *Do I really have to teach reading?: Content comprehension, grades 6–12.* Portland, ME: Stenhouse.

WestEd. (2000). *Teachers who learn: Kids who achieve: A look at schools with model staff development programs.* Oakland, CA: Author.

Strategy Guides

Billmeyer, R., & Barton, M. L. (1998). *Teaching reading in the content areas: If not me, then who?* (2nd ed.). Denver, CO: McREL.

Buehl, D. (2004). *Classroom strategies for interactive learning.* Newark, DE: International Reading Association.

Burke, J., Klemp, R., & Schwartz, W. (2002). *Reader's handbook: A student guide for reading and learning.* Wilmington, MA: Great Source.

Strong, R. W., Silver, H. F., Perini, M. J., & Tuculescu, G. M. (2002). *Reading for academic success.* Thousand Oaks, CA: Corwin Press.

Other Resources

Alliance for Excellent Education. (2004). *Reading next: A vision for action and research in middle and high school literacy: A report to the Carnegie Corporation of New York.* Washington, DC: Author.

International Reading Association. (2005). *Standards for middle and high school literacy coaches.* Newark, DE: International Reading Association.

REFERENCES

Alliance for Excellent Education. (2004). *Reading next: A vision for action and research in middle and high school literacy: A report to the Carnegie Corporation of New York.* Washington, DC: Author.

Alvermann, D. (2004). Effective literacy instruction for adolescents. *Journal of Literacy Research, 34,* 189–208.

Alvermann, D. E., & Rush, L. S. (2004). Literacy intervention programs at the middle and high school levels. In T. L. Jetton & J. A. Dole (Eds.), *Adolescent literacy research and practice* (pp. 210–227). New York: Guilford Press.

Anderson, V., & Roit, M. (1993). Planning and implementing collaborative strategy instruction for delayed readers in grades 6–10. *Elementary School Journal, 94*(2), 121–137.

Ball, A. F. (2005). Culture and language: Bidialectical issues in literacy: A response to Carol Lee. In J. Flood & P. L. Anders (Eds.), *Literacy development of students in urban schools: Research and policy* (pp. 275–287). Newark, DE: International Reading Association.

Bean, T. W. (1997). Pre-service teachers' selection and use of content area literacy strategies. *Journal of Educational Research, 90,* 154–163.

Bean, T. W. (2000). Reading in the content areas: Social constructivist dimensions. In M. Kamil, P. B. Mosenthal, P. D. Pearson, & R. Barr (Eds.), *Handbook of reading research* (Vol. 3, pp. 629–644). Mahwah, NJ: Erlbaum.

Beck, I. L., McKeown, M. G., Hamilton, R. L., & Kucan, L. (1997). *Questioning the author: An approach for enhancing student engagement with text.* Newark, DE: International Reading Association.

Bereiter, C., & Bird, M. (1985). Use of thinking aloud in identification and teaching of reading comprehension strategies. *Cognition and Instruction, 2*(2), 131–156.

Boudah, D. J., Deshler, D. D., Schumaker, J. B., Lenz, K., & Cook, B. (1997). Student-centered or content-centered?: A case study of a middle school teacher's lesson planning and instruction in inclusive classes. *Teacher Education and Special Education, 20*(3), 189–203.

Bransford, J. D., Brown, A. L., & Cocking, R. R. (1999). *How people learn: Brain, mind, experience and school.* Washington, DC: National Research Council.

Close, E., Hull, M., & Langer, J. A. (2005). Writing and reading relationships in literacy learning. In R. Indrisano & J. R. Paratore (Eds.), *Learning to write/writing to learn.* Newark, DE: International Reading Association.

Cole, N. (1997). *The ETS gender study: How females and males perform in educational settings.* Princeton, NJ: Educational Testing Service.

Conley, M. W. (2005, October). *Reconsidering adolescent literacy: From competing agendas to shared commitment.* Paper presented at Michigan State Symposium on Literacy Achievement, East Lansing, MI.

Cooper, E. (2005). It begins with belief: Social demographics is not destiny. *Voices from the Middle, 13,* 1.

Deshler, D., Schumaker, B., Lenz, K., Bulgren, J., Hock, M., Knight, J. (2001). Ensuring content-area learning by secondary students with learning disabilities. *Learning Disabilities Research and Practice, 16*(2), 96–108.

El Dinary, P. B. (2002). Challenges of implementing transactional strategies instruction for reading comprehension. In C. C. Block & M. Pressley (Eds.), *Comprehension instruction: Research-based best practices* (pp. 201–215). New York: Guilford Press.

Graves, M. F. (2004). Theories and constructs that have made a significant difference in adolescent literacy—but have the potential to produce still more positive benefits. In T. L. Jetton & J. A. Dole (Eds.), *Adolescent literacy research and practice* (pp. 433–452). New York: Guilford Press.

Greenleaf, C. L., & Schoenbach, R. (2004). Building capacity for the responsive teaching of reading in the academic disciplines: Strategic inquiry designs for middle and high school teachers' professional development. In D. Strickland & M. L. Kamil (Eds.), *Improving reading achievement through professional development* (pp. 97–127). Norwood, MA: Christopher-Gordon.

Greenleaf, C. L., Schoenbach, R., Cziko, C. & Mueller, F. L. (2001). Apprenticing adolescent readers to academic literacy. *Harvard Educational Review, 71,* 79–129.

Guthrie, J. T., Alao, S., & Rinehart, J. M. (1997). Engagement in reading for young adolescents. *Journal of Adolescent and Adult Literacy, 40*, 438–446.

Guthrie, J. T., & Davis, M. H. (2003). Motivating struggling readers in middle school through an engagement model of classroom practice. *Reading and Writing Quarterly, 19*, 59–85.

Gutierrez, K. D. (2005). The persistence of inequality: English-language learners and educational reform. In J. Flood & P. L. Anders (Eds.), *Literacy development of students in urban schools: Research and policy* (pp. 288–304). Newark, DE: International Reading Association.

Hinchman, K. A., & Zalewski, P. (1996). Reading for success in a tenth grade global-studies class: A qualitative study. *Journal of Literacy Research, 28*, 91–106.

Ivey, G. (2004). Content counts with struggling urban readers. In D. Lapp, C. C. Block, E. Cooper, J. Flood, N. Roser, & J. V. Tinajero (Eds.), *Teaching all the children: Strategies for developing literacy in an urban setting* (pp. 316–326). New York: Guilford Press.

Jetton, T. L., & Alexander, P. A. (2004). Domains, teaching and literacy. In T. L. Jetton & J. A. Dole (Eds.), *Adolescent literacy research and practice* (pp. 15–39). New York: Guilford Press.

Lee, C. D. (2005). Culture and language: Bidialectical issues in literacy. In J. Flood & P. L. Anders (Eds.), *Literacy development of students in urban schools: Research and policy* (pp. 241–274). Newark, DE: International Reading Association.

Luke, A., & Elkins, J. (2000). Re/mediating adolescent literacies. *Journal of adolescent and Adult Literacy, 43*, 396–398.

Moore, D. W., Bean, T. W., Birdyshaw, D., & Rycik, J. A. (2000). *Adolescent literacy: A position statement for the commission on adolescent literacy of the International Reading Association.* Newark, DE: International Reading Association.

Moore, P. J., & Scevak, J. J. (1997). Learning from texts and visual aids: A developmental perspective. *Journal of Research in Reading, 24*, 293–306.

Ogle, D. (2000). Make it visual: A picture is worth a thousand words. In M. McLaughlin & M. E. Vogt (Eds.), *Creativity and innovation in content area teaching.* Norwood, MA: Christopher-Gordon.

Ogle, D., & Hunter, K. (2000). Developing leadership in literacy at Amundsen High School: A case study of change. In M. Bizar & R. Barr (Eds.), *School leadership in times of urban reform* (pp. 179–194). Mahwah, NJ: Erlbuam.

Ogle, D., Newman, M., & Spirou, C. (2005, March). *Visual literacy (reading maps and photographs) in teaching history.* Presentation at the Association of Teacher Educators Conference, Chicago.

Oldfather, P. (2002). Students' experiences when not initially motivated for literacy learning. *Reading and Writing Quarterly, 18*, 231–256.

Oldfather, P., & McLaughlin, H. J. (1993). Gaining and losing voice: A longitudinal study of students' continuing impulse to learn across elementary and middle school contexts. *Research in Middle Level Education, 3*, 1–25.

Paris, S. G., Cross, D. R., & Lipson, M. Y. (1984). Informed strategies for learning: A program to improve children's reading awareness and comprehension. *Journal of Educational Research, 76*, 1239–1252.

Pearson, P. D., & Gallagher, M. (1983). The instruction of reading comprehension. *Contemporary Educational Psychology, 8*, 317–344.

Pressley, M., & Afflerbach, P. (1995). *Verbal protocol of reading: The nature of constructively responsive reading.* Mahwah, NJ: Erlbaum.

Pressley, M., Almasi, J., Schuder, T., Bergman, J., Hite, S., El-Dinary, P. B., et al. (1994). Transactional instruction of comprehension strategies: The Montgomery County, Maryland SAIL program. *Reading and Writing Quarterly: Overcoming Learning Difficulties, 10,* 5–19.

Pressley, M., Wharton-McDonald, R., Hampson, J. M., & Echevarria, M. (1998). Strategies that improve children's memory and comprehension of text. *Elementary School Journal, 90,* 3–32.

Raphael, T. E., & Au, K. H. (2005). QAR: Enhancing comprehension and test-taking across grades and content areas. *The Reading Teacher, 59*(3), 206–221.

Raphael, T., & McMahon, S. (1994). Book club: An alternative framework for reading instruction. *The Reading Teacher, 48,* 102–116.

Reed, J. H., Schallert, D. L., Beth, A. D., & Woodruff, A. L. (2004). Motivated reader, engaged writer: The role of motivation in the literate acts of adolescents. In T. L. Jetton & J. A. Dole (Eds.), *Adolescent literacy research and practice* (pp. 251–282). New York: Guilford Press.

Robnolt, V. J., Rhodes, J. A., & Richardson, J. S. (2005, December 1). *Study skills for the twenty-first century "demographic group differences."* Paper presented at the National Reading Conference, Miami.

Santa, C., Havens, L., & Maycumber, E. (2005). *Creating independence through student-owned strategies.* Dubuque, IA: Kendall/Hunt.

Schallert, D. L., & Reed, J. H. (1997). The pull of the text and the process of involvement in reading. In J. T. Guthrie & A. Wigfield (Eds.), *Reading engagement: Motivating readers through integrated instruction* (pp. 68–85). Newark, DE: International Reading Association.

Shoenbach, R., Greenfield, C. L,. Cziko, C., & Hurwitz, L. (1999). *Reading for understanding: A guide to improving reading in middle and high school classrooms.* San Francisco: Jossey-Bass.

Smith, M., & Wilhelm, J. D. (2004). "I just like being good at it": The importance of competence in the literate lives of young men. *Journal of Adolescent and Adult Literacy, 47*(6), 454–461.

Snow, C. E. (2002). *Reading for understanding: Toward an R & D program in reading comprehension.* Santa Monica, CA: RAND Corporation.

Sturtevant, E. G. (1996). Beyond the content literacy course: Influences on beginning mathematics teachers' uses of literacy in student teaching. In D. J. Leu, C. K. Kinzer, & K. A. Hinchman (Eds.), *Literacies for the 21st century: Research and practice: Forty-fifth yearbook of the National Reading Conference* (pp. 146–158). Chicago: National Reading Conference.

Tovani, C. (2004). *Do I really have to reach reading?: Content comprehension, grades 6–12.* Portland, ME: Stenhouse.

U.S. Department of Education. (2006). *Striving readers.* Retrieved January 25, 2006, from www.ed/gov/programs/strivingreaders

Unrau, N. J., & Ruddell, R. B. (1995). Interpreting texts in classroom contexts. *Journal of Adolescent and Adult Literacy, 39*(1), 16–27.

Part III

EVIDENCE-BASED STRATEGIES FOR LITERACY LEARNING AND TEACHING

Chapter 7

BEST PRACTICES IN TEACHING PHONOLOGICAL AWARENESS AND PHONICS

Patricia M. Cunningham

This chapter will:

- Describe the role of phonemic awareness in learning to read.
- Explore what research says about the best way to teach phonics.
- Summarize what we know about multisyllabic word decoding.
- Describe classroom practices consistent with what we know about phonemic awareness, phonics, and multisyllabic word decoding.

Phonics is and has been the most controversial issue in reading. Since 1955, when Rudolph Flesch's book *Why Johnny Can't Read* became a national best-seller, educators and parents have debated the role of phonics in beginning-reading instruction. A variety of published phonics programs have been touted as the "cure-all" for everyone's reading problems. Enthusiasm for these programs has lasted just long enough for everyone to relearn that thoughtful reading requires much more than just the ability to quickly decode words. As the chapters of this book demonstrate, the most effective literacy frameworks include a variety of instruction and activities that provide children with a balanced literacy diet. This chapter focuses on phonemic awareness and phonics. When the knowledge from this chapter is combined with that from all the other chapters, good balanced research-based literacy instruction will result.

EVIDENCE-BASED BEST PRACTICES

To become good readers and writers, children must learn to decode words. In the beginning stages of learning to read, phonemic awareness is crucial to success. As children move through the primary grades, their phonics strategies must be developed. Successful reading in the intermediate grades requires children to have strategies for decoding multisyllabic words. There is research to guide us as we guide children through all stages of successful decoding.

Phonemic Awareness

One of the understandings that many children gain from early reading and writing encounters is the realization that spoken words are made up of sounds. These sounds (phonemes) are not separate and distinct. In fact, their existence is quite abstract. Phonemic awareness has many levels and includes the concept of rhyme and the ability to blend and segment words and to manipulate phonemes to form different words. Phonemic awareness develops gradually for many children through exposure to songs, nursery rhymes, and books with rhymes and alliteration that promote word play.

Phonemic awareness is one of the best predictors of success in learning to read (Ehri & Nunes, 2002; National Reading Panel, 2000). Upon learning that phonemic awareness is such an important concept, some people have concluded that phonemic awareness is all we need to worry about in preparing children to read. Phonemic awareness training programs have been developed and mandated for every child every day for 30–40 minutes. The classroom reality is that there are only so many minutes in a day, and if something gets 30–40 minutes, other important things get less time. In addition to phonemic awareness, children who are going to learn to read successfully must develop print tracking skills and begin to learn some letter names and sounds. They need to develop cognitive clarity about what reading and writing are for, which you can only learn when you spend some of your time each day in the presence of reading and writing.

Another problem with the overreaction to the phonemic awareness findings is that some children enter school with sufficient phonemic awareness to begin to learn to read and others will develop it solely from engaging in emergent literacy activities such as shared reading of books that play with sounds and writing with invented spelling. Yopp and Yopp

(2000) argue for phonemic awareness instruction as only *one* part of a beginning literacy program:

> Our concern is that in some classrooms phonemic awareness instruction will replace other crucial areas of instruction. Phonemic awareness supports reading development only if it is part of a broader program that includes—among other things—development of students' vocabulary, syntax, comprehension, strategic reading abilities, decoding strategies, and writing across all content areas. (p. 142)

Phonics

While there is general agreement on the need to develop children's decoding strategies, there is little agreement on which methods are most successful in doing this. Stahl, Duffy-Hester, and Stahl (1998) reviewed the research on phonics instruction and concluded that there are several types of good phonics instruction and that there is no research base to support the superiority of any one particular type. The National Reading Panel (NRP, 2000) reviewed the experimental research on teaching phonics and determined that explicit and systematic phonics is superior to nonsystematic or no phonics but that there is no significant difference in effectiveness among the kinds of systematic phonics instruction:

> In teaching phonics explicitly and systematically, several different instructional approaches have been used. These include synthetic phonics, analytic phonics, embedded phonics, analogy phonics, onset-rime phonics, and phonics through spelling. . . . Phonics-through-spelling programs teach children to transform sounds into letters to write words. Phonics in context approaches teach children to use sound–letter correspondences along with context clues to identify unfamiliar words they encounter in text. Analogy phonics programs teach children to use parts of written words they already know to identify new words. The distinctions between systematic phonics approaches are not absolute, however, and some phonics programs combine two or more of these types of instruction. (p. 2-89)

Several studies published since the NRP report suggest that effective phonics instruction might include a variety of approaches. Davis (2000) found that spelling-based decoding instruction was as effective as reading-based decoding instruction for all her students but more effective for children with poor phonological awareness. Juel and Minden-Cupp (2000) noted that the most effective teachers they observed of children who entered first grade with few literacy skills combined systematic letter-sound instruction with onset/rime analogy instruction and taught these units for application in both reading and writing. McCandliss, Beck,

Sandak, and Perfetti (2003) investigated the effectiveness of Isabel Beck's instructional strategy, Word Building, with students who had failed to benefit from traditional phonics instruction. They found that the children who received this word building instruction demonstrated significantly greater improvements on standardized measures of decoding, comprehension, and phonological awareness.

Multisyllabic Word Decoding

Little research has been conducted on multisyllabic word decoding, but what we do know leads us to believe that morphemes—prefixes, suffixes, and roots—are the building blocks of big words. In 1984, Nagy and Anderson published a landmark study in which they analyzed a sample of 7,260 words found in books commonly read in grades 3–9. They found that most of these words were polysyllabic words and that many of these big words were related semantically through their morphology. Some of these relationships are easily noticed. The words *hunter, redness, foglights,* and *stringy* are clearly related to the words *hunt, red, fog,* and *string.* Other, more complex, word relationships exist between such words as *planet/planetarium, vice/vicious,* and *apart/apartment.* Nagy and Anderson hypothesized that if children knew or learned how to interpret morphological relationships, they could comprehend six or seven words for every basic word known. To move children along in their decoding and spelling abilities in upper grades, instruction needs to focus on morphemes—prefixes, suffixes, and roots—and how these morphemes help us decode, spell, and gain meaning for polysyllabic words.

BEST PRACTICES IN ACTION

While research does not tell us what kind of phonemic awareness and phonics instruction is most effective, we can use some research-based findings to evaluate classroom activities. Activities designed to develop phonemic awareness should be done in the context of reading and writing so that children develop the other concepts necessary for successful beginning reading. Because children vary in their level of phonemic awareness, phonics activities for young children should include opportunities to develop phonemic awareness. Because it is not clear how phonics is best taught (and because all children might not learn best with any single method), phonics instruction should include a variety of activities, including letter-sound, spelling, and analogy instruction. As children encounter more big words in their reading, they should learn to use morphemes to unlock the pronunciation, spelling, and meaning of polysyllabic words. The remainder of this section will describe activities to teach phonemic awareness, phonics, and multi-syllabic word decoding in ways that are consistent with research.

Focus on Rhymes to Develop Phonemic Awareness

Children who come to school with well-developed phonemic awareness abilities have usually come from homes in which rhyming chants, jingles, and songs were part of their daily experience. These same chants, jingles, and songs should be a part of every young child's day in the classroom.

There are so many wonderful rhyming books, but because of their potential to develop phonemic awareness, two deserve special mention. Along with other great rhyming books, Dr. Seuss wrote *There's a Wocket in My Pocket* (1974). In this book, all kinds of Seusssian creatures are found in various places. In addition to the wocket in the pocket, there is a vug under the rug, a nureau in the bureau and a yottle in the bottle! After several readings, children delight in chiming in to provide the nonsensical word and scary creature which lurks in harmless-looking places. After reading the book a few times, it is fun to decide what creatures might be lurking in your classroom. Let children make up the creatures, and accept whatever they say as long as it rhymes with their object:

"There's a pock on our clock!"
"There's a zindow looking in our window!"
"There's a zencil on my pencil!"

Another wonderful rhyming book for phonemic awareness is *The Hungry Thing* by Jan Slepian and Ann Seidler. In this book, a large friendly dinosaur-looking creature (You have to see him to love him!) comes to town, wearing a sign that says "Feed Me." When asked what he would like to eat, he responds, "Shmancakes." After much deliberation, a clever little boy offers him some pancakes. The Hungry Thing eats them all up and demands, "Tickles." Again, after much deliberation the boy figures out he wants pickles. As the story continues, it becomes obvious that The Hungry Thing wants specific foods and that he asks for them by making them rhyme with what he wants. He asks for *feetloaf* and gobbles down the meatloaf. For dessert, he wants *hookies* and *gollipops*!

The Hungry Thing is a delightful book, and in many classrooms teachers have made a poster-size Hungry Thing, complete with his sign that reads "Feed Me" on one side and "Thank You!" on the other. Armed with real foods or pictures of foods the children try to feed The Hungry Thing. Of course, he won't eat the food unless they make it rhyme. If they offer him spaghetti, they have to say "What some bagetti?" (or "zagetti," or "ragetti"—any silly word that rhymes with *spaghetti*!) To feed him Cheerios, they have to offer him "seerios," "theerios," or "leerios"!

Focus on Blending and Segmenting to Develop Phonemic Awareness

In addition to hearing and producing rhymes, the ability to put sounds together to make a word—blending—and the ability to separate out the sounds in a word—segmenting—are critical components of phonemic awareness. Blending and segmenting are not easy for many children. In general, it is easier for them to segment off the beginning letters—the onset—from the rest of the word—the rhyme—than it is to separate all the sounds. In other words, children can usually separate *bat* into /b/ and /at/ before they can produce the three sounds /b/ /a/ and /t/. The same is true for blending. Most children can blend /S/ and /am/ to produce the name Sam before they can blend /S/ /a/and /m/. Most teachers begin by having children blend and segment the onset from the rime and then move to blending and segmenting individual letters.

There are lots of games children enjoy that can help them learn to blend and segment. The most versatile is a simple riddle-guessing game. The teacher begins the game by naming the category and giving the clue: "I'm thinking of an animal that lives in the water and is a /f/ /ish/ [or /f/ /i/ /sh/, depending on what level of blending you are working on]." The child who correctly guesses "fish" gives the next riddle: "I'm thinking of an animal that goes quack and is a /d/ /uck/ [or /d/ /u/ /ck/]." This sounds simplistic but children love it, and you can use different categories to go along with units you are studying.

A wonderful variation on this guessing game is to put objects in a bag and let children reach in the bag and stretch out the name of an object they choose and then call on someone to guess "What is it?" Choose small common objects you find in the room—a cap, a ball, chalk, a book—and let the children watch you load the bag and help you stretch out the words for practice as you put them in.

Children also like to talk like "ghosts." One child chooses an object in the room to say as a ghost would—stretching the word out very slowly—"dddoooorrr." The child who correctly guesses "door" gets to ghost-talk another object—"bbbooookkk." Both the ghost-talk game and the guessing game provide practice in both segmenting and blending as children segment words by stretching them out and other children blend the words together to guess them.

Encourage Writing with Invented Spelling

When young children write, they need to spell many words that they have not yet learned to spell. If teachers demonstrate how you can stretch out words and put down letters for the sounds you hear, young children will write a lot more than if they think they have to spell all the words correctly or wait for someone to spell the words for them. As they stretch out words, they are segmenting those words into their component sounds. Segmenting is an important—and difficult—phonemic awareness ability that will develop more quickly if children are encouraged to stretch out words while writing.

How Emphasizing Rhyme, Segmenting, and Blending Reflects What We Know

Rhyme awareness—the ability to make and recognize rhymes—is one of the earliest developed phonemic awareness abilities. Many children come to kindergarten with developed rhyme awareness. These children were not given any direct instruction in rhyme, but they were immersed in an environment of songs, jingles, and books in which rhyme played a large role. Including rhyming songs, jingles, and books as part of every early-childhood day allows all children to begin developing their phonemic awareness.

Segmenting and blending words are two of the more difficult phonemic awareness abilities. Children need lots of practice with oral activities in which they put sounds together to create words and pull words apart into their component sounds. When children are encouraged to stretch out words while writing, they get a lot of practice with segmenting. Writing also gives students a way to apply the letter-sound knowledge they are learning. Many children can read their own writing before they can read the same words in books.

Make Words to Include a Variety of Phonics Approaches

Making Words is a popular activity with both teachers and children. Children love manipulating letters to make words and figuring out the secret word that can be made with all the letters. While children are having fun making words, they are also learning important information about phonics and spelling. As children manipulate the letters to make the words, they learn how small changes, such as changing just one letter or moving the letters around, result in completely new words. Children develop phonemic awareness as they stretch out words and listen for the sounds they hear and the order of those sounds.

Making Words lessons are an example of a type of instruction called Guided Discovery. In order to truly learn and retain strategies, children must discover them. But some children do not make discoveries about words on their own. In Making Words lessons, children are guided toward those discoveries.

Making Words lessons have three steps. In the first step, the children make words. The lesson begins with short easy words and moves to longer, more complex, words. The last word is always the secret word—a word that can be made with *all* the letters. As children create the words in their seats, one who has made a word successfully goes up to the pocket chart and makes the word with big letters. Children who don't have the word made correctly in their seats quickly fix their word to be ready for the next word. The small changes between most words encourages even those children who have not made a word perfectly to fix it because they soon realize that having the current word correctly spelled increases their chances of spelling the next word correctly. Each lesson includes 10–15 words that can be made, including the secret word that can be made with all the letters.

In step 2 of a Making Words lesson, children sort the words into patterns. Many children discover patterns just through making the words in the carefully sequenced order, but some children need more explicit guidance. This guidance happens when all the words have been made and the teacher guides the children to sort them into patterns. Depending on the sophistication of the children and the words available in the lesson, words might be sorted according to their beginning letters—all the letters up to the vowel. Another pattern that children need to discover is that many words have the same root word. If they can pronounce and spell the root word and if they recognize root words with endings, prefixes, or suffixes added, they are able to decode and spell many additional words. Every Making Words lesson contains several sets of rhyming words. Children sort the words into rhyming words and notice that words that rhyme have the same spelling pattern.

Many children know letter sounds and patterns and yet may not apply these to decode an unknown word encountered during reading or spell a word they need while writing. This is the reason that every Making Words lesson ends with a transfer step. Once words are sorted according to rhyme, children use these rhyming words to decode two new words and spell two new words. Here is an example of how you might conduct a Making Words lesson and cue the children to the changes and words you want them to make.

Beginning the Lesson

The children all have the letters *a o o c n r s t*. These same letters—big enough for all to see—are displayed in a pocket chart. The vowels are in

a different color, and the letter cards have lower-cased letters on one side and capital letters on the other side.

The words the children are going to make are written on index cards. These words will be placed in the pocket chart as the words are made and will be used for the sort and transfer steps of the lesson.

The teacher begins the lesson by having the children hold up and name each letter as the teacher holds up the big letters in the pocket chart.

> "Hold up and name each letter as I hold up the big letter. Let's start with your vowels. Show me your *a* and your two *o*'s. Now show me your *c, n, r, s,* and *t.* You all have eight letters. In a few minutes, we will see if anyone can figure out the secret word which uses all eight letters."

Step 1: Making Words.

"Use three letters to spell the word *act.* We will all *act* in our class play."

Find someone with *act* spelled correctly and send that child to spell *act* with the big letters.

"Use the same three letters in *act* to spell *cat.* My *cat* likes music."
"Change the vowel in *cat* to spell *cot.* At camp, I sleep on a *cot.*"
"Change just one letter in *cot* to spell *not.* Spelling *not* is not hard."
"Start over and use four letters to spell *soon. Soon* we will go to lunch."

Quickly send someone with the correct spelling to the big letters. Keep the pace brisk. Do not wait until everyone has *soon* spelled with their little letters. It is fine if some children are making *soon* as *soon* is being spelled with the big letters.

"Start over and use four letters to spell *torn.* The sleeve on his jacket is *torn.*"

"Change just one letter to spell *corn.* I love *corn* on the cob."

"Change the last two letters to spell *coat.* When it is cold, I wear my warm *coat.*"

"Add one letter to *coat* to spell *coast.* Virginia is on the Atlantic *coast.*"

"Change one letter in *coast* to spell *roast.* At camp, we *roast* marshmallows."

"Use six letters to spell *acorns.* The *acorns* fell off the big oak tree."

"Use six letters to spell *actors.* We will all be *actors* in our play."

"I have just one word left. It is the secret word you can make with all your letters. See if you can figure it out."

Give the students 1 minute to figure out the secret word, and then gives clues if needed. Let someone who figures it out go to the big letters and spell the secret word—*cartoons.*

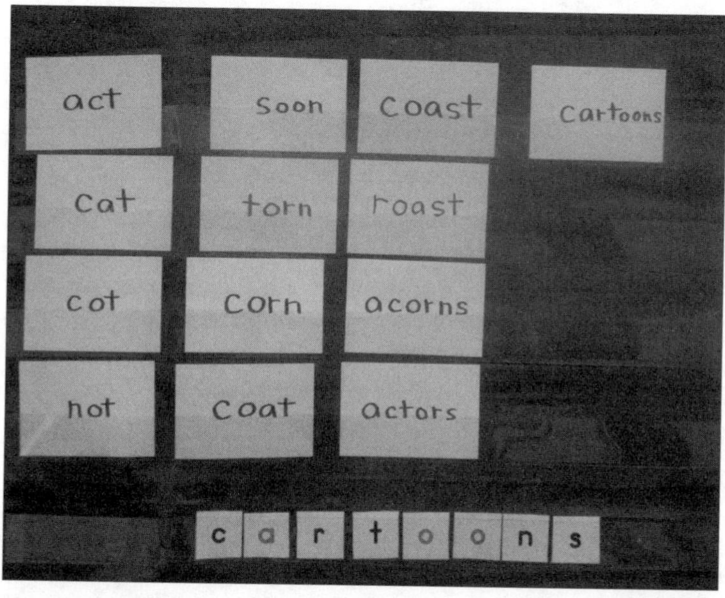

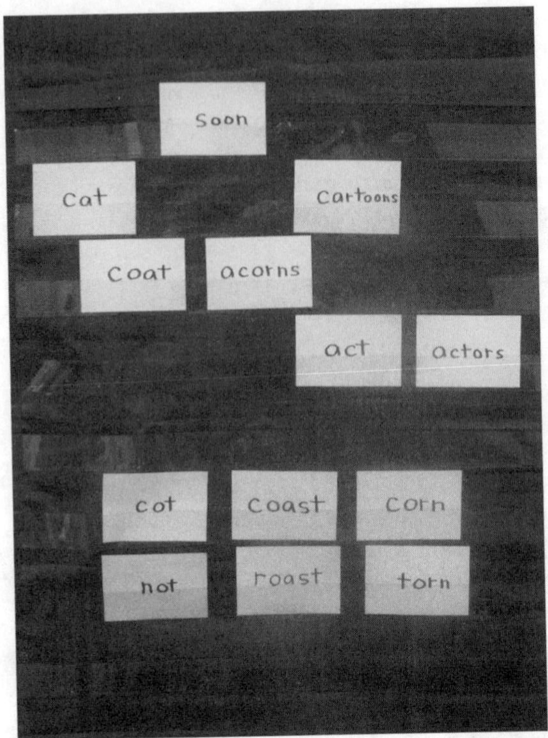

Step 2: Sorting the Words into Patterns. Have the children read aloud with you all the words made in the lesson. Then have them sort out the related words. Remind the children that related words share a root word and some meaning. Say a sentence to show how these words are related. "The people who *act* in a play are called *actors.*"

act   actors

Next have the children sort the rhyming words.

cot	coast	torn
not	roast	corn

Step 3: Transfer. Tell the children to pretend they are reading and they come to a new word. Show one child the word *born* written on an index card. Let that child put *born* under *torn* and *corn,* and have all the children pronounce all three words, using the rhyming words they made to decode the new word, *born.* Do the same thing with *boast.*

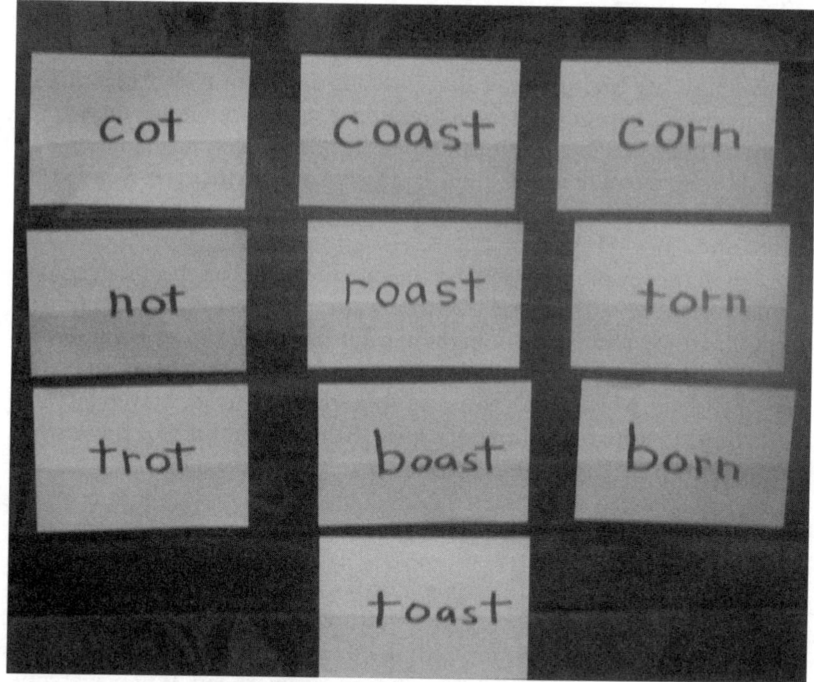

Next, tell children to pretend they are writing and need to spell a word: "Let's pretend Terry is writing and is trying to spell the word *toast.*" Have the children tell you that *toast* begins with *t,* and write *t* on an index card. Then have the children pronounce the sets of rhyming words in the pocket chart and decide that *toast* rhymes with *coast* and *roast* and use the *oast* pattern to finish spelling *toast.* Do the same thing with *trot.* When you finish the lesson, the rhyming words you made will be lined up in the pocket chart along with two new words the children helped you read and two new words they helped you spell.

Teach Children to Use the Words They Know to Decode and Spell Other Words

Another activity that includes a variety of approaches to phonics is called Using Words You Know. To plan a Using Words You Know lesson, we pick three or four words that our children can read and spell and that have many rhyming words spelled the same way. You can use any words your students know that have lots of rhyming words. *Play,* for example, will help you decode many other words, including *stray, spray, clay, delay* and *betray. Rain* helps you decode and spell *brain, Spain, chain, sprain,* and *complain.* You can also use brand names that have lots of rhyming words. Bring in packages with the product names, and then use those names as the known words. Children are highly motivated by these products and are fascinated to see how many other words these products can help them read and spell. Here is a sample lesson (adapted from Cunningham, 2005) using ice cream and Cool Whip.

Begin the lesson by displaying the products, and let the children talk a little about them. Draw the children's attention to the names, and tell them that these names will help them spell and read a lot of other words. Using the board, chart, or overhead, make columns and head each with one of the key words, underlining the spelling pattern. Have your students do the same on a sheet of paper. At the beginning of the lesson, their papers look like this:

ice cream cool whip

Show the students words that rhyme with *ice, cream, cool,* or *whip.* Do not say these words and do not allow them to say the words but rather have them write them in the column with the same spelling pattern. Send one child to write the word on the chart, board, or overhead. When everyone has the rhyming word written under the original word that will help them read it, have them say the known word and the rhyming word. Help them to verbalize the strategy they are using by saying something like "If c-r-e-a-m is *cream,* d-r-e-a-m must be *dream.*" "If c-o-o-l is *cool,* d-r-o-o-l is *drool.*" After showing them eight to ten words and having them use the known word to decode them, help them practice using known words to spell unknown words. To help them spell, don't show them a word. Instead, say a word, such as *twice,* and have them say the word and write it under the word that it rhymes with. Again, help them verbalize their strategy by leading them to explain:

> "If *ice* is spelled i-c-e, *twice* is probably spelled t-w-i-c-e."
> "If *whip* is spelled w-h-i-p, *strip* is probably spelled s-t-r-i-p."

To show children how they can decode and spell bigger words based on rhyming words, end the lesson by showing them a few longer words and having them write them under the rhymes and use the rhymes to decode them. Finally, say a few longer words, help them with the spelling of the first syllables and have them use the rhyme to spell the last syllable. Here is what their papers would look like with some added longer words:

ice	cr*eam*	c*ool*	wh*ip*
nice	dream	drool	tip
mice	stream	pool	skip
slice	scream	fool	trip
twice	gleam	spool	strip
dice	beam	stool	clip
sacrifice	mainstream	whirlpool	equip
device	downstream	preschool	spaceship

It is very important for Using Words You Know lessons that you choose the rhyming words for them to read and spell rather than ask them for rhyming words. In English, there are often two spelling patterns for the same rhyme. If you ask them what rhymes with *cream,* or *cool,* they may come up with words with the *e-e-m* pattern such as *seem* and words with the *u-l-e* pattern such as *rule.* The fact that there are two common patterns for many rhymes does not hinder us while reading. When we see the word *drool,* our brain thinks of other o-o-l words such as *cool* and *school.* We make this new word *drool* rhyme with *cool* and *school* and then check out this pronunciation with the meaning of whatever we are reading. If we were going to write the word *drool* for the first time, we wouldn't know for sure which spelling pattern to use, and we might think of the rhyming word *rule* and use that pattern. Spelling requires both a sense of word patterns and a visual checking sense. When you write a word and then think "That doesn't look right!" and then write it using a different pattern, you are demonstrating that you have developed a visual checking sense. Once children become good at spelling by pattern, you can help them develop their visual checking sense. During Using Words You Know lessons, we are trying to get them to spell based on pattern, and we "finesse" the problem of two patterns by choosing the words we present to them.

Using Words You Know lessons are easy to plan if you use a good rhyming dictionary, such as the *Scholastic Rhyming Dictionary* (Young, 1994). Children enjoy Using Words You Know, especially if the words you use are popular products such as *Coke, Crest, Tang,* and *Cat Chow.*

How Making Words and Using Words You Know Reflect What We Know

Making Words and Using Words You Know are examples of lesson formats that teach phonics in a variety of ways. When the children are making words with their letters, they are engaging in a spelling approach to phonics. They are told the word, and they must figure out which of their letters to use to spell it. This spelling approach is also used in Using Words

You Know when the teacher says a word that rhymes with the key words and the children decide how to spell them based on their known rhyming words.

Both lesson formats also teach children to decode words based on pattern and analogy. In a Making Words lesson, there are always several sets of rhymes with the same spelling pattern. Children sort out these rhyming words and then use these words to decode two new words and spell two new words with the same pattern. Analogy and pattern instruction is also obvious in Using Words You Know lessons in which children use known words to decode and spell rhyming words with the same pattern.

While not the focus of the lesson, both Making Words and Using Words You Know provide opportunities for children to develop phonemic awareness and firm up their beginning letter knowledge if they still need to do that. Teachers encourage the children to stretch out words as they are making them. In the transfer step, children blend the beginning letters with the rhyming patterns to read the new words.

Sorting rhyming words is included in every Making Words lessons, but there are also opportunities to sort for beginning letter patterns if children still need their attention focused on those. Whenever possible, we include words such as *act* and *actors,* which share the same base word. Although this is not the focus of instruction in primary grades, children do need to begin to notice the morphemic patterns that are the basis for the decoding and spelling of polysyllabic words. In Using Words You Know lessons, we always include some words with two or more syllables to help children extend their decoding strategies to longer words.

Word Detectives

Word Detectives is an activity we do with children when introducing big words to them. We teach the children to ask themselves two questions to "solve the mystery of big words."

> "Do I know any other words that look and sound like this word?"
> "Are any of these look-alike/sound-alike words related to one another?"

The answer to the first question helps children with pronouncing and spelling the word. The answer to the second question helps children discover what, if any, meaning relationships exist between this new word and others in their meaning vocabulary stores. To be most effective, children need to be word detectives throughout the school day in every subject area. Imagine that during math students encounter the new word *equation.* The teacher demonstrates and gives examples of equations and helps build meaning for the concept. Finally, the teacher asks the students to pronounce *equation* and to see whether they know any other words that look and sound like *equation.* Students think of words that end like *equation* such as *addition, multiplication, nation,* and *vacation.* For the beginning chunk, they think of *equal* and *equator.*

The teacher lists the words, underlining the parts that are the same and having the students pronounce the words, emphasizing the part that is pronounced the same. The teacher then points out to the students that thinking of a word that looks and sounds the same as a new word will help you quickly remember how to pronounce the new word and will also help you spell the new word.

Next the teacher explains that words, like people, sometimes look and sound alike but are not related. If this is the first time this analogy is used, the teacher will want to spend some time talking with the students about people with red hair, green eyes, and so on who have some parts that look alike but are not related and others who are.

> "Not all people who look alike are related, but some are. This is how words work too. Words are related if there is something about their meaning that is the same. After we find look-alike, sound-alike words that will help us spell and pronounce new words, we try to think of any ways these words might be in the same meaning family. "

With help from the teacher, the children discover that *equal, equator,* and *equation* are related because the meaning of *equal* is in all three. An *equation* has to have *equal* quantities on both sides of the *equal* signs. The *equator* is an imaginary line that divides the earth into two *equal* halves.

Later, during science time, the students are doing some experiments using thermometers and barometers. At the close of the lesson, the teacher points to these words and asks the students to once again be word detectives. The children notice that the *meters* chunk is pronounced and spelled the same. The teacher then asks the students if they think these words are just look-alikes or are related to one another. The students conclude that you use them both to measure things and the *meters* chunk must be related to measuring, as in *kilometers.* Students also notice that *thermometer* begins like *thermostat* and decide that *thermometer* and *thermostat* are related because they both involve heat or temperature.

Throughout their school day, children encounter many new big words. Because English is such a morphologically related language, most new words can be connected to other words by their spelling and pronunciation, and many new words have meaning-related words already known to the student. Children who use clues from other big words to figure out the decoding, spelling, and meaning of new big words are being word detectives.

How Word Detectives Reflects What We Know

Word Detectives is an activity specifically designed to help children become sensitive to morphology prefixes, suffixes, and roots that provide links to the spelling, pronunciation, and meanings of big words. Because the words chosen always come out of the context of what is being studied, children learn to use morphology and context together as clues to solve the mysteries of big words.

CONCLUSIONS AND LOOKING TO THE FUTURE

This chapter has summarized what we know from research about how to teach phonemic awareness and phonics. The key conclusion of this research is that children do need systematic phonics instruction but there is no one best way to teach phonics. This conclusion is disturbing to those who would like for there to be a specified best way so that everyone could be mandated to do it in that way. In many schools, one approach to phonics has been mandated despite the lack of proof that that approach is any better than others teachers might favor.

In order to improve reading instruction for all children, we need to look to the research on effective literacy instruction (Allington & Johnston, 2002; Pressley, Allington, Wharton-McDonald, Block, & Morrow, 2001). These nationwide studies identified effective first- and fourth-grade classrooms and analyzed the literacy instruction that occurred in those classrooms. They found that there were many differences in these classrooms but also many commonalities. The classrooms of the most effective teachers were characterized by high academic engagement, excellent and positive classroom management, explicit teaching of skills, large amounts of reading and writing, and integration across the curriculum. Within these commonalities, there were huge differences in the way the components were orchestrated. How we teach phonics has not been demonstrated to have a huge effect on achievement, but how we orchestrate classrooms has shown that effect. To improve beginning literacy achievement, we need to continue our efforts to research how to create, maintain, and support excellent classroom teachers.

ENGAGEMENT ACTIVITIES

1. Consider other phonics activities you have done or read about. How well do they reflect what we know about how children learn phonics. Is phonemic awareness developed as an integral part of that activity? Does the activity include a variety of approaches to learning phonics strategies?

2. Almost all the key words encountered in science and social studies are polysyllabic words. These big words are stumbling blocks for many children who don't know how to use prefixes, suffixes, and roots as keys to spelling, decoding, and meaning. Examine the materials and activities you have available for teaching phonics, and determine how much attention they pay to helping children discover morphemic links.

REFERENCES

Professional Literature

Allington, R. L., & Johnston, P. H. (2002). *Reading to learn: Lessons from exemplary fourth-grade classrooms.* New York: Guilford Press.

Cunningham. P. M. (2005). *Phonics they use: Words for reading and writing* (4th ed.). Boston: Pearson Education.

Davis, L. H. (2000). The effects of rime-based analogy training on word reading and spelling of first-grade children with good and poor phonological awareness (doctoral dissertation, Northwestern University). *Dissertation Abstracts International, 61,* 2253A

Ehri, L. C., & Nunes, S. R. (2002). The role of phonemic awareness in learning to read. *What research has to say about reading instruction* (pp. 110–139). Newark, DE: International Reading Association.

Flesch, R. (1955). *Why Johnny can't read.* New York: Harper & Row.

Juel, C., & Minden-Cupp, C. (2000). Learning to read words: Linguistic units and instructional strategies. *Reading Research Quarterly, 35,* 458–492.

McCandliss, B., Beck, I. L., Sandak, R., & Perfetti, C. (2003). Focusing attention on decoding for children with poor reading skills: Design and preliminary tests of the Word Building intervention. *Scientific Studies of Reading, 7,* 75–104.

Nagy, W., & Anderson, R. C. (1984). How many words are there in printed school English? *Reading Research Quarterly, 19,* 304–330.

National Reading Panel. (2000). *Teaching children to read: An evidence-based assessment of the scientific research literature on reading and its implications for reading instruction* (National Institute of Health Publication No. 00-4769). Washington, DC: National Institute of Child Health and Human Development.

Pressley, M., Allington, R. L., Wharton-McDonald, R., Block, C. C., & Morrow, L. M. (2001). *Learning to read: Lessons from exemplary first-grade classrooms.* New York: Guilford Press.

Stahl, S. A, Duffy-Hester, A. M., & Stahl, K. A. (1998). Everything you wanted to know about phonics (but were afraid to ask). *Reading Research Quarterly, 33,* 338–355.

Yopp, H. K., & Yopp, R. H. (2000). Supporting phonemic awareness development in the classroom. *The Reading Teacher, 54,* 130–143

Young, S. (1994). *The Scholastic rhyming dictionary.* New York: Scholastic.

Children's Literature

Seuss, Dr. (1974). *There's a wocket in my pocket.* New York: Random House.

Slepian, J., & Seidler, A. (1967). *The hungry thing.* New York: Scholastic.

Chapter 8

BEST PRACTICES IN VOCABULARY INSTRUCTION

Camille L. Z. Blachowicz
Peter J. Fisher

This chapter will:

- Present five research-based guidelines for vocabulary instruction.
- Share the research that underpins each and give examples of instruction reflecting the targeted guideline.
- Describe a classroom that utilizes this type of instruction.
- Share resources for vocabulary instruction.

EVIDENCE-BASED BEST PRACTICES

The term *vocabulary instruction* can encompass a number of activities that occur in a classroom. we often ask teachers to make a list of word study activities that normally occur during a single day in their classroom. a typical list from a fourth-grade teacher included the following:

- Teach the suggested words prior to the reading selection from the basal.
- Brainstorm synonyms for the word *said* as part of a minilesson in writing.
- List word families as part of spelling instruction.
- Teach the meaning of *quadrant* for word problems in math.

- Have the Mexican American and Arab American students teach the rest of the students the Spanish and Arabic words for *plains, rivers, clouds, mountains,* and *rain* as part of social studies on the Great Plains.
- Develop a semantic web for the Great Plains, including words learned so far in the unit.
- Talk about *honesty* in relation to one student's having "borrowed" a marker from another without permission.
- Clarify the meanings of some difficult words in the teacher read-aloud at the end of the day.

Clearly, for each of these teaching events, the nature of the learning task was somewhat different. In some cases, students were learning unfamiliar words (the Spanish and Arabic words) for familiar concepts (*plains, rivers,* etc.), whereas in others they were learning new concepts (*quadrant*). In addition, we might expect that students would remember some words and use them almost immediately (synonyms for *said*), whereas students might recognize other words in a story but not choose to use them in their own writing (which largely features basal words). Vocabulary instruction occurs in our classrooms every day at a variety of levels and for a variety of purposes. After all, words are the currency of education. However, teachers are increasingly faced with a diverse group of learners in terms of current word knowledge, linguistic background, learning styles, and literacy abilities. It is up to us as teachers to make word learning enjoyable, meaningful, and effective.

How, then, does a teacher meet all these needs in a classroom of diverse learners? Like much in education, there is no simple answer. However, research has suggested several guidelines that apply across most situations (Blachowicz & Fisher, 2000; National Reading Panel, 2000):

- *Guideline 1.* The effective vocabulary teacher builds a word-rich environment in which students are immersed in words for both incidental and intentional learning and the development of "word awareness."
- *Guideline 2.* The effective vocabulary teacher helps students develop as independent word learners.
- *Guideline 3.* The effective vocabulary teacher uses instructional strategies that not only teach vocabulary but also model good word-learning behaviors.
- *Guideline 4.* The effective vocabulary teacher provides explicit instruction for important content and concept vocabulary, drawing on multiple sources of meaning.
- *Guideline 5.* The effective vocabulary teacher uses assessment that matches the goal of instruction.

In the next section, we look at each guideline in turn, presenting an evidence base and then some examples of instruction consistent with this guideline.

Vocabulary Instruction: The Evidence Base

In today's world, it is important to model good practice in our classrooms and be able to articulate an evidence base for our instruction drawn from research and best practices. The research base on good practice in vocabulary instruction strongly supports the guidelines we have presented, and we examine each in more depth.

> *Guideline 1. The effective vocabulary teacher builds a word-rich environment in which students are immersed in words for both incidental and intentional learning and the development of "word awareness."*

Vocabulary and Emergent Readers

This guideline is supported by research in several areas: the importance of rich oral language in the classroom; the need for wide reading; the importance of vocabulary learning as a metalinguistic process. Just as teachers use the term *flood of books* to talk about situations in which students have many and varied opportunities to read, so *flood of words* is an important concept for general vocabulary development (Scott, Asselin, Henry, & Butler, 1997); both rich oral and rich book language provide important input for students' vocabulary growth.

The variance in vocabulary knowledge of young children is well established. In 1995 Betty Hart and Todd Risley, two researchers at the University of Kansas who looked at parent–child interactions among different social groups, found some striking differences among preschoolers. On average, professional parents talked to their toddlers more than three times as much as parents of families on welfare did. Not surprisingly, that difference resulted in a big discrepancy in the children's vocabulary size. The average 3-year-old from a welfare family demonstrated an active vocabulary of around 500 words, whereas a 3-year-old from a professional family demonstrated a vocabulary of over 1,000 words.

Those differences become more pronounced as children get older—by the time the low-income children get to school and start to learn to read, they're already at an enormous disadvantage. It is estimated that children from economically privileged homes enter kindergarten having heard some 30 million more words than students from economically disadvantaged homes. Further, the difference in time spent in "lap reading"—

sitting in the lap of an adult and listening to a book being read—may be of the magnitude of 4,000–6,000 hours.

Read-alouds, reading aloud to children—sometimes also referred to as shared storybook reading—is a productive means for giving students opportunities to develop new-meaning vocabulary. Because children's books present more advanced and less familiar vocabulary than everyday speech (Cunningham & Stanovich, 1998), listening to books that are read helps students to go beyond their existing oral vocabularies and presents them with new concepts and vocabulary. Discussions after shared storybook reading also give students opportunities to use new vocabulary in the more decontextualized setting of a book discussion.

Numerous studies have documented the fact that young students can learn word meanings incidentally from read-aloud experiences (Eller, Pappas, & Brown, 1988; Elley, 1988; Robbins & Ehri, 1994). In school settings, the effect is large for students age 5 and older and smaller for those under age 4. Involving students in discussions during and after listening to a book has also produced significant word learning, especially when the teacher scaffolds this learning by asking questions, adding information or prompting students to describe what they heard. Whitehurst and his associates (Whitehurst et al., 1994, 1999) have called this process "dialogic reading."

However, teachers are amazed when they hear that storybook reading with young children is not always a positive experience. Some reading situations are less optimal than others, and research also suggests that this scaffolding (providing explanations, asking questions, clarifying) may be more essential to those students who are less likely to learn new vocabulary easily. Children with less rich initial vocabularies are less likely to learn new vocabulary incidentally and need a thoughtful, well-designed scaffolded approach to maximize learning from shared storybook reading (Robbins & Ehri, 1994; Senechal, Thomas, & Monker, 1995).

De Temple and Snow (2003) draw the contrast between talk around shared storybook reading that is cognitively challenging and talk that is not. There has been substantial research on the nature and effects of storybook reading in both home and school settings that supports their view and suggests ways in which read-alouds can maximize student vocabulary learning (Neuman & Dickinson, 2001). Some of the findings include:

- Children can learn the meaning of unknown words through incidental exposure during storybook reading.
- With traditional storybook readings, in the absence of scaffolding for those with less rich initial vocabularies, the vocabulary differences between children continue to grow over time.
- Children learn more words when books are read multiple times.

- Children do not benefit from being talked *at* or read *to*, but from being talked *with* and read *with* in ways requiring their response and activity.
- Natural scaffolded reading can result in more learning than highly dramatic "performance" reading by the adult.
- Children learn more words when books are read in small groups.

In sum, most researchers agree on several principles related to developing vocabulary with read-aloud storybook reading in schools. First, there should be some direct teaching and explanation of vocabulary during storybook reading in school settings. Second, adult–child discussion should be interactive, and discussion should focus on cognitively challenging ways to interact with the text rather than literal one-word or yes/no questions. The students need to be able to contribute to the discussion in a substantial way, and smaller groups of five or six allow for this type of interaction. Third, the rereading of texts in which vocabulary is repeated can maximize learning; informational texts and text sets can both capitalize on children's interest in "real" things (trucks, dinosaurs, pandas) as well as providing satisfaction on thematically related words. Lastly, the nature of the learning that occurs is different with familiar versus unfamiliar books. In an initial reading the children may focus on the plot or storyline. In subsequent readings the reasons for characters' actions, and especially unfamiliar vocabulary, may become the focus of their interest. Read-alouds can be a potent tool in exposing students to new vocabulary in a meaningful and pleasurable way.

Wide Reading

Wide reading is another hallmark of word learning, with many studies suggesting that word learning occurs normally and incidentally during normal reading (Herman, Anderson, Pearson, & Nagy, 1987; Nagy, Herman, & Anderson, 1985). Furthermore, discussion in the classroom (Stahl & Vancil, 1986) and around the dinner table (Snow, 1991) is another correlate of incidental word learning. Although this type of learning through exposure cannot guarantee the learning of specific vocabulary words, it does develop a wide, flexible, and usable general vocabulary.

Models

Teachers should also be models of word learning. We all remember the year we learned many new words in school. We had a teacher who was an avid punster, crossword puzzle aficionado, or otherwise involved in wordplay. Teachers can be sure that they and their classrooms are models of best practices by being good models of enthusiastic and pleasurable word learning. Using word games such as Hinky Pinkies, puns, puzzles, contests, and other playful activity develops this awareness in a playful and motivating way (Blachowicz & Fisher, 2004). In a detailed study of word learning in the middle elementary grades, Beck, Perfetti, and McKeown (1982) found one classroom in which the students outperformed others in word learning. Looking around the classroom, they saw a 79¢ piece of posterboard on the wall, with words entered on it by different students. When the researchers asked about this, they were told by the teacher, "Oh, that's just a little something we do each day. If the kids encounter a new and interesting word, they can tell the rest of the class about it, put it on the chart, and earn points for their team." The students became attuned to listening for new and interesting words, and this interest was validated in the classroom on a regular basis. Techniques such as "word of the day" and "mystery word" are easy, low-maintenance, inexpensive, and time-effective ways of making sure that kids are intentionally exposed to words each day and motivated to do their own word learning.

When the goal is to have students gain control of vocabulary to use for their own expression, students need many experiences that allow them to use words in meaningful ways. Use in writing and conversation, where feedback is available, is essential to durable and deep learning. Creating personal word books and dictionaries is a good first step toward ownership; use in many situations is a second step. Using new words in discussion, writing, independent projects, and wordplay develops real ownership and moves new words into students' personal vocabularies.

Wordplay

Wordplay is also an important part of the word-rich classroom. The ability to reflect on, manipulate, combine, and recombine the components of words is an important part of vocabulary learning and develops metalinguistic reflection on words as objects to be manipulated intelligently and for humor (Nagy & Scott, 2001; Tunmer, Herriman, & Nesdale, 1988). Phonemic awareness (being able to segment phonemes, such as the *am* in *ambulance*), morphological awareness (of word part meanings), and syntactic awareness (how a word functions in language) all play important parts in word learning (Carlisle, 1995; Willows & Ryan, 1986). There is also evidence that this type of learning is developmental over the school years (Johnson & Anglin, 1995; Roth, Speece, Cooper, & De la Paz, 1996).

Part of creating a "positive environment for word learning" involves having activities, games, materials, and other resources that allow students to play with words. Who would not enjoy spending a few minutes each day figuring out a *wuzzle* or word puzzle? Wuzzles and other word games and puzzles call on students to think flexibly and metacognitively about words. Much of the fun stems from the fact that words can be used in multiple ways with humorous results (see Figure 8.1).

So, our students need "word-rich" and "word-aware" classrooms, where new vocabulary is presented in rich listening and personal reading experiences, time is taken to stop and discuss new words, language is a part of all activities, and words, dictionaries, puzzles and word games, word calendars, books on riddles, and rhymes round out the environment for enthusiastic word learning.

> *Guideline 2. The effective vocabulary teacher helps students develop as independent word learners.*

Control of Learning

Good learners take control of their own learning. They can select words to study and use context, word structure, and word references to get information about important vocabulary they need to know. Studies that focus on self-selection of vocabulary suggest that when students choose words that they need to learn, they learn the word meanings more successfully and retain the meanings longer than when a teacher chooses the words. Haggard (1982) interviewed adults and secondary school learners about their memories of learning new words and found that these learners most easily retained words that were usable in their peer groups—popular among peers, occurring frequently in their readings, buzzwords

jobsinjobs

Q. Can you tell what phrase this Wuzzle (Word Puzzle) represents?

A. In between jobs

FIGURE 8.1. Wuzzle example.

in the media. Her subsequent teaching studies involving self-selection of words to be learned (Haggard, 1982, 1985; Ruddell & Shearer, 2002) suggested that the control offered by self-selection is an important factor in building a generalized vocabulary. Moreover, for students for whom English is a second language, some self-selection is critical to getting a true picture of words that confound learning (Jiminez, 1997).

With the popularity of wide reading approaches and cooperative group models of classroom instruction, Fisher, Blachowicz, and Smith (1991) examined the effects of self-selection in cooperative reading groups on word learning. The fourth-grade groups analyzed in this study were highly successful in learning a majority of the words chosen for study. In a later study with fifth- and seventh-grade readers (Blachowicz, Fisher, Costa, & Pozzi, 1993) the results were repeated and new information was added. The teachers who were coresearchers in the study were interested not only in whether the words were learned but also in whether the students chose challenging words for study. In all groups studied, the students consistently chose words at or above grade level for study. These and other studies indicate that self-selection and self-study processes can work effectively in the classroom. Collaborative word choice, with the students selecting some words to be learned and the teacher also contributing words for study, may be called for in content-area learning and with new difficult conceptual topics (Beyersdorfer, 1991). Combined with teacher selection and support, helping students learn to select words for self-study is a powerful tool for independent learning.

Context

Researchers suggest that learning words from context is an important part of vocabulary development but point out that it is unreasonable to expect single new contextual exposures to do the job (Baldwin & Schatz, 1985). Students need to understand context and how to use it.

Although several studies have provided intensive instruction in contextual analysis with mixed results, recent instructional studies suggest that successful context-use instruction involves explicit instruction, good planning, practice and feedback, scaffolding that leads to more student responsibility, and a metacognitive focus (Blachowicz & Fisher, 2006; Buikema & Graves, 1993; Kuhn & Stahl, 1998). For example, a teacher might choose particular words from students' reading to teach how to predict meaning and look for clues. Similarly, instruction focusing on structural analysis or morphology (the learning of word parts, such as the Greek roots *tele-* and *graph*) can be helpful in learning new words while reading, as long as a teacher emphasizes problem solving.

Dictionary

Students also need supportive instruction in learning how to use the dictionary—an important word-learning tool. Every teacher who has watched a student struggle to look up a word knows that using a dictionary can be a complex and difficult task. Stories of dictionary use often take on a "kids say the darndest things" aura: The student whose only meaning of *sharp* has to do with good looks feels vindicated by finding "acute" as one meaning for *sharp* in the dictionary ("That sure is acute boy in my class"). Another, noting that *erode* is defined as "eats out," produces the sentence "Since my mom went back to work my family erodes a lot" (Miller & Gildea, 1987). Aside from providing humorous anecdotes for the teacher's room, dictionaries and dictionary use are coming under closer scrutiny by those involved in instruction. Students do not automatically understand how dictionaries work or how they can most effectively take information from them.

The use of morphology, word parts such as prefixes, suffixes, roots, and the other elements needed to break a word's meaning apart, is also an important strategy. Breaking words apart not only helps students learn and remember those specific words but also supplies them with the building blocks to understand new words they encounter (Carlisle, 2000). For morphology instruction, contextual analysis, and work with dictionaries, it is wise to remember to work from the known to the unknown. As students engage in learning any one of these processes, it is important for them to understand the underlying rationale. This is best achieved through exploration of the "how-to" with familiar words and phrases. Once they have mastered easy words, they can practice with more and more difficult words until the process becomes automatic.

> *Guideline 3. The effective vocabulary teacher uses instructional strategies that not only teach vocabulary but also model good word-learning behaviors.*

The effective vocabulary teacher presents new vocabulary in ways that model good learning. This involves developing learners who are active, who personalize their learning and look for multiple sources of information to build meaning, and who are playful with words.

Good learners are active. As in all learning situations, a hallmark of good instruction is having the learners actively attempt to construct their own meanings. Learning new words as we have new experiences is one of the most durable and long-lasting ways to develop a rich vocabulary. For example, the words *thread, needle, selvage, pattern,* and *dart* may be learned naturally in the context of learning to sew, just as *hit, run, base,* and *fly* take on special meanings for a baseball player. This is particularly important with students whose primary language is not English. They may need the additional contextual help of physical objects and movement to internalize English vocabulary. Another way for students to become actively involved in discovering meaning is by answering questions that ask them to evaluate different features of word meaning (Beck & McKeown, 1983). For example, answering and explaining one's answer to the question "Would a recluse enjoy parties?" helps students focus on the important features of the word *recluse,* a person who chooses to be alone rather than with others. As noted earlier, discussion is another way to involve learners in examining facets of word meaning.

Graphic Organizers

Making word meanings and relationships visible is another way to involve students actively in constructing word meaning. Semantic webs, maps, organizers, or other relational charts, such as the one in Figure 8.2, not only graphically display attributes of meanings but also provide a memory organizer for later word use. Many studies have shown the efficacy of putting word meaning into a graphic form such as a map or web (Heimlich

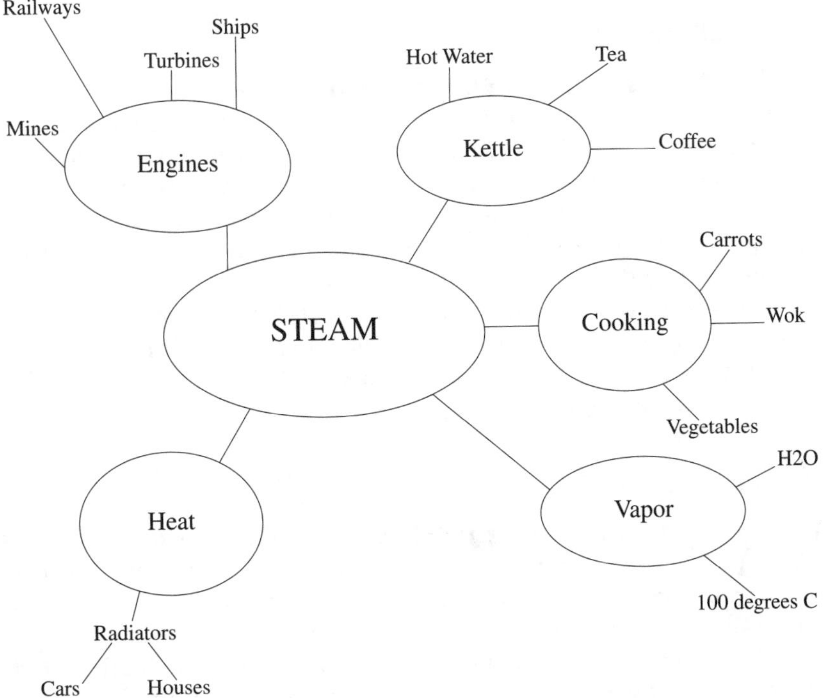

FIGURE 8.2. Web/map.

& Pittelman, 1986) or a semantic feature chart (Pittelman, Heimlich, Berglund, & French, 1991), advanced organizer, or other graphic form. It is critical to note, however, that mere construction of such maps, without discussion, is not effective (Stahl & Vancil, 1986).

Clustering Techniques

Other approaches that stress actively relating words to one another are clustering strategies that call for students to group words into related sets, brainstorming, grouping and labeling (Marzano & Marzano, 1988), designing concept hierarchies (Wixson, 1986), or constructing definition maps related to conceptual hierarchies (Bannon, Fisher, Pozzi, & Wessell, 1990–1991; Schwartz & Raphael, 1985) mapping words according to their relation to story structure categories (Blachowicz, 1986). All these approaches involve student construction of maps, graphs, charts, webs, or clusters that represent the semantic relatedness of words under study to other words and concepts. Again, discussion, sharing, and use of the words are necessary components of active involvement, as are feedback and scaffolding on the part of the teacher.

Personalizing Learning

Effective learners make learning personal. We have already commented that one of the most durable ways to learn words is in the context of learning some important skill. When we do so, word meanings are personalized by our experiences. Words not learned in firsthand experiences can also be personalized; relating new words to one's own past experiences has been a component of many successful studies. Eeds and Cockrum (1985) had students provide prior knowledge cues for new words, a method related to that used by Carr and Mazur-Stewart (1988), who asked students to construct personal cues to meaning, along with graphic and other methods. Acting out word meaning (Duffelmeyer, 1980) has also led to increased word learning.

Mnemonic Strategies

Creating one's own mnemonic or image is another way to personalize meaning. While active, semantically rich instruction and learning seem best for learning new concepts, tagging a new label onto a well-established concept can be done through the creation of associations. For example, we all know that feeling of being happy, when everything is right with the world, so we have a concept for the word *euphoria*. Mnemonic strategies, those strategies aimed at helping us remember, such as ROY G. BIV for the colors of the spectrum (red, orange, yellow, green, blue, indigo, violet), are time-honored ways to assist memory. Keyword methods are the best known of these word-learning strategies. They involve the creation of a verbal connection, an image, or a picture to help cement the meaning in memory. For example, to remember *phototropism*, the bending of plants toward light, a student created the picture in Figure 8.3 as a visual mnemonic. The verbal labels *photographer* and *tropical plant* aided in memorizing the word; the bending toward the light supplied a visual image to support it. Another student created a keyword sentence, "A photo was taken of the plant bending toward light." When trying to remember, one student would call up the picture in her mind; the other would think of the sentence, with "photo" providing an acoustic cue and "bending toward light" a meaning clue.

A significant amount of research has examined the use of the keyword method as a remembering technique (Levin, 1993) for special education students (Scruggs, Mastropieri, & Levin, 1985), for second-language learners, and for adult learners (McCarville, 1993). Although reviews of the research suggest that the keyword may be limited in its application, it remains a useful approach for remembering specific word labels, especially combined with imagery, drawing, and other tools for personalization.

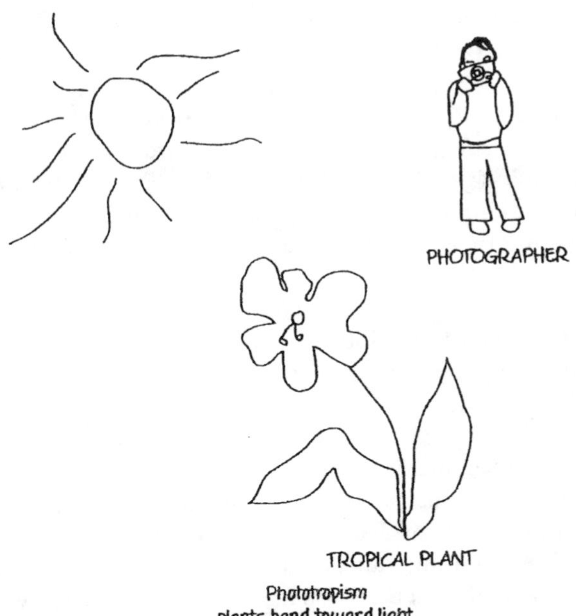

FIGURE 8.3. Keyword for *phototropism*. From Blachowicz and Fisher (2002). Copyright 2002 by Camille Blachowicz. Reprinted by permission.

Guideline 4. The effective vocabulary teacher provides explicit instruction for important content and concept vocabulary, drawing on multiple sources of meaning.

Although contextualized word learning in wide reading, discussion, listening, and engaging in firsthand learning provides a great deal of word learning, explicit instruction can also contribute to vocabulary development (Biemiller, 2001). This is most appropriate in the content areas, where students need a shared set of vocabulary to progress in their learning. It is hard to have a discussion about phototropism if the words *plant, sun, bend,* and *light* have not already been established in the learner's vocabulary. Shared content vocabulary is required for group learning.

Numerous studies comparing definitional instruction with incidental learning from context or with no-instruction control conditions support the notion that teaching definitions results in learning. However, students who received instructions that combined definitional information with other active processing, such as adding contextual information, writing contextual discovery, or rich manipulation of words, all exceeded the performance of students who received only definitional instruction (see Blachowicz & Fisher, 2000, for a review of this research). A meta-analysis of studies that compared different types of instruction (Stahl & Fairbanks, 1986) concluded that methods with multiple sources of information for students provide superior word learning. In effective classrooms, students encounter words in context and work to create or understand appropriate definitions, synonyms, and other word relations.

Therefore, teachers can model mature word-learning strategies by helping students gather information across texts and sources. Students should keep looking for different types of information that will flesh out the meaning they need to understand. Students benefit from the following:

- Definitional information
- Contextual information
- Usage examples

They also profit from manipulating words in many contexts.

Definitional information can be provided in many ways. Giving synonyms and antonyms provides information on what a word is or is not. Creating definitions using frames (see Figure 8.4) or other models helps students understand what a dictionary can provide. Example sentences clue students into nuance as well as usage. Semantic maps (as exemplified earlier), webs, feature analysis, and comparing and contrasting words all help students gain definitional information.

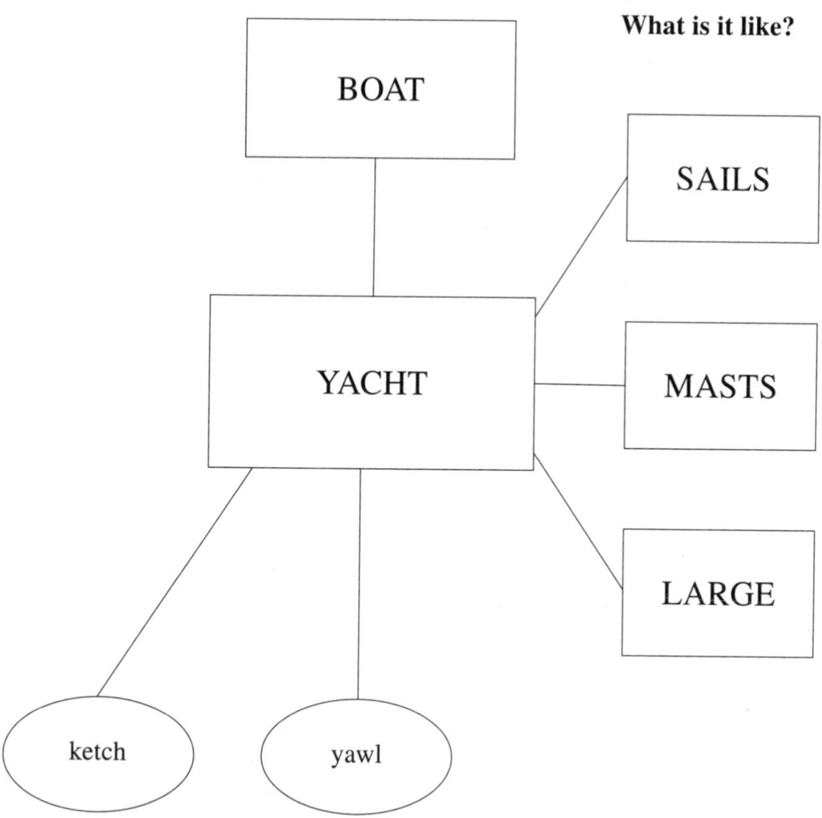

FIGURE 8.4. Concept of definition map.

Care must be taken that the students see the words in context and have chances to use the words with feedback. Teachers often present usage sentences for choice and discussion. For example, for the word *feedback,* the teacher might present the following and ask students to choose the correct usage.

We gave him feedback on his choices.
We were feedbacked by the teacher.

As in all vocabulary activities, discussion is the key. After choice and discussion, the teacher could ask each student to do two things: (1) Locate a sentence or paragraph in the text where the word is used and explain the meaning, and/or (2) write and illustrate an original sentence.

Guideline 5. The effective vocabulary teacher uses assessment that matches the goal of instruction.

The final guideline relates to the complexity of the vocabulary instruction suggested in our introduction. We teach words for so many different purposes and require varying levels and types of understanding according to the task, the word, and the subject area. In general, it is helpful to think of two main dimensions for vocabulary knowledge—depth and breadth.

Depth refers to how much is known about a particular word: Can you recognize the meaning in text or conversation, can you use it appropriately, or can you define it? We all have the experience of being asked "What does *energetic* mean?" and replying "Well, Lassie is energetic when she runs all over the house and barks at everything." We tend to supply examples to illustrate meaning rather than to give a definition. This is probably appropriate in many situations and relies on the questioner's ability to use the context we provide to elaborate on the basic meaning of the word. We often do this even when we could give a definition, but on many occasions we do it because we know how to use a word, perhaps *calligraphy*, but are unsure of the precise meaning. Other times we can understand some of the meaning of a word when we hear or see someone use it—and yet not feel comfortable about using it ourselves. We learn more about words each time we see or hear them; that is, we increase our depth of understanding. In relation to classrooms, it is helpful to consider what level of understanding is needed for successful completion of the task. Perhaps, when reading a particular selection, it is enough to know that a *pallet* is a form of bed, or maybe it is necessary to know what distinguishes it from other beds (it is made of straw) because it is part of a social studies unit that connects living styles to the environment.

Breadth of knowledge of a word is related to depth insofar as it can add layers of understanding, but breadth is concerned primarily with how a word is connected to other words in a domain of learning. For example, do students understand the relations among the words *plains, rivers, mountains, foothills,* and *erosion*? Students in the fourth grade may need to see how each relates to the other when studying a unit on the Great Plains. However, their depth of understanding of *erosion* may be limited as compared to that of a high school geography student or a geomorphologist.

Baker, Simmons, and Kameenui (1995) have argued that an important principle of vocabulary instruction is that it should be aligned with the depth of word knowledge required in any setting. We understand this to mean that teachers should decide how much students need to know about a word's meaning before teaching it. For example, is it enough that students learn that an *echidna* is a small Australian mammal, or do they need to know more about its appearance and habitat? We would add that the assessment should match the instruction in relation to both depth and breadth of word knowledge. This may sound complicated, but it is not. Many instructional techniques can also be used as assessment techniques, so that a teacher can evaluate a student's understanding in authentic learning situations.

Assessing Vocabulary Breadth

One way to know what students have learned about a broad range of words is to use and analyze pre- and postinstruction graphic organizers that ask students to work with sets of related words. Knowledge ratings, semantic mapping and webbing, Vocab-O-Grams, semantic feature analysis, structured overviews, and other graphic organizers can reveal to a teacher what students have learned about groups of terms. Mapping activities can be done individually or in groups and allow a teacher to keep tabs on word learning without testing. Alternatively, a teacher can test what individuals have learned by presenting graphic organizers that are partially completed.

Assessing Vocabulary Depth

Sometimes, rather than assessing breadth of knowledge, we want to analyze how deeply students understand central terms. If we expect students to have a deep knowledge, such as a definition, an alternative to writing a definition is to have them complete a concept of definition map (Schwartz & Raphael, 1985; see Figure 8.4). Using this alternative allows a teacher to see where students' knowledge is incomplete: Do they know a category, distinguishing characteristics, and examples, or only some of these parts of a definition?

The ability to use a term is often regarded as less difficult than defining it. When you want to know about students' ability to use a new term correctly, rather than resorting to such a simplistic method as "See how many of this week's new words you can use in one story"—a technique sure to produce distorted and contrived usage—you can ask students to use vocabulary in meaningful ways in the context of some larger activities. The most direct way to do this is to ask students to incorporate particular words in their responses to questions, and their summaries and retellings. Observing students' use of words in discussion, in lessons, and in writing is a means of evaluating their vocabulary usage in the most authentic way. Many teachers compose their own "rubrics," or structured ways of looking at vocabulary and rating usage. If you keep a notebook with a page for each student, you can pull out sheets for a few students each day to make observations or enter information on the sheet when you notice something in your daily anecdotal records. In addition to observing students in action in discussion and writing, you might ask students to keep lists of words that interest them and that they encounter in reading. You can designate specific words as journal additions, and review can serve as assessment.

Another alternative for evaluating word usage is to use word monitors for discussion. A student in a discussion group can be designated as a "word monitor" to chart the number of times particular teacher-selected words are used. The monitor for that word can also be charged to survey each student in the group about the word's meaning and ask each to supply a usage for a designated word or words. Records turned into the teacher can be used as assessment.

Some teachers use Word Walls or vocabulary charts as part of assessment. Students can be assigned to construct a collection of new words in a word bank, list, or dictionary, or on a Word Wall or bulletin board. A teacher can have periodic 3-minute meetings in which she selects 10 words from the collections and asks students to use them in a meaningful way.

Along with the use of teacher assessment methods, it may be important to ask students to evaluate themselves in terms of their word learning. Using knowledge ratings and other techniques, you can encourage students to become self-reflective about the words they need to learn and the ways they need to go about learning them.

Finally, for assessing students' ability to recognize a meaning for a word, teacher-constructed tests may be appropriate. These tests can take many forms and usually test recognition (the ability to select an appropriate answer) rather than the more difficult recall (the ability to provide a word from memory). Typical teacher-made tests are types of recall assessment that involve defining a word by

1. Giving/choosing a synonym (a *diadem* is a *crown*).
2. Giving/choosing a classification (a *shrimp* is a *crustacean*).
3. Giving/choosing examples (*flowers* are things, such as daisies, roses, mums).
4. Giving/choosing an explanation of how something is used (a *shovel* is a *tool* used to dig holes).
5. Giving/choosing an opposite.
6. Giving/choosing a definition.
7. Giving/choosing a picture.
8. Giving/choosing a word to complete a context.

Tests that you make for the classroom should be easy and efficient to use. You will also want to ask the following questions:

1. Do the items and the process call on students to do the same things you typically ask them to do in class? If your normal question in class asks that students supply a synonym, then asking for an antonym on a test does not make much sense.
2. Will answering the item provide useful repetition of vocabulary or make students think more deeply about it? If the test item is an exact repetition of something you did earlier, then it may be testing rote memory rather than more creative or extensive thinking.
3. Will the knowledge you draw on be useful and relevant to the course in which the assessment is taking place? If you are testing aspects of word knowledge not relevant to the topic, your efforts may be counterproductive.
4. Does your test format match your instructional format? If you have stressed usage in instruction, test for usage. If you have emphasized word recognition, test for recognition.

An important part of all assessment is keeping records to show growth and change. Both students and teachers can keep records in the classroom to record change and growth. Students may use word files and notebooks to record their developing knowledge. These may become part of a portfolio. In addition to test records, you may also want to keep anecdotal records, using the type of techniques already suggested. The records that you keep will help you become a more effective vocabulary teacher by aligning your assessment with instruction and vice versa.

BEST PRACTICES IN ACTION

You can tell that Angela, a fourth-grade teacher, loves words and wordplay from the moment you walk into her classroom. A poster headed "New Words We Like" is displayed prominently on the front wall. It is filled with entries from students, with some words spilling over onto the wall on index cards. For each word, there is an entry, a description of where the student encountered the word, such as the one for *vile,* which the student illustrated with a drawing and verbal description of her sister's shoes (see Figure 8.5). Each student who used the word during the week could add his or her initials to the picture with another example.

In the library area, a shelf of riddle, joke, and pun books holds many well-thumbed volumes, and a "joke of the day" is posted on the wall. The

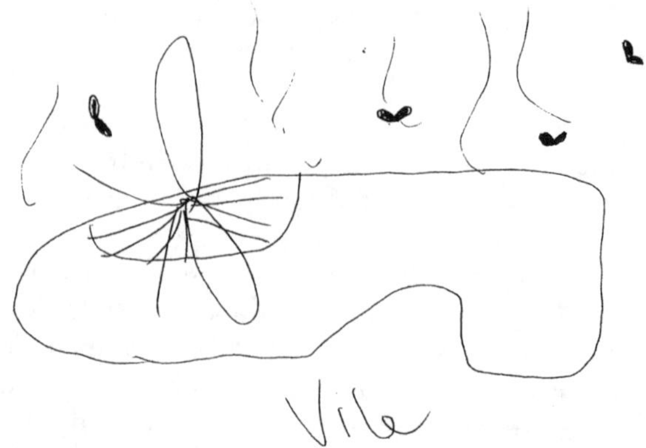

FIGURE 8.5. Personal word record: *vile.* "My brother says my sister's shoes smell vile. *Vile* = really bad, nasty."

bookcase also has a multitude of dictionaries—sports dictionaries, animal dictionaries, dictionaries of tools, and others. On the bottom shelf, a number of word games are stored, including Boggle, Scrabble, Pictionary, and their junior versions. There is also a basket of crossword books nearby and blank forms for making crossword puzzles. The nearby computer has a crossword puzzle program that is well used. There is also a box of discs called "Personal Dictionaries" on which students keep their own word lists. For some, a simple list in table form is used. These can be easily alphabetized and realphabetized with each addition. Other students like to use HyperCard stacks to keep their word files, so that they can resort them in different ways.

Rather than having a set of dictionaries stored on her bookshelf, Angela has dictionaries in convenient locations around the room. These range from hardbound collegiate dictionaries to more accessible softbacks at a range of levels. She also has several "learner's dictionaries" (e.g., *American Heritage Dictionary*, 2000), which are intended for students who are learning English. These define words functionally instead of classically, and Angela finds that many students like to use them, not just her English-as-a-second-language (ESL) students.

Angela's day starts with a word of the week, in which she poses a puzzle such as "Would a *ruthless* person be a good social worker?" If some students have a view, they answer and explain their reasoning. If no one has anything to offer, Angela presents the word in a few context sentences and then provides a definition. No more than 5 minutes are spent on this activity, and she varies the format. Sometimes she presents a word as a puzzle, sometimes as a guessing game, and so forth.

Today the class is starting a new unit on whales, so Angela begins with a Vocab-O-Gram (Blachowicz, 1986) brainstorming. She puts up a piece of chart paper (see Figure 8.6) and begins by having students brainstorm the words they already know about whales and enter these words on the chart in the categories related to the "grammar" of the selection. As the unit progresses, more and more words will be added, and new categories will be drawn out of the "Other interesting words" category. Because she has many ESL students in her class, Angela uses the "Vocabulary Visit" (Blachowicz & Obrochta, 2005) model of scaffolding, recording and revisiting thematic content material over the course of the unit.

In math class, students are busy working on their graphic dictionary of math terms, showing types of angles labeled with their names. In literature time, students are engaged in self-selection words for study from *The Castle in the Attic* (Winthrop, 1986), their core book for the unit. As they read their self-selected books on medieval life, they add to their personal lists.

At the end of each school day, Angela reads from a chapter book that her class has chosen. She asks the students to choose from a list of conceptually rich books that are too difficult for most of the children to read on their own. Each day, at the end of the reading, she asks students to pick a "wonderful word" the author used from that day's reading, and they add it to their wonderful word list. The day ends, as it began, with the wonder of words.

REFLECTIONS AND FUTURE DIRECTIONS

In 2003, Hispanic students represented 19% of public school enrollment, up from 6% in 1972 (National Center for Educational Statistics, 2005). This is only part of the increase in English language learners in the schools system. While we know all children are language learners, educating an increasingly diverse student population whose first language is not English presents a special challenge, particularly in the area of vocabulary development (Blachowicz & Fisher, 2000). Finding creative and effective

Habitat/home	Description/types	Food
Predators/prey	Life/cycle	Other interesting words

FIGURE 8.6. Vocab-O-Gram.

means for developing the vocabularies of diverse learners will be a major challenge of this decade. This is a critical issue for equity as well as for instruction.

CONCLUDING COMMENTS

All of us are vocabulary teachers when we work with students in classrooms. We teach them new ways of looking at the world and, in doing so, develop new concepts and understandings. Every day, we teach words in a variety of ways. Our obligation to the students is not just to be vocabulary teachers but the best vocabulary teachers that we can be. Following the five evidence-based guidelines will make our classrooms homes for motivated word learners whose interest and skill in learning new words will grow along with their vocabularies.

ENGAGEMENT ACTIVITIES

1. Choose a vocabulary word from a text selection you will use with students. Construct a vocabulary frame for that word (see Figure 8.3 for an example). Then develop three contextual sentences, each of which gives a clue to the meaning. Lastly, develop two usage-choice sentences. Try them out with a classmate or with students in class. Write a reflection on what worked and what did not. How would you modify what you did?
2. Choose a vocabulary website below to use with your students. Describe the directions you would give them to use it. (See the Reading Center website—*www2.nl.edu/reading_center*—for some other sites to start with or search in your browser.)
3. Develop a Vocab-O-Gram for a selection. Use it to select the words you would teach. Try it out with a classmate or with students in class. Write a reflection on what worked and what did not. How would you modify what you did?

RESOURCES FOR FURTHER LEARNING

Books for Further Reading

Allen, J. (1999). *Words, words, words: Teaching vocabulary in grades 4–12.* York, ME: Stenhouse.

Beck, I. L., McKeown, M. G., & Kucan, L. (2002). *Bringing words to life: Robust vocabulary instruction.* New York: Guilford Press.

Blachowicz, C., & Fisher, P. (2002). *Teaching vocabulary in all classrooms* (2nd ed.). Columbus, OH: Prentice-Hall.

Ganske, K. (2000). *Word journeys: Assessment-guided phonics, spelling, and vocabulary instruction.* New York: Guilford Press.

Johnson, D. D. (2000). *Vocabulary in the elementary and middle school.* Boston: Allyn & Bacon.

Stahl, S. S. (1999). *Vocabulary development.* Cambridge, MA: Brookline Books.

Websites

General

Vocabulary websites on the National College of Education Reading Center website.

www2.nl.edu/reading_center

Research

National Center to Improve the Tools of Educators (NCITE) Reading Research Synthesis
NCITE Research Synthesis: Reading and Diverse Learners NCITE staff reviewed reading research on the design of instructional materials for diverse learners in six general areas: vocabulary acquisition, word recognition, text organization, emergent literacy, fluency, and comprehension.

idea.uoregon.edu/~ncite/documents/techre. . . .

Vocabulary Acquisition Research Group
Centre for Applied Language Studies
University of Wales
Swansea Vocabulary Research Group

www.swan.ac.uk/cals/calsres.html

Vocabulary Improvement Project (VIP)
The VIP is a national research program funded by the U.S. Department of Education. The Project's main goal is to develop intervention strategies aimed at helping children who are learning English.

mind.ucsc.edu/vip

Games

Vocabulary.com
Vocabulary puzzles and games

www.vocabulary.com

The Word Detective
Ezine with column about words and their meanings

www.word-detective.com

Adventures of Vocabulary Van
Learn new things and meet new friends in this adventure of words and creative fun. Meet Vocabulary Van and join her in her adventures.

kidslangarts.about.com/kids/kidslangarts . . .

ESL

Interactive Audio–Picture English Lessons
Offers interactive ESL with pronunciation and pictures.
www.web-books.com/Language

EnglishCLUB.net
Features grammar and vocabulary activities, word games, pen pal listings, and question-and-answer service. Includes free classroom handouts for ESL teachers.
www.englishclub.net

Learn English—Have Fun
Offers online English crosswords, ESL word games, jokes, tests, and word-search puzzles. New games and crosswords added regularly.
www.englishday.com

Interesting Things for ESL Students
Free Web-based textbook and fun study site. Daily Page for English, proverbs, slang, anagrams, quizzes, and more.
www.aitech.ac.jp/~itesls

REFERENCES

American Heritage Dictionary for learners of English. (2000). Boston: Houghton Mifflin.

Baker, S. K., Simmons, D. C., & Kameenui, E. J. (1995). *Vocabulary acquisition: Curricular and instructional implications for diverse learners* (Technical Report No. 14). Eugene, OR: National Center to Improve the Tools of Educators, University of Oregon.

Baldwin, R. S., & Schatz, E. I. (1985). Context clues are ineffective with low frequency words in naturally occurring prose. In J. A. Niles & R. V. Lalik (Eds.), *Issues in literacy: A research perspective* (34th Yearbook of the National Reading Conference, pp. 132–135). Rochester, NY: National Reading Conference.

Bannon, E., Fisher, P. J. L., Pozzi, L., & Wessel, D. (1990–1991). Effective definitions for word learning. *Journal of Reading, 34,* 301–303.

Beck, I. L., & McKeown, M. G. (1983). Learning words well—a program to enhance vocabulary and comprehension. *The Reading Teacher, 36,* 622–625.

Beck, I., Perfetti, C., & McKeown, M. (1982). The effects of long-term vocabulary instruction on lexical access and reading comprehension. *Journal of Educational Psychology, 74,* 506–521.

Beyersdorfer, J. M. (1991). *Middle school students' strategies for selection of vocabulary in science texts.* Unpublished doctoral dissertation, National-Louis University, Evanston, IL.

Biemiller, A. (2001). Teaching vocabulary: Early, direct, and sequential. *American Educator, 25*(1), 24–28, 47.

Blachowicz, C. L. Z. (1986). Making connections: Alternatives to vocabulary notebook. *Journal of Reading, 29,* 643–649.

Blachowicz, C. L. Z., & Fisher, P. J. L. (2000). Vocabulary instruction. In R. Barr, M. L. Kamil, P. B. Mosenthal, & P. D. Pearson (Eds.), *Handbook of reading research* (Vol. 3, pp. 503–523). New York: Longman.

Blachowicz, C., & Fisher, P. (2004). Putting the "fun" back in fundamental: Word play in the classroom. In J. F. Baumann & E. J. Kame'enui (Eds.), *Vocabulary instruction: Research to practice.* New York: Guilford Press.

Blachowicz, C., & Fisher, P. (2006). *Teaching vocabulary in all classrooms* (3rd ed.). Columbus, OH: Prentice-Hall.

Blachowicz, C. L. Z., Fisher, P. J. L., Costa, M., & Pozzi, M. (1993, November). *Researching vocabulary learning in middle school cooperative reading groups: A teacher–researcher collaboration.* Paper presented at the 10th Great Lakes Regional Reading Conference, Chicago.

Blachowicz, C. L. Z., & Obrochta, C. (2005). Vocabulary visits: Developing content vocabulary in the primary grades. *Reading Teacher, 59,* 262–269.

Buikema, J. L., & Graves, M. F. (1993). Teaching students to use context clues to infer word meanings. *Journal of Reading, 36,* 450–457.

Carlisle, J. (1995). Morphological awareness and early reading achievement. In L. Feldman (Ed.), *Morphological aspects of language processing* (pp. 189–209). Hillsdale, NJ: Erlbaum.

Carlisle, J. F. (2000). Awareness of the structure and meaning of morphologically complex words: Impact on reading. *Reading and Writing: An Interdisciplinary Journal, 12,* 169–190.

Carr, E. M., & Mazur-Stewart, M. (1988). The effects of the vocabulary overview guide on vocabulary comprehension and retention. *Journal of Reading Behavior, 20,* 43–62.

Cunningham, A. E., & Stanovich, K. E. (1998, spring/summer). What reading does for the mind. *American Educator,* pp. 8–17.

De Temple, J., & Snow, C. (2003). Learning words from books. In A. V. Kleeck, S. A. Stahl, & E. B. Bauer (Eds.), *On reading books to children: Parents and teachers* (pp. 16–36). Mahwah, NJ: Erlbaum.

Duffelmeyer, F. A. (1980). The influence of experience-based vocabulary instruction on learning word meanings. *Journal of Reading, 24,* 35–40.

Eeds, M., & Cockrum, W. A. (1985). Teaching word meanings by expanding schemata vs. dictionary work vs. reading in context. *Journal of Reading, 28,* 492–497.

Eller, R. G., Pappas, C. C., & Brown, E. (1988). The lexical development of kindergartners: Learning from written context. *Journal of Reading Behavior, 20,* 5–24.

Elley, W. B. (1988). Vocabulary acquisition from listening to stories. *Reading Research Quarterly, 24,* 174–187.

Fisher, P. J. L., Blachowicz, C. L. Z., & Smith, J. C. (1991). Vocabulary learning in literature discussion groups. In J. Zutell & S. McCormick (Eds.), *Learner factors/teacher factors: Issues in literacy research and instruction* (40th Yearbook of the National Reading Conference, pp. 201–209). Chicago: National Reading Conference.

Haggard, M. R. (1982). The vocabulary self-selection strategy: An active approach to word learning. *Journal of Reading, 26,* 634–642.

Haggard, M. R. (1985). An interactive strategies approach to content reading. *Journal of Reading, 29,* 204–210.

Hart, B., & Risley, T. R. (1995). *Meaningful differences in the everyday experience of young American children.* Baltimore: Brookes.

Heimlich, J. E., & Pittelman, S. D. (1986). *Semantic mapping: Classroom applications.* Newark, DE: International Reading Association.

Herman, P. A., Anderson, R. C., Pearson, P. D., & Nagy, W. E. (1987). Incidental acquisition of word meaning from expositions with varied text features. *Reading Research Quarterly, 22,* 263–284.

Jiminez, R. J. (1997). The strategic reading abilities and potential of five low-literacy Latina/o readers in middle school. *Reading Research Quarterly, 32,* 224–243.

Johnson, C. J., & Anglin, J. M. (1995). Qualitative developments in the content and form of children's definitions. *Journal of Speech and Hearing Research, 38,* 612–629.

Kuhn, M., & Stahl, S. (1998). Teaching children to learn word meanings from con-text: A synthesis and some questions. *Journal of Literacy Research, 30,* 119–138.

Levin, J. R. (1993). Mnemonic strategies and classroom learning: A twenty year report card. *Elementary School Journal, 94,* 235–244.

Marzano, R. J., & Marzano, J. S. (1988). *A cluster approach to elementary vocabulary instruction.* Newark, DE: International Reading Association.

McCarville, K. B. (1993). Keyword mnemonic and vocabulary acquisition for developmental college students. *Journal of Developmental Education, 16*(3), 2–4, 6.

Miller, G. A., & Gildea, P. M. (1987). How children learn words. *Scientific American, 257,* 94–99.

Nagy, W. E., Herman, P. A., & Anderson, R. C. (1985). Learning words from context. *Reading Research Quarterly, 20,* 233–253.

Nagy, W., & Scott, J. (2001). Vocabulary processes. In M. L. Kamil, P. B. Mosenthal, P. D. Pearson, & R. Barr (Eds.), *Handbook of reading research* (Vol. III, pp. 269–283). New York: Longman.

National Center for Educational Statistics. Retrieved August 11, 2005, from *nces.ed.gov/programs/coe/2005/section1/indicator04.asp.*

National Reading Panel. (2000). *Report of the National Reading Panel: Teaching children to read.* Washington, DC: National Academy Press.

Neuman, S. B., & Dickinson, D. K. (2001). *Handbook of early literacy research* (Vol. 1). New York: Guilford Press.

Pittelman, S. D., Heimlich, J. E., Berglund, R. L., & French, M. P. (1991). *Semantic feature analysis: Classroom applications.* Newark, DE: International Reading Association.

Robbins, C., & Ehri, L. C. (1994), Reading storybooks to kindergarteners helps them learn new vocabulary words. *Journal of Educational Psychology, 86,* 54–64.

Roth, F., Speece, D., Cooper, D., & Dela Paz, S. (1996). Unresolved mysteries: How do metalinguistic and narrative skills connect with early reading? *Journal of Special Education, 30,* 257–277.

Ruddell, M. R., & Shearer, B. A. (2002). "Extraordinary," "tremendous," "exhilarating," "magnificent": Middle school at-risk students become avid word learners with the vocabulary self-collection strategy (VSS). *Journal of Adolescent and Adult Literacy, 45,* 352–363.

Schwartz, R. M., & Raphael, T. E. (1985). Concept of definition: A key to improving students' vocabulary. *Reading Teacher, 39,* 198–205.

Scott, J., Asselin, M., Henry, S., & Butler, C. (1997, June). *Making rich language visible: Reports from a multi-dimensional study on word learning.* Paper presented at the annual meeting of the Canadian Society for the Study of Education, St. John's, Newfoundland.

Scruggs, T. E., Mastropieri, M. A., & Levin, J. R. (1985). Vocabulary acquisition of retarded students under direct mnemonic instruction. *American Journal of Mental Deficiency, 89,* 5451–5456.

Senechal, M., Thomas, E., & Monker, J. (1995). Individual differences in 5-year-olds' acquisition of vocabulary during storybook reading. *Journal of Educational Psychology, 87,* 218–229.

Snow, C. (1991). The theoretical basis of the home-school study of language and literacy development. *Journal of Research in Childhood Education, 6,* 5–10.

Stahl, S. A., & Fairbanks, M. M. (1986). The effects of vocabulary instruction: A model-based meta-analysis. *Review of Educational Research, 56,* 72–110.

Stahl, S., & Vancil, S. (1986). Discussion is what makes semantic maps work in vocabulary instruction. *Reading Teacher, 40,* 62–69.

Tunmer, W. E., Herriman, M. L., & Nesdale, A. R. (1988). Metalinguistic abilities and beginning reading. *Reading Research Quarterly, 23,* 134–158.

Whitehurst, G. J., Epstein, J. N., Angell, A. L., Payne, A. C., Crone, D. A., & Fischel, J. E. (1994). Outcomes of an emergent literacy intervention in Head Start. *Journal of Educational Psychology, 86,* 542–555.

Whitehurst, G. J., Zevenberg, A. A., Crone, D. A., Schultz, M. D., Velting, O. N., & Fischel, J. E. (1999). Outcomes of an emergent literacy intervention from Head Start through second grade. *Journal of Educational Psychology, 91,* 261–272.

Willows, D. M., & Ryan, E. B. (1986). The development of grammatical sensitivity and its relationship to early reading achievement. *Reading Research Quarterly, 21,* 253–266.

Winthrop, E. (1986). *The castle in the attic.* New York: Yearlong Books.

Wixson, K. K. (1986). Vocabulary instruction and children's comprehension of basal stories. *Reading Research Quarterly, 21,* 317–329.

Chapter 9

BEST PRACTICES IN FLUENCY INSTRUCTION

Melanie R. Kuhn
Timothy Rasinski

This chapter will:

- Describe the role of fluency in the overall reading process.
- Discuss components for effective instruction.
- Present approaches for integrating fluency instruction into the classroom.
- Suggest possible assessment options.
- Summarize future directions for research.

EVIDENCE-BASED BEST PRACTICES

According to the National Reading Panel (2000), fluency plays a critical role in the overall reading process. This is because fluent reading incorporates accurate, automatic word recognition along with the expressive rendering of text and serves as a bridge between decoding instruction and comprehension (Kuhn & Stahl, 2003; Rasinski & Hoffman, 2003). Over the past several years, it has gained an increasing amount of attention in terms of classroom practice as well. This is because fluency can make a significant difference in a student's success as a reader (e.g., Pikulski & Chard, 2005; Hudson, Lane, & Pullen, 2005).

As part of this chapter, we plan to present a range of instructional approaches that are effective for students who are both developing fluency (usually in the second and third grade) and those who have experienced difficulty with their fluency development (that is, older struggling readers). These will also cover a range of grouping situations, including individual students, pairs of learners, and flexible groups. Before delving into these strategies, however, we want to discuss why it is worth integrating fluency instruction into regular classroom instruction.

While we alluded to the importance of fluency's role in reading above, there are two aspects of fluency that are integral to reading development (Kuhn & Stahl, 2003); these are automaticity and prosody. Importantly, these elements not only characterize what it means to be a fluent word reader but also contribute to a learner's ability to construct meaning from text.

Contribution of Automatic Word Recognition to Comprehension

When it comes to word recognition, proficient readers not only identify words accurately but also recognize the vast majority of them instantly and effortlessly. In other words, they no longer need to spend a great deal of time on word recognition. This is important because, as with any cognitive task, individuals have a limited amount of attention available while reading (Adams, 1990; Laberge & Samuels, 1974; Samuels, 2004; Stanovich, 1980). As a result, whatever attention they expend on word recognition is, necessarily, attention that is unavailable for comprehension. This is especially the case for early readers. Because they are developing their decoding skills, they need to focus a great deal of their attention on word recognition, which leaves little attention for comprehension. For us as educators, the question becomes: What do students need to do to move from the point where their decoding is purposeful and effortful to the point where their word identification becomes automatic and effortless? There is a general consensus that this can best occur through practice—practice that consists of the supported reading of a wide variety of connected text (e.g., Kuhn & Stahl, 2003; Mostow & Beck, 2005; Rasinski & Hoffman, 2003). As learners repeatedly encounter words in print, they need to direct progressively less attention toward decoding them, until they eventually become part of a reader's sight word vocabulary (according to Torgesen, 2005, this occurs over the course of three to eight repetitions).

Contribution of Prosody to Reading Fluency

The second component of fluency is prosody. As we mentioned in the introduction to this chapter, fluent reading consists of more than simply reading words quickly and accurately; it also involves prosodic reading, or those elements of language that, when taken together, constitute expressive reading (Dowhower, 1991; Erekson, 2003; Schreiber, 1991). These include intonation, stress, tempo, and the use of appropriate phrasing. If you think about students who are not yet fluent readers, they tend to read either in a word-by-word manner or by grouping words in ways that deviate from oral language. On the other hand, appropriate phrasing, intonation and stress are all seen as indicators of fluent reading. And, when applied correctly, they allow written text to take on the qualities of speech. Further, when readers incorporate prosody into their oral reading, they are providing clues to an otherwise invisible process, that of comprehension. This is because prosodic elements contribute to shades of meaning and a richer understanding of what is written. While we know that prosody is closely tied to comprehension, exactly how the two are related is a matter for additional research (e.g., is the relationship reciprocal, does understanding the text allow for prosody, or does prosody lead to better comprehension? Erekson, 2003; Schwanenflugel, Hamilton, Kuhn, Wisenbaker, & Stahl, 2004). No matter what the relationship, however, the use of expression contributes to learners' engagement with text, helping to bring text to life and adding nuance to their reading.

BEST PRACTICES IN ACTION

Fluency Instruction and the Literacy Curriculum

Given the role of fluency in the reading process, it is important to determine ways to promote fluent reading in the classroom. While fluency is something we always strive for in our oral reading, it is a primary focus of reading development during the second and third grades (Chall, 1996; Stahl & Heubach, 2005). Prior to this, there is a greater emphasis on emergent literacy (kindergarten) and conscious word recognition strategies (first grade). Throughout these years, it is also important to provide modeling of literate behavior for students and to give them extensive opportunities to practice the skills they are learning as part of their literacy development. It is also essential that students be taught that reading is a meaning-making process and that comprehension is the principal reason for reading any text from the outset. However, there is a shift toward fluency, or the development of automaticity and the use of expression, during the second and third grades. Such an emphasis allows students to consolidate their growing knowledge of print and their comfort with text.

Importantly, there are a number of traits that underlie effective fluency instruction in all its forms (Rasinski, 2003). We outline these principles because it is possible to integrate some aspect of these qualities across a range of literacy curricula, depending on the needs of your learners. In addition, we outline approaches for individual learners (reading-while-listening), pairs of readers (paired repeated readings), flexible groups (authentic repeated readings, Fluency Oriented Oral Reading), and synthesized fluency routines that can become an integral part of regular classroom instruction (Fluency Development Lesson). These approaches can become regular components of your lesson plans for younger readers who are making the transition to fluency or integrated into your literacy curriculum as needed for older struggling readers who are have not achieved fluency to date.

Principles of Fluency Instruction

Rasinski (2003) outlined four basic principles that can help teachers and curriculum designers develop effective fluency instruction: (1) the teacher or some other fluent reader's modeling of fluent reading for students; (2) providing oral support for students while they themselves are reading (that support can come in the form of choral reading with a group, paired reading with a partner, or reading while listening to a prerecorded version of the text read orally); (3) practicing repeated readings of a given text (usually best done when students have a chance to perform the rehearsed text for an audience); and (4) focusing attention on reading syntactically appropriate and meaningful phrases (Rasinski, 1990). These basic principles or fluency-building blocks can be used for instruction and can be combined to create synergistic instructional routines. In the following sections we present various approaches to fluency instruction that are based on these principles.

Reading-While-Listening

Reading-while-listening, a strategy that uses audiotapes to help students develop their reading fluency, incorporates all of the principles outlined above. This approach was designed by Chomsky (1976) as a way to assist five third graders identified by their teacher as reading between 1 and 2 years below grade level. Although the students had received extensive instruction in decoding strategies, they had difficulty applying this knowledge to connected text. Since the students were competent decoders, an alternative approach to additional word recognition instruction seemed to be called for—one that would support their reading of significant amounts of connected text in an accessible format.

As such, Chomsky decided to try using tape-recorded books, since they had the potential to provide the readers with support for their word recognition, lots of opportunities to practice reading connected text, and a model of what fluent reading sounds like. She began by tape-recording two dozen books that ranged in reading level from second to fifth grade, texts that were at the upper end of the students' instructional level and that would therefore be considered challenging for the children. The children selected the books they wanted to read from among the choices available and were asked to listen to the books while reading along with the text. They also set the pace for their own reading. However, unlike a listening center in which children often listen to a story for pleasure or to develop a sense of story structure or other emergent literacy skills, the children were asked to listen to and read the story repeatedly until they were able to render the material fluently.

At first, the students encountered some difficulty coordinating their eye movements with the tape recordings, but, as they continued to work with the tapes, they became increasingly capable of following along with the story. Further, as they repeatedly listened to and read along with the tapes, the students became more fluent with the material. When they felt they were able to read their selection independently, they asked the teacher to listen to their rendering of the story. If the teacher felt the student had mastered the text, the student moved on to a new selection; otherwise, he or she was asked to continue practicing with the same text. It is also worth noting that the process became increasingly easier for the students and that it took them less time to become fluent on each subsequent selection. Perhaps even more important, however, is the fact that, as a result of the strategy, students began reading independently and began to engage in writing activities as well. This approach has been used repeatedly over the years and in various formats and has been found to be a successful way to assist learners with their fluency development (Rasinski & Hoffman, 2003).

Paired Repeated Readings

The next strategy, that of paired repeated readings, was designed as a means of taking repeated readings, a successful approach to fluency development for individual learners, and adapting it to the classroom. Repeated readings, itself, was created in response to the common classroom practice of having students read new material each day in order to develop their word recognition skills (Dahl, 1979; Samuels, 1979). However, this approach was unsuccessful with many learners. As a result, Samuels wondered whether it might be easier for students to develop automatic word recognition by increasing their practice through repetition of a given passage rather than constantly encountering new text. The procedure was designed for students who were decoding text accurately but slowly and requires that their reading rate and number of miscues be recorded after each reading. As such, it is most easily implemented in a one-on-one setting.

While repeated readings has proven to be effective across a number of studies (see Dowhower, 1989), Koskinen and Blum (1984, 1986) recognized that it was not easy to implement with large numbers of students. With this in mind, they developed an alternative approach, paired repeated reading. Like the original, this strategy allows students to read a short passage several times as a means of improving their word recognition. However, rather than working with the teacher in order to improve their reading fluency, it is designed to allow the students to work with one another. The process requires learners to practice a text they have already encountered as part of their classroom literacy curriculum, whether as part of their shared or their guided reading lessons. Ideally, the teacher will have introduced the text through an expressive oral reading of the selection so students will know what a fluent rendering of the selection sounds like.

At this point, it is also useful to discuss with your students how to provide each other with positive feedback, something that will be required of them during the rereading component of the activity. Suggestions such as "I thought your reading was quicker," "I think you are getting more words right," or "You read that with more expression" are all examples of the type of appropriate encouragement students can give to each other. After discussing a range of encouraging comments, the class is divided into pairs. This can best be accomplished by making a list of your students, starting with your most skilled reader and working your way toward your most struggling reader. Once the list is compiled, it should be divided in half, and the names should be matched across so that your most skilled reader is paired with one of your average students (at the top) and one of your average students is paired with your most struggling reader (at the bottom) in order to ensure that a reasonable but not excessive gap exists between the readers.

The next step in this process requires each student in the pair to select approximately a 50- to 100-word passage from their texts. It is worth noting that, if the students are reading from the same selection, each student should be asked to choose a different passage in order to prevent the students from directly comparing their reading ability to each other. Students can also decide who is to read aloud first, although the creation of an alternating schedule can again help to minimize disputes. The students are then asked to read their passages through four times, once silently and three times aloud. The initial silent reading allows students to become comfortable with the passage. This is followed by the first student reading his or her passage aloud. After completing each reading of the passage, the reader assesses his or her own performance, recording how well they did on a self-evaluation sheet. Additionally, the partner is also expected to listen carefully and, after the second and third attempt, comment on ways in which the performance has improved. The listener then records his or her comments on a listening sheet. After the first reader is done, the pair switches roles, and the second student takes over as the reader while the first reader serves as the listener.

Because paired repeated reading can be used with the entire class or with smaller reading groups, it is easy to integrate into the literacy curriculum. For example, it can be used in a whole-class format as part of the class's shared reading time, or it can be used as an alternative to independent seatwork while the teacher works with a particular group of students. Further, the research conducted with paired repeated readings (Koskinen & Blum, 1984, 1986) indicates that students using the approach improve in terms of both accurate and automatic word recognition, a key component of fluent reading. And, since reading with expression is emphasized as part of the performance criteria, it seems likely that students will begin to integrate this element into their reading as well. Finally, it appears that the improvements made on the practiced passages transfer to previously unread text, thereby improving learners' overall fluency, the ultimate goal for any of these procedures.

Authentic Repeated Reading

Repeated readings of a given text can be done for a number of reasons—to increase reading rate, accuracy, or expression. Most commercial programs aimed at developing fluency through repeated reading focus on improving students' reading rate. This practice tends to take students' focus off the main reason for reading—comprehension—and may eventually cause the procedure to become a tedious and meaningless activity for students.

Another goal for repeated readings is performance (Rasinski, 2003)—students rehearse a text several times in order to prepare for a performance of the text to an audience. This approach makes repeated readings (rehearsal) a more authentic experience for students and gives them an authentic purpose for the practice. Certain genres of texts are designed for performance. Among these are scripts (Readers' Theatre), poetry, song lyrics, oratory (speeches), chants, and other texts rich in the author's voice.

Incorporating performance—and the use of texts that are meant to be performed—can provide students with authentic motivation to practice and to make their oral rendering of a passage meaningful and expressive, not simply fast. Classroom studies of the use of performance as the basis for repeated reading have been positive (Griffith & Rasinski, 2004; Martinez, Roser, & Strecker, 1999). In both studies, teachers divided students into small repertory groups that rehearsed authentic performance passages throughout the week. At the end of the week the groups performed their scripts, poems, or other texts to their classmates and classroom visitors who constituted the authentic audience.

Fluency Oriented Oral Reading

One element all of the foregoing approaches have in common is the expectation that learners reread a given text until they can read it fluently. For many years, repetition was considered a key element in aiding the fluency development of many learners. However, in their review of research on fluency interventions, Kuhn and Stahl (2003) noted that when students who were using a repeated readings approach were compared with students who read equivalent amounts of text with support, both groups made equivalent gains. In order to explore this possibility further, Kuhn (2004–2005) compared two forms of small-group fluency instruction with second-grade struggling readers, one using repetition and the other using the wide reading of a number of texts. Additionally, she included a group that listened to, but did not read, the texts used by the fluency groups and a control group.

The program involved working with small groups of students (five to six per group) for 15–20 minutes per session three times per week. Since the students were struggling second-grade readers, and since the goal was to scaffold, or support, the students' reading of texts slightly beyond their instructional level, the texts they read ranged from a late first to an early third-grade reading level (FEP/Booksource, 1998; Fountas & Pinnell, 1999) and included titles such as *Big Max* (Platt, 1992), *The Golly Sisters Go West* (Byars, 1985), and *Whistle for Willie* (Keats, 1977). The first group of learners used a modified repeated readings technique, or Fluency Oriented Oral Reading (FOOR). This consisted of echo or choral reading a single trade book three times over the course of a week (i.e., the same book was read for each of the week's three 15- to 20-minute sessions). The second condition, or Wide Reading approach, involved a single echo or choral reading of three different texts, or one text for each session. The third group listened to all the stories that were presented to the Wide Reading group but did not read the texts themselves, and the control group did not receive any extra reading instruction beyond what was occurring in their classroom.

The approaches were very simple, but the results were quite interesting. Kuhn found that both intervention groups did better than either the control group or the students who simply listened to the texts in terms of word recognition in isolation, prosody, and correct words per minute. However, only the Wide Reading group made greater growth on comprehension. Kuhn considers that this may be the result of the nature of the task; that is, students in the FOOR felt the implicit purpose of the repeated reading was improving word recognition and prosody, while the students in the Wide Reading group felt the implicit purpose of their multiple texts also included construction of meaning, and these differences were reflected in the differences in their outcomes. It is important to note that, while there was some discussion surrounding both the stories and unfamiliar vocabulary as part of the sessions, there was no direct instruction in these areas. It may be that, simply by introducing these elements into the lessons, the students in the FOOR group would have made gains in comprehension similar to the students in the Wide Reading group.

Fluency Development Lesson

The Fluency Development Lesson (FDL) (Rasinski, Padak, Linek, & Sturtevant, 1994) integrates several of the principles of effective fluency instruction mentioned earlier into a coherent classroom routine. In the FDL, students work with a daily text. First, the passage is read to students two to three times by the teacher while the students follow along silently. Next, students read it chorally as a group, with each student providing oral support for his or her classmates. Students then divide into pairs and engage in paired repeated reading, with each student reading the text two to three times while their partner follows along silently and provides support and encouragement. After completing this practice, students are offered the chance to perform the daily text for their classmates, alone or in small groups. Finally, students and the teacher choose words from the text for word study. As an option, students may also take the assigned passage home for further practice with family members.

Implementation of the FDL with second-grade students demonstrated gains in overall fluency and a trend for improved overall achievement in reading (Rasinski et al., 1994). Fast Start (Padak & Rasinski, 2005) is a variation of the FDL for home involvement. In Fast Start, students work with a caregiver on a daily rhyme or other short text. Caregivers read the passage to their child two to three times while pointing to the words; next, caregiver and child read the passage together two to three times; then the caregiver listens to the child read the passage to him or her a couple of times. Finally, caregiver and child engage in a brief word study activity with one or more words from the passage (e.g., if the word *wall* was found in the passage, caregiver and child may write and read other words within the same word family—*ball, call, stall, mall,* and so on). In an implementation of Fast Start with first-grade students, Rasinski and Stevenson (2005) found that Fast Start had a profound and positive impact on the reading development of the most at-risk students—Fast Start students made nearly twice the gain in fluency than their peers who did not participate in the program.

Assessing Fluency

Before leaving this discussion on fluency instruction, we consider it important to briefly discuss ways in which fluent reading can be assessed. We present two different types of measures here. The first is suggested by the Oral Reading Fluency (ORF) Target Rate Norms (Rasinski, 2004)—an assessment designed to assess students' rate (correct words per minute) and word recognition accuracy. This provides a sense of how students are developing in terms of accurate and automatic word recognition—according to both their grade level and the time of year (see Table 9.1). Our one concern regarding this approach to assessing fluency is the tendency for students to develop the understanding that fast reading, as opposed to meaningful reading, is the goal of reading instruction. When using this approach, we remind students to focus on meaning while reading, not simply speed.

The second assessment is the National Assessment of Educational Progress's (NAEP) Oral Reading Fluency Scale (1995), a measure that looks at fluency more broadly—incorporating phrasing, smoothness,

TABLE 9.1. Oral Reading Fluency (ORF) Target Rate Norms

Grade	Fall (wcpm)	Winter (wcpm)	Spring (wcpm)
1		10–30	30–60
2	30–60	50–80	70–100
3	50–90	70–100	80–110
4	70–110	80–120	100–140
5	80–120	100–140	110–150
6	100–140	110–150	120–160
7	110–150	120–160	130–170
8	120–160	130–170	140–180

Note. wcpm, words correct per minute. Adapted from "AIMSweb: Charting the Path to Literacy" (2003; available at *www.aimsweb.com/norms/reading_fluency.htm*). Data are also adapted from Hasbrouck and Tindal (1992).

pace, and expression—and evaluates children's oral reading against a range of behaviors, from reading that is primarily word-by-word and monotonous to reading that incorporates higher-level attributes in a fluent rendering of a text (see Table 9.2). By using this simple scale (or a variation of the scale) along with the correct words per minute norms, it is possible to decide whether students will benefit from a fluency-oriented instructional approach—either as part of the general literacy curriculum or as part of an intervention designed for individuals or a small group of learners—or whether they have already achieved oral reading fluency and are ready to focus on another aspect of their reading development.

REFLECTIONS AND FUTURE DIRECTIONS

While a review of the research indicates that the foregoing approaches are all effective in promoting fluent reading (e.g., Kuhn & Stahl, 2003; National Reading Panel, 2000), there are still a number of questions relating to flu-

TABLE 9.2. National Assessment of Educational Progress's Oral Reading Fluency Scale

Level 4

Reads primarily in larger meaningful phrase groups. Although some regressions, repetitions, and deviations from text may be present, those do not appear to detract from the overall structure of the story. Preservation of the author's syntax is consistent. Some or most of the story is read with expressive interpretation.

Level 3

Reads primarily in three- or four-word phrase groups. Some smaller groupings may be present. However, the majority of phrasing seems appropriate and preserves the syntax of the author. Little or no expressive interpretation is present.

Level 2

Reads primarily in two-word phrases with some three- or four-word groupings. Some word-by-word reading may be present. Word groupings may seem awkward and unrelated to larger context of sentence or passage.

Level 1

Reads primarily word-by-word. Occasionally two-word or three-word phrases may occur, but these are infrequent and/or they do not preserve meaningful syntax.

ency development and its instruction that need to be answered. Perhaps the most important concerns the nature of the relationship between prosody and comprehension. While it is clear that, in general, as prosody improves, so does comprehension, it is less clear whether improvements in comprehension result from improvements in prosody, whether improvements in prosody result from improvements in comprehension, or whether there is an interaction between the two that supports improvements in both aspects of reading development. Given that the primary goal of reading is comprehension, this is a key area for further study.

Secondly, recent research (Kuhn et al., in press; Mostow & Beck, 2005) indicates that improvements in fluency do not result specifically from the repetition of text but instead from a more generalized increase in the amount of challenging connected text that students are responsible for reading with appropriate support. Previous studies that have compared the repeated reading of a small number of texts to the scaffolded reading of a larger number of texts without repetition have produced similar results (Kuhn & Stahl, 2003). If it is the case that fluency development can occur simply by increasing the amount of text students read with support, then there may be a range of approaches that are as effective as those discussed here. Research in this area may allow us to create additional instructional approaches while simultaneously developing a better understanding of how fluency contributes to learners' overall reading development.

Along these same lines, the appropriate level of text difficulty used in fluency instruction is an issue worth further consideration. Conventional wisdom suggests that fluency is best developed through practice with easier independent-level material. However, recent research by Stahl and Heubach (2005) found that greater progress was made when students were given more challenging materials for repeated readings.

Finally, the role of the teacher in fluency instruction has not been thoroughly investigated. While the wide or repeated practice of a text may seem to be an activity engaged in alone, we feel that the teacher plays a significant role in fluency instruction through choosing appropriate texts, modeling fluent reading, encouraging and providing feedback and support for students, and setting the stage for performance. Clearly the appropriate role of the teacher during fluency instruction needs further examination.

CONCLUDING COMMENTS

Prior to publication of the National Reading Panel, fluency was considered to be the "neglected reading goal" (Allington, 1983, p. 556). In recent years, there has been a renewed focus on approaches that assist learners with their fluency development. We believe the approaches and principles presented here will help you begin to integrate effective fluency instruction into your classroom. By doing so, your students will not only develop automatic word recognition and integrate expression into their oral reading but also will be better able to read challenging text with understanding, thereby achieving the ultimate goal of reading instruction.

Although several issues related to reading fluency still need to be resolved, we feel strongly that appropriate fluency instruction offers a key to success in reading for many developing and struggling readers. We hope you agree and are willing to give fluency instruction a try!

ENGAGEMENT ACTIVITIES

1. Select two short poems or passages from a story. Try to select passages that have a good sense of voice—that lend themselves well to oral expressive and meaningful reading. Pair up your students, and have them practice repeatedly reading the texts using the paired repeated reading approach. Tell them to emphasize expression and their own interpretation of the piece. After the students have had the opportunity to practice their passage, ask for volunteers to perform their interpretation of the piece in front of their classmates.
2. Select a range of texts and follow the format outlined for two recommended approaches (authentic repeated reading, Fluency Oriented Oral Reading, Fluency Development Lesson, or Wide Reading) for several weeks. See which approach your students enjoy more as well as how easy it is to implement these in your classroom!
3. Purchase or make an audiotape of a book for an individual student who is a disfluent reader. Allow him or her to listen to the entire book for enjoyment, and then ask the learner to listen to and read along with the first few pages several times. When he or she feels ready, have the student read the text aloud to you. You should hear some improvement in his or her oral reading. Encourage the student to continue the process until he or she has mastered the text (or a chapter in the text, depending on the selection).
4. Select a text that your class will be reading. Have each of your students read a passage from the text aloud to you without practicing it ahead of time. Use the Oral Reading Fluency (ORF) Target Rate Norms and the NAEP Oral Reading Fluency Scale (National Assessment of Educational Progress, 1995) to evaluate their oral reading level. This will give you a sense of which students in your class need to work on their fluency development in order to be successful with the material you are expected to cover.

REFERENCES

Adams, M. J. (1990). *Beginning to read: Thinking and learning about print.* Cambridge, MA: MIT Press.

Allington, R. L. (1983). Fluency: The neglected reading goal. *The Reading Teacher, 36,* 556–561.

Byars, B. (1985). *The Golly sisters go west.* New York: HarperCollins.

Chall, J. S. (1996). *Stages of reading development.* Orlando, FL: Harcourt, Brace & Company.

Chomsky, C. (1976). After decoding: What? *Language Arts, 53,* 288–296.

Dahl, P. R. (1979). An experimental program for teaching high speed word recognition and comprehension skills. In J. E. Button, T. Lovitt, & T. Rowland (Eds.), *Communications research in learning disabilities and mental retardation* (pp. 33–65). Baltimore: University Park Press.

Dowhower, S. (1989). Repeated reading: Research into practice. *The Reading Teacher, 42,* 502–507.

Dowhower, S. L. (1991). Speaking of prosody: Fluency's unattended bedfellow. *Theory into Practice, 30*(3), 158–164.

Erekson, J. (2003, May). *Prosody: The problem of expression in fluency.* Paper presented at the International Reading Association Preconvention Institute, Orlando, FL.

FEP/Booksource. (1998). *1998 books for early childhood to adult.* St. Louis, MO: The Booksource.

Fountas, I. C., & Pinnell, G. S. (1999). *Guided reading: Good first teaching for all children.* Portsmouth, NH: Heinemann.

Griffith, L. W., & Rasinski, T. V. (2004). A focus on fluency: How one teacher incorporated fluency with her reading curriculum. *The Reading Teacher, 58,* 126–137.

Hasbrouck, J. E., & Tindal, G. (1992). Curriculum-based oral reading fluency norms for students in grades 2 through 5. *Teaching Exceptional Children, 24,* 41–44.

Hudson, R. F., Lane, H. B., & Pullen, P. C. (2005). Reading fluency assessment and instruction: What, why and how? *The Reading Teacher, 58,* 702–713.

Keats, E. J. (1977). *Whistle for Willie.* New York: Puffin Books USA.

Koskinen, P. S., & Blum, I. H. (1984). Repeated oral reading and the acquisition of fluency. In J. A. Niles & L. A. Harris (Eds.), *Changing perspectives on research in reading/language processing and instruction: Thirty-third yearbook of the National Reading Conference* (pp. 183–187). Rochester, NY: National Reading Conference.

Koskinen, P. S., & Blum, I. H. (1986). Paired repeated reading: A classroom strategy for developing fluent reading. *The Reading Teacher, 40,* 70–75.

Kuhn, M. R. (2004–2005). Helping students become accurate, expressive readers: Fluency instruction for small groups. *The Reading Teacher, 58,* 338–344.

Kuhn, M. R., Schwanenflugel, P. J., Morris, R. D., Morrow, L. M., Woo, D. G., Meisinger, B., et al. (in press). Teaching children to become fluent and automatic readers. *Journal of Literacy Research.*

Kuhn, M. R., & Stahl, S. A. (2003). Fluency: A review of developmental and remedial practices. *Journal of Educational Psychology, 95,* 3–22.

LaBerge, D., & Samuels, S. A. (1974). Toward a theory of automatic information processing in reading. *Cognitive Psychology, 6,* 293–323.

Martinez, M., Roser, N., & Strecker, S. (1999). "I never thought I could be a star": A Readers Theatre ticket to reading fluency. *The Reading Teacher, 52,* 326–334.

Mostow, J., & Beck, J. (2005, June). *Micro-analysis of fluency gains in a reading tutor that listens.* Paper presented at the annual meeting of Society for the Scientific Study of Reading, Toronto, Ontario.

National Assessment of Educational Progress. (1995). *Listening to Children Read Aloud, 15.* Washington, DC: U.S. Department of Education, National Center for Education Statistics.

National Reading Panel. (2000). *Teaching children to read: An evidence-based assessment of the scientific research literature on reading and its implications for reading instruction. Reports of the subgroups.* Bethesda, MD: National Institutes of Health. Available at *www.nichd.nih.gov/publications/nrp/.*

Padak, N., & Rasinski, T. (2005). *Fast start for early readers: A research-based send-home literacy program.* New York: Scholastic.

Pikulski, J. J., & Chard, D. J. (2005). Fluency: Bridge between decoding and reading comprehension. *The Reading Teacher, 58,* 510–519.

Platt, K. (1992). *Big Max.* New York: HarperCollins.

Rasinski, T. V. (1990). *The effects of cued phrase boundaries in texts.* Bloomington, IN: ERIC Clearinghouse on Reading and Communication Skills (ED 313 689).

Rasinski, T. V. (2003). *The fluent reader: Oral reading strategies for building word recognition, fluency, and comprehension.* New York: Scholastic Professional Books.

Rasinski, T. V. (2004). *Assessing reading fluency.* Honolulu: Pacific Resources for Education and Learning. Available at *www.prel.org/products/re_/assessing-fluency.htm.*

Rasinski, T. V., & Hoffman, J. V. (2003). Oral reading in the school curriculum. *Reading Research Quarterly, 38,* 510–522.

Rasinski, T. V., Padak, N. D., Linek, W. L., & Sturtevant, E. (1994). Effects of fluency development on urban second-grade readers. *Journal of Educational Research, 87,* 158–165.

Rasinski, T., & Stevenson, B. (2005). The effects of Fast Start Reading, a fluency based home involvement reading program, on the reading achievement of beginning readers. *Reading Psychology: An International Quarterly, 26,* 109–125.

Samuels, S. J. (1979). The method of repeated readings. *The Reading Teacher, 32,* 403–408.

Samuels, S. J. (2004). Toward a theory of automatic information processing in reading, revisited. In R. B. Ruddell & N. J. Unrau, *Theoretical models and processes of reading* (5th ed., pp. 1127–1148). Newark, DE: International Reading Association.

Schreiber, P. A. (1991). Understanding prosody's role in reading acquisition. *Theory into Practice, 30,* 158–164.

Schwanenflugel, P. J., Hamilton, A. M., Kuhn, M. R., Wisenbaker, J., & Stahl, S. A. (2004). Becoming a fluent reader: Reading skill and prosodic features in the oral reading of young readers. *The Journal of Educational Psychology, 96,* 119–129.

Stahl, S. A., & Heubach, K. (2005). Fluency-Oriented Reading Instruction. *Journal of Literacy Research, 37,* 25–60.

Stanovich, K. E. (1980). Toward an interactive–compensatory model of individual differences in the development of reading fluency. *Reading Research Quarterly, 21,* 360–407.

Torgesen, J. (2005, September). *Teaching every child to read: What every teacher needs to know.* Georgia Reading First Pre-Service Conference, Atlanta.

Chapter 10

BEST PRACTICES IN TEACHING COMPREHENSION

Cathy Collins Block
Michael Pressley

This chapter will:

- Present research, current issues, and best practices of teaching comprehension.
- Discuss the evolution of teaching methods upon which today's highly effective comprehension instruction is based.
- Describe evidence-based best comprehension practices in action.
- Suggest directions for future research and instruction.

Prior to this chapter, many components of successful reading instruction have been described. Each discussion contained information about important skills that assist students in learning how to read. Since 1978, however, researchers have defined the topic of this chapter, comprehension, as the "essence of reading" (Durkin, 1978–1979), and the ultimate goal of successful literacy (Pressley, 2006). Highly effective comprehension instruction comprises the learning activities that enable students to leave a reading experience with fresh perspectives, vital information, and new ideas. Through it, readers also learn how to use the other important skills described in this book as they execute the complex comprehension processes needed to create meaning.

To achieve these goals, today's teachers must assist readers in (1) actively interacting with all genres to decode authors' stated and implied meanings; (2) independently reflecting upon the information in a text before, during, and after they read; (3) determining reading purposes that are uniquely their own; (4) processing information immediately; (5) remembering, connecting, and anticipating intentions; (6) inferring, reasoning, and decoding without losing an author's train of thought; (7) assigning accurate meaning to unique vocabulary terms; (8) relating facts, imagining concepts, savoring connotations, and, interpreting figurative language without teacher prompting; and (9) integrating new information for personal use within students' culturally influenced lives. The purpose of this chapter is to present research-based best comprehension instructional practices that can enable more students to obtain such highly advanced self-governed abilities.

EVIDENCE-BASED BEST PRACTICES

In preparing this chapter, we reviewed research that occurred from 2001 to 2006 and observed numerous classrooms. We explored exemplary instructional methods that produced exceptional student comprehension (see Block, 2004, 2005a, 2005c; Block & Mangieri, 2003; Pressley, 2006, for a summary of these bodies of research). When we compared these findings to similar research that we conducted 7 years ago, we found that the comprehension tasks students complete today are more informed by historically and contemporarily based comprehension research than was true in the past. These developments are noteworthy, especially when we realize how much progress comprehension instruction has made since 1999 (Block & Pressley, 2003). At that time, many teachers reported that they did not know how to provide effective comprehension instruction. Still others believed that students could learn how to comprehend simply by doing massive amounts of reading.

Research Update: Word-Level Processing Effects on Comprehension

For half a century, research has demonstrated that when readers cannot decode or decode only with great effort, comprehension is either impossible or severely restricted. When students have difficulty decoding, they cannot direct their attention to understanding continuous text because their attention capacity is limited (i.e., the 7 ± 2 chunks of short-term memory capacity is focused on decoding or vocabulary processing [Miller, 1956]). Thus, without highly effective fluency, word recognition, vocabulary, and fluent word recognition instruction (as described in earlier chapters), comprehension will be compromised. For instance, when students encounter a word they do not recognize (i.e., cannot read automatically), students can lose the comprehension gained to that point unless we urge them first to attempt to sound the word out, stimulating listening comprehension. Once they have done that, we must ask them to check whether the word makes sense in the context—based on the text already read, the author's word choices, graphics, pictures, and the students' interpretation of the author's train of thought (Pressley, 2006).

Eighteen years after Miller's important study, LaBerge & Samuels (1974) demonstrated that with increased automaticity in decoding, readers' attention capacity can be freed up to permit greater comprehension. Since that time, research has repeatedly documented that fluent recognition of sight words (e.g., Goswami, 2004) and fluent reading developed through effective instruction and practice (e.g., Breznitz, 1997a, 1997b; Tan & Nicholson, 1997) can significantly increase comprehension. Moreover, for accurate decoding and comprehension to occur simultaneously, readers must learn how to coordinate sound-, letter-, and word-level cues and contextual cues, temporally prioritizing the former, as they tackle challenging words and ideas independently. This ability has been labeled as active, self-guided (metacognitively aware) comprehension (Israel, Block, Bauserman, & Kinnucan-Welsh, 2005; Pressley, 2006).

We now also know that good readers use comprehension processes even at the word level (Block, 2005a, 2005b). These students use every little bit of understanding that they have created up to the point that they have to decode an unknown word, and they activate many comprehension strategies to derive that word's meaning. For instance, good readers may read from beginning to end while occasionally omitting words, skipping around, and rereading words, sentences, and paragraphs. They use the author's choice of words, depth of vocabulary, level of detail, and a text's organizational pattern to anticipate the meaning of an unknown word and to self-monitor their understanding of sentences, paragraphs, and full texts (Block, Gambrell, & Pressley, 2002; Flavell, 1977).

Direct instruction in vocabulary is also important. When students have at least six multiple exposures to a word in a variety of contexts, they develop significantly higher levels of comprehension (Block, Hasni, & Mangieri, 2005; Block, 2005b; Carlo et al., 2004; National Reading Panel, 2000; RAND Reading Study Group, 2002; Stahl & Kapinus, 2001). Within the past 5 years, better methods of building students' vocabularies have been developed (Beck, McKeown, & Kucan, 2002; Block & Mangieri, 2005; Bravo, Hiebert, & Pearson, 2007; Carlisle, Fleming, & Gudbrandsen, 2000; and see Baumann & Kame'enui, 2004, for a review of recent vocabulary research and its implications for reading comprehension). In summary, research has repeatedly confirmed that comprehension processes are used at and beyond the word level. To comprehend even a single word requires much more mental processing than previously thought—merely applying phonics, decoding, calling words, or immediately retelling what was read is not enough (Pressley & Afflerbach, 1995).

For these reasons, we suggest that the traditional methods of classifying essential comprehension processes for instructional purposes need to be updated. In the past, comprehension processes were grouped either (1) as strategies that should be activated before, during, or after reading or (2) as processes that enabled literal, inferential, applicative, or metacognitive understandings. Neither of these grouping systems reflects the facts that readers must (1) apply comprehension processes at the word learning level; (2) actively engage cognitive and metacognitive comprehension processes continuously without teacher prompting; (3) use a lot of the same comprehension processes before, during, throughout, and after a reading experience; and (4) apply several processes repeatedly from the onset to the end of a reading. We suggest that teachers group their comprehension instruction into the following categories (presented in more detail in Table 10.1):

- Comprehension processes needed to understand words
- Comprehension processes needed to interpret sentences and paragraphs
- Comprehension processes needed to understand text well
- Comprehension processes needed to shape and use the knowledge gained

Research Update: Comprehension Process Instruction

Thirty-seven years of research, from 1970 to 2006, have created an exceptionally strong theoretical foundation upon which today's best practices rely. As a brief overview, during the 1970s and 1980s many scientists determined that successful comprehension involved several cognitive and metacognitive abilities that enabled readers to interrelate numerous mental representations of meaning (Doctorow, Wittrock, & Marks, 1978; Taylor, 1982; van Dijk & Kintsch, 1983). Readers taught to construct complex networks of associated verbal and imaged representations significantly increased their comprehension (Clark & Paivio, 1991; Levin, 1973; Pressley, 1976, 1977). Even weak readers who learned to attend to story grammar elements could use this new skill to increase their understanding and retention of material read (Mandler, 1984; Short & Ryan, 1984; Stein & Glenn, 1979). These and other major advancements in our knowledge base led to the important findings that (1) metacognition (Flavell,

1977; Paris, Lipson, & Wixson, 1983; Pressley, Heisel, McCormick, & Nakamura, 1982), (2) constructivism and scaffolding (Vygotsky, 1978; Meichenbaum, 1977), and (3) validating interpretive variability (perspectives and information interact differently for different readers, based on their personal, cultural, historical, and social contexts [Beach & Hynds, 1991; Rosenblatt, 1978]) are important in comprehension instruction.

By 2000, the National Reading Panel (2000) collapsed these major theoretical concepts into the recommendation that comprehension programs should include direct instruction (Duffy & Roehler, 1989) and be delivered through transactional strategy lessons, a method of teaching in which multiple comprehension abilities are learned, automatized, and applied to one's own cultural and experiential base (Pressley, Gaskins, Wile, Cunicelli, & Sheridan, 1991). Transactional strategies instruction is the teaching of self-regulated comprehension processes, "developing students who, on their own, use the comprehension strategies that excellent readers use [as identified by Pressley & Afflerbach, 1995]" (Pressley, 2006, p. 319).

Since 2000, contemporary researchers have engaged in numerous multiyear projects designed to (1) increase students' comprehension of nonfiction (Pearson, 2005; Hiebert, Pearson, & Ayra, 2005; Purcell & Duke, 2005); (2) build the metacognitive abilities of less able, young and adolescent readers (Baker, 2005; Afflerbach & Meuwissen, 2005; Schmitt, 2005); (3) assess more complex comprehension and metacomprehension processes (Block, 2005c; Paris & Flukes, 2005); (4) enhance the effectiveness of teacher- and student-generated think-alouds (Block & Israel, 2004; Duffy, 2005; Israel & Massey, 2005); (5) strengthen inservice and preservice teacher education programs so as to enhance literacy coaches' and reading teachers' abilities to advance students' comprehension of text and technology (Bean, 2004; Leu, 2005; Risko, Roskos, & Vukelich, 2005); and (6) identify the developmental factors that have an impact on students' abilities to internalize, automatize, and transfer comprehension processes to new contexts without teacher prompting (Cummins, Stewart, & Block, 2005; Paris & Flukes, 2005).

To illustrate the depth and breadth of knowledge that each of these projects is producing, we will summarize the results to date from one of them. For years, researchers have known that it usually takes longer to develop automaticity in comprehension than in decoding (e.g., Fielding & Pearson, 1994; National Reading Panel, 2000; Samuels, 2002; Stewart, 2004); however, we have not known exactly how long it takes to develop automaticity in specific comprehension processes at each grade level. Prior to 2000, research suggested that students could transfer comprehension processes to standardized tests if they had direct instruction for 8 months (Anderson & Pearson, 1984; Block, 1993; Collins, 1991). Each of these studies found that various factors could prolong the time required for automaticity to be achieved. The most common reason was that students did not have a mechanism (such as a visual aid) to help them learn how to elicit more than one comprehension process during a single reading experience.

We now know that the internalization of a comprehension process can take less time than previously believed when such aids are available. We also know that automaticity is developmentally sensitive. By first and second grade, for instance, students taught to use more than one comprehension process in a single lesson scored significantly higher on the Stanford Nine Comprehension Subtest, enjoyed what they read more, compared what they read to other texts more, and drew more conclusions as they read nonfiction than control groups. Third graders also became significantly better at using nonfictional textual clues than control subjects. By fifth grade, experimental subjects were better able to predict from what they read in nonfictional texts (Block, 2005a; Stewart, 2004). Teachers in each of these grades reported that teaching higher-level comprehension skills and more than one comprehension process in a single lesson was difficult to learn how to do (Cummins et al., 2005; Stewart, 2004).

Lastly, this multiyear study taught students to use from 3 to 15 strategies in a single reading, and at the end of 8 weeks experimental subjects used more strategies continually (and increased their abilities continuously to do so from week 1 to week 8). On average, they applied 4.5 comprehension processes without teacher prompting as they read a full book (K–2) or a chapter in a nonfictional text (grades 3–5) by week 8. In contrast, control subjects were inconsistent in how many strategies they used from week 1 to 8, and by week 8 they were no higher in their abilities to independently apply comprehension processes than they had been in week l. They averaged only 2.5 strategies per book or chapter. These data have implications as to how many strategies we should teach per grade level, whether the comprehension strategies being taught should vary by grade level, and how long (on average) it takes for less able readers to master more than three of the comprehension processes employed by good readers.

In summary, past and present research programs are producing new understandings of how to teach comprehension. Data suggest that comprehension instruction should increase students' ability to understand text- and technology-based print by encouraging readers to be active in the ways that good comprehenders are active. We should teach students how to:

- Activate many comprehension strategies to decode and derive word meanings.
- Size up a text in advance by looking at titles, text features, sections, pictures, and captions, continuously updating and making predictions about what will be in a text.

- Stop to reread and initiate comprehension processes when the meaning of single sentences or paragraphs is unclear.
- Generate interpretations that make sense, confirm or change predictions based on the text, construct images expressed in the text, ask questions (i.e., wonder), and notice or generate answers as they read.
- Come to a fictional text expecting to (and making certain that they do) note the setting, characters, and story grammar early on; and making certain that they watch for problems to develop, solutions to be attempted, and resolutions to occur.
- Come to an informational text watching for textual features, access features, unique types of information that appear in a specific genre, important points, the sequence of details, and conclusions.
- Connect to ideas in the text based on their personal experiences, knowledge of other texts, and general world knowledge, making certain that these connections are made quickly and do not divert attention from the actual text but rather help the reader understand the text better.
- Summarize the text, making sure it includes information gained from story grammar or textual features, and, if they can't, teach the students that this is a signal to reread.
- Continue to reflect on the text after reading, deciding how to shape the knowledge base for their personal use.

BEST PRACTICES IN ACTION

The following best practices are consistent with the experiments reported in this chapter as well as those conducted prior to 1997 (e.g., Anderson, 1992; Brown, Pressley, Van Meter, & Schuder, 1996; Collins, 1991) that have validated the teaching of a small repertoire of comprehension strategies, with large effects on comprehension. In each method, students are "mentally active while reading." Evidence of this is that they report the comprehension processes they are executing as they read (e.g., "I have a great image of the witch! And she is really tall but very pretty, like it says in the story." "I predict she is going to use her magic to try to harm the kids, but I don't think it will work").

The Basic Research-Based Comprehension Lesson Plan

How do you teach students to become active comprehenders and to independently initiate the processes described in Table 10.1?

TABLE 10.1 Processes Involved in Comprehension

Understanding the words

- Can I fluently read the words in the sentence without pausing?
- Can I use my background to make sense of the words?
- Does this word meaning make sense?

Interpreting sentences and paragraphs

- Does it make sense?
- Can I recall what I just read?
- Can I determine what the author thinks is most important in each paragraph by selecting, deleting, condensing, and integrating the key information in every paragraph?

Understanding text well

- Can I see the characters, . . . the setting, . . . the actions?
- Can I use my sensory images to make a movie in my mind?
- Can I use story grammar and text features to follow an author's train of thought?
- Have I looked for the author's writing style so I can follow the compare/contrast, descriptive, problem/solution, cause/effect, descriptive, or sequential patterns through which information is being presented?
- Can I interpret, predict, and update my knowledge by scanning the titles, headings, and pictures and relating the information gained to prior knowledge?
- Can I summarize the text, making sure my summary includes information gained from the story and eliminates duplication, restates in fewer words, and uses summary words? If I can't, did I interpret this as a sign to reread?
- Have I reread for clarification?
- Have I used fix-up comprehension strategies?
- Are there still questions or concepts that were explored in the text that I missed?
- Can I use the "W" and "H" questions, and ask questions about why things are the way they are in the fictional or nonfictional story or informational text?
- Can I draw inferences or create images by filling in details missing from the text or by elaborating on what I read?

Shaping and using the knowledge gained

- How is my knowledge different now?
- Do I need to be acquiring more knowledge in this area? Have I come up with a plan to do so?
- Have I connected the ideas in this text to my personal reference of knowledge from other texts and general word knowledge, making certain that these connections do not divert my attention away from the actual text?
- Have I used cultural knowledge to comprehend and use what I read?

1. Select one of the strategies or processes described in Table 10.1.

2. Explain it to the students through at least six distinctive think-alouds while you read aloud and students follow the text with you as they read silently.

3. Reteach the comprehension process in use as active good readers do in think-alouds throughout the next six days.

4. Ask students to use the strategy as they read silently. Move from student to student when they have difficulty. As they raise their hands, ask them what they have tried, perform a think-aloud about how they can elicit the comprehension process that will help at that point and at similar places in future texts. Tell them that you will return to see if they can describe what they are thinking at a similar point in the text. Before the end of that silent reading period, return and ask each student you helped to read at a new point in the text that is similar to the one that previously caused difficulty. Have that student describe his or her thought processes to better gain meaning. Praise or reteach as appropriate.

5. Reteach comprehension strategies and processes to students who need them in small teacher- or student-led reading groups, as described on pages 232–233.

6. Most students will not independently use the comprehension process or strategy that was just taught, at first. Cue them, but let them know you want them to use the strategies or processes on their own and to be able to report aloud when they are using it as they read. It might take a while for students to consistently use the strategy independently. After a while, they will. Then, it is time to . . .

7. Introduce another strategy or process, following steps 1–6, above, with the following steps added to this instructional process.

8. Model the use of the second strategy while you read, but continue to model the use of the first strategy in conjunction with the think alouds you performed to introduce the second comprehension process. Let students know that good readers activate a variety of strategies as they read.

9. Begin to expect students to use both comprehension processes as they read aloud, cuing them at first. How you cue is important, with the clear message being that students must choose when to use each strategy. When they are reading silently and encounter confusion, you can say: "Is there a strategy or process that you might choose to use here? Are you actively thinking as you read? If you are, let me know what strategies or processes you are using."

In kindergarten and first grade, if, over the course of a school year, children automatize three to five comprehension processes and use them continuously, metacognitively, without your prompting, you will have had a great year. Throughout every lesson, encourage students to use the actual name of these strategies and processes when they report what they are doing, but also require that they tell you more than its name. They should tell you what they are predicting and why. They should tell you what their images look like. You want to hear the questions they are asking and the connections they are making. They should let you know what is confusing and what they are doing to clarify. They should summarize rather than just say that they are summarizing.

In kindergarten, we recommend that you begin by teaching how to predict, image, make connections, and summarize. In this and the other early grades, you should perform think-alouds with every read-aloud—and there should be lots of read-alouds so as to model how to use multiple comprehension processes. You should perform think-alouds as you read both fiction and nonfiction texts—making predictions, talking about images that come to mind, formulating questions (and noting when the questions are answered in the text), seeking clarification if something is confusing, making connections, and summarizing. (If you want more information about how to create think-alouds and explain each of the processes listed in Table 10.1, and more, see Block & Israel, 2004; Block & Mangieri, 2005; Zimmermann & Hutchins, 2003).

A word of caution: One way of being reading-disabled that you must discourage is for students to make images and connections, and so on, that are purely *tangential.* For instance, if a student is reading *Little Red Riding Hood* and, at any point in the steps of the lesson plan on page 228, he or she makes the connection that red is his or her favorite color and then starts talking about fire trucks, this student needs for you to point out that some images and connections help the reader to understand the text better and others do not. This reader must be made to see how the connections, images, or questions he or she is thinking should connect directly to the text. In small-group discussions, spend time commenting on how the images reported, the connections made, and the summaries suggested show that the reader understood the text. Urge readers to react to the central ideas in every text, and tell them that using such comprehension processing may be difficult at first.

Lastly, you likely noted that the silent reading experience in step 4 of the basic lesson plan was not a sustained silent reading experience (SSR), with SSR being defined as a time for the students and their teacher to read silently a book of their choice. Research has found that for silent reading periods to produce significant comprehension gains for all readers, teachers must perform one or more of the following actions (Block & Reed, 2005; Block, Parris, Reed, & Whiteley, in press). Teachers must monitor, intercede, reteach, and assess students individually as they read silently, as described in step 4 of the basic lesson plan. Alternatively, or in conjunction with these actions, when students are reading nonfictional texts, teachers can encourage students to select books of interest but require that each student read two nonfiction books on the same topic, back to back, before they choose to read about a different topic. Books that students are allowed to choose among should have been introduced by the teacher as relating to a theme or story that the class has experienced or is studying. If teachers choose the books that students are to read, books should be selected to match students' independent reading levels and discussed so readers can share the insights gained from individual books that relate to a global class theme.

Teaching Multiple Strategies in One Lesson

Because reading comprehension is not an isolated process but a network of conscious and metacognitive processes, the newest instructional methods teach multiple strategies in single lessons. These methods help students learn comprehension processes that can work together to bring about meaning. For years, children have been taught to find main ideas, to predict based on pictures, to think about an authorial writing pattern, and to think metacognitively as they read. Unfortunately, much of this instruction occurred as a prelude to actual reading. Students were taught these comprehension processes as stand-alone procedures, making it difficult for them to understand when, where, and why to initiate these processes in conjunction with others while they read.

By teaching them how to use more than one comprehension process in a single lesson, students may be shown how to view their comprehension and metacomprehension as a unified self-controlled ability (Block, 2004). The research program that supports these lessons has found that even kindergarten students can use multiple strategies after 1 week of direct instruction, and the result is normally significantly higher achievement than in control groups in predicting, identifying main ideas, knowing how much they have learned from their teacher's instruction, identifying the author's purpose, internalizing comprehension processes, and using nonfiction textual features (Block, 2005a; Block, Rodgers, & Johnson, 2004; Cummins, Stewart, & Block, 2005; Stewart, 2004). Three instructional practices were validated in this research.

The first evidence-based practice is to construct a chart that tracks students' previewing; predicting; questioning; identifying vocabulary, recognizing text structure or access features, and knowing an author's purpose; thinking critically; and creating graphic organizers or mind maps as students participate in a read-aloud. When these processes were taught with nonfictional text, a GO! Chart (Benton & Cummins, 2001) proved beneficial. Research findings suggest that this format may be enhanced by teaching fewer of the comprehensions processes cited above in each lesson. One modified version of the GO! Chart that we recommend appears in Figure 10.1.

The second research-based practice is to teach students to write their thoughts about three comprehension processes on post-it notes placed strategically on three pages of a book. This lesson enables less able readers to practice using expert reading processes in context. Each post-it note is placed at a point in the text where the comprehension processes described on the note would be elicited automatically by expert readers. Students pause at each post-it note to write the thoughts they are having at that point in the text by using the comprehension process depicted on the post-it. See Figure 10.2 for the three processes that significantly led to increased comprehension for less able readers using this method. We recommend using these and other processes described in Table 10.1 to further document the effects of this practice on student's comprehension abilities.

The third research-based practice is to use a trifolded bookmark, with two varieties shown in Block and Israel (2004) and Cummins, Stewart, and Block (2005). Such bookmarks are visual aids designed to elicit more active metacognitively driven reading. These bookmarks are placed at three points in a book so that students can think and write about their metacognitive experiences at parts of a book where each process is used often. Students see five comprehension processes on the first bookmark placed at about page 5 of a book, three processes at the middle of a reading experience (on the bookmark placed at the middle of a book), and

Preview/ Predictions	Interpretations	Connections	Organizing
What will this text be about? What is the purpose of this text? • Animals that live in Florida • Animals that are endangered • People hurting sea animals • Animals that live in cold water • Ocean animals that move from place to place	*What clues did you find for the Author's Message?* <u>Author's Purpose</u>: to describe things about manatees and dugongs *What are you still wondering* • If people are still trying to hurt them • Why Columbus thought they looked like mermaids • How they are related to elephants • Why the author wrote more about manatees than dugongs	*What does this information remind you of?* • The time I went to Florida and saw the manatee signs • The text we read about the endangered tigers • The time I helped animals by working at the animal shelter	*What mindmap will best help you sort the facts into concepts?* 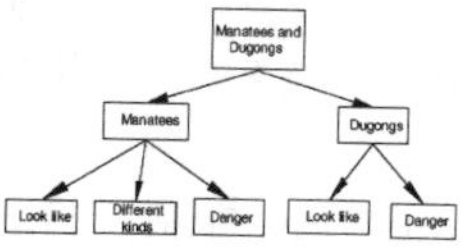 Manatees and Dugongs Manatees: Look like; Different kinds; Danger Dugongs: Look like; Danger

FIGURE 10.1. Example of a GO! Chart for the book *Manatees and Dugongs.*

- Weeks 5-8
- Grades K-2
- After reading about 2-4 pages, establish purpose
- About 1/3 of way through, make inferences
- Near end of book, have students give conclusions before author gives conclusions

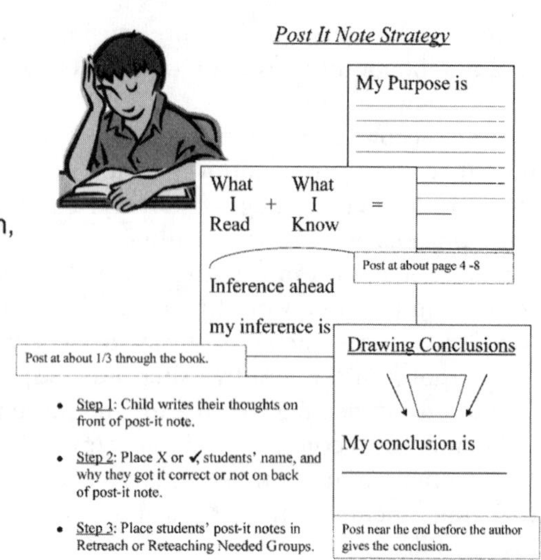

FIGURE 10.2. Post-it note strategy.

four processes at the final pages of a text (on the bookmark placed at the page before the conclusion or resolution in the book occurs). When students come to each bookmark, they are to stop reading and apply the three-to-five comprehension processes described on the bookmark to the section of text just completed. After each reflection, they write on the bookmark's lines (beneath each process's name) what they thought as they applied each comprehension process. Lastly, the class discusses their application of the processes described on all bookmarks after the book is finished.

Finally, we recommend putting a poster in the reading corner—and elsewhere, listing the comprehension strategies and processes that students have learned at each point during a school year. When students are not obviously using the strategies independently, remind them to make the choice to be strategic readers and to use the comprehension processes that are listed on the chart.

Teaching Comprehension Processes in Small-Group Settings

Research documents the value of teaching comprehension in the context of a reading group so that a teacher can initially explain and model comprehension processes for students "but quickly transfer responsibility to the members of the group, with individual students taking turns leading the reading group" (Pressley, 2006, p. 306). Small-group instruction such as reciprocal teaching, both without technological supports

(Brown & Palincsar, 1989) and with them (Dalton & Robinson, 2005), and teacher-reader groups (Block, 2004) have proven to be highly effective. They contain many research-based practices. Reciprocal teaching involves group leaders who assist their peers in (1) making predictions when reading, (2) questioning themselves about the ideas in the text, (3) seeking clarifications when confused, and (4) summarizing content.

Teacher-reader groups enable students to select these or other comprehension processes to discuss and learn more about through reading from more than one book. The difference between teacher-reader groups and reciprocal teaching is that in the former students select which comprehension process in Table 10.1 they want to discuss. Group members bring texts to the group. These books are ones in which they successfully or did not successfully (but wished to) complete the process(es) that the group has chosen to discuss. The group leader (i.e., the "teacher"), and in turn all group members, reads from his or her text and describes how he or she performed the process being discussed, suggests ways that others can perform that comprehension process better, and/or asks questions about how he or she can use that process more effectively in the future.

Both of these research-based approaches employ multiple learning modalities, use think-alouds, and provide multiple descriptions of several comprehension processes. They demonstrate how to execute several comprehension processes at appropriate points in a text to clarify or enhance meaning. They enable students to execute a sequence of comprehension strategies required to understand texts. Peers also model how to reason as one reads, having to justify and back up their claims about what they do to read well. Moreover, when smart people discuss text in small groups, they more rapidly realize the great power of these comprehension processes because their engagement in discussion customizes their learning. Such skilled small-group discussions have proven to be the heart of language arts achievement even as late as the middle and high school years (Applebee, Langer, Nystrand, & Gamoran, 2003). These group lessons can go far in encouraging better dialogue, and, as students dialogue more effectively to describe their enhanced comprehension abilities, their verbalizations further encourage internalization of oral discourse skills as well as more automatic application of comprehension strategies and processes when they read.

Teaching Comprehension Processes for Information Texts

Shouldn't the strategies for informational texts be different than those that are taught for fiction? Some nonfictional texts are laid out in a clear cause-and-effect pattern, or logical sequence or are ordered naturally by the specific attributes of a concept, but most are not! When students are taught the classic information text structures and apply them to texts with exactly that structure, they, in fact, zero in on that information, comprehending and remembering it very well. The problem is that most information texts are not constructed consistently with classic informational text structures.

In most nonfictional texts, predictions can be made, images can be generated about causes and effects, sequences can be determined, logical questions can be asked, and connections can be made. When there is confusion, students should clarify, and definitely we want students to summarize what they read. If they cannot do so, or cannot recall what they are supposed to have gotten out of the text, then rereading is in order. The major difference in teaching nonfiction is that the depth of the vocabulary, the lack of background experience with the topic, and a greater likelihood for misconceptions make comprehension more difficult. Numerous nonfictional instructional practices are presently being created and tested. As stated previously, we already know that reading two nonfictional texts on the same topic, back to back, can overcome these challenges, as does teaching nonfictional text features. We recommend both of these practices.

A third highly effective practice for increasing comprehension of nonfictional texts is to teach students to ask themselves (and answer) "why" questions as they read. Show them how to basically boil down the textual information to the question "Why does this new fact make sense (based on my prior knowledge and what I have read in the text already)?" For example, model for students and perform think-alouds to show students how to ask themselves such *why* questions as "Why is the author talking about extortion in this chapter on the reconstruction period?" *Why* questions and the mental process of answering them produce huge positive effects on learning from nonfictional text (Pressley, 2006).

A fourth research-based practice is to encourage students to take notes as they read nonfiction (Pressley, 2006). Often it makes sense to take notes, especially if the information is going to be used later. Encourage students to take notes on those occasions. Feel free to add a text-mapping approach to note taking while reading informational texts. We recommend that you also try semantic mapping, with the main idea as the central node on the map and all other information related to that node. Virtually all informational texts can be semantically mapped in this way.

Unfortunately, a common objection to the reading of nonfiction (and often fiction as well) is that students would rather read straight through without stopping to ask *why* questions, reread, or take notes. It should be emphasized to students that not stopping to think is passive reading and that they are therefore reading in a way that weak readers read. Good readers respond to ideas in text and often pause to reflect on them. Predicting (and associated previewing) before reading, doing all the comprehension strategies and processes listed in Table 10.1 as reading proceeds, and especially thinking about the summary (even going back to see what else should be added) after completing a reading is how expert comprehenders behave.

WHAT COMPREHENSION STRATEGIES INSTRUCTION IS NOT!

It is not research-based best comprehension strategies instruction to have students fill out worksheets *after* reading a text—in which they report, for example, the predictions they made, images that occurred to them, questions that occurred to them, and/or a summary. Comprehension processes must be employed in real-time, and the best evidence of their use is students' responses *as* they read, not in response to questions (or worksheets) afterward. There is no evidence that a steady diet of completing such postreading sheets, in fact, leads to active reading (Pressley, 2006). Although worksheets and answering postreading comprehension questions may help prepare students for standardized tests, they fall short of building active comprehension processing per se—the habit of mind we want students to internalize and use forever. The key to internalization—owning active comprehension—is to experience several years of practicing comprehension processes in context every day. Thus, a student reading group is not evidencing active reading on its own until its individual members' discussions and think-alouds consistently manifest these processes.

REFLECTIONS AND FUTURE DIRECTIONS

We wish that we were just beginning our careers there are so many important questions concerning comprehension instruction that need to be answered. Yet we are reassured that these and many more inquiries will be addressed capably by the highly gifted teams of new young comprehension researchers who are accepting the responsibility to do so. Because many of the broader-based understandings concerning how comprehension occurs have been uncovered during the past half-century, a new younger generation of researchers is already focusing its work on more specific instructional challenges and issues. We suggest that such research be continued so more evidence-based comprehension practices can be created that will enable all students to learn to enjoy rich, continuous comprehension. For instance, we suggest that future scientists find ways to improve our present practices of teaching decoding and vocabulary skills so that this instruction does not occur as often in isolation of active, ongoing comprehension processing and instruction. We also need to learn more about how we can build *all* students' abilities to decode accurately during the comprehension process.

Since we know that accurate comprehension requires the mastery of several interrelated mental processes, we must learn to teach all readers to initiate these processes automatically and independently. Since we know that best practices include direct instruction and transactional strategy lessons, how can we enhance these lessons to better meet the needs of less able and ELL readers? Since we know that many of today's students cannot read with high levels of comprehension, we must develop more instructionally dense small-group guided-practice experiences such as reciprocal teaching and teacher-reader groups. The extended modeling that students need over time should come from more voices than any single teacher can supply.

Since we know that sustained silent reading alone does not produce consistently significant comprehension growth for all students, such methods as those described in step 4 of the basic lesson plan, the reading of multiple nonfiction books back to back, note taking, and reflection must all be tried so that independent practice sessions of comprehension lessons bear fruit for all readers. We must learn how to help students find information they want and use that information once found. More research should address the specific age level at which given comprehension processes are best introduced. Since we know that many teachers find it difficult to learn how to teach comprehension processes, we must increase our research base concerning best teacher education practices.

These are but a few of the exciting new discoveries that await us. We can't wait to see how these and other potential new findings will affect the comprehension practices in future classrooms. When new research becomes available, we are certain that more students will learn how to comprehend with greater ease and pleasure, and they will do so more rapidly through the rich learning experience with the strategies and processes we have described in this chapter.

CONCLUDING COMMENTS

In this chapter we have described research from 1956 to 2006 that informs best-comprehension instructional practices. The synthesis of this body of knowledge can lead our educational community to a deeper appreciation of the comprehension processes that are necessary even at the word-learning level and that all readers must become active, self-guided, metacognitively aware meaning makers. We presented a new instructional categorization for the teaching of comprehension processes: Students need comprehension processes to (1) understand words, (2) interpret sentences and paragraphs, (3) understand full texts well, and (4) shape and use the knowledge gained. We described several evidence-based best practices, including a basic comprehension lesson plan; how to teach multiple strategies in a single lesson with charts, post-it notes, and bookmarks; and how to teach students to better comprehend informational texts using *why* questions, note taking, and semantic mapping. We also discussed what best-comprehension instruction is *not*.

ENGAGEMENT ACTIVITIES

1. Readers of this chapter can examine their abilities to teach best comprehension practices. They can set a goal of adding one or more of these methods to their classroom program this year.
2. Readers can review their comprehension objectives to determine how many of the research-based goals they include in their instruction. Those that are not present can be incorporated and evaluated as to their effect on increasing students' abilities to become more active self-guided comprehenders.
3. Readers can set their own agendas as to how they would like to improve their teaching of comprehension. They might make pre- and post- audio- or videotapes of the teaching of one of the essential comprehension processes. They can share their tapes with colleagues as they work as a team to improve the comprehension instruction in their classrooms, school, and district.
4. Teachers, literacy coaches, administrators, and central office leaders can work together to implement the approaches covered in this chapter, including using this volume as a book study so that methods presented can be taught and shared on a monthly basis at school- and district-wide meetings.

REFERENCES

Afflerbach, P., & Meuwissen, K. (2005). Teaching and learning self-assessment strategies in middle school. In S. E. Israel, C. C. Block, K. L. Bauserman, & K. Kinnucan-Welsh (Eds.), *Metacognition in literacy learning: Theory, assessment, instruction, and professional development* (pp. 141–165). Mahwah, NJ: Erlbaum.

Anderson, R. C., & Pearson, P. D. (1984). A schema-theoretic view of basic processes in reading. In P. D. Pearson (Ed.), *Handbook of reading research* (pp. 255–291). New York: Longman.

Anderson, V. (1992). A teacher development project in transactional strategy instruction for teachers of severely reading disabled adolescents. *Teacher and Teacher Education, 8,* 391–403.

Applebee, A. N., Langer, J. A., Nystrand, M., & Gamoran, A. (2003). Discussion-based approaches to developing understanding: Classroom instruction and student performance in middle and high school English. *American Educational Research Journal, 40,* 685–730.

Baker, L. (2005). Developmental differences in metacognition: Implications for metacognitively oriented reading instruction. In S. E. Israel, C. C. Block, K. L. Bauserman, & K. Kinnucan-Welsh (Eds.), *Metacognition in literacy learning: Theory, assessment, instruction, and professional development* (pp. 61–81). Mahwah, NJ: Erlbaum.

Baumann, J. F., & Kame'enui, E. (Eds.). (2004). *Vocabulary instruction: Research to practice.* New York: Guilford Press.

Beach, R., & Hynds, S. (1991). Research on response to literature. In R. Barr, M. L. Kamil, P. Mosenthal, & P. D. Pearson (Eds.), *Handbook of reading research* (Vol. 2, pp. 453–489). White Plains, NY: Longman.

Bean, R. M. (2004). *The reading specialist: Leadership for the classroom, school, and community.* New York: Guilford Press.

Beck, I. L., McKeown, M. G., & Kucan, L. (2002). *Bringing words to life: Robust vocabulary instruction.* New York: Guilford Press.

Benton, V., & Cummins, C. (2000). *Nonfiction retelling: Teaching literacy skills through informational texts.* Bothell, WA: Wright Group/McGraw-Hill.

Block, C. C. (1993). Strategy instruction in a student-centered classroom. *The Elementary School Journal, 94*(2), 137–153.

Block, C. C. (2004). *Teaching comprehension: The comprehension process approach.* Boston: Allyn & Bacon.

Block, C. C. (2005a, December). *Effects of multiple comprehension process instruction on kindergarten through grade 5 students' achievement.* Paper presented at the annual meeting of the National Reading Conference, Miami.

Block, C. C. (2005b, December). *Effects of 8 weeks of direct vocabulary instruction on students achievement.* Paper presented at the annual meeting of the National Reading Conference, Miami.

Block, C. C. (2005c). What are metacognitive assessments? In S. E. Israel, C. C. Block, K. L. Bauserman, & K. Kinnucan-Welsh (Eds.), *Metacognition in literacy learning: Theory, assessment, instruction, and professional development* (pp. 83–101). Mahwah, NJ: Erlbaum.

Block, C. C., Gambrell, L. B., & Pressley, M. (2002). *Improving comprehension instruction: Rethinking theory, research and classroom practices.* San Francisco: Jossey-Bass.

Block, C. C., Hasni, J., & Mangieri, J. N. (2005, December). Effects of direct vocabulary instruction on students' vocabulary, comprehension and affective development. Paper presented at the annual meeting of the National Reading Conference, Miami, FL.

Block, C. C., & Israel, S. (2004). The ABCs of performing highly-effective think-alouds. *The Reading Teacher, 58*(2), 154–167.

Block, C. C., & Mangieri, J. N. (2003). *Exemplary literacy teachers: Promoting successs for all students in grades K–5.* New York: Guilford Press.

Block, C. C., & Mangieri, J. N. (2005). *Powerful vocabulary for reading success: Grades 3, 4, 5, and 6.* New York: Scholastic.

Block, C. C., Parris, S. R., Reed, K., & Whiteley, C. (in press). Learning environment effects on comprehension abilities. *Journal of Educational Psychology.*

Block, C. C., & Pressley, M. (2003). Best practices in comprehension instruction. In L. M. Morrow, L. B. Gambrell, & M. Pressley (Eds.), *Best practices in literacy instruction* (2nd ed., pp. 111–126). New York: Guilford Press.

Block, C. C., & Reed, K. (2005). *Effects of trade book reading on comprehension, vocabulary, fluency and attitudes* (Research Report No. 110224). Charlotte, NC: Institute for Literacy Enhancement.

Block, C. C., Rodgers, L., & Johnson, R. B. (2004). *Comprehension process instruction: Creating reading success in grades K–3.* New York: Guilford Press.

Bravo, M. A., Hiebert, E. H., & Pearson, P. D. (2007).Tapping the linguistic resources of Spanish–English bilinguals: The role of cognates in science. In R. K. Wagner, A. E. Muse, & K. R. Tannenbaum (Eds.), *Vocabulary acquisition: Implications for reading comprehension* (pp. 140–156). New York: Guilford Press.

Breznitz, Z. (1997a). Effects of accelerated rate on memory for text among dyslexic readers. *Journal of Educational Psychology, 89,* 289–297.

Breznitz, Z. (1997b). Enhancing the reading of dyslexic children by reading acceleration and auditory masking. *Journal of Educational Psychology, 89,* 103–113.

Brown, A. L., & Palincsar, A. S. (1989). Guided, cooperative learning and individual knowledge acquisition. In L. B. Resnick (Ed.), *Knowing, learning, and instruction: Essays in honor of Robert Glaser* (pp. 393–451). Hillsdale, NJ: Erlbaum.

Brown, R., Pressley, M., Van Meter, P., & Schuder, T. (1996). A quasi-experimental validation of transactional strategies instruction with low-achieving second grade readers. *Journal of Educational Psychology, 88,* 18–37.

Carlisle, J. F., Fleming, J. E., & Gudbrandsen, B. (2000). Incidental word learning in science classes. *Contemporary Educational Psychology, 25,* 184–211.

Carlo, M. S., August, D., McLaughlin, B., Snow, C. E., Dressler, C., Lippman, et al. (2004). Closing the gap: Addressing the vocabulary needs of English-language learners in bilingual and mainstream classrooms. *Reading Research Quarterly, 39*(3), 188–215.

Clark, J. M., & Paivio, A. (1991). Dual coding theory and education. *Educational Psychology Review, 3,* 149–210.

Collins, C. (1991). Reading instruction that increases thinking ability. *Journal of Reading, 34,* 510–516.

Cummins, C., Stewart, M. T., & Block, C. C. (2005). Teaching several metacognitive strategies together increases students' independent metacognition. In S. E. Israel, C. C. Block, K. L. Bauserman, & K. Kinnucan-Welsh (Eds.), *Metacognition in literacy learning: Theory, assessment, instruction, and professional development* (pp. 277–295). Mahwah, NJ: Erlbaum.

Dalton, B., & Robinson, F. (2005, December). *A comparison of teachers' enactment of reciprocal teaching in a print versus digital strategic reading environment.* Paper presented at the annual meeting of the National Reading Conference, Miami.

Doctorow, M., Wittrock, M. C., & Marks, C. (1978). Generative processes in reading comprehension. *Journal of Educational Psychology, 70,* 109–118.

Duffy, G. G. (2005). Developing metacognitive teachers: Visioning and the expert's changing role in teacher education and professional development. In S. E. Israel, C. C. Block, K. L. Bauserman, & K. Kinnucan-Welsh. (Eds.), *Metacognition in literacy learning: Theory, assessment, instruction, and professional development* (pp. 299–315). Mahwah, NJ: Erlbaum.

Duffy, G. G., & Roehler, L. R. (1989). Why strategy instruction is so difficult and what we need to do about it. In C. B. McCormick, G. Miller, & M. Pressley (Eds.), *Cognitive strategy research: From basic research to educational applications* (pp. 133–154). New York: Springer-Verlag.

Durkin, D. (1978–1979). What classroom observations reveal about reading comprehension instruction. *Reading Research Quarterly, 37,* 734–744.

Fielding, L. G., & Pearson, P. D. (1994). Synthesis of research: Reading comprehension: What works? *Educational Leadership, 51* (5), 62–67.

Flavell, J. (1977). *Cognitive development.* Englewood Cliffs, NJ: Prentice Hall.

Goswami, U. (2004). Neoscience and education. *British Journal of Educational Psychology, 74,* 1–14.

Hiebert, E. H., Pearson, D., & Ayra, D. J. (2005, December). *Learning Complex Vocabulary in a science text.* Paper presented at the annual meeting of the National Reading Conference, Miami.

Israel, S. E., Block, C. C., Bauserman, K. L., & Kinnucan-Welsh, K. (Eds.). (2005). *Metacognition in literacy learning: Theory, assessment, instruction, and professional development.* Mahwah, NJ: Erlbaum.

Israel, S. E., & Massey, D. (2005). Metacognitive think-alouds: Using a gradual release model with middle school students. In S. E. Israel, C. C. Block, K. L. Bauserman, & K. Kinnucan-Welsh (Eds.), *Metacognition in literacy learning: Theory, assessment, instruction, and professional development* (pp. 183–199). Mahwah, NJ: Erlbaum.

LaBerge, D., & Samuels, S. J. (1974). Toward a theory of automatic information processing in reading. *Cognitive Psychology, 6,* 293–323.

Leu, D. (2005, December). *New advancements in instruction relative to technology comprehension.* Presidential address presented at the annual meeting of the National Reading Conference, Miami.

Levin, J. R. (1973). Inducing comprehension in poor readers: A test of a recent model. *Journal of Educational Psychology, 65,* 9–24.

Mandler, J. M. (1984). *Stories, scripts, and scenes: Aspects of schema theory.* Hillsdale, NJ: Erlbaum.

Meichenbaum, D. (1977). *Cognitive behavior modification.* New York: Plenum.

Miller, G. A. (1956). The magical number seven, plus-or-minus two: Some limits on our capacity for processing information. *Psychological Review, 63,* 81–97.

National Reading Panel. (2000). *Report of the National Reading Panel Subgroups: Teaching children to read* (No. 00-4754). Washington, DC: Government Printing Office.

Paris, S. G., & Flukes, J. (2005). Assessing children's metacognition about strategic reading. In S. E. Israel, C. C. Block, K. Bauserman, & K. Kinnucan-Welsh (Eds.), *Metacognition in literacy learning: Theory, assessment, instruction, and professional development* (pp. 121–141). Mahwah, NJ: Erlbaum.

Paris, S. G., Lipson, M. Y., & Wixson, K. K. (1983). Becoming a strategic reader. *Contemporary Educational Psychology, 8*, 293–316.

Pearson, P. D. (2005, December). *The impact of text genre on students' acquisition of science.* Paper presented at the annual meeting of the National Reading Conference, Miami.

Pressley, M. (1976). Mental imagery helps eight-year-olds remember what they read. *Journal of Educational Psychology, 68*, 355–359.

Pressley, M. (1977). Imagery and children's learning: Putting the picture in developmental perspective. *Review of Educational Research, 47*, 586–622.

Pressley, M. (2006). *Reading instruction that works: The case for balanced teaching* (3rd ed.). New York: Guilford Press.

Pressley, M., & Afflerbach, P. (1995). *Verbal protocols of reading: The nature of constructively responsive reading.* Hillsdale, NJ: Erlbaum.

Pressley, M., Gaskins, I. W., Wile, D., Cunicelli, B., & Sheridan, J. (1991). Teaching literacy strategies across the curriculum: A case study at Benchmark School. In J. Zutell & S. McCormick (Eds.), *Learner factors/teacher factors: Issues in literacy research and instruction: Fortieth yearbook of the National Reading Conference* (pp. 219–228). Chicago: National Reading Conference.

Pressley, M., Heisel, B. E., McCormick, C. G., & Nakamura, G. V. (1982). Memory strategy instruction with children. In C. J. Brainerd & M. Pressley (Eds.), *Progress in cognitive development research: Vol. 2. Verbal processes in children* (pp. 125–159). New York: Springer-Verlag.

Purcell, V., & Duke, N. (2005, December). *Comprehending non-fictional text.* Paper presented at the annual meeting of the National Reading Conference. Miami.

RAND Reading Study Group. (2002). *Reading for understanding: Towards an R & D program in reading comprehension.* Washington, DC: RAND Education.

Risko, V. J., Roskos, K., & Vukelich, C. (2005). Reflection and the self-analytic turn of mind: Toward more robust instruction in teacher in education. In S. E. Israel, C. C. Block, K. L. Bauserman, & K. Kinnucan-Welsh (Eds.), *Metacognition in literacy learning: Theory, assessment, instruction, and professional development* (pp. 315–335). Mahwah, NJ: Erlbaum.

Rosenblatt, L. M. (1978). *The reader, the text, the poem: The transactional theory of the literary work.* Carbondale, IL: Southern Illinois University Press.

Samuels, J. (2002). Fluency instruction. In A. Farstrup & J. Samuels (Eds.), *What research has to say about reading instruction* (2nd ed., pp. 347–369). Newark, DE: International Reading Association.

Schmitt, M. C. (2005). Measuring students' awareness and control of strategic processes. In S. E. Israel, C. C. Block, K. L. Bauserman, & K. Kinnucan-Welsh (Eds.), *Metacognition in literacy learning: Theory, assessment, instruction, and professional development* (pp. 101–121). Mahwah, NJ: Erlbaum.

Short, E. J., & Ryan, E. B. (1984). Metacognitive differences between skilled and less-skilled readers: Remediating deficits through story grammar and attribution training. *Journal of Educational Psychology, 76*, 225–235.

Stahl, S., & Kapinus, B. (2001). Word power: What every educator needs to know about vocabulary. Washington, DC: NEA Professional Library.

Stein, N. L., & Glenn, C. G. (1979). An analysis of story comprehension in elementary school children. In R. O. Freedle (Ed.), *New directions in discourse processing.* (Vol. 2, pp. 53–120). Norwood, NJ: Ablex.

Stewart, M. T. (2004). Early literacy instruction in the climate of No Child Left Behind. *The Reading Teacher, 57*(8), 732–753.

Tan, A., & Nicholson, T. (1997). Flashcards revisited: Training poor readers to read words faster improves their comprehension of text. *Journal of Educational Psychology, 89,* 276–288.

Taylor, B. M. (1982). Text structure and children's comprehension and memory for expository material. *Journal of Educational Psychology, 74,* 323–340.

van Dijk, T., & Kintsch, W. (1983). *Strategies of discourse comprehension.* New York: Academic Press.

Vygotsky, L. S. (1978). *Mind in society: The development of higher psychological processes.* Cambridge, MA: Harvard University Press.

Zimmermann, S., & Hutchins, C. (2003). *7 keys to comprehension: How to help your kids read it and get it!* New York: Three Rivers Press.

Chapter 11

BEST PRACTICES IN TEACHING WRITING

Karen Bromley

This chapter will:

- Discuss theory and research on writing.
- Present evidence-based practices for K–8 writing instruction.
- Suggest future directions for literacy instruction.

> "State testing isn't affecting my writing instruction all that much. I believe that if I can give students confidence to write and the skills to write well, then that will be reflected in their tests. We will do one parallel writing task this year—but I feel that spending too much time on test format and not good quality writing is a waste of our time."

This statement by Dodie, a sixth-grade literacy teacher in a suburban school district, reflects the feelings of teachers who find that within the context of state assessments they can provide best practices in writing instruction to students. Although testing drives teaching in many classrooms, there are teachers like Dodie who believe they need to help students develop as writers first so that achievement on tests is a natural outcome. These teachers use a writing process approach and direct instruction in skills to develop good writers. They believe that when students can articulate ideas confidently and write in organized, fluent, and clear ways, they will do well on writing tests.

Tracy, a grade 3–5 curriculum coordinator in a large urban school district with a diverse student population, says:

> "I have a somewhat negative view of these tests since I see the stress they place on teachers and the imbalance between on-demand writing and planned, thoughtful writing. The tests require the use of text-based details with little opportunity for independent thinking or use of prior knowledge. They send students mixed messages about what reading and writing are *really* all about."

Tracy works with teachers like Dodie and others who struggle to make writing interesting and authentic as they teach the skills students need to do well on tests. Many of these teachers want to remain loyal to a writing process approach because they believe it develops thoughtful and effective writers. Yet, they must also prepare students for "on-demand" writing tasks that include little opportunity for planning and revising. These teachers regularly have students complete "parallel tasks" that mirror the kinds of writing on the tests. But, theory and research show that both a writing process approach and direct skill instruction help students become good writers. This chapter explores writing and the kind of writing instruction teachers like Dodie and curriculum coordinators like Tracy use to develop good writers and prepare students for tests.

EVIDENCE-BASED BEST PRACTICES

Writing is a complex interaction of cognitive and physical factors. It involves the hand, eye, and both sides of the brain. Writing requires making connections and constructing meaning. It is a way to explore thinking and create new knowledge. It requires knowing the conventions of grammar, spelling, punctuation, and form. It involves small-muscle development and eye–hand coordination to form letters, words, and paragraphs with a pen, pencil, or keys on a computer keyboard. It requires having a vocabulary that permits effective self-expression. Writing can be a personal process done solely for oneself or a social process done for and with others.

Writing Theory

Cambourne's (1988) model of learning applied to literacy provides a framework for understanding writing. He suggests that authentic *engagement* accompanied by *immersion* and *demonstration* result in good writing. Cambourne believes that students learn to write when they are surrounded with examples and models, given expectations, allowed to make decisions and mistakes, provided with feedback, and given time to practice in realistic ways. To be fully and successfully engaged in writing, what students write about must be relevant to them.

Oral language is an important contributor to writing, because both depend on the same cognitive abilities. Vygotsky (1978) theorized that children's early speech is a precursor to inner speech, which in turn results in the ability to think in words. This self-talk is like an inner commentator that develops into a mature writer's voice (Armstrong, 2003). Although no consistent body of research supports the specifics of the relationship, it is likely that oral language ability is a valuable foundation for writing (Shanahan, 2006). Vygotsky (1978) believed thought and knowledge emerge from oral language that is embedded in social interaction. He believed that this co-construction of meaning leads to learning. Writing can be a social act and is often stronger because of interactions that result when students talk and create new meanings together.

Social interaction around a shared experience is the foundation of the language experience approach. When students talk about an experience and that talk is transcribed, they can then read the written story or report. Young children learn how to write and how to read as a result of the social interaction that is part of the language experience approach. Similar substantive discussions or "curricular conversations" focused on content strengthen middle school students' writing, as well as their reading, speaking, and thinking abilities (Angelis, 2003). This kind of *demonstration* and *immersion* in talking, writing, and reading as students create meaning together is the *engagement* Cambourne (1988) says is at the heart of all learning.

Graves's (1983, 1994) work with young children resulted in a model of the writing process that is also based on relevance and engagement in the recursive steps of *planning, drafting, revising, editing,* and *publishing* for a real audience. This process approach to writing is part of a writing workshop format (Fletcher & Portaluppi, 2001) in which the teacher sets up the structure and allows students plenty of choice in what they write. Atwell's (1998) work with middle-school students also supports the use of writing process in a writing workshop.

Grammar, Spelling, and Other Conventions

Research has shown grammar instruction to have little positive effect on writing. Studies over time indicate that teaching formal grammar to students has "a negligible or even harmful effect on improving students' writing" (Routman, 1996; p. 119). In fact, "a heavy emphasis on mechanics and usage results in significant losses in overall quality" (Hillocks, 1987, p. 74). Thus, The National Council of Teachers of English (NCTE) published a resolution urging teachers to discard traditional school grammar instruction (Brozo, 2003).

In a climate of standards-based mandated tests that often require students to correct errors, teachers may need to focus student attention on identifying and correcting errors (Smith, Cheville, & Hillocks, 2006). Alerting students to the pattern of errors they commit within and across their own writing assignments is one way to do this (Weaver, 1998). Using strategies and lesson plans for examining and correcting errors gives teachers and students another window into using standard grammar and conventions in writing.

Research suggests a strong relationship between spelling and writing. Good writing depends on the automatic use of spelling skills. When students struggle with spelling, they use up valuable cognitive resources that they might otherwise use for other aspects of writing (Singer & Bashir, 2004). Students who try to use standard spelling but do not possess this skill may labor over every word and use words that he or she can readily spell rather than words that are more difficult. Thus, accurate and automatic spelling can improve fluency (McCutcheon, 2006), and the quality and length of a written piece is affected as well as a writer's confidence.

In fact, Moats (2005–2006) calls for automatic knowledge of spelling and other conventions. She says, "Even more than reading, writing is a mental juggling act that depends on automatic deployment of basic skills such as handwriting, spelling, grammar, and punctuation so that the writer can keep track of such concerns as topic, organization, word choice, and audience needs" (p. 12). Knowledge of conventions is important whether students write with pencil and paper or use a computer and word processor. While grammar checkers may underline grammatical problems and spell checkers may correct misspellings of commonly used words, these devices do not catch all errors, and students still need knowledge of standard grammar and spelling.

But, students can become more metacognitively aware of their own thinking and may produce better writing when they use a word processor, since it does change some spelling and correct some grammar (Berninger & Winn, 2006). Baker (2000) found word processors eased the difficulties many young children have with fine motor control as they try to form letters and helped them better understand revision. Baker also found that, through student interaction with the Web and Information and Communication Technology the writing abilities of students improved. They found support for their writing efforts, increased their awareness of audience, and gained useful feedback.

Although vocabulary is not considered a writing convention, it is an important contributor to good writing. Zarry (1999) found that students who received vocabulary instruction that engaged them in playful activities used the words they learned more often in their writing and wrote narratives of a higher quality than students who did not receive such instruction. The students each received a thesaurus and were encouraged to select their own words to use in their writing and create their own definitions and sentences for each word.

Special Populations

Research on gender differences in the writing of elementary and middle-school students is striking. On standardized writing tests, girls in the 4th, 8th, and 12th grades consistently outperformed boys in narrative, persuasive, and informative writing (National Assessment of Educational Progress [NAEP], 2002). Peterson (2006) found that the writing of boys was more action-filled, competitive, and assertive than the writing of girls, which was more nurturing and focused on domestic topics. Boys more often wrote in the first person and wrote shorter pieces, while girls wrote in the third person and wrote longer pieces using more adjectives than boys. Girls were more confident and were viewed as better writers by both boys and girls.

Studies of students with learning disabilities indicate these students possess limited metacognitive awareness of the knowledge, skills, and strategies necessary to be good writers (Troia, 2006). So, writing instruction that incorporates self-monitoring, goal setting, and self-evaluation is important for these students. Troia reported that these students often skip the planning stage, have problems generating and transcribing ideas, and often do not revise. He notes that students with learning disabilities need more time provided for writing, and they need intensive, individualized, and explicit instruction in self-regulation skills and writing strategies.

NAEP (2002) results also showed that Asian–Pacific Islanders and white students outperformed black and Hispanic students in the 4th, 8th, and 12th grades in writing. Other students from diverse cultural and language backgrounds do not do well on NAEP and other standardized tests. They often come from urban schools in poor communities that lack the resources of more affluent schools. In an analysis of 50 studies of K–12 writing with racial or ethnic minorities, Ball (2006) observed that teaching strategies that include a balance between process and product writing and reflect cultural understandings and influences on students' writing are necessary to help these students meet the demands of school and work.

Casey and Hemenway (2001) conducted a 10-year study of students from third grade to high school graduation, and the conclusion they arrived at is important. They found that a balance between structure and freedom results in "more dynamic writers excited about their abilities" (p. 68). Their study suggests that providing instruction that is intentional, socially interactive, and authentic can build a bridge between structure and freedom that supports good writing.

The previous discussion briefly examines some of the theory and research evidence that supports writing instruction. In the next section, the classroom practices of several K–8 teachers provide examples of some best practices for sound writing instruction.

BEST PRACTICES IN ACTION

Mandated assessments, higher standards, and accountability issues cause some teachers to reduce time for writing, teach writing artificially, and fragment the curriculum (Strickland et al., 2001). In some classrooms, the focus may be away from the writing process and toward writing skills and the written product. While proponents of a process approach to writing instruction are sometimes criticized for overlooking direct instruction, conventions, and legibility, a skills-product approach, including grammar and punctuation practice and teacher-provided prompts and rubrics, is sometimes criticized for its teacher-centeredness and tending to overlook student motivation, purpose, and voice. However, good writers need *simultaneous* opportunities to engage in the process and to learn the skills of writing. The following discussion explores three areas to include in a best-practices writing program, namely, context for writing, intentional writing instruction, and writing assessment.

Context for Writing

The context or environment for writing is critical to best-practices instruction. A context for writing includes individual, physical, and social aspects that impact instruction. The individual teacher's attitude and commitment are critical. For example, when teachers identify and commit to improving student writing as a school-wide goal, the focus of their professional development can be on writing. Teachers can study writing, have conversations about their students' writing, analyze writing tests and test results to see what their students do and don't do, develop writing curriculum, and create a vision of exemplary student performance and specify criteria for it. A place to begin to teach writing well is to examine present practices with questions like these:

- What choices do my students have in their writing?
- How much and what kind of writing do they do daily?
- Who do my students write for besides me? Who gives them feedback on their writing?

- Are they writing in a variety of forms in all content areas?
- How do I use the writing process? What kind of direct instruction do I provide?
- What opportunities do I provide students to use word processors and email?

Self-evaluation is also important for students because it encourages them to take responsibility for their own writing progress. A writing attitude survey can provide information about how students feel about writing (Kear, Coffman, McKenna, & Ambrosio, 2000). Periodic self-evaluation with questions like these also helps students reflect and set goals for themselves:

- What do I do well as a writer?
- What is one thing I have learned most recently as a writer?
- What do I need to learn to be a better writer?
- How can I improve?

Creating a context for writing includes creating a physical environment that is rich with words for students to use when they write. In the following classrooms, two teachers recognize the value of environmental print for teaching reading and writing. In Kelly's first grade, she adds several words to the *word wall* every week so students can use them in their writing. The class composes a daily Morning Message as they convert spoken language to writing and learn to spell, form letters, and use punctuation. There are printed 5 × 8 labels identifying the *wastebasket*, the *pencil sharpener*, and other classroom objects. In Sean's classroom, like Kelly's, there is a writing corner with baskets of pencils, felt-tip markers, calligraphy pens, colored pencils, ballpoint pens, and paper. In both classrooms, each student has a dictionary and thesaurus. Sean's classroom also has word walls for science and social studies terms. They are especially helpful for the five English-language learners in the class. Sean says Lev, who is newly from Russia, and a buddy use the word walls each day as Lev learns English and teaches his buddy Russian.

Another aspect of context for writing is the social interactions teachers provide to develop good writing. Both classrooms are wired for Internet access, and every student uses a computer on a regular basis. Students locate information on the Internet and plan, draft, revise, and publish their stories, poems, and reports using a variety of software including *Inspiration* and *Publisher*. In Sean's classroom, his sixth graders use Blackboard, an online classroom program where students discuss books they are reading and respond to one another's postings.

Kelly and Sean set aside blocks of time when students write on topics of their choice during writing workshop (Atwell, 1998; Calkins, 1994;

Fletcher & Portaluppi, 2001). Calkins (1994) suggests that writing workshop should include minilessons, work time for writing, peer conferring and/or response groups, share sessions, and publication celebrations. Teachers who use Atwell's (1998) and Fletcher and Portaluppi's (2001) model spend an hour a day in writing workshop that includes a brief lesson on a demonstrated need of a group of students. These teachers also spend time sharing and discussing a well-written piece of literature to help students improve their writing and learn to respond to a piece of work. Writing is also integrated with content-area learning so that students in these classrooms are writing to learn as they are learning to write.

Many teachers encourage buddy reading, discussion, and collaborative writing, which is particularly helpful for students who may have ideas to contribute but who may not yet have the language skills, motivation, or confidence to write without this stimulation. Both students who are learning English and those who struggle with it are supported and encouraged to develop their abilities when they work in pairs with students who possess strong skills. Both Kelly and Sean share models with their students of the kinds of writing they expect them to do. They compose reports, poems, and other written forms with the class as a whole so that students have opportunities to learn from one another as they see a piece develop.

Establishing a writing community in the classroom and school is also critical to building a social context and improving student writing. Calling students "authors" and "writers" can have a positive effect on how students view themselves, and whether or not and how they write. Posting writing in the classroom of every student validates them as writers as well. Inviting authors and illustrators of children's books to share their work with students can nudge even the most reluctant writer to write. The entire school can study the work of an author before a visit so students know the author's style and content and can interact in substantive ways with him or her. A visit from an author like Jerry Pallotta (*www.alphabetman.com/*), who talks about his writing and shares the many alphabet books he has written can spark students of all ages to read his work and write like him.

Intentional Writing Instruction

Writers need direct intentional instruction in writing as well as time to write (Tompkins, 2004). Students need to learn how to use the traits of writing effectively—ideas, organization, voice, word choice, sentence fluency, conventions, and presentation (Culham, 2003). They need opportunities for enough instruction, guidance, and practice to allow them to become accomplished. Good writing teachers balance writing process and product as they celebrate and encourage clarity of meaning, creativity, and standard English.

NCTE promotes teaching standard conventions and correctness by having students edit writing they do for real purposes (Brozo, 2003). Other alternatives to isolated grammar instruction include teaching grammar during writing instruction, having grammar debates, teaching students to use style manuals, creating assignments that require writing for real audiences, and studying grammar controversies (Dunn & Lindblom, 2003). When teachers engage students in the writing process, teach and discuss word usage, and teach students to construct sentences using their own work, students can use grammar to improve their writing.

Many teachers incorporate direct instruction in composing and the conventions of grammar, spelling, form, and handwriting into writing workshop (Peterson, 2000). For example, teaching terms like *purpose, audience, form, voice, noun, verb,* and *adjective* gives students a common vocabulary for discussing and improving their writing. Talking about sentence construction, grammar, and usage makes sense to students when they are writing for a specific audience that is real. Many teachers use "fix-the-error exercises" to teach specific grammar skills with examples from real literature that students are familiar with (Kane, 1997). Like Kelly and Sean, they teach minilessons using their own writing and volunteers' writing to show how quotation marks, commas, and periods should be used.

Karen, a third-grade teacher who has been using writing workshop for several years, begins with a lesson on one aspect of writing that she knows a group of students needs help with, such as organization, run-on sentences, adjectives, verbs, or punctuation. Recently, Karen taught a minilesson on common and proper nouns after noticing the overuse of pronouns in several of her third-grade students' narrative stories. Part of the lesson included revising the work of a draft volunteered by a student. On another day she reviewed with the class the function and placement of topic sentences in expository writing and a five-paragraph report (a one-paragraph introduction, three-paragraph body, and one-paragraph conclusion).

Often in a minilesson Karen shares a piece of writing as a model so that her students will know what good writing looks and sounds like (Calkins, 1994; McElveen & Dierking, 2001). Reading and listening to literature helps students think like writers and write with an audience in mind. Good narrative and expository writing lets students see how an author holds the reader's attention and uses conventions. Then students can begin to use this knowledge in their own writing. For example, one third grader had read several of R. L. Stine's books in which "*THE END*" is used in the final sentence, as in "It doesn't really matter in . . . THE END." The student borrowed this technique and concluded his nonfiction report with "Volcanoes are very cool but when they erupt it's . . . THE END."

To extend her students' writing beyond topics they choose themselves, Karen uses a *genre study* (Calkins, 1994), where students immerse themselves in a particular kind of literature and then write in this form. For example, during recent writing workshops and in conjunction with a social studies unit, Karen's students read nonfiction books about animals, gathered information from a CD-ROM encyclopedia, took an electronic field trip to a zoo, and then created their own informative report about an animal. She compiled these reports into a book that her students shared with a first-grade class. Karen encourages students to coauthor at least one story or report because she believes collaboration is a catalyst for learning.

Even first and second graders can immerse themselves in a genre, such as informational text for example, and learn to write in that format (Moss, 2005). Read (2005) found that instructional practices in primary grades underestimate the ability of these students. She says, "Given appropriate instruction in the skills of writing and a topic that they've chosen and find interesting, young students are fully capable of dealing with the complex problems that occur when reading and writing informational texts" (Read, 2005, p. 44).

Teachers of writing need to be writers themselves. Tracy, the curriculum coordinator whose quote also introduced this chapter, keeps a personal journal, uses email, and writes curriculum, lesson plans, and grant proposals. She believes that writing regularly is a powerful strategy for learning subject matter. She says:

> "Writing is a process of constructing meaning, and I never realize what I know until I start writing. I come up with ideas I didn't have before I begin writing. For this reason, I believe writing should be part of every content area."

When students write in a variety of forms in the content areas to explain or share information, they construct new meaning and demonstrate their science and social studies knowledge, too.

Expository writing across the curriculum can take many forms. In first grade, Kelly linked math, social studies, and language arts in a unit called "Quilt Connections." After students had read and heard stories about quilts, researched other cultures' quilts in the library and on the Internet, visited a museum exhibit, and learned about shapes, equal parts, and fractions, a final activity involved creating a quilt. The finished quilt, made of special fabrics and designs contributed by students, went home each day with a different student along with a journal. Students and parents wrote about the quilt in the journal, giving parents an opportunity for involvement in their child's classroom learning.

In third grade, during a study of the Cheyenne, Iroquois, Navaho, Sioux, and Seminole tribes, Karen had students write daily "on-demand" responses to questions she posed to them. In this on-demand writing, students have only a short time to think, perhaps list a few ideas, and then write. Karen does not grade this work, but she reads it and responds and/or she has students read and respond to one another's entries. Karen's students, like Dodie's sixth graders, also engage in writing an occasional "parallel task," which mirrors the kind of writing task found on the state tests. For example, at the conclusion of the study of Indians, Karen had her students read a short nonfiction article and a poem about Indian reservations, compare the information offered in each, and write an essay from the perspective of a member of one of the tribes they studied. In the finished pieces they compared and contrasted information from both sources and presented them to the class.

Writing to explain is part of many mandated math tests. Colleen's eighth-grade students use journals as a way to explain math concepts. This is a way to explore students' thinking, and it is an example of on-demand writing. Colleen's students also write to her in their journals to explain what they believe they do well, what they don't understand, and, for extra credit, how to correct test items they missed. This kind of expository writing exposes students' reasoning so that Colleen can reteach a concept if needed. For Colleen, writing is an assessment tool that helps to measure math learning and misconceptions.

Because graphic organizers are visual representations of information that show relationships and contain key vocabulary, they make excellent planning tools for writing (Bromley, in press-b; Irwin-DeVitis, Bromley, & Modlo, 1999). They also appear on many mandated tests, thus making it important that even young students learn to use them. For students learning English or those with learning disabilities in literacy, graphic organizers are particularly useful, because they simplify information, use key words, and help organize ideas before writing. When Karen's third graders compared and contrasted a nonfiction selection and poem as part of the parallel task cited above, they used Venn diagrams and t-charts to plan their writing.

Graphic organizers also support research. For example, in a study of Mexico, Rebecca's second-grade students gathered information from several sources on data charts before they wrote about what they learned. As part of a sixth-grade unit on immigration, Michele's students took the perspective of a person in the story or focused on relationships among characters in *Esperanza Rising* by Pam Munoz Ryan (2000). Before writing, students used a character map and character relationship map to record evidence and page numbers where it appeared.

Central to good writing instruction is giving students choices in the topics to write about and choices among teacher-provided topics. Choices in both topic and format can build interest and commitment to writing. For example, to conclude a study of pollution and the environment, Sean and his class identified several writing options. Then students signed up in groups of four for the project they wanted to complete. One group wrote and performed a play, a second group wrote an article for the local newspaper accompanied by digital pictures, two groups created PowerPoint presentations, and another group updated entries on the Internet encyclopedia Wikipedia about the effects of river pollution on local bird life.

Today, many students use computers to do research for written reports and presentations and publish their work on the Internet (Wepner & Tao, 2002). Both students and teachers use the Internet, CD-ROM encyclopedias, and primary sources on the Web such as historical documents or secondary sources like museum or observatory websites (Leu, 2000; Owens, Hester, & Teale, 2002). Research in K–6 classrooms indicates that teachers report an increase in student motivation to write when their work is published on the Internet (Karchmer, 2001). In addition to skills in viewing and analyzing, when students write for the Internet they build skills in keyboarding, word processing, and navigating with browsers and search engines. Some examples follow for using the computer to develop student writers:

- Establish electronic key pal exchanges with students in other states or countries that can be social and/or related to science or social studies.
- Help students use a software program to write items for a monthly classroom newsletter; use clip art, formatted text, and emails, or take hard copies to parents.
- Alert students and parents to Internet sites that publish student work, such as:
  - *www.kidsbookshelf.com/index.asp* (publishes book reviews, poems, short stories)
  - *Writing With Writers teacher.scholastic.com/writewit/index.htm* (provides a workshop environment in which students can email their work to professional writers who will comment on it)
  - *www.kidpub.com/kidpub/* (publishes stories; students can read works by other students and participate in a never-ending interactive story)

Writing Assessment

"Writing instruction has improved dramatically over the last 25 years" (Lenski & Johns, 2000, p. 1). Much of this improvement can be attributed to better writing assessments that inform more effective writing instruction. Of course, not all writing needs formal assessment, but, whether formal or informal, assessment should be ongoing. Teachers need to assess their writing instruction, and students need to regularly assess their own written products (Bromley, in press-a). Portfolios, rubrics, and checklists offer opportunities for writing assessment by both students and teachers.

Students often keep their writing in all its stages in writing folders or portfolios. This collection of work creates a record of student progress and can show a student's growth as a writer. But, students need to examine their work, reflect on the patterns they see, and set new goals for themselves as well. Teachers, students, and parents can examine written work in a folder or portfolio to determine what skills a student possesses and needs to develop. As well, conversations with parents and assigning grades are more easily accomplished when there is a body of written work from which to make observations.

Rubrics and checklists can also help identify students' strengths and needs (Bromley, in press-a; Tompkins, 2004). Dodie says her team of teachers often develops rubrics and checklists based on the priorities for grading a particular project. One project Dodie uses to develop students' careful reading and to build expository and persuasive writing skills is the "Classic" Inspiration Project (see Figure 11.1). The project introduces the class to books they may not have read yet and integrates reading, writing, and technology. In this essay students consider whether or not they believe a book is a "classic" (one that reflects quality, a universal theme, and the potential for longevity). Dodie wants students to develop arguments based on evidence and share their arguments with the class. Students must read a book or choose a book they have read and either defend it or be critical of it. In their essays, students use Inspiration software and are graded with the rubric in Figure 11.1. They must produce a pleasing and readable visual layout with appropriate computer graphics, and present the finished essays to the class. Dodie allocates points for specific components, spelling, layout, and graphics, for a total of 100 points. She often has students give themselves a grade using this rubric. She also completes a grading, and then she conferences with students to determine whether and how they agree with her assessment, which she believes helps improve their writing and accuracy in self-assessment.

Dodie also has her sixth graders create checklists and rubrics with her, because "They seem to understand the assignment better and have confidence that they can achieve a higher grade when they have a say in rubric development." First, she explains the project or writing piece and shares an exemplar. She has students brainstorm characteristics or criteria for an excellent paper. Then they group the characteristics into categories and students rate them for importance. Lastly, Dodie creates a draft,

Name____Date_______Period_____
Book Title____
Author____

	4	3	2	1
All three components included	• 2 reasons book is a *classic* with examples • 2 exciting or engaging parts • Theme and why it is universal (30 pts.)	3–4 components explained accurately (25 pts.)	1–2 components explained accurately (20 pts.)	1 component explained accurately (10 pts.)
Spelling	All spelling accurate (20 pts.)	All but 1–3 words spelled accurately (17 pts.)	All but 4–5 words spelled accurately (12 pts.)	All but 5 or more words spelled accurately (15 pts.)
Layout	• Flows in a way that is organized and easy to understand • Shows creativity • Graphics do not interfere with info (30 pts.)	• Layout is mostly under-standable • Organiza-tion is present, but little creativity • Some graphics get in way of info (25 pts.)	• Layout is partly under-standable • Weak orga-nization • Little creativity • Graphics interfere with info (20 pts.)	• Layout is confusing • Lacks orga-nization • Graphics interfere with info (15 pts.)
Graphics	• Pictures and graphics used are appropriate • They aid creativity (20 pts.)	• Most pic-tures and graphics used are appropriate (17 pts.)	• Some pictures and graphics are appropriate (12 pts.)	• Pictures and graphics are not appropriate • Pictures and graphics hinder pre-sentation of info (8 pts.)

Comments:

FIGURE 11.1. "Classic" Inspiration Project rubric.

shares it on the overhead, and the class edits it as needed and votes to accept it. When students create criteria for a written piece, such as the Descriptive Writing Checklist in Figure 11.2, Dodie feels it has a dramatic effect on the finished product. When students have finished writing and revising, they check off the presence of each component and then have a peer read the piece and do the same. Based on this feedback, students revise before they hand the paper to Dodie. She says, "You can't possibly do this for every checklist or rubric. But once the process is completed, you can use some of the criteria for other projects or pieces, as I did to create the rubric for this essay" (see Figure 11.3).

Knowing the key components of a good piece of writing provides students with goals for writing and the characteristics of a good report, essay, letter, PowerPoint presentation, play, or poem, for example, before they write. It also gives the teacher and students an objective way to assess the finished product after writing. Rubrics show teachers what to reteach, and rubrics can help parents understand a student's grade. Of course, teachers don't use them for every piece of writing, but they can improve the quality of writing on key assignments and final projects.

Name____________________________________Date________Period______

Title of Essay____

My Editing Peer____

Directions: Use this checklist as you work on your essay. Your essay will be scored according to the rubric on the attached sheet.

Literary Style	Self	Peer
Includes title	____	____
Varies sentence structure and length	____	____
Includes at least 2 similes	____	____
Includes at least 1 metaphor	____	____
Uses adjectives, adverbs, and vivid verbs	____	____
Refers to a minimum of 3 senses	____	____
Organization		
Introductory paragraph has a clear topic	____	____
Introductory paragraph grabs the reader's attention	____	____
All paragraphs include a main idea and supporting details	____	____
A clear and logical order of information is evident	____	____
Details let the reader develop a clear mental picture	____	____
Concluding paragraph is a summary and restates the central idea	____	____
Mechanics		
Uses capital letters correctly	____	____
Uses all punctuation correctly	____	____
Essay is free of spelling errors	____	____
Essay is free of run-on sentences and fragments	____	____

FIGURE 11.2. Descriptive Writing Checklist.

Name____Date__________Period_____

Title of Essay____

	4	3	2	1	0
Descriptive components	Unique language that engages the senses—2 similes, 1 metaphor, adverbs, adjectives, and vivid verbs (35 pts.)	Language is often precise and appropriate. Vivid vocabulary present with 1 missing component (29 pts.)	Some language is precise and appropriate. Vivid vocabulary minimal with 2–3 missing components (25 pts.)	Limited use of vivid vocabulary and figurative language, with 4 or more components missing (21 pts.)	Lacks descriptive components. Not developed as a descriptive writing piece (0 pts.)
Mechanics	Varied sentence structure. All correct grammar, capitals, punctuation (15 pts.)	Most sentences show variety. Correct grammar, capitals, punctuation except 1–2 errors (13 pts.)	Some sentence variety. Correct grammar, capitals, punctuation except 3–4 errors (11 pts.)	Little sentence variety. Correct grammar, capitals, punctuation except 5 or more errors (9 pts.)	No sentence variety. Incomplete sentences. Grammar and other errors hinder message (0 pts.)
Spelling	All spelling correct (15 pts.)	All but 1 word spelled correctly (13 pts.)	All but 2–3 words spelled correctly (11 pts.)	All but 4 or more words spelled correctly (9 pts.)	Many spelling errors that affect message (0 pts.)
Organization	All paragraphs include topic and conclusion sentences with details. Clear connections and smooth transitions (35 pts.)	Most paragraphs include topic and conclusion sentences and details. Some unclear connections and transitions (29 pts.)	Some paragraphs include topic and conclusion sentences and details. Weak organization and sequence of ideas (25 pts.)	Some organization. Transitions and connections not present or weak (21 pts.)	Organization, connections, and transitions not evident (0 pts.)

Comments:

Dodie and her fellow teachers often use the rubric templates found at these three websites: Rubistar (*rubistar.4teachers.org*), which contains existing criteria she can add to herself or edit; Rubrician (*www.rubrician.com*), with links by subject area; and the Schrock Guide for Educators (*school.discovery.com/schrockguide/assess.html*).

Peers can also assess one another's written work and provide feedback (se Figure 11.2). Besides conferencing with students one-on-one, many teachers use peer conferences to give students real and immediate audience feedback on their work. Often, when a student reads his or her work to a peer or hears it read to him or her, the student discovers what to revise. Kelly uses writing groups of two to three students and has students read each other's work and give feedback on drafts. She uses *TAG* (*Tell, Ask, Give*), in which peers *tell* the writer one thing they like about a piece, *ask* a question about something they don't understand, and *give* a piece of advice. One student's handwriting improved dramatically when a peer wrote "You should write neater so I can read it!" When Karen's third graders work in pairs or small groups to give each other feedback, she uses a different version of *TAG*. She uses the language of *PQS* (*Praise, Question, Suggest*). To help frame constructive feedback, both teachers model responses first by thinking aloud about a volunteer's draft and then have students respond to the draft with three statements.

Conferencing with students during writing workshop is a good way to assess and improve writing. Dodie, the sixth-grade teacher whose quote opened this chapter, makes conferences a priority even though she works with 125 students daily in 42-minute classes. She has a sign-up sheet for conferences, and she tries to see five students for a few minutes every day. To make the most of a conference, Dodie has students come with a question they have about their writing. For example, "This sentence doesn't sound right to me. What do you think?" or "Is my introduction strong enough?" Requiring students to reflect on their own work and wonder about some aspect of it shifts responsibility for improved writing to the student. But, Dodie also asks pointed questions to prompt each student to rethink and revise his or her writing as well.

Teachers can also assess student writing with "The Word Writing CAFÉ" (Leal, 2006), which is a "*C*omplexity, *A*ccuracy, and *F*luency *E*valuation." This group-administered assessment is "an objective writing assessment of a whole class at one time" (p. 341). It is an inventory of words students know how to write. It is not meant to measure sentence or paragraph creation but rather the ability to write and spell words correctly. It can be used at the beginning and end of the year to assess what words students can write coming into the classroom and how this changes over the year. It can also show interests, strengths, and weaknesses. While it does not measure text writing ability, the Word Writing CAFÉ shows the teacher the complexity of vocabulary words students use and write.

Along with writing portfolios, rubrics, checklists, peer feedback, and of course teacher conferencing, students need to become accurate in making self-assessments of their own work. Students need to regularly ask questions about their writing such as the ones suggested earlier in this chapter. This self-assessment needs to be ongoing, because students improve as writers when they regularly examine their work with an eye toward making it more organized, fluent, and clear.

REFLECTIONS AND FUTURE DIRECTIONS

Today, perhaps more than ever before, technology is transforming writing (Bromley, 2005). Writing practices in classrooms of the future will need to reflect the roles computers and the Internet increasingly play in work-related writing. Although outside school many students use email and instant messaging, which do not always conform to standard grammar, spelling, or punctuation, students still need to possess basic skills in standard written conventions to be successful in the work world. Accountability, mandates, and tests will undoubtedly continue to affect what and how writing is taught. Thus, teachers need to be flexible, open to collaboration with others, and creative in blending the in-school and out-of-school writing students do. Research is needed that examines technology and writing and best-practices instruction for increasingly diverse classrooms. We need to understand better what sound instruction should look like for students who differ in cultural, ethnic, language, learning backgrounds, and gender.

CONCLUDING COMMENTS

The goal of a best-practices writing program ought to be to develop writers who enjoy and learn from writing as they write well in a range of forms for a variety of purposes and audiences. Vygotsky's (1978) ideas about *thought, knowledge,* and *social interaction,* and Cambourne's (1988) model of *engagement,* through *immersion* and *demonstration,* provide a foundation for this kind of program, as does the research briefly presented in this chapter. Establishing a classroom context for writing, providing intentional instruction, and regularly assessing writing can build student writers who are fluent, competent, and independent. Classroom practices that give students plenty of opportunities for writing and self-assessment at every grade level, both individually and together, are critical in developing strong writers.

ENGAGEMENT ACTIVITIES

1. Read *6 + 1 Traits of Writing: The Complete Guide Grades 3 and Up* by Ruth Culham (2003). Do you agree or disagree with the traits Culham says should be taught at different grade levels? Why? Choose a lesson and teach it to students.
2. Collaboratively create a rubric with a class of students for something they will write. Using students' ideas and your own ideas, group comments into categories. Have you included the 6 + 1 traits? What are the benefits and drawbacks of this kind of lesson?
3. Visit *www.readingonline.org* and bookmark this electronic journal of the International Reading Association for future reading. Read an article on the teaching of writing. How does it connect (or not connect) to what you just read in this chapter?
4. Do you agree with Dodie's rubrics? Would you change them? If so, why and how?

REFERENCES

Angelis, J. (2003). Conversation in the middle school classroom: Developing reading, writing, and other language abilities. *Middle School Journal, 34*(3), 57–61.

Armstrong, T. (2003). *The multiple intelligences of reading and writing: Making the words come alive.* Alexandria, VA: Association for Supervision and Curriculum Development.

Atwell, N. (1998). *In the middle: New understandings about writing, reading and learning* (2nd ed.). Portsmouth, NH: Boynton Cook.

Baker, E. A. (2000). Instructional approaches used to integrate literacy and technology. *Reading Online, 4*(1). Retrieved December 23, 2005, from *www.readingonline.org/articles/art_index.asp?HREF=baker/index.html.*

Ball, A. F. (2006). Teaching writing in culturally diverse classrooms. In C. A. MacArthur, S. Graham, & J. Fitzgerald (Eds.), *Handbook of writing research* (pp. 293–310). New York: Guilford Press.

Berninger, V. W., & Winn, W. D. (2006). Implications of advancements in brain research and technology for writing development, writing instruction, and educational evolution. In C. A. MacArthur, S. Graham, & J. Fitzgerald (Eds.), *Handbook of writing research* (pp. 96–114). New York: Guilford Press.

Bromley, K. (in press-a). Assessing student writing. In J. Paratore & R. McCormack (Eds.), *Classroom literacy assessment: Making sense of what students know and do.* New York: Guilford Press.

Bromley, K. (in press-b). From drawing to digital creations: Graphic organizers in the classroom. In D. Strickland & N. Roser (Eds.), *Handbook of research on teaching literacy through the communicative and visual arts,* (Vol. 2). Mahwah, NJ: Erlbaum.

Bromley, K. (2005). Writing and technology. In M. McKenna, L. Labbo,

R. Kieffer, & D. Reinking (Eds.), *Handbook of literacy and technology* (Vol. 2, pp. 349–354). Mahwah, NJ: Erlbaum.

Brozo, W. (2003). Literary license. *Voices from the Middle, 10*(3), 43–45.

Calkins, L. (1994). *The art of teaching writing* (*new ed.*). Portsmouth, NH: Heinemann.

Cambourne, B. (1988). *The whole story: Natural learning and the acquisition of literacy in the classroom.* Auckland, New Zealand: Scholastic.

Casey, M., & Hemenway, S. (2001). Structure and freedom: Achieving a balanced writing curriculum. *English Journal, 90*(6), 68–75.

Culham, R. (2003). *6 + 1 traits of writing: The complete guide: grades 3 and up.* New York: Scholastic.

Dunn, P. A., & Lindblom, K. (2003). Why revitalize grammar? *English Journal, 92*(3), 43–50.

Fletcher, R., & Portaluppi, J. (2001). *Writing workshop: The essential guide.* Portsmouth, NH: Heinemann.

Graves, D. (1983). *Writing: Teachers and children at work.* Portsmouth, NH: Heinemann.

Graves, D. (1994). *A fresh look at writing.* Portsmouth, NH: Heinemann.

Hillocks, G. (1987). Synthesis of research in teaching writing. *Educational Leadership, 11,* 71–82.

Irwin-DeVitis, L., Bromley, K. & Modlo, M. (1999). *50 graphic organizers for reading, writing and more.* New York: Scholastic.

Kane, S. (1997). Favorite sentences: Grammar in action. *The Reading Teacher, 51*(1), 70–72.

Karchmer, R. A. (2001). The journey ahead: Thirteen teachers report how the internet influences literacy and literacy instruction in their K–12 classrooms. *Reading Research Quarterly, 36*(4), 442–480.

Kear, D. J., Coffman, G. A., McKenna, M. C., & Ambrosio, A. L. (2000). Measuring attitude toward writing: A new tool for teachers. *The Reading Teacher, 54*(1), 10–23.

Leal, D. J. (2005). The word writing CAFÉ: Assessing student writing for complexity, accuracy and fluency. *The Reading Teacher, 59*(4), 340–350.

Lenski, S. D., & Johns, J. L. (2000). *Improving writing: Resources, strategies, assessments,* Dubuque, IA: Kendall Hunt.

Leu, D. J. (2000). Our children's future: Changing the focus of literacy and literacy instruction. *The Reading Teacher, 53*(5), 424–429.

McCutcheon, C. (2006). Cognitive factors in the development of children's writing. In C. A. MacArthur, S. Graham, & J. Fitzgerald (Eds.), *Handbook of writing research* (pp. 115–130). New York: Guilford Press.

McElveen, S. A., & Dierking, C. C. (2001). Children's books as models to teach writing. *The Reading Teacher, 54*(4), 362–364.

Moats, L. C. (2005–2006, Winter). How spelling supports reading: And why it is more regular and predictable than you may think. *American Educator,* 12–22, 42–43.

Moss, B. (2005). Making a case and a place for effective content area literacy instruction in the elementary grades. *The Reading Teacher 59*(1), 46–55.

National Assessment of Educational Progress. (2002). Retrieved December 21, 2005, from *nces.ed.gov/nationsreportcard/writing/results2002/.*

Owens, R. F., Hester, J. L., & Teale, W. H. (2002). Where do you want to go today? Inquiry-based learning and technology integration. *The Reading Teacher, 55*(7), 616–641.

Peterson, S. (2000). Yes, we do teach writing conventions! (Though the methods may be unconventional). *Ohio Reading Teacher, 34*(1), 38–44.

Peterson, S. (2006). Influence of gender on writing development. In C. A. MacArthur, S. Graham, & J. Fitzgerald (Eds.), *Handbook of writing research* (pp. 311–323). New York: Guilford Press.

Read, S. (2005). First and second graders writing informational text. *The Reading Teacher, 59*(1), 36–44.

Routman, R. (1996). *Literacy at the crossroads: Crucial talk about reading, writing and other teaching dilemmas.* Portsmouth, NH: Heinemann.

Ryan, P. M. (2000). *Esperanza rising.* New York: Scholastic.

Shanahan, T. (2006). Relations among oral language, reading and writing development. In C. A. MacArthur, S. Graham, & J. Fitzgerald (Eds.), *Handbook of writing research* (pp. 171–186). New York: Guilford Press.

Singer, B., & Bashir, A. (2004). Developmental variations in writing. In C. A. Stone, R. R. Silliman, B. J. Ehren, & K. Apel (Eds.). *Handbook of language and literacy: Development and disorders* (pp. 559–582). New York: Guilford Press.

Smith, M. W., Cheville, J., & Hillocks, G. (2006). "I guess I'd better watch my English": Grammars and the teaching of the English language arts. In C. A. MacArthur, S. Graham, & J. Fitzgerald (Eds.), *Handbook of writing research* (pp. 263–274). New York: Guilford Press.

Strickland, D. S., Bodino, A., Buchan, K., Jones, K. M., Nelson, A., & Rosen, M. (2001). Teaching writing in a time of reform. *The elementary school journal, 101*(4), 385–397.

Tompkins, G. E. (2004). *Teaching writing: Balancing process and product.* Upper Saddle River, NJ: Prentice Hall.

Troia, G. A. (2006). Writing instruction for students with learning disabilities. In C. A. MacArthur, S. Graham, & J. Fitzgerald (Eds.), *Handbook of writing research* (pp. 324–336). New York: Guilford Press.

Vygotsky, L. (1978). *Mind in society.* Cambridge, MA: Harvard University Press.

Weaver, C. (1998). *Lessons to share on teaching grammar in context.* Portsmouth, NH: Boynton/Cook.

Wepner, S. B., & Tao, L. (2002). From master teacher to master novice: Shifting responsibilities in technology-infused classrooms. *The Reading Teacher, 55*(7), 642–661.

Zarry, L. (1999). Vocabulary enrichment in composition. *Education, 120*, 267–271.

Chapter 12

BEST PRACTICES IN LITERACY ASSESSMENT

Peter Afflerbach

This chapter will:

- Describe the current state of literacy assessment.
- Examine a series of imbalances in current literacy assessment that have an impact on the positive contributions of literacy assessment.
- Suggest means for achieving balance and best practice in literacy assessment.
- Provide examples of balanced approaches and best practices with literacy assessment.

This chapter focuses on classroom-based reading assessments, assessments that hold considerable promise to enhance the teaching and learning of reading. The chapter begins with an overview of the context in which reading assessment is conceptualized and conducted. In this context, curriculum and instruction, teachers and students, and tradition and politics interact. A result of this interaction is that certain reading assessments are privileged and others are underutilized or ignored. This creates a series of imbalances in reading assessment. In the chapter I identify six areas within reading assessment that are in need of balance as well as the means for working toward balance. I describe particular classroom-based assessments that are capable of measuring the depth and breadth of students' reading development while attaining standards of validity and reliability that are the hallmarks of useful reading assessment.

EVIDENCE-BASED BEST PRACTICES

Setting the Context

Any consideration of best practices in reading assessment must take into account the contexts (often contentious contexts) in which teaching and learning happen and reading assessments are proposed, mandated, developed, bought, administered, and conducted. The current context of reading assessment is marked by imbalance. A significant portion of this imbalance is attributable to the inordinate attention given to high-stakes testing and a resultant lack of attention to classroom-based reading assessment that might help change the teaching and learning of reading. Correcting these imbalances can provide one basis for superior teaching and learning, while ignoring them may diminish the achievements of teachers and their students. The most pressing challenges to best practices in classroom assessment of reading relate to a lack of balance in:

- The assessment of reading processes and reading products.
- The assessment of reading skills and strategies and the assessment of how students use what they understand from reading.
- The assessment of cognitive and affective reading factors.
- Formative reading assessment and summative reading assessment.
- The reading assessment that is done to or for students and the reading assessment that is done with and by students.
- The demands for teacher and school accountability and professional development opportunities that help teachers develop expertise in reading assessment.

The promise to meet these challenges emanates from the depth and breadth of knowledge we possess about the reading construct (National Reading Panel, 2000; Snow, 2002) and the means to develop effective reading assessments (Pellegrino, Chudowsky, & Glaser, 2001). Never before have we had such detailed understanding of reading and its development, and never before have we possessed as many potentially valid reading assessment options.

We have rich conceptualizations of reading, its development, and influences on its development. Further, the necessary skills and strategies for accomplished reading are generally well researched (Pressley & Afflerbach, 1995), providing detail that should inform both our instruction and assessment. Informing our understanding is research from fields as diverse as critical discourse (Rogers, 2003), human development (Alexander, 2005), information processing (LaBerge & Samuels, 1974), economics (Hart & Risley, 1995), and anthropology (Heath, 1983). Thus, our ability to describe the nature of reading and what student readers need to succeed is greatly enhanced, as is our means to provide instruction that fosters student readers' growth.

As our knowledge about reading evolves, so to does our understanding of effective reading assessment. Many forms of reading assessment, informed by research in educational measurement, have the potential to positively influence instruction and learning. Pellegrino et al. (2001) suggest that, when we carefully chart the territory of what we will assess, we are then in a good position to produce the assessment materials and procedures that will best demonstrate the nature of students' development. Insofar as we have confidence in our full account of the construct of reading and we utilize our knowledge from assessment and psychometrics, we should have confidence in the assessments we design and use. In turn, this should give us confidence in the inferences we make from assessment results. Thoughtful assessment seeks to use knowledge or the collected wisdom about the construct to be measured and combine this with our best understanding of effective assessment so that the inferences we make from reading assessment information are accurate and useful.

Consider an example of how this should work. We know from research that successful readers decode printed text, often relying on phonics early in their development. Part of decoding involves learning to identify pairs of consonants as they appear in words and learn the unique sounds that these consonant blends make. Allowing for dialect variations, we know that the *ch* consonant blend makes predictable sounds, and we can design assessments to measure students' ability to accurately recognize *ch* in print, to determine its sound counterparts, and to correctly pronounce, or "say," the *ch* blend. As we are careful with our understanding of the *ch* blend and how we assess students' ability to produce the sounds, we can make accurate inferences about their developing ability to do so. We can examine students' ability to decode the *ch* blend using assessments that include words that contain the *ch* blend in words within meaningful text, as the *ch* blend occurs in whole words, and with the *ch* blend in isolation.

From student performance on these assessments we may infer phonics skills and decoding strategies. With confidence in our conceptualization of phonics and in our attempt to assess phonics as students use them, we have confidence in our inferences drawn from assessment results. We can use the results of our assessment in a formative manner, to immediately shape our understanding of the developing reader and related instruction. We can also use the results in a summative manner, as they provide evidence that the student has (or has not) met a key learning goal. Likewise, we understand that students' reading comprehension can be conceptualized as literal, inferential, critical, and evaluative (National Assessment Governing Board, 2005). We can formulate questions that require of students literal, inferential, critical, and evaluative comprehension of the texts they read, and from students' responses we make inferences about the development of their reading comprehension.

As broad as our understanding of reading is, we must strive to develop assessments that describe the complexity of student reading growth. Davis (1998) reminds us that we must be vigilant in our development and use of assessments and that assessment is always but a sample of the thing we are wanting to describe. Davis also urges that we acknowledge that many of our assessments are "thin"; that is, they yield results that describe but a portion of reading. This acknowledgment should temper the inferences we make about students' complex growth and learning.

While theoretical and practical knowledge of reading and reading assessment is rich, the implementation of useful and effective reading assessment is impoverished. We have reading assessment habits that are informed by tradition rather than by current conceptualizations of accomplished reading and effective teaching. Given the considerable advances in our understanding of reading and reading assessment, shouldn't we find it puzzling that our students' adequate yearly progress is measured by tests much like those we took in elementary and middle school? In addition, the use of single test scores to judge students' reading achievement and teachers' accountability skews schools' reading assessment agendas and funding (Afflerbach, 2005). Despite the fact that using single test scores to make highly consequential decisions is indefensible, much school capital is invested in these single score events. The purchasing, training, practicing, administering, scoring, and teaching related to high-stakes tests all take from limited school resources and create a paucity of alternatives and the means to pursue them.

BEST PRACTICES IN ACTION

Assessment must reflect the evolution of our understanding of the construct of reading, and assessment must be informed by state-of-the-art knowledge in the science of educational measurement. Reading assessment must reflect a series of balances that produces information that is useful to different audiences, for their different purposes. And it is within classrooms that the promise of reading assessment must be realized. In spite of the considerable growth in our understanding of how to develop and use classroom based reading assessments (Calfee & Hiebert, 1996), implementation is generally slow.

Effective reading assessment is that which informs important educational decisions. A first concern for classroom teachers is collecting and using reading assessment information that can be used to shape instruction and learning. Consider the students who populate our classrooms. In a classroom of 25 or 30 students, we expect that each will vary in terms of reading skills and strategies, prior knowledge of texts, motivation, and self-esteem as a reader. Each student will vary in the attributions he or she makes for reading success or failure and in terms of agency, or the degree to which he or she feels in control of the reading he or she does. These differences contribute to varied performances and achievements in reading. We need assessments that describe the characteristics of student readers in diverse classrooms, characteristics that can influence their reading achievement. Talented teachers use their understanding of each of these student characteristics to shape reading instruction, and careful classroom-based assessment informs teachers and serves as a basis for this instruction. Throughout reading lessons and on a daily basis, over marking periods and across the school year, *this is* high-stakes assessment, for without it there is no progress toward daily, weekly, or annual reading goals.

Best practices in reading assessment are balanced so that they provide teachers with rich and current information about their students' reading development. Vygotsky (1978) defines the zone of proximal development as the place in which students learn new things in relation to their knowledge and competencies and in relation to teachers' instruction and support. If you believe, as I do, that teacher accountability is related to identifying students' zones of proximal development and teaching in these zones, then the centrality of classroom-based assessment becomes evident. We need regular classroom-based assessments that help us identify teachable moments for each student, that give us the detail we need to effectively teach to students' needs, and that describe the important outcomes of effective reading instruction.

Over the course of a school year, carefully teaching to students' individual needs can obviate the need to teach to the test. We must know where students are in terms of their skill and strategy development, motivation and engagement, prior knowledge of the texts they read, and self-esteem as readers. When reading assessment provides us with this information, we can identify the next steps for student learning and for our teaching. A robust classroom assessment program continually provides detailed information about students' current competencies and next steps: it informs our ongoing work in the zone of proximal development while richly describing student reading.

Addressing Imbalance in Reading Assessment

In the next section, I describe necessary balances that promote best practices in classroom-based reading assessment. I examine the important work that must be done in balancing:

- Assessments that focus on reading processes and reading products.
- The assessment of reading skills and strategies and the assessment of how students use what they understand from reading.
- The assessment of cognitive and affective reading outcomes and reader characteristics.
- Formative reading assessment and summative reading assessment.
- The reading assessment that is done to or for students and the reading assessment that is done with and by students.
- The demands for teacher and school accountability and professional development opportunities to develop expertise in reading assessment.

In each case I provide an overview of the imbalance, explain why we would do well to fix it, and describe means to achieving balance. In doing so, I refer to specific reading assessments that can provide valid and reliable assessment information. These assessments include reading inventories and miscue analysis, performance assessments, teacher questioning, observations and surveys of student growth, and checklists.

Balancing Assessments That Focus on Reading Processes and Reading Products

All of our reading assessment involves making inferences about students' growth and achievement. We reason about the extent of students' reading development using our assessment of the processes and products of their reading. In general, process assessments focus on students' skills, strategies, and work as they unfold. In contrast, product assessments focus on what students produce as a result of reading. Much attention is now given to product assessments, especially tests, and this creates an imbalance that favors product assessment at the expense of process assessment.

Reading processes are those skills and strategies that readers use when they decode words, determine vocabulary meaning, read fluently, and comprehend. Process-oriented reading assessment focuses on these skills and strategies that students use to construct meaning from text. Such assessment allows teachers to assess in the midst of students' reading. For example, as we listen to the student applying phonics knowledge to sound out the *ch* consonant blend, we are in the midst of the student using decoding processes. When we observe a student rereading a sentence to clarify meaning, we are in the midst of a metacognitive process. Our process assessment helps us determine the skills and strategies that work or do not work as the student attempts to construct meaning. Moreover, assessment of reading processes can be situated in the context of a student's actual reading, providing insights into how reading skills and strategies work together.

In contrast, product-oriented reading assessment provides an after-the-fact account of student reading achievement. The information provided by product assessments can help us determine students' achievement in relation to important reading goals, ranging from benchmark reading performances to content-area learning. Typical reading product assessments are quizzes, tests, and questions related to students' comprehension of text. When we examine test scores, we can make strong inferences about students' achievement in relation to benchmarks and curriculum standards, but we must make large retrospective inferences about what worked (or didn't work) as the student read. If we are interested in making inferences about how our instruction contributed (or didn't contribute) to the students' achievement, a similar series of retrospective inferences is necessary.

This is an important fact about product assessments: they are relatively limited in their ability to provide detail on what students can and can't do as they read. An apt analogy is one in which we try to determine why a basketball team won or lost a game by examining the final score. Certainly the final score is important, but it tells us little about the means by which it was achieved. In both cases, there may be very little for us to go on if we are interested in gaining useful information from the assessment about how to do better.

In contrast, some emphasis on classroom-based assessment of reading processes can provide us with detailed information on how students process text and construct meaning. Here, our inferences are based on our assessment of the processes themselves. A prime example of assessment that focuses on readers' processes is reading inventories and miscue analyses (Clay, 1993; Goodman & Goodman, 1977). Assessment is "on-line," and we get information about students' reading processes as they read. Consider the miscue analysis of students' oral reading: such assessment can illustrate how students decode print, engage prior knowledge, read fluently, construct meaning, and monitor the comprehension process. The inferences we make about students' strengths and needs best derive from the richest account available of reading processes. When we observe oral reading firsthand, we can see when a student is not consistently comprehending, as we can readily observe when meaning-changing miscues are being made. We are able to pinpoint the problem more precisely, and we may be better able to provide instruction to address the specific student need based on our process-oriented reading assessment information.

Balancing the Assessment of Reading Skills and Strategies with the Assessment of How Students Use What They Understand from Reading

Students must comprehend the texts they read, and students must also be able to use the information they gain from reading to perform reading-related tasks. Current reading assessment focuses on the former: the bulk of assessment seeks to describe the reader's comprehension of text. We can assess students' ability to determine or construct main ideas, and we can ask students to locate or identify details in texts. When we ask students to summarize the texts they read, we are continuing a focus on constructing meaning. Each of these assessments focuses on comprehension as the final goal of reading.

In many reading assessment scenarios and increasingly when students have demonstrated the ability to process text and establish the literal meaning of text, students read to answer teacher questions or to do well on quizzes and tests that measure comprehension. We must remember that reading to answer comprehension questions, while a common school practice, is not nearly as common in the reading done outside of school. Our reading assessment should also focus on using what we have understood in reading-related tasks. When students read guidelines for conducting hands-on experiments to help guide their science inquiry or they read colonists' diaries so that they can create a dramatic presentation on the struggles in Jamestown, reading involves these two goals: to comprehend text and to use what is comprehended in a related task or performance. Of course, such purposes for reading are the norm outside of the classroom. So should it be in classrooms.

If students are assessed only to determine what they have comprehended from text, we are but halfway there. We must balance and complement this type of assessment with information about how a student uses what is comprehended. Performance assessment, a form of authentic assessment, can focus on the types of reading that students do and the types of things we expect them to do with knowledge gained from reading (Baxter & Glaser, 1998). For example, fifth grade students read instructions and guidelines for conducting a hands-on science experiment. Of course, we focus on their comprehension, but we are also very interested in their application of what is learned (or comprehended) in the conducting of the science experiment. This includes the correct sequencing of steps in the scientific inquiry, the identification of laboratory tools, and the implementation of the detailed scientific procedures accurately.

The performance assessment accommodates our need to measure and describe the link between comprehension of text and how students use what they comprehend. Performance assessment has the added attraction of rubrics that help students conceptualize suitable levels of performance at a specific task: they provide students with a blueprint of what they must do to achieve a superior score, with the performance assessment illustrating for students what is needed. The rubric also provides the means for students to check their progress toward a particular performance level and to practice self-assessment. The assessment uncovers the black box of assessment (Black & William, 1998) and helps students continue to learn how to do assessment for themselves.

Balancing the Assessment of Cognitive and Affective Reading Outcomes and Reader Characteristics

Currently used high-stakes assessments, early reading screening instruments and the majority of classroom reading assessments focus on the reading skills and strategies that make comprehension possible. Assessment measures the cognitive development of student readers, but little or no attention is paid to the factors that can support and enhance reading development. Experienced classroom teachers and parents recognize that possession of reading skills and strategies is essential to students' reading success, but mere posession of them does not guarantee success.

Successful readers are engaged readers (Guthrie & Wigfield, 1997). These readers are motivated to read, they identify themselves as readers, they persevere in the face of reading challenges and they consider reading to be an important part of their daily life. When we think of our teaching successes, do we think only of students who scored high on tests under our guidance, or do we also think of students who went from reluctant readers to enthusiastic readers? Do we think of students who evolved from easily discouraged readers to readers whose motivation helped them persevere through reading challenges? Do we remember students who avoided reading at all costs evolving to students who learned to love reading? Surely, we count such students and our positive influence on them as among our most noteworthy teaching accomplishments.

If we are serious about accountability, we need to have balance in the assessment that demonstrates that high-quality teaching and effective reading programs change student readers' lives. To achieve balance we need assessments that are capable of measuring and describing student growth that is complementary to reading skill and reading strategy development. This growth can include positive motivation, perseverance in the face of difficulties, appropriate attributions made for reading success and failure, and increased self-esteem as a reader. We are fortunate to have such measures, including surveys and inventories of students' reading motivations (Gambrell, Palmer, Codling, & Mazzoni, 1996), attitudes toward reading (McKenna & Kear, 1990), and reading self-concepts (Chapman & Tunmer, 1995). These and related assessments can help us understand and describe growth that is related to the already much-assessed cognitive development. They move us toward a fuller measure of the accomplishments of students and their teachers. Achieving balance would result in more of these assessments being built into the routines of classrooms and schools and greater attention and respect being given to the information these assessments provide.

Balancing Formative Reading Assessment and Summative Reading Assessment

We are a society enamored of numbers. Schools, school districts, classrooms, states, teachers, and students are evaluated and ranked in relation to annual series of tests or summative reading assessments. These assessments report important summary information about students' reading skills and strategies. They summarize reading achievement as a level, a raw score, or a percentile rank. Summative assessment is important, as it helps us understand whether students have reached grade-level benchmarks, unit and lesson goals, and standards in classrooms, districts, and states. However, summative assessment is, by its nature, an after-the-fact of teaching events. We do not have as rich an opportunity with summative assessment to inform instruction and to address students' individual needs as they are developing.

In spite of this limitation, summative assessment is used to make highly consequential decisions. Accountability, sanction, reward, school success, and school failure are all determined by single summative assessment scores. The pressure to focus on such summative assessment creates an imbalance vis-à-vis formative assessment efforts, the very type of assessment that could help teachers and schools demonstrate accountability on a daily basis. Formative assessment, after all, is conducted with the specific goal of informing our instruction and improving student learning. At the heart of effective reading instruction is the classroom teacher's detailed knowledge of each student. This knowledge is constructed through ongoing formative assessments, conducted across the school day and the school year, like the process-oriented reading assessment discussed earlier in this chapter.

Teacher questioning may be tailored so that it provides formative assessment information. The teacher adept at asking questions during instruction can develop a detailed sense of how well students are "getting" the lesson. Teachers' questions can focus on both skills and strategies, cognitive and affective influences on reading achievement, and content-area learning that is a result of reading. The information provided by students' responses to questions is used by the teacher to build a detailed sense of how students are progressing toward lesson goals and where the ongoing instructional focus should be. Consider a third-grade teacher's questions to her students as they read a chapter on ecosystems in a science textbook: What is an ecosystem? Is our schoolyard an ecosystem? Can you explain your reasoning? How do you know? Where do you get the information contained in your explanation? Questions like these evoke student responses that demonstrate the degree of student understanding. From students' responses, the teacher constructs her own understanding of their achievement. And from this understanding comes action: a decision to move ahead or to reteach, a decision to slow the pace of instruction or speed it up, a decision to have more class discussion around the key concept being taught.

Formative assessment is conducted *in situ*, or as the process of teaching and learning unfolds. The degree of detail that is provided by formative assessment may help a classroom teacher determine a teachable moment, identify the need for reteaching an important concept or skill, or move forward to new instruction with confidence that students possess the requisite knowledge to succeed. Creating balance will result in formative assessment describing students' ongoing reading growth as it occurs and summative assessment providing summary statements about students' literacy achievement.

Balancing the Reading Assessment That Is Done to or for Students with the Reading Assessment That Is Done with and by Students

Many students move through school with reading assessment done solely to them or for them. A result is that many students think of assessment as a "black box" (Black & William, 1998). That is, the common practice is that students read, take a quiz or test, and hand it in. It is evaluated and graded and then returned to the student. The student earns a score but gains no understanding of how assessment works. A consequence of this approach to reading assessment is that students do not learn to do reading assessment for themselves. Even though teachers ask questions in class, unless we explain why we ask these questions or how we arrive at our evaluations of student responses, students will not understand how the evaluation of their reading is made. Over the school years there may be countless lost opportunities for students to learn to conduct reading assessment on their own; instead, students remain outsiders to the culture of reading assessment.

While our classroom-based assessment should contribute to the collection of valuable information that can inform our understanding of students and our instruction, it must also provide students with the means to eventually assume responsibility for assessing their own reading. Accomplished readers regularly assess their ongoing comprehension of text and their progress toward reading-related goals. This ability is not innate: it is learned from models of doing assessment that the student eventually internalizes. In fact, a hallmark of the successful reader is the ability to monitor his or her reading and conduct ongoing assessment of reading progress (Pressley & Afflerbach, 1995).

As we strive to create balance, we should provide opportunities in which students learn the value of self-assessment and the means to do accurate and useful assessment for themselves. This can be a long and challenging process. A good start is modeling simple and straightforward assessment routines and helping students learn to initiate and successfully complete the routines independently. Consider the checklist used by a second-grade teacher. As the students read, she regularly asks them to refer to the checklist and engage in the assessment thinking that it requires. She models using the checklist and expects that her students will learn to use it as they read independently. The checklist includes the following:

_____ I check to see if what I read makes sense.
_____ I remind myself why I am reading.
_____ I focus on the goal of my reading while I read.
_____ I check to see if I can summarize sentences and paragraphs.
_____ If reading gets hard, I ask myself if there are any problems.
_____ I try to identify the problem.
_____ I try to fix the problem.
_____ When the problem is fixed, I get back to my reading, making sure I understand what I've read so far.

The teacher also models the use of the checklist by asking related questions of herself when she reads to the students, and thinks aloud about why she asks the questions and about her answers to the questions. This predictable presentation of self-assessment routines can help set developing readers on a healthy path to self-assessment.

The checklist is also scalable: it can be constructed to reflect specific instructional goals. If we are interested in helping students learn to assess critical reading abilities, we may supplement the preceding items with two more as students continue their development:

_____ I check the text to see if the author provides evidence to support claims.
_____ I compare the information in the text with what I already know about the topic.

We do not give up our responsibility to conduct valuable classroom-based reading assessments when we promote student self-assessment. Rather, we look for opportunities when using our assessments to help students learn assessment themselves (Afflerbach, 2002). Creating balance is imperative, for if in all our teaching related to reading the student does not begin to learn how to do self-assessment, how will the student ever become a truly independent reader?

Balancing the Demands for Teacher and School Accountability with Professional Development Opportunities to Develop Expertise in Reading Assessment

Each of the necessary balances described in this chapter is dependent on teachers' professional development in assessment. Successful classroom-based reading assessment demands teacher expertise, and professional development is the means for helping teachers develop expertise and achieve balance in each area of reading assessment. Accomplished reading teachers and effective schools take accountability to heart each and every day. This accountability is demonstrated through the care and professionalism with which teachers work with their students. In addition, teacher and school accountability are determined by the results of high-stakes testing. The costs involved in developing, buying, administering, and scoring these assessments are considerable. Unfortunately, the school funds spent on high-stakes tests are taken from school budgets that are otherwise limited. This means that money spent on tests cannot be spent on initiatives that would actually help teachers become better at classroom-based assessment.

Lack of professional development opportunities prevents many teachers from becoming practicing experts in classroom-based reading assessment (Black & William, 1998). Teachers become expert at classroom assessment when they are supported by their administrators and school districts (Johnston, 1987). Specifically, professional development can help teachers learn, develop, and use effective reading assessment materials and procedures that best influence the daily teaching and learning in the classroom (Stiggins, 1999). This support helps teacher develop and refine the formative and process-oriented reading assessments that are so critical to daily successes in the classroom. Regular and detailed assessments provide information that helps teachers recognize and utilize the teachable moment. These daily successes are summed up in the accomplished teaching and learning that is reflected in accountability tests. But accountability is not achieved through testing—it is achieved through the hard work that surrounds successful classroom assessment and instruction. Professional development also helps teachers construct reliable product assessments, such as quizzes, tests, and report cards. Professional development helps teachers become educated consumers and users of the variety of reading assessments that are available.

There needs to be a better balance between the call for teacher and school accountability and the means to help teachers and schools maintain that accountability. The balance here is related to funding and vision. Teachers' professional development is the means by which classroom-based assessment can be learned, practiced, and used expertly. To provide effective professional development, school districts must create balance in the manner of funding for reading assessments. Too much money given to tests and their related costs will continue to deprive teachers of much-needed professional development opportunities.

Summary

Effective reading assessment is necessary for reading program success, and balance is necessary for effective reading assessment. Current reading assessment practice reflects a series of imbalances that can have negative effects on our teaching and on our students' learning. As teachers we are challenged to provide effective instruction for each and every student. Effective instruction is dependent on assessment that helps teachers and students move toward and attain daily and annual reading goals. This chapter has described the imbalances that must be addressed if reading assessment is to reflect our best and most recent understanding of reading and how to measure reading development. We do not lack descriptions or details of how classroom-based reading assessment helps our teaching and how our teaching helps student readers to develop. There must be a concerted effort to bring classroom-based reading assessment into the spotlight and, when the time arrives, to make it deliver on its promise.

High-quality classroom assessment of reading is as much a product of teacher expertise and effort as it is of political power, popular will, and continuing education. Many people believe that tests are at worst a nuisance and at best a key to school excellence; but a populace that automatically equates testing with best practice in assessment needs further education. Additionally, fully accounting for the costs of current reading assessment programs, especially high-stakes tests, should help the general public better understand how massive amounts of resources are funneled to reading assessments that yield relatively little useful information. Teachers must earn and they work to maintain the trust that is currently invested in high-stakes standardized tests. If, in correcting imbalances in our schools and classrooms we are able to demonstrate the superior nature of particular reading assessment information, we may gain needed new converts to classroom assessment.

The imbalances identified in this chapter require our attention. Righting these imbalances should lead to an assessment program that is more integral to the daily life of teachers, students, and classrooms. When we focus on process assessment, we can accurately determine what aspect of a summarization strategy students do and don't understand. When we assess and determine how a student's motivation grows as the result of gaining control of the act of reading, we are describing a compelling success story. And when we share our reading assessment knowledge with our students, we are preparing them to bring a balanced approach to the assessment of their own reading, fostering personal independence.

REFLECTIONS AND FUTURE DIRECTIONS

A balanced approach to classroom reading assessment will be achieved when classroom teachers can conduct assessment in a reliable and valid manner, thus gaining the public trust. Earlier I sketched the importance of professional development to teachers' growing ability to conduct classroom reading assessments and effectively use their results. However, there is little research that describes how teachers develop as assessment experts or that demonstrates what types of classroom assessment training most benefit teachers and their students.

A related area for future research and action is the public perception of assessment. We are a society that purports to value scientific inquiry, research results, and agendas for action that are informed by such inquiry and results. Why, then, are our most consequential assessments uninformed by our most recent research-based understanding? Similarly, why do states and school districts spend the bulk of their assessment budgets on test purchasing, administering, scoring, and reporting? This problem is exacerbated by the federal mandate of testing all students in grades 3 through 8 in reading, but it existed prior to the passage of No Child Left Behind.

A final area for future research relates to the effects of reading assessment on student reading achievement. Despite the importance of reading assessment in determining student achievement and related consequences, reading assessment itself is not a common focus of research. Reading assessment is used as the measure of student achievement in many research designs. There are few studies that describe how assessment can contribute to student learning and achievement, although work in this area is promising (Black & William, 2005; Crooks, 1988). Research should help us determine the relationship of reading assessment to students' reading achievement. Classroom-based reading assessments, especially those that focus on formative assessment, assessment of processes, and the application of knowledge gained from reading, should impact teaching and learning, as they operate within the zone of proximal development.

CONCLUDING COMMENTS

Early in this chapter I framed best practices in reading assessment in terms of balance and imbalance. As I conclude this chapter, I am trying to balance pessimism and optimism. My pessimism is fueled by the fact that during the past few years we have witnessed an actual deterioration in reading assessment. Positive developments in assessment, including the use of performance assessments in statewide and large school district testing to measure complexities in students' reading growth (Maryland State Department of Education, 2006; Valencia, Hiebert, & Afflerbach, 1994), have been abandoned and left behind as a result of new federal laws. The many factors that combine in students' successful reading performances are ignored when assessment's exclusive focus is on cognitive gain. And politicians and the general public continue to privilege high-stakes tests over all other forms of reading assessment, using a single annual "read" of students to make hugely consequential decisions despite the fact that no professional organization supports such practice.

In contrast, my optimism is fueled by the fact that eminently useful reading assessment materials and procedures exist, indicating that part of the hard work is already done. We have the means to develop reading assessment that is central to the identification and accomplishment of teachable moments and reading assessment that reflects student achievement in relation to our most recent understanding of reading. This must be complemented by teachers' professional development and the public commitment to examine our new conceptualizations of reading and reading assessment and to support those assessments that best describe students' reading achievement.

ENGAGEMENT ACTIVITIES

The following activities are designed to encourage readers of this chapter to investigate balance and imbalance and reading assessment:

1. Conduct an inventory of the reading assessments used in your classroom and school. Evaluate the current assessments in relation to the balances described in this chapter. Is there ample opportunity for the collection and use of formative assessment information that might inform ongoing reading instruction? Do the assessments provide opportunity to observe

students' reading *processes* as well as the products of reading? Do assessments help us understand how students develop in areas related to their cognitive growth, motivation, and self-esteem? Are there opportunities for students to learn to do assessment for themselves? Look for gaps, redundancies, and how well the collection of reading assessments honors the rich construct of reading. Prepare to use the results of your inventory to argue for change or maintenance of the current assessment program.

2. Conduct task analyses of the reading and reading-related work that is asked of your students. When our reading assessments require that students summarize text or locate important details, we should be familiar with the means with which students accomplish this. Task analyses give us detailed knowledge of the things we ask students to do. This puts us in a position to assess our assessments. Are they sensitive to all the growth that students may exhibit? Do they favor one type of achievement while ignoring others? Task analyses not only help us determine the suitability of the assessment but also direct our attention to aspects of reading strategies and tasks that may be the focus of instruction. Knowing the assessment, in this case helps us think about teaching, assessment, and balance in assessment.
3. Learn to advocate for those reading assessments that you find most useful. It is important to know the benefits and shortcomings of different reading assessments. Be prepared to demonstrate the particular benefits of an assessment to fellow teachers and administrators. Develop reasoned and detailed explanations of those assessments that could do better as replacements to or complements of current materials and procedures, and frame your claims in relation to the different audiences and purposes that reading assessment should serve. Choose a type of assessment, and become expert at it. Demonstrate your expertise at this assessment, and demonstrate how it provides valuable assessment information to different audiences in your school community. This, in essence, is the most effective means to create change.
4. Lobby for professional development opportunities that promote teachers' expertise in developing and using high-quality classroom assessments of reading. Demonstrate the value of a particular type of reading assessment, such as performance assessment, so that you can then lobby for the need to support teachers in this effort.

REFERENCES

Afflerbach, P. (2002). Teaching reading self-assessment strategies. In C. C. Block & M. Pressley (Eds.), *Comprehension instruction: Research-based best practices* (pp. 96–111). New York: Guilford Press.

Afflerbach, P. (2005). High stakes testing and reading assessment. *Journal of Literacy Research, 37*, 1–12.

Alexander, P. (2005). The path to competence: A lifespan developmental perspective on reading. Retrieved from *www.nrconline.org/*.

Baxter, G., & Glaser, R. (1998). Investigating the cognitive complexity of science assessments. *Educational Measurement: Issues and Practice, 17*(3), 37–45.

Black, P., & William, D. (1998). Assessment and classroom learning. *Educational Assessment: Principles, Policy and Practice, 5*, 7–74.

Black, P., & William, D. (2005). Assessment for learning in the classroom. In J. Gardner (Ed.), *Assessment and learning*. London: Sage.

Calfee, R., & Hiebert, E. (1996). Classroom assessment of reading. In R. Barr, M. Kamil, P. Mosenthal, & D. Pearson (Eds.), *Handbook of reading research* (2nd ed., pp. 281–309). Mahwah, NJ: Erlbaum.

Chapman, J. W., & Tunmer, W. E. (1995). Development of young children's reading self-concepts: An examination of emerging subcomponents and their relationship with reading achievement. *Journal of Educational Psychology, 87*, 154–167.

Clay, M. (1993). *Reading Recovery : A guidebook for teachers in training*. Portsmouth, NH: Heinemann.

Crooks, T. (1988). The impact of classroom evaluation on students. *Review of Educational Research, 58*, 438–481.

Davis, A. (1998). *The limits of educational assessment*. Oxford, UK: Blackwell.

Gambrell, L., Palmer, B., Codling, R., & Mazzoni, S. (1996). Assessing motivation to read. *The Reading Teacher, 49*, 518–533.

Goodman, K., & Goodman, Y. (1977). Learning about psycholinguistic processes by analyzing oral reading. *Harvard Educational Review, 47*, 317–333.

Guthrie, J., & Wigfield, A. (1997). *Reading engagement: Motivating readers through integrated instruction*. Newark, DE: International Reading Association.

Hart, B., & Risley, T. (1995) *Meaningful differences in the everyday experience of young American children*. Baltimore: Brookes.

Heath, S. (1983). *Ways with words: Language, life and work in communities and classrooms*. Cambridge, UK: Cambridge University Press.

Johnston, P. (1987). Teachers as evaluation experts. *The Reading Teacher, 40*, 744–748.

LaBerge, D., & Samuels, S. (1974). Toward a theory of automatic information processing in reading. *Cognitive Psychology, 6*, 293–323.

Maryland State Department of Education. (2006). *How did we test what students learned from 1993–2002?* Baltimore: Author.

McKenna, M. C., & Kear, D. J. (1990). Measuring attitude towards reading: A new tool for teachers. *The Reading Teacher, 43*, 626–639.

National Assessment Governing Board. (2005). *Reading framework for the 2009 National Assessment of Educational Progress*. Washington, DC: American Institutes for Research.

National Reading Panel. (2000). Report of the National Reading Panel: Teaching children to read. Washington, DC: National Institute of Child Health and Human Development.

Pellegrino, J., Chudowsky, N., & Glaser, R. (2001). *Knowing what students know: The science and design of educational assessment*. Washington, DC: National Academy Press.

Pressley, M., & Afflerbach, P. (1995). *Verbal reports of reading: The nature of constructively responsive reading*. Hillsdale, NJ: Erlbaum.

Rogers, R. (2003). *An introduction to critical discourse analysis in education.* Mahwah, NJ: Erlbaum.

Snow, C. (2002). *Reading for understanding: Toward an R&D program in reading comprehension.* Washington, DC: RAND.

Stiggins, R. (1999). Evaluating classroom assessment training in teacher education. *Educational Measurement: Issues and Practices, 18,* 23–27.

Valencia, S., Hiebert, E., & Afflerbach, P. (Eds.). (1994). *Authentic reading assessment: Practices and possibilities.* Newark, DE: International Reading Association.

Vygotsky, L. (1978). *Mind in society: The development of higher psychological processes.* Cambridge, MA: Harvard University Press.

Part IV

PERSPECTIVES ON SPECIAL ISSUES

Chapter 13

INSTRUCTIONAL RESOURCES IN THE CLASSROOM: DEEPENING UNDERSTANDING THROUGH INTERACTIONS WITH MULTIPLE TEXTS AND MULTIPLE MEDIA

Linda Kucan
Diane Lapp
James Flood
Douglas Fisher

This chapter will:

- Present research that supports integrated multisource instruction.
- Present classroom vignettes that illustrate integrated multisource instruction.
- Suggest procedures that enable teachers to design integrated multisource instruction.
- Explain how classroom teachers can make use of a variety of topically and thematically related information resources to promote student engagement, interest, and learning.
- Describe strategies that support learning through multisource instruction.

EVIDENCE-BASED BEST PRACTICES

In many classrooms today teachers are designing and implementing literacy experiences that encourage students to investigate themes and topics that are not constrained by curricular boundaries (e.g., Barton & Smith, 2000; Guthrie & Wigfield, 1997; Jones, 2000; Roser & Keehn, 2002; Smith & Johnson, 1994). Interdisciplinary learning experiences that engage students in investigating themes and topics across content areas create a rich context for learning. An important aspect of the richness in such contexts is the opportunity for students to interact with multiple and diverse texts and media sets. As students use these information sources in integrated investigations, they construct disciplinary knowledge in social studies, science, and mathematics as they gain insights into literature and literacy.

According to Guthrie and Wigfield (1997), "Frequency, amount, and diversity of reading activity increase reading achievement" (p. 5). Current notions about text argue for diversity in genre, format, and presentation. Hartman and Allison (1996) suggested that a text is "anything that communicates meaning" (p. 111). Thus, while linguistic texts, such as books, diaries, and letters, once dominated ideas about literacy, current notions recognize that texts can also be semiotic, including films, music, architecture, and cuisine. Digital and multimedia resources in hypermedia environments are texts as well (Reinking, 1998).

Making connections among multiple and diverse texts is one way that experienced readers make sense of what they read. For example, the Harry Potter books and films (e.g., Rowling, 1999) are linked to cinematic and linguistic versions of *The Lord of the Rings* (e.g., Tolkien, 1954/1982), *The Wizard of Oz* (Baum, 1900), and *The Chronicles of Narnia* (Lewis, 1950) not only because they all involve a conflict between the forces of good and evil but also because they trace the progress of individuals who discover the values of courage, loyalty, and friendship as well as their own identities. The dialogue that ensues when texts speak to other texts in these ways becomes a model for the internal dialogue in which involved readers engage as they read and reflect on their reading.

There are cognitive as well as literary consequences for students who interact with multiple texts. Hynd (1999) suggests that students who make use of multiple textual resources engage in processing that involves evaluating the importance, credibility, and relevance of individual texts. The result of such processing is that students are able to construct more elaborated representations of people, events, and concepts (Perfetti, Britt, & Georgi, 1995).

Literacy researchers and educators emphasize that inviting students to notice and participate in the ongoing conversation among texts is an enterprise of critical importance (e. g., Frey & Fisher, 2006; Hartman, 1995; Lapp & Flood, 1993; Lenski, 1998; Lipson, Valencia, Wixson, & Peters, 1993). For example, Short (1992) provided groups of students in the third and sixth grades with Text Sets, Collections of 7–15 books in a variety of genres related to a topic, theme, or author. Students read and talked about individual books and then thought about possible connections among them. Students successfully focused on common literary elements across books such as character or plot, as well as themes and symbols. Some students did research to find out about authors and illustrators and then considered how biographical information helped them to interpret specific elements in the books. Students also made personal connections to the characters and plots of the stories they had read.

Thoughtful talk around multiple texts was also described by Roser and Hoffman (1992), who developed Language Charts to organize, record, and display connections across texts related by theme, topic, genre, author, or illustrator. Primary-grade teachers were given sets of 10 books with guidelines for constructing a chart with specific categories to support students in thinking about the texts. Completing the charts allowed students to see patterns across the books.

Worthy and Bloodgood (1992) also provided categories for students to use in thinking about various Cinderella tales. The categories supported students in investigating the Cinderella variants in a number of thoughtful ways. One analysis focused on the antagonists in the stories: the stepmother, siblings, and father. Another charted information about setting, characters, events, and magical elements so that patterns of similarities and differences emerged.

Palincsar, Parecki, and McPhail (1996) developed a 6-week thematic unit about friendship for third- and fourth-grade students with learning disabilities. Interactive read-alouds of a variety of texts involved students in talking about their personal experiences as well as other stories they knew that dealt with friendship. After the readings, students wrote in their journals. They were specifically encouraged to express how each reading had added to or changed their ideas about friendship. Pre- and post-interviews revealed that students were able to broaden their notions about friendship by making use of ideas from several texts.

Ms. Eyres-Wright, a teacher-researcher whose work was described by Lapp, Flood, and Fisher (1999), compared the depth of understanding constructed by students who read two biographical books about a person and students who read only one book but also viewed a film. Students' journal entries and the teacher's field notes during small-group discussions revealed that "students comprehended more when they were exposed to and were required to use multiple but different sources of information (intermediality)" (p. 779).

The studies described above provide examples of how teachers can support students in developing intertextual understandings by investigating multiple and diverse texts. While each text provides information and insights, it is the accumulation of insights from multiple texts and multiple media that expands and reinforces students' developing understanding.

BEST PRACTICES IN ACTION

In the sections that follow, we present two examples of integrated multisource explorations: one with preservice and inservice teachers reading and responding to *Catherine, Called Birdy* (Cushman, 1994), historical fiction set in the Middle Ages, and another with fourth-grade students working through an integrated unit about rocks and minerals and the California Gold Rush.

Into the Middle Ages

As students enter the classroom, they hear the lyrical voices of four women chanting medieval verses (Anonymous 4, 1995). The melodic sound creates an "otherworldly" atmosphere, recalls a distant time and place and way of life. When class begins, students study a timeline and map. Their journey to England in the year 1290 has begun. The place and time become even more real as they watch the beginning of *A Knight's Tale* (Rellim, Black, & Helgeland, 2000). The film tells the story of William Thatcher (Heath Ledger), a peasant squire who hides his identity and dares to compete against nobles in the tournaments. Thatcher's desire to break the rules is a desire shared by Birdy, the 14-year-old heroine of Karen Cushman's (1994) *Catherine, Called Birdy*, the novel that students will experience over the next few weeks. As students read the novel, they participate in a variety of literary and multimedia activities. They do research and use information from the novel to find out about medieval clothing. They come to class dressed as peasants, lords, ladies, monks, knights, and squires. They select 1 of 26 possible topics and use the Internet to create an illustrated page for a class Abcedarium, an alphabet book with entries for medieval terms. Their ideas about medieval life are enriched by watching excerpts from the films *Robin and Marian* (Stark, Shepherd, & Lester, 1976), *The Name of the Rose* (Eichinger & Annaud, 1986), and *The Saints with Sister Wendy* (Willcock, 1997), and by becoming actors in a Robin Hood play. These experiences deepen and enrich not only their appreciation and understanding of *Catherine, Called Birdy* but also their ideas about reading and texts.

Exploring Themes and Symbols in Catherine, Called Birdy

Catherine, Called Birdy (Cushman, 1994) underscores the conflict between Birdy and the social norms of her time. It draws attention to Birdy's struggle for freedom and of flight as a symbol for that freedom. It is also a "coming of age" novel in which Birdy changes as she discovers who she is and what she values.

The integrated multisource exploration described below was designed for upper elementary students and was used as a model with undergraduates and graduates in reading methods courses. The central activity of this intertextual exploration involves completing a Literature Chart to organize information about *Catherine, Called Birdy* and a variety of related picture books from an array of genres.

Selecting Texts

The three themes selected for students to explore related to *Catherine, Called Birdy* were (1) people at odds with their situation in society, (2) flights to freedom, and (3) transformation. The themes are broad enough to allow for the use of a wide range of literature. Traditional literature from a variety of cultures and time periods and literature from a diverse array of genres including poetry, biography, and informational texts were selected. The books are short but also substantial enough to support authentic investigation. The books, which at first glance seem quite different from *Birdy*, elicit students' curiosity and prompt genuine inquiry. A number of picture books were selected because such books are sophisticated sources of fiction and nonfiction presented in dramatic and motivating formats (Fuhler, 2002; Martinez, Roser, & Strecker, 2000). Picture books also allow readers to look for visual as well as verbal connections.

For each exploration, four or five texts were selected, and a Literature Chart was developed with categories specifically related to those texts (see below).

Setting Up the Process

Students formed groups with four or five members. Each group member was given a different book, but all the books were related in some way. Students had to read their assigned book and then share its content with other group members. After all group members shared their books, the group had to figure out what connected the books to *Catherine, Called Birdy* and to one another. The group had to create a Literature Chart to share with the rest of the class, using the template provided. Finally, they had to generate a descriptive title for the chart, revealing the theme that the books shared with *Birdy*.

People at Odds with Their Situation in Society. The students in Group 1 were given the books *Theodoric's Rainbow* (Kramer, 1995), *Starry Messenger: Galileo Galilei* (Sis, 1996), *Aunt Harriet's Underground Railroad in the Sky* (Ringgold, 1992), *Frida* (Winter, 2002), and *Frida Kahlo: The Artist Who Painted Herself* (Frith, 2003). Students were also given the following template:

Book title/ Author	Who is featured?	When/where did the person live?	What obstacles did the person face?	What did the person accomplish?	What are some connections between the person and Birdy?

Your ideas: books, stories, movies, songs, works of art, personal experiences, and how they connect

The last cell on the chart reflects the suggestion from Hartman and Allison (1996) that "Students should be encouraged to look for their own links between texts, to make judgments about what is relevant to connect, and to synthesize information in ways that make sense to them" (p. 117). This notion was also emphasized by Beach, Appleman, and Dorsey (1994).

After sharing their books and ideas, the members of Group 1 created the Literature Chart shown in Figure 13.1. The information on the chart includes ideas from two groups of students, one group of preservice teachers (A) and another group of inservice teachers (B). The undergraduates created the title "Going Against the Grain." The graduate students decided on the title "We Have What It Takes."

Figure 13.1 shows that the connections between and among the picture books and between the picture books and *Birdy* were quite robust. The books spanned a large expanse of time (1200s to 1900s) and space (Germany, Italy, United States, and Mexico); yet, all described people who would not accept the social norms of their society, people who had what it took to go against the prevailing notions of their times.

The entries on Figure 13.1 reflect careful attention to visual as well as verbal information. For example, students noted that the books about Frida Kahlo included many references to birds—from the cover illustration that shows her flying on the back of a bird to the title page illustration that shows her wing-shaped eyebrows. Students also noted the affectionate name Frida's father used for her: "dove." The chart entries also reveal that students attended to symbolic as well as literal or factual connections. For example, they included the notion that Frida's corset was like a cage.

Flights to Freedom. The students in Group 2 were given the books *D'Aulaires' Book of Greek Myths* (D'Aulaire & D'Aulaire, 1962/1992), *The*

People Could Fly (Hamilton, 1985/2004), *Amelia and Eleanor Go for a Ride* (Ryan, 1999), and two poems: "Sympathy" (Dunbar, 1913) and "The Cormorant's Tale" (Fleischman, 1985). Students were also given the following template:

Book title/ Author	Characters/ People	Setting: Time and Place	Main Conflict	How do character/plot/ theme relate to *Catherine, Called Birdy*?

Your ideas: books, stories, movies, songs, works of art, personal experiences, and how they connect

After discussing their books and possible connections among them, the members of Group 2 created the Literature Chart shown in Figure 13.2. The undergraduates chose the title "Freedom," around which they drew wings; the graduates chose "Flights to Freedom."

Like the entries on Figure 13.1, those in Figure 13.2 reference symbolic as well as factual information. For example, the students connected the ring around the cormorant's neck with the wedding ring that Birdy believed would restrict her freedom. They noted the references to cages in the novel and connected those to the poem "Sympathy." They referred to the fact that Birdy kept birds in cages until near the end of the novel, when she set them free.

The entries also refer to verbal and visual elements. For instance, students remarked on the opening lines of *Amelia and Eleanor Go for a Ride*, "Amelia and Eleanor were birds of a feather," and they noted the feathers on the endpapers of *The People Could Fly*.

Transformation. The students in Group 3 were given the books *Where Butterflies Grow* (Ryder, 1989), *Eyewitness: Knight* (Gravett, 2004), *Life of a Medieval Knight* (Corrick, 2001), *Birdsong* (Haley, 1984), and *The Ugly Duckling* (Anderson, 1844/1999). Students were also given the following template:

Book title/ Author	Who or what is transformed? What are they like at the beginning? How are they changed at the end? What stages in development or changes do they experience?	How do the changes/events relate to changes/events in Birdy's life?

Your ideas: books, stories, movies, songs, works of art, personal experiences and how they connect

After sharing their books and ideas, members of Group 3 created the Literature Chart in Figure 13.3. The undergraduates called the chart

FIGURE 13.1. Literature Chart created by Group 1.

A: Going Against the Grain B: We Have What It Takes					
Book Title / Author	Who is featured?	When/where did the person live?	What obstacles did the person face?	What did the person accomplish?	What are some connections between the person and Birdy?
Theodoric's Rainbow Stephen Kramer	Theodoric of Theodoric of Freiberg, a Dominican friar	Sometime around 1250 to about 1311; Germany	Theodoric lived in a time when people were superstitious. As a monk, most of his day was taken up with work and prayer, so he didn't have much time for experiments.	Theodoric was able to figure out how light is reflected and refracted by water drops to form rainbows.	Like Birdy, Theodoric was observant, curious, had many questions, and wondered about things; he wrote and drew. He didn't believe the magical stories about rainbows; he wanted to find out about them himself. Birdy once wanted to be a monk (p. 28).
Starry Messenger: Galileo Galilei Peter Sis	Galileo Galilei	1564–1641; Pisa, Italy	Galileo lived in a time when the Church was very powerful and made decisions about what people could believe. He was imprisonsed because of his beliefs about the sun being in the center of the universe instead of the earth.	Galileo invented and perfected many instruments: thermometer, compass, microscope, telescope. He used the telescope to observe objects in the sky, discovering the moons of Jupiter, sunspots.	Like Birdy, Galileo was curious and argumentative. He did not just accept ideas. Like Birdy, he was imprisoned in his home as a punishment.
Aunt Harriet's Underground Railroad in the Sky Faith Ringgold	Harriet Tubman	1820–1913; United States	Harriet Tubman was a black woman and a slave.	Harriet Tubman led more than 300 slaves to freedom.	Like Harriet Tubman, Birdy risked her own freedom to help others be free: she bargained to get a cottage so that Meg and Alf could marry; she gave silver to Perkin so he could become a scholar; she purchased freedom for the bear

					Harriet Tubman and Birdy knew how to use herbs for healing. Both Harriet Tubman and Birdy had dreams. When she was near death, Harriet Tubman dreamed about flying to freedom. Birdy dreamed that she was an angel. Harriet Tubman learned how to imitate bird calls and used them to warn slaves of danger.
Frida Jonah Winter *Frida Kahlo: The Artist Who Painted Herself* Margaret Frith	Frida Kahlo	1907–1954; Mexico	Frida wanted to be an artist at a time when women were not encouraged to be artists. She had polio and was in an accident that caused her great pain. She was put into a cast and had to use a cane. She also had to wear a brace or corset.	Frida created many fascinating paintings. Her courage is an inspiration to many.	Both Frida and Birdy were painters and kept journals or diaries. Both also kept birds. Both lived in societies in which men had more freedom than women. Frida's father called her "the dove." Frida painted herself with eyebrows that look like birds' wings. In both books about Frida, the illustrators used birds on the cover and title pages. There are many illustrations of birds throughout the books. Frida's brace or corset was like a cage.
Your ideas: books, stories, movies, songs, photographs, works of art, personal experiences and how they connect Lance Armstrong Helen Keller William Thatcher (the protagonist in the film *A Knight's Tale* (2001) played by Heath Ledger, a commoner who becomes a knight)					

FIGURE 13.2. Literature Chart created by Group 2.

A: Freedom B: Flights to Freedom				
Book Title / Author	Characters/People	Setting: Time and Place	Main Conflict	How do character/plot/theme relate to *Catherine, Called Birdy*?
Daedalus and Icarus in *D'Aulaires' Book of Greek Myths* Ingri D'Aulaire and Edgar Parin D'Aulaire	Daedalus, architect and inventor; Icarus, his son	Ancient Greece	Daedalus and Icarus were imprisoned by King Minos. Daedalus designed wings of wax and feathers for himself and his son. They used the wings to escape, but Icarus flew too close to the sun, his wings melted, and he plunged to his death.	Like Birdy, Daedalus and Icarus were imprisoned and wanted their freedom. Icarus took a risk in disobeying his father. Birdy, too, defied her father.
The People Could Fly Virginia Hamilton	Toby, Sarah, and other slaves; Overseer, Driver	Africa and the United States; sometime before the Civil War	In Africa, the people had wings and could fly. When they were brought to the United States as slaves, they gave up their wings and forgot how to fly. When the Overseer was cruel to Sarah, Toby said the magic words and she flew away with her baby. Toby told other slaves the words, and they flew away, too.	Like the slaves, Birdy was not free. She, too, longed to fly away to freedom. Like the people in Africa, Birdy dreamed that she was an angel with wings. Like the slaves, Birdy was free all along, but she just didn't know the words that would allow her to understand that reality. The endpapers of the book are covered with beautiful black feathers.

Amelia and Eleanor Go for a Ride Pam Muñoz Ryan	Amelia Earhart, aviator, first woman to fly solo across the Atlantic; Eleanor Roosevelt, wife of President Franklin D. Roosevelt	Washington, DC; April 20, 1933	Amelia Earhart and Eleanor Roosevelt were independent spirits who lived during a time when women were not expected to do things like fly or drive cars. Both women were concerned about and worked for equal rights for women. On April 20, 1933, Amelia and Eleanor left a White House function to take a ride in an airplane.	Although Amelia Earhart and Eleanor Roosevelt were famous women, they, like Birdy, knew what it was like to be considered too outspoken and independent. Ryan's book begins: "Amelia and Eleanor were birds of a feather. Eleanor was outspoken and determined. So was Amelia. Amelia was daring and liked to try things other women wouldn't even consider. Eleanor was the very same." Birdy, too, shared the qualities of Eleanor and Amelia. Birdy's sister was named Eleanor (p. 194)
"Sympathy" poem by Paul Laurence Dunbar	Narrator is someone who "knows why the caged bird sings."		The narrator is trapped and longs for freedom.	The poem includes references to the caged bird who "beats his bars and would be free." Birdy's mother said to her, "You are so much already, Little Bird. Why not cease your fearful pounding against the bars of your cage and be content?" (p. 53). Birdy herself referred to being caged at the end of the book: "In any event, I am, if not free, at least less painfully caged" (p. 205). Birdy kept birds in cages in her room, but eventually freed them.

FIGURE 13.2. (*continued*)

FIGURE 13.2. (*continued*)

A: Freedom	B: Flights to Freedom			
Book Title / Author	Characters/People	Setting: Time and Place	Main Conflict	How do character/plot/theme relate to *Catherine, Called Birdy*?
"The Cormorant's Tale" poem by Paul Fleischman	cormorant, bird used for fishing		The cormorant was forced to catch fish but was prevented from swallowing them by a ring placed around its neck.	The poem begins with the cormorant saying, "As free as a bird." It continues with the cormorant describing its life, which consists of fishing with a ring around its neck. For Birdy, a wedding ring seems to be preventing her from being free. The cormorant desires to be free as it imagines fish are free. The last lines of the poem are "As free as a fish." Birdy, too, imagined that being a monk, a Crusader, and even a pig boy would allow her to be free. She made a list of things that girls are not allowed to do (pp. 83–84).
Your ideas: books, stories, movies, songs, photographs, works of art, personal experiences, and how they connect *The Shawshank Redemption* (1994), a film starring Tim Robbins and Morgan Freeman about a man who, while in prison, devises a way to secure books for the library, manages an ingenious escape for himself, and makes it possible for his friend to achieve freedom from a narrow life once he is released from prison.				

"Metamorphosis," the graduates chose "Ch-ch-ch-ch-changes," a line from David Bowie's song "Changes" (Bowie, 1976, track 3).

Like the other groups, members of Group 3 were able to link the themes in their books to Birdy in thoughtful ways, noting particular instances in the novel that related to specific elements in the picture books. For example, students coupled the cocoon stage in the butterfly's life cycle and the time when Birdy was mostly wrapped up in herself. They connected the vigil of the knight with Birdy's night vigil under the pear tree. They acknowledged that changes could be positive or negative, comparing Birdy's compassion and generosity to Jorinella's hardness of heart and greed. They noted how Birdy, like the Ugly Duckling, discovered happiness after enduring torments.

Connections Beyond the Texts

All three groups were asked to include personal connections to the theme of their Literature Chart. It is interesting that, of the nine connections noted on the three charts, five were films and only one was another book.

One of the advantages of using the Literature Chart activity with picture books is that students are exposed to many literary works. For instance, the students who completed the Literature Charts related to *Catherine, Called Birdy* read at least one book in addition to *Birdy* and learned about 12 other books and two poems.

Reflecting on the Experience

After the chart presentations, students reflected on the process of constructing them. In her reflection, JA, a graduate student and teacher, offered a response revealing that the process of connecting one book to other books was something new and different for her.

> "I really didn't realize how many connections could be made between Birdy and the rest of the world—other books, movies, poems, etc. . . . I learned that books from various genres, time periods, authors, etc. can all be connected if you look at the right elements. I had not noticed this connection previously."

This idea was echoed in the discussions that took place during class sessions. Several students commented that they had never thought of engaging in such an activity before and felt that they, and their students, had missed out on something important.

Most students referred to the importance of working in a group. For instance, MP wrote:

FIGURE 13.3. Literature Chart created by Group 3.

A: Metamorphosis B: Ch-Ch-Ch-Ch-Changes		
Book Title / Author	Who or what is transformed? What are they like at the beginning? How are they changed at the end? What stages in development or changes do they experience?	How do the changes/events relate to changes/events in Birdy's life?
Where Butterflies Grow Joanne Ryder	An egg is transformed into a butterfly. Stages: egg, caterpillar, pupa, butterfly. Each stage involves a change in form and capability: movement, from no movement (egg), to crawling (caterpillar), to no movement again (pupa), to flying (butterfly).	Like a butterfly, Birdy went through a series of changes. At first, she was wrapped up in herself, rebellious and stubborn. Next, she decided to give up her freedom for something that she believed in: the well-being of the bear. Then, she decided that no one could take away her freedom, her identity. When she discovered that she would not have to marry Shaggy Beard, she said that it was "like moving from darkness into the light" (p. 204), like a pupa moves from its dark covering into the light of day. At the end of her book, Ryder addresses the butterfly with these words: "You have grown and changed and your world has grown, too." These words apply to Birdy, too.
Making a knight in *Eyewitness: Knight* Christopher Gravett The Training of the Knight in *Life of a Medieveal Knight* James A. Corrick	To become a knight, a boy had to progress through a series of learning experiences that extended over a period of almost 20 years. The stages in the training were: page, squire, and knight. A page began serving at the age of 7. He would wait on tables and run errands for the knight. At age 14, he would become a squire and the real training would begin. He would wear armor and learn to use a lance. He would also assist the knight. At the age of 21, the squire would be dubbed a knight. The dubbing ceremony took place after the squire had kept a nightlong vigil in the castle chapel. After the vigil, the squire would bathe at dawn and be clothed in white for the ceremony.	Birdy, too, underwent a kind of training. Birdy matured throughout the novel, and learned to understand what her "teachers"—other women like the old Jewish woman and Madame Joanne—had told her. She also took on more responsibility. For example, she took care of her mother when she was pregnant and confined to her bed. Birdy also kept a kind of vigil during the night she spent with Ethelfritha, particularly the time she spent in the rain under the pear tree thinking about the options available to her (pp. 200–203). Birdy wanted to be a Crusader (pp. 8, 35).
Birdsong Gail E. Haley	When a young orphan girl plays the pipes, birds gather around her. A woman who traps and sells birds, Jorinella, tricks the girl into living with her. She calls	Like Birdsong, Birdy freed birds from their cages. The illustrations show an eagle attacking Jorinella as she tries to whip Birdsong. Birdy describes her Uncle

	the birds, but then she became greedy and trapped the birds to sell. Birdsong also finds out that Jorinella captures the birds who come to hear her songs. She releases the birds, who then carry her to a new kingdom.	The illustrations also show Birdsong in a cage, a situation that Birdy described as her own. Unlike Jorinella, Birdy did not become hard of heart and greedy. Rather, she became more compassionate and generous: buying the bear's freedom and giving silver to Perkin.
The Ugly Duckling Hans Christian Anderson; adapted by Jerry Pinkney	An egg hatches into an ugly duckling, but eventually grows into a beautiful swan.	The ugly duckling was teased and tormented and decided to leave its home. On its journey, which lasted through the fall and winter, the duckling met other birds and animals and people, some were kind but others were cruel. In the spring, the duckling discovered that it could fly and that it was a swan. When it heard children calling it the best swan of all, "The swan knew that it was worth having undergone all the suffering and loneliness that he had. Otherwise, he would never have known what it was to be really happy." Birdy, too, felt tormented and ugly. She described herself as "no beauty, being sun-browned and gray-eyed with poor eyesight and a stubborn disposition" (p. 6). She also referred to herself as a "plain gray and brown goose" (p. 33). Near the end of the book, Birdy changed her opinion of her appearance, referring to herself as a "gray-eyed, sun-browned beauty" (p. 203).

Your ideas: books, stories, movies, songs, photographs, works of art, personal experiences, and how they connect
Pretty Woman (1990), a film starring Julia Roberts and Richard Gere, in which a call girl and the man who hires her are changed as a result of their relationship.
Remember the Titans (2000), a film starring Denzel Washington, in which an African American coach and his team are transformed over the course of a football season.
Finding Nemo (2003), an animated film about a young fish and his father, who complete a journey that results in profound changes for both of them.
Ida B. (2004), a novel for children by Katherine Hannigan, in which a young girl, Ida B., experiences a number of dramatic changes in her life and is changed in the process.
Tadpoles, because they change dramatically in form when they become frogs.

> "I didn't realize how many little details I skipped over about Birdy until I met with my group and discussed the chart. For example, I knew Birdy wrote a lot, but I forgot about her writing songs and drawing. This helped me understand more how 'well-rounded' Birdy was. She was a very talented young lady."

Students acknowledged that the Literature Charts themselves supported their thinking. EV explained:

> "I'm a very visual learner, so seeing a chart laid out like the ones we made was an awesome way to see the connections between stories and really understand the dynamics of them all."

For several students, the experience of constructing the Literature Charts had an impact on how they thought about the reading process itself. LW wrote:

> "I will now more often look for themes in other books that I read and try to make connections. I think if we can get students to do this it will open a new door to the world of reading for them."

Other students noted:

> "I learned that when reading any book to look for themes and relationships to the real world, other books, and other stories" (NP).

> "[Making] connections between plots, characters, themes, etc. . . . will help you become a more aware reader, an active reader . . . [to experience] insights and revelations" (EV).

The remarks of these students suggest that the experience of constructing the Literature Charts had introduced them to larger literary ideas and had helped them to notice overarching themes and recurring symbols such as those referred to by Temple (1990). Nurturing such noticing is of critical importance because it is in developing such awareness that literary experiences are enriched and deepened.

Back to the Gold Rush

As students enter their fourth-grade classroom, they wonder why ads from newspapers are on their desks. Their teacher, Ms. Sutton, explains that they should gather into groups of four, look through the ads, and make a list of all the items that are made from gold. Once the lists are made, Ms. Sutton and the students discuss the many items made of gold that are part of everyday life. Ms. Sutton then asks students if they know anything about the California Gold Rush. She explains that the mineral known as gold was first discovered in California about 150 years ago. The discovery was the beginning of a series of events referred to as the California Gold Rush. During the next few weeks, students will learn about gold, the people and places involved in the discovery of gold in California, and the effects that this discovery had not only on the settlement of California but also on the history of the United States.

Back to the Drawing Board

JoAnne Sutton and her colleagues wanted to create a learning environment that was motivating to their fourth-grade students, aligned with the California curriculum standards, and able to support student interactions with a wide array of text and online experiences. Together they decided that they would design an integrated unit that would involve students in working together and individually on projects that promoted literacy and content-area integration. They also had decided that an effective way to think about organizing their unit was through "backward planning" (McTighe & Wiggins, 1999). "Backward planning" begins with educators thinking about the final outcomes of a unit of study rather than specific activities. As such, backward planning involves three critical steps: (1) identifying student learning outcomes; (2) determining acceptable evidence or performance for the learning outcomes; and (3) planning text and online learning activities by taking into account the intended learning outcomes and evidence and performance criteria.

Using the backward planning framework, JoAnne and her fourth-grade colleagues began to plan a unit of study that would involve their students in the study of rocks and minerals (science) and the Gold Rush (social studies) through a variety of oral and written activities (language arts and visual and performing arts).

Identifying Student Learning Outcomes

JoAnne and her colleagues reviewed the information about the Gold Rush available in their social studies and science textbooks. They also gathered children's literature, historical fiction as well as information books, magazines, and websites related to the topic. They listed important concepts presented in these resources. They also reviewed the fourth-grade California content standards for social studies, science, language arts, and the visual and performing arts. These sources informed their decision making about the student learning outcomes that they would address in the Gold Rush unit. For example, while learning about the historical context of the Gold Rush, a social studies standard, students would also investigate rocks and minerals, which are earth science standards.

Determining Acceptable Evidence or Performance for the Learning Outcomes

After identifying and prioritizing student learning outcomes for the Gold Rush unit, JoAnne and her colleagues designed tasks that would provide information about what students had learned. For example, to demonstrate their understanding of the effects of the Gold Rush on the daily life of Californians as well as on the physical environment, students should be able to explain those effects. To show that they understood how music can convey historical information, students should be able to analyze music composed during the Gold Rush to identify historical facts.

Planning Learning Activities

Knowing that each student comes to school with a different set of background experiences, prior knowledge, language proficiencies, and literacy skills, JoAnne and her colleagues realized that they needed to design activities and provide resources for students with a range of abilities. Thus, they planned for students to work in a variety of participation structures such as small groups and partners. They also made sure that students had access to a variety of resources: printed as well as electronic texts, verbal as well as visual and aural resources.

The result of the thoughtful planning completed by JoAnne and her colleagues is summarized in Figure 13.4. As the figure shows, students were engaged in a variety of activities based on interactions with multiple texts and multiple media. They worked in a variety of participation structures to create products and performances to demonstrate their understanding of specific concepts and topics.

REFLECTIONS AND FUTURE DIRECTIONS

For several reasons, we expect that integrated multisource instruction will become the approach of choice for teachers at all grade levels. First, current trends in literacy reform initiatives provide support for such instruction because it: (1) makes the most of limited instructional time; (2) supports students in exploring concepts and themes in more depth; (3) creates a context in which multiple texts and multiple media can be used; (4) encourages diverse products and performances, thus providing greater opportunities for addressing the special needs of a diverse student population; and (5) allows teachers to engage students in the kinds of authentic tasks that they will encounter in the world beyond the classroom (Barton & Smith, 2000).

[*text continues on p. 309*]

FIGURE 13.4. Integrated Unit: The California Gold Rush.

Content Areas / Standards	Tasks	Resources
History / Social Science **Standard:** Students explain the economic, social, and political life in California from the establishment of the Bear Flag Republic through the Mexican-American War, the Gold Rush, and the granting of statehood.	In groups, students will create posters depicting the effects of the Gold Rush on settlements, daily life, politics, and the physical environment. Students may draw from multiple online and text sources, including biographies of John Sutter, Mariano Guadalupe Vallejo, and Louise Clapp.	**Websites:** California's Natural Resources: A Brief History of the Gold Rush *ceres.ca.gov/ceres/calweb/geology/goldrush.html* Discovery of Gold by John A. Sutter—1848 *www.sfmuseum.org/hist2/gold.html* The 2005 Clapp Family Yearbook *www.ourfamilyyearbook.com* Settlements, daily life, politics, and the physical environment *www.museumca.org/goldrush/curriculum/4v2p1standards.html* Oregon–California Trail—A complete compendium on the great western journey *www.isu.edu/~trinmich/Oregontrail.html* *www.isu.edu/%7Etrinmich/home.html* **Newspaper:** Debnam, B. (1998) *Newspaper: The California Gold Rush.* The San Diego Union-Tribune Special Feature for Kids. July 20, pp. E7–10. **Magazine:** California Gold Rush. (1997, December). *Cobblestone Magazine.* Petersborough, NH: Carus Publishing. **Texts:** Holliday, J. S. (1981). *The World Rushed In.* New York: Simon & Schuster. National Park Service (1980). *The Overland Migrations.* Washington, DC: U.S. Superintendent of Documents. (Brief and readable, with helpful maps and illustrations.) Unruh, J. (1993). *The Plains Across.* Champion, IL: University of Illinois Press. (Widely praised definitive work on the overland journey.) **Basal Social Studies Text:** White, William. (2006). *Gold Rush.* Grade 4. Scott Foresman History/Social Science for CA (pp. 75–80, 97–102). Glenview, IL: ScottForesman.

FIGURE 13.4. (*continued*).

		Images Sutter *www.kn.pacbell.com/wired/ca* Gold Rush Map *www.colorpix.ca/goldrushmap.html* Gold Rush *www.library.cagov/goldrush*
Mathematics / Measurement and Geometry **Standard:** Visualize, describe, and make models of geometric solids.	Using clay, students will make models of geometric solids (gold nuggets) in terms of the number and shape of faces, edges, and vertices. Students' gold nugget prisms will include varied bases (e.g., cube, rectangle, triangle, pentagon, hexagon).	**Websites:** Famous People of the Gold Rush by Betty Rios *projects.edtech.sandi.net/balboa/goldrush* Gold Fever! The Lure and Legacy of the California Gold Rush *www.museumca.org/goldrush/fever.html* **Text:** O'Donnell, K. (2005). *The California Gold Rush: Multiplying and Dividing Three- and Four-Digit Numbers.* New York: Powerkids Press.
Earth Sciences **Standard:** Students know how to differentiate among igneous, sedimentary, and metamorphic rocks by referring to their properties and methods of formation (the rock cycle).	In pairs, students will design a brochure for the National Park Services, including rock properties and methods of formation. 	**Websites:** Rocks & Minerals *www.fi.edu/tfi/units/rocks/rocks.html* Rocks & Minerals slide show *volcano.und.edu/vwdocs/vwlessons/lessons/Slideshow/Slideindex.html* Rocks & Minerals Webquest *cte.jhu.edu/techacademy/fellows/brannon/webquest/kmbindex.html* Gold *www.desertusa.com/mag98/june/papr/geo_gold.html* Quest for Gold *www.nationalgeographic.com/xpeditions/activities/16/questgold.html*

		Texts: Kay,V. (1999). *Gold Fever.* New York: Putnam. Levy, JoAnn. (1992). *They Saw the Elephant: Women in the California Gold Rush.* Norman: University of Oklahoma Press. **Basal Science Text:** Cooney, T. M., Ostlund, K., Ukens, L., & Romance, N. (2006). *Minerals and Rocks.* Grade 4, Chapter 6, pp. 177–212. Glenview, IL: ScottForesman. **Images:** Panning _Gold.jpg *www.sitnews.net* Gold1.gif *www.sd52bc.ca* Video: 1-hour documentary on the Gold Rush *www.isu.edu/~trinmich/storegrvideo.html*
Writing Strategies and Applications **Standards:** Write an information report. Quote or paraphrase information sources, citing them appropriately. Locate information in reference texts by using organizational features (e.g., prefaces, appendices). Use various reference materials (e.g., dictionary, thesaurus, card catalog, encyclopedia, online	Using poster boards, students will create information reports relating to the central question: How can the specific economic activity in a region (Gold Rush) facilitate the creation of towns, which often turn into ghost towns if the economic activity ends? Students will include facts and details for focus and will draw from more than one source of information	**Websites:** John Sutter & James Marshall *www.mtdemocrat.com/columist/hughey1.shtml* **Texts:** Chambers, C. E. (1998). *California Gold Rush.* New York: Troll. Levine, E. (1992). *If You Traveled West in a Covered Wagon.* New York: Scholastic. Brands, H. W. (2002). *The Age of Gold: The California Gold Rush and the Birth of Modern America.* New York: Random House. **Images:** Gold Rush.jpg *www.publications.water.ca.gov* The Land of Glittering Dreams—CA Gold Rush *www.zigseek.com/search/site1listall.*

FIGURE 13.4. (*continued*).

FIGURE 13.4. (*continued*).

information) as an aid to writing. Understand the organization of almanacs, newspapers, and periodicals and how to use those print materials. Demonstrate basic keyboarding skills and familiarity with computer terminology.	(e.g., speakers, books, newspapers, other media sources). Students will create, present, and share with a friend a news headline that would convince others to journey to California in search of gold.	
Speaking Applications **Standard:** Deliver oral summaries of articles and books that contain the main ideas of the event or article and the most significant details.	Students will work in pairs (Student 1 is the interviewer and Student 2 is John Sutter) to present an interview to the entire class. Student 1 will ask John Sutter about his life, the details of his trip to California, and the memorable experience of creating Sutter's Mill.	**Websites:** Sutter's Mill *www.eraoftheclipperships.com/page10web.html* John Augustus Sutter *www.syix.com/yubacity/johnsutter.html* "The West" on PBS Links to biographies of pertinent people (e.g., James Marshall, John Sutter, Sam Brannan), as well as related classroom activities. Episode 3, "A Speck of the Future," focuses on the Gold Rush *www.pbs.org/weta/thewest/* **Magazine:** Shea, M. (January 2000). Blacks in the gold rush. *Cobblestone Magazine.* Peterborough, NH: Carus Publishing. **Texts:** Rawls, J. J., & Orsi, R. J. (Eds.). (1999). *A Golden State: Mining and Economic Development in Gold Rush California.* Berkeley & Los Angeles: University of California Press. Walker, D. L. (2003). *Eldorado: The California Gold Rush.* New York: Tom Doherty Associates.

Reading Comprehension **Standard:** Read and understand grade-level-appropriate material (e.g., classic and contemporary literature, magazines, newspapers, online information). Draw upon a variety of comprehension strategies as needed (e.g., generating and responding to essential questions, making predictions, comparing information from several sources).	In groups of three, students will complete a chart after reading several passages or articles on the same topic. The three columns of the chart should be: rock or mineral, influence on California history, and evidence/source of information. Students will use at least three different sources.	**Websites:** "The American Experience: Gold Fever" on PBS *www.pgs.org/wgbh/amex/gold/about.html* Related online resources, teacher's guide, and pertinent links to gold rush sites California Historical Society (an excellent collection of California history books) *www.californiahistoricalsociety.org/* **Texts:** Kelly, L. A. (1997). *California's Gold Rush Country.* Baldwin Park, CA: Gem Guides Book Company. Kelly, L. A. (1997). *Traveling California's Gold Rush Country.* New York: Falcon. Mattes, M. (1988). *The Great Platte River Road.* Lincoln, NE: University of Nebraska. (Definitive work on the first half of the Oregon–California Trail. Exhaustive.) **Graphic Novel:** Western comic depicting the Gold Rush: *www.toonopedia.com/ruggles.htm*
Listening/Speaking Strategies **Standard:** Evaluate the role of the media in focusing attention on events and in forming opinions on issues.	Two students will pretend to talk on the telephone while the rest of the class listens in. Student 1 tries to convince Student 2 to come to California to search for gold. Student 2 is unsure about the long trip, the existence of gold, and the unsettled territory. Other students can "call in," helping to persuade Student 2 about the chance of a lifetime.	**Website:** The California Gold Rush, from the State of California's CERES. *ceres.ca.gov/ceres/calweb/geology/goldrush.html* **Poetry:** Gioia, D., Yost, C., & Hicks, J. (Eds.). 2003. *California Poetry: From the Gold Rush to the Present.* (California Legacy). New York: Heyday Books. **Texts:** Stein, R. (2001). *California Gold Rush.* New York: Sagebrush. Bo Boessenecker, J. (1999). *Gold Dust and Gunsmoke: Tales of Gold Rush Outlaws, Gunfighters, Lawmen, and Vigilantes.* New York: Wiley. **Video & Graphic Novel:** Gold Rush book and video: *www.pbs.org/goldrush/prbook.html*

FIGURE 13.4. (*continued*).

FIGURE 13.4. (*continued*).

Visual and Performing Arts / Historical and Cultural Context **Standard:** Understand the diversity of dance, song, and folk history/tales	After listening to songs written by Gold Rush immigrants, students will be able to discuss in small groups how history was told through song and tall tales as miner's worked and visited. They will be helped to perform and identify folk/traditional and social dances from California history.	**Websites:** Eyewitness account of Mr. Shufelt's Gold Rush experience *www.eyewitnesstohistory.com/californiagoldrush.htm* Women in the Gold Rush *www.goldrush.com/~joann/* Untold stories *www.over-land.com/trgold.html* Popular music of the California Gold Rush before the discovery of gold at Sutter's Mill near Sacramento *www.sbgmusic.com/html/teacher/reference/historical/goldrush.html* Music of the Alaska-Klondike Gold Rush *www.uaf.edu/uapress/books/MusicoftheAlaska.htm* **Texts:** Erickson, P. (1997). *Daily Life in a Covered Wagon.* New York: Puffin Books. Hill, W. (1986). *The California Trail: Yesterday and Today.* Boulder, CO: Pruett Publishing Co. Minnick, S. S. (1988). *Samfow: The San Joaquin Chinese Legacy.* Fresno, CA: Panorama West Publishing. (Covering much more than just the Gold Rush period, a good primer on the Chinese in the region.) **Musical Play about the Gold Rush:** Benson, Mary Ann (1994). *Days of 49: Being the (almost) true tale of one TOM MOORE who lived through the California Gold Rush.* Oakland, CA: Calicanto Associates. (*www.calicantoassociates.com*)

Second, the resources needed to support integrated multisource instruction, particularly multimedia and electronic resources, will become increasingly available (Leu, Karchmer, & Leu, 1999). Publishers are also responding to the call for information texts in all the content areas at various reading levels (e.g., Freeman & Person, 1998; Moss, 2003).

Perhaps most important of all, as teachers design and implement integrated multisource units and refine them across several cycles, their experiences will provide the most compelling evidence that such an approach is influencing the motivation, engagement, and understanding of their students in remarkable ways.

CONCLUDING COMMENTS

In this chapter we have provided a research-based rationale supporting multisource integrated instruction and have supplied two classroom examples of activities and resources supporting this kind of instruction. We have emphasized the importance of diverse texts not only as sources of motivation but also as sites for cognitive engagement and deeper processing.

ENGAGEMENT ACTIVITIES

1. Select a novel that your students will be reading. Identify the important themes and symbols in the book. Locate multiple resources—books, poems, music, and films—that relate to the themes and symbols. Construct a Literature Chart with appropriate categories that will support students in using the resources to develop a deeper understanding of the themes and symbols.
2. Identify a topic in your social studies or science curriculum that lends itself to a unit of study using an integrated multisource approach. Locate multiple resources related to the topic. List the important concepts that the resources can support students in constructing. Identify the student learning outcomes in your state's social studies, science, and language arts content standards that the unit will address.
3. Design an activity that engages students in using multiple and diverse resources to address a specific learning goal.

REFERENCES

Andersen, H. C. (1999). *The ugly duckling.* (J. Pinkney, Adapt.). New York: Morrow. (Originally published 1844).

Anonymous 4. (1995). *The lily and the lamb* [CD]. USA: harmonia mundi usa.

Barton, K. C., & Smith, L. A. (2000). Themes or motifs? Aiming for coherence through interdisciplinary outlines. *The Reading Teacher, 54*(1), 54–63.

Baum, L. F. (1900). *The Wizard of Oz.* Chicago: Rand McNally.

Beach, R., Appleman, D., & Dorsey, S. (1994). Adolescents' use of intertextual links to understand literature. In R. B. Ruddell, M. R. Ruddell, & H. Singer (Eds.), *Theoretical models and processes of reading* (4th ed., pp. 695–714). Newark, DE: International Reading Association. (Reprinted from *Developing discourse practices in adolescence and adulthood,* by R. Beach & C. Hynds, Eds., Norwood, NJ: Ablex).

Bowie, D. (1976). Changes. On *Changes One Bowie* [CD]. UK: RCA.

Corrick, J. A. (2001). *Life of a medieval knight.* San Diego, CA: Lucent Books.

Cushman, K. (1994). *Catherine, called Birdy.* New York: HarperTrophy.

D'Aulaire, I., & D'Aulaire, E. P. (1992). *D'Aulaires' book of Greek myths.* New York: Dell. (Originally published 1962).

Dunbar, P. L. (1913). *The complete poems of Paul Laurence Dunbar.* New York: Dodd, Mead.

Eichinger, B. (producer), & Annaud, J. J. (director). (1986). *The name of the rose* [motion picture]. Los Angeles, CA: Embassy Home Entertainment.

Fleischman, P. (1985). *I am phoenix: Poems for two voices.* New York: HarperTrophy.

Freeman, E. B., & Person, D. G. (1998). *Connecting informational children's books with content area learning.* Boston: Allyn & Bacon.

Frey, N., & Fisher, D. (2006). *Language arts workshop: Purposeful reading and writing instruction.* Upper Saddle River, NJ: Merrill/Prentice Hall.

Frith, M. (2003). *Frida Kahlo: The artist who painted herself.* New York: Grosset & Dunlap.

Fuhler, C. J. (2002). Picture books for older readers: Passports for teaching and learning across the curriculum. In J. B. Elliott & M. M Dupuis (Eds.), *Young adult literature in the classroom: Reading it, teaching it, loving it* (pp. 170–192). Newark, DE: International Reading Association.

Gravett, C. (2004). *Eyewitness: Knight.* New York: DK Publishing.

Guthrie, J. T., & Wigfield, A. (Eds.). (1997). *Reading engagement: Motivating readers through integrated instruction.* Newark, DE: International Reading Association.

Haley, G. E. (1984). *Birdsong.* New York: Crown.

Hamilton, V. (2004). *The people could fly: The picture book.* New York: Knopf. (Originally published 1985).

Hartman, D. K. (1995). Eight readers reading: The intertextual links of proficient readers reading multiple passages. *Reading Research Quarterly, 30*(3), 520–560.

Hartman, D. K., & Allison, J. (1996). Promoting inquiry-oriented discussions using multiple texts. In L. B. Gambrell & J. F. Almasi (Eds.), *Lively discussions!: Fostering engaged reading* (pp. 106–133). Newark, DE: International Reading Association.

Hynd, C. R. (1999). Teaching students to think critically using multiple texts in history. *Journal of Adolescent and Adult Literacy, 42*(6), 428–436.

Jones, J. P. (2000). Interdisciplinary units: An introduction to integrated curriculum in the intermediate and middle school. In K. D. Wood & T. S. Dickinson (Eds.), *Promoting literacy in grades 4–9: A handbook for teachers and administrators* (pp. 207–219)). Boston: Allyn & Bacon.

Kramer, S. (1995). *Theodoric's rainbow.* New York: Freeman.

Lapp, D., & Flood, J. (1993). Literature in the science program. In B. E. Cullinan (Ed.), *Fact and fiction: Literature across the curriculum* (pp. 68–79). Newark, DE: International Reading Association.

Lapp, D., Flood, J., & Fisher, D. (1999). Intermediality: How the use of multiple media enhances learning. *The Reading Teacher, 52*(7), 776–780.

Lenski, S. D. (1998). Intertextual intentions: Making connections across texts. *The Clearing House, 72*(2), 74–80. Retrieved January 11, 2005, from *0-infotrac.galegroup.com.*

Leu, D. J., Karchmer, R. A., & Leu, D. D. (1999). The Miss Rumphius effect: Envisionments for literacy and learning that transform the Internet. *The Reading Teacher, 52*(6), 636–642.

Lewis, C. S. (1950). *The lion, the witch, and the wardrobe.* New York: Macmillan.

Lipson, M. Y., Valencia, S. W., Wixson, K. K., & Peters, C. W. (1993). Integration and thematic teaching: Integration to improve teaching and learning. *Language Arts, 70,* 252–263.

McTighe, J., & Wiggins, G. (1999). *The understanding by design handbook.* Alexandria, VA: Association for Supervision and Curriculum Development.

Martinez, M. G., Roser, N. L., & Strecker, S. (2000). Using picture books with older children. In K. D. Wood & T. S. Dickinson (Eds.), *Promoting literacy in grades 4–9: A handbook for teachers and administrators* (pp. 250–262). Boston: Allyn & Bacon.

Moss, B. (2003). *Exploring the literature of fact: Children's nonfiction trade books in the elementary classroom.* New York: Guilford Press.

Palinscar, A. S., Parecki, A. D., & McPhail, J. C. (1995). Friendship and literacy through literature. *Journal of Learning Disabilities, 28*(8), 503–510, 522.

Perfetti, C. A., Britt, M. A., & Georgi, M. C. (1995). *Text-based learning and reasoning: Studies in history.* Mahwah, NJ: Erlbaum.

Reinking, D. (1998). Introduction: Synthesizing technological transformations in a post-typographic world. In D. Reinking, M. C. McKenna, L. D. Labbo, & R. D. Kieffer (Eds.), *Handbook of literacy and technology: Transformations in a post-typographic world* (pp. xi–xxx). Mahwah, NJ: Erlbaum.

Rellim, T. V., & Black, T. (producers) & Helgeland, B. (director). (2000). *A knight's tale* [motion picture]. Culver City, CA: Columbia Tristar Home Entertainment.

Ringgold, F. (1992). *Aunt Harriet's underground railroad in the sky.* New York: Crown.

Roser, N. L., & Hoffman, J. V. (1992). Language charts: A record of story time talk. *Language Arts, 69,* 44–52.

Roser, N. L., & Keehn, S. (2002). Fostering thought, talk, and inquiry: Linking literature and social studies. *The Reading Teacher, 55*(5), 416–526.

Rowling, J. K. (1997). *Harry Potter and the sorcerer's stone.* New York: Scholastic.

Ryan, P. M. (1999). *Amelia and Eleanor go for a ride: Based on a true story.* New York: Scholastic.

Ryder, J. (1989). *Where butterflies grow.* New York: Penguin.

Short, K. G. (1992). Intertextuality: Searching for patterns that connect. In C. K. Kinzer & D. J. Leu (Eds.), *Literacy research, theory, and practice: Views from many perspectives, Forty-first yearbook of the National Reading Conference* (pp. 187–197). Chicago: National Reading Conference.

Sis, P. (1996). *Starry messenger: A book depicting the life of a famous scientist, mathematician, astronomer, philosopher, physicist, Galileo Galilei.* New York: Farrar Straus, & Giroux.

Smith, J. L., & Johnson, H. (1994). Models for implementing literature in content studies. *The Reading Teacher, 48*(3), 198–209.

Stark, R., & Shepherd, R., (producers), & Lester, R. (director). (1976). *Robin and Marian* [motion picture]. Burbank, CA: RCA/Columbia Pictures Home Video.

Temple, C. (1990). How literary theory expands our expectations for children's reading and writing. In T. Shanahan (Ed.), *Reading and writing together: New perspectives for the classroom* (pp. 23–56). Norwood, MA: Christopher-Gordon.

Tolkien, J. R. R. (1982). *The fellowship of the ring: Being the first part of the lord of the rings.* Boston, MA: Houghton Mifflin. (Originally published 1954).

Willcock, D. (producer and director). (1997). *The saints with Sister Wendy* [motion picture]. USA: PBS Home Video.

Winter, J. (2002). *Frida.* New York: Scholastic.

Worthy, M. J., & Bloodgood, J. W. (1992). Enhancing reading instruction through Cinderella tales. *The Reading Teacher, 46*(4), 290–301.

Chapter 14

ORGANIZING EFFECTIVE LITERACY INSTRUCTION: DIFFERENTIATING INSTRUCTION TO MEET THE NEEDS OF ALL CHILDREN

D. Ray Reutzel

This chapter will:

- Provide a theoretical and research overview of differentiated literacy instruction.
- Present the essential elements of differentiated literacy instruction.
- Discuss the use of assessment data to inform differentiated literacy instruction.
- Describe the use of an array of effective literacy instructional practices.
- Offer alternative grouping approaches as a part of differentiated literacy instruction.
- Illustrate the scheduling of the literacy instructional block to support differentiated literacy instruction.

EVIDENCE-BASED BEST PRACTICES: DIFFERENTIATING LITERACY INSTRUCTION

Because teachers' experiences and expertise in managing the complexity of classrooms vary greatly, and because students' needs are equally complex and challenging in today's increasingly diverse classroom environments, the question of how to differentiate instruction is of critical importance for all teachers—novice and experienced alike (Gregory & Chapman, 2002). When teachers determine to differentiate literacy instruction, they consciously or unconsciously add to the complexity of managing the classroom environment while at the same time providing necessary accommodations to meet diverse student needs. The tension between increasing management complexity for the teacher and meeting diverse student needs is a tenuous balancing act (Tomlinson, 2001).

For example, let us assume that a teacher has chosen to use whole-class literacy instruction to reduce the difficulty of management in the classroom. The potential moral consequences of such a choice may be that individual student needs are not met or, worse yet, that selected children, perhaps the most at-risk, may be denied access to literacy knowledge, instruction, and an opportunity to learn (Goodlad & Oakes, 1988; Oakes, 1986, 1988). Thus, a decision to use a particular literacy grouping strategy in order to reduce management problems in the classroom must be made in full appreciation of the potential social, instructional, psychological, and moral outcomes of such a choice on children, not based solely the ease or convenience for the teacher. On the other hand, an overtaxed, stressed-out teacher with too many small-group or individual literacy learning activities may not be as emotionally available to sensitively respond to the diverse needs of all children. A workable model for many teachers begins with a simple, limited, and manageable small-group differentiated instructional plan. Such a model may then gradually expand toward effectively using an increasing range of instructional differentiation strategies (including intensive, extensive teacher-guided instruction to meet individual differences), which allows for free choice within a clear, bounded, and explicit framework that allocates space and determines rules, directions, schedules, and familiar routines; that fosters social collaboration and interaction; that provides access to coherent knowledge domains and structures; that supports individual literacy learners' development; and that encourages children to become self-regulated and independent literacy learners (Gregory & Chapman, 2002; Raphael et al., 2003; Tomlinson, 2001; Tyner, 2004).

Differentiating literacy instruction implies at least two moral imperatives. First, teachers need to recognize that the process of becoming literate follows a developmental path from the simple to the complex, from the unconventional to the conventional, from the cradle to the grave. Second, the tendency of some schools is to create a "one size fits all" curriculum will not reach all of the children (Raphael et al., 2003; Tyner, 2004). In order to reach all of the children, teachers must be willing to provide instruction that is responsive to the needs of each child based upon assessment results. To meet the diverse needs of all children, teachers will need to know how to effectively implement many instructional interventions and management techniques (Tomlinson, 1999). In this chapter we will discuss only a few of the important ways teachers can meet the needs of all children in becoming readers and writers, including (1) providing the essentials of literacy instruction, (2) using assessment data to inform literacy instruction, (3) using an array of effective literacy instructional practices, (4) properly grouping participants for differentiated literacy instruction, and (5) scheduling time effectively to support differentiated literacy instruction.

Providing the Essentials of Literacy Instruction

Although attention to the activities, techniques, methods, or the *how* of teaching literacy has shown some moderate effects on young children's early literacy learning, teaching children the essential or critical components of the literacy process is of even greater significance (Mathes et al., 2005; Rathvon, 2004). Children, depending upon their level of literacy development, need daily, sustained, and high-quality literacy instruction in (1) oral language, (2) concepts about print, (3) phonological and phonemic awareness, (4) alphabetic principle to include letter names, and phonics, (5) fluency, (6) vocabulary, (7) comprehension strategies, and (8) writing and spelling to make satisfactory progress in early literacy development. Current research also strongly suggests that knowledge of these critical components of the reading and writing process needs to be taught *explicitly*—meaning that teachers need to directly explain, model, and scaffold children's practice and acquisition of the concepts, skills, and strategies attendant to each of these critical components of early literacy.

In addition, recent work by Shanahan (2004) harkens back to well-known research on the effects of allocated learning time and academic learning time on students' academic achievement. So, while teaching the critical components of the literacy process is important, so too is allocating sufficient time for the literacy block each day. Shanahan (2004) recommends that a minimum of 120 total minutes of the available daily instructional time in the elementary classroom be allocated to the literacy block. It is beneficial when that time can be a single block of uninterrupted time, but, if not, smaller time blocks should be scheduled as contiguous to one another as possible.

Furthermore, Shanahan (2004) strongly urges that sufficient daily time, within the literacy block, be allocated for teaching the critical components of the literacy process to young children. Consequently, it is recommended that four 30-minute time blocks, or 120 minutes be scheduled for explicit teacher-directed instruction in the following:

1. *Word Work* (30 minutes): This includes instruction in letter recognition, phonological and phonemic awareness, concepts about print, and phonics.
2. *Writing* (30 minutes): This would include instruction in composition, mechanics, grammar, and spelling.
3. *Fluency* (30 minutes): This time would be devoted to increasing students' reading and writing accuracy, rate, and expression through some instruction and copious amount of reading and writing practice.
4. *Comprehension Strategy Instruction* (30 minutes): Instruction in this time block would focus on vocabulary acquisition and study as well as teaching children effective comprehension strategies for constructing meaning with text and becoming self-regulated learners.

Using Assessment Data to Inform Instruction

"Assessment drives instruction!" is an accepted, almost axiomatic, saying in educational circles. Although this may be true at some level, its implicit message is also highly exaggerated in the best sense of the phrase. For the most part the role current high-stakes or outcomes assessment has played in instruction is to lead to reductionistic instructional approaches. This means that high-stakes or outcomes testing and assessment have often led to teachers to engage in instruction that mimics the content and format of the testing or assessment—or, worse yet, to engage in simplistic gimmicks such as giving children food during testing, providing test prep courses, or offering rewards for high test performance. Thus, in this case, assessment is driving instruction in the worst sense of the phrase. Conversely, in the recent past it has been rare to observe teachers consistently gathering assessment data for the purpose of monitoring students' progress and then actually using these data to inform the selection of instructional approaches, strategies, interventions, or content. So, in the best sense of the phrase, assessment hasn't been driving instruction.

It seems that the relationship between assessment and instruction always has been a tenuous one. In the past assessment was viewed as an intrusion into the curriculum and instruction of the classroom rather than seen as an integral part of selecting and designing instructional interventions based upon informed decision making. In short, assessment was like a cold; it was something to get over and then go on with classroom life. In today's educational context, such a position is no longer viable. Assessment and using assessment data are at the very heart of differentiating instruction to meet the diverse literacy learning needs of all children in the classroom.

Also, assessment no longer serves the singular purpose of determining the outcomes of reading or writing instruction. Rather, assessment in today's classrooms is much more sophisticated and is used for a variety of purposes. There are four general categories or types of assessment in literacy, each used for a different specific purpose: (1) screening assessment, (2) diagnostic assessment, (3) progress-monitoring assessment, and (4) outcomes assessment. *Screening assessments* are given to all students to determine if there are pre-existing concerns about any given child's literacy development and growth prior to offering instruction. If children perform well on literacy screening assessments, there is no need for additional assessment or the selection of special interventions. These children are likely to be well served by providing a high-quality classroom core literacy program. The literacy instruction or program offered to all children in a classroom irrespective of their individual needs is often referred to as *Tier 1* intervention.

On the other hand, if children perform poorly on literacy screening assessments, then this signals the need for additional *diagnostic assessment* to pinpoint the source of the problem as well as to design specific, targeted interventions to redress the problem. *Tier 2* instructional interventions are determined by using the results of diagnostic assessments in literacy and often occur in small groups in the classroom. In some cases, after or in conjunction with Tier 2 interventions in literacy, children are found to be in need of additional special services in literacy such as *Title I* or *Special Education,* often referred to as *Tier 3* interventions, to redress literacy learning problems. As Tier 1, 2, or 3 interventions are used with children, teachers carefully track their literacy development using *progress-monitoring assessments.* These progress-monitoring literacy assessments are typically quick, reliable, valid, and fairly frequent assessments, such as DIBELS (Dynamic Indicators of Basic Early Literacy Skills), used to determine the effectiveness of the literacy interventions selected (Good & Kaminski, 2002). If progress monitoring shows acceptable student literacy growth, then one concludes the literacy intervention selected can continue to be used effectively. If progress monitoring demonstrates little or no student progress in literacy, then the literacy instructional intervention select isn't having the desired effect, and another or additional literacy instructional interventions may be needed to promote literacy growth and progress. Finally, after a specified period of instruction has taken place, such as an academic or school year, state and federal laws require that *outcomes assessments* be used to determine overall literacy growth for students, classrooms, and schools as compared with other students' progress nationally or against an established standard at the state or local level.

As a result, assessment has taken on a different purpose for many classroom teachers in today's classrooms, and that purpose is to inform their decisions about which interventions to use with whom, when, and where for teaching a specific component of the literacy process. In fact, progress-monitoring assessment has largely displaced the calendaring discussions in faculty meetings of yesteryear with discussions among teachers about student data and how specific children can be helped. In schools where I routinely work with teachers, these teachers use an assessment data board like the one shown in the photo below during faculty meetings and in team meetings. Children who are falling behind or who are achieving below the local, state, or national standard are discussed as individuals, and teachers make specific plans with one another about how to help these children make improved literacy progress.

As a result, assessment is truly influencing classroom teachers' literacy instructional choices; in the very best sense of the phrase, assessment really is driving instruction!

BEST PRACTICES IN ACTION

A Classroom Vignette

It's the first day of school for 20 excited and somewhat frightened first-grade children. Like most young children, they arrive fully expecting that this is the year, perhaps even the day, when they learn to read and write! Ms. Songi, first-grade teacher at Sunset Elementary School, greets each child with a warm smile as each one enters a classroom that has been carefully crafted to support a variety of literacy teaching and learning situations to meet the diverse needs of children in today's classrooms.

The classroom is organized into several areas—each thoughtfully designed to meet the differing needs of children—including whole-class, small-group, and individual learning opportunities. The classroom is filled with print—labeled objects, posters, charts, daily schedules, message centers, books, word walls, word chunks, environmental print collections, signs, work board or classroom routine displays, etc. A multicolored carpet with black squares for each child is located in the front of the room near the dry-erase white board. Near this location there is an electronic music keyboard and an easel stocked with large chart paper readied for whole-class instruction. A small horseshoe-shaped table in a distant corner of the classroom awaits a variety of instructional activities organized for small groups of children.

Literacy and content-area learning centers are placed around the perimeter of the classroom. A publishing center runs along one side of the room opposite the windows; on a cupboard top in this area, a full line of writing tools and materials awaits anxious but willing hands for writing and publishing. A small carpeted reading nook, complete with a large rocking chair for one-to-one reading and several beanbag chairs for independent reading by children, is neatly organized in a quiet area of the room. Near the front of the room is a play office area complete with typewriter, adding machine, telephone, desk, writing tablets, pencils, pens, erasers, markers, rubber stamps, dictionary, speller, liquid white-out, and a dry-erase board for business planning and messages. Across the room sits a small center stocked with everything from stencils and magnetic letters to Alpha-Bits cereal, a center designed to enable children to explore letters of the alphabet and engage in word play, exploration, sorting, and study. Near the classroom door is a listening center complete with: cassette tape recorder, headphones, audiocassette tapes of books, six-pack copies of selected children's book titles, and a computer and monitor loaded with children's books on compact discs (CDs). A storage area with 20 large plastic trays is located on the other side of the classroom door. The classroom has no desks, only tables and chairs organized into many interesting and exciting learning areas. Children are instructed to each find a chair with his or her own nametag carefully written in manuscript on a cartoon bookworm character, a nametag to be pinned to each child's shirt. Each child writes a duplicate nametag and places his or her nametag on a tray to be used for storing books and personal supplies. School is ready to start.

If permitted, Ms. Songi would tell us that much study, reading, planning, thought, and preparation have preceded this momentous day. It is common knowledge that effective classroom environments, use of grouping strategies, and implementing effective classroom routines, management, and interventions do not occur by accident. These complex organizational components, like so much of effective literacy instruction, are the products of teacher knowledge, skill, and ingenuity.

Using an Array of Effective Literacy Instructional Practices

As you can tell from the vignette, Ms. Songi attends to the differences children bring to school with them, since she is well aware that not all children respond to instruction in the same way or with similar enthusiasm. Despite the fact that every child needs to be taught, to varying degrees, all of the critical components of the literacy process (Rathvon, 2004), this is also not meant to imply that a one-size-fits-all instructional approach is either desirable or would be equally effective with all children. Conversely, neither does differentiating classroom literacy instruction excuse teachers from teaching the critical components of the literacy process, but rather suggests to teachers that each critical literacy component will be taught in differing amounts or with differing emphasis dependent upon the needs of each learner. What's more, the instructional approach used to teach and practice each critical component of the literacy process may also need to be differentiated dependent upon the needs of each learner.

Research findings have helped most teachers understand that, although some children will learn to read and write with almost any kind or quality of instruction, there are other children—usually those who struggle the most—who will not learn to read or write sufficiently well without instruction that is sequenced, systematic, intentional, teacher-directed, and explicit (Chall, 2000; Delpit, 1988; National Reading Panel, 2000; Duffy, 2003).

Explicit instruction is difficult for most teachers to accomplish, because, as Duffy (2003) points out, "It is often difficult for us to provide explicit explanations for how to read. To do so, we must become aware ourselves of the processes we use as we read. However, because we are expert readers we no longer think about the processes we use to read" (p. 10). As previously noted in this chapter, explicit instruction is composed of three interlocking sequenced phases: (1) explanations, (2) modeling, and (3) scaffolding.

What do we do when we *explain* reading or writing concepts, skills, or strategies to children? First and of absolute importance, we must immerse children in the reading of or writing of texts! Concepts, skills, or strategies learned and practiced in isolation seldom transfer to the actual act of reading or writing (Taylor, Pearson, Clark, & Walpole, 1999). Second, within this text-based or text-production environment, we explain to students which reading or writing concept, skill, or strategy they are to learn, when or where it will be used in reading or writing, and why learning this concept, skill, or strategy is important for becoming a successful reader or writer.

Next, we systematically model for children the application of a literacy concept, skill, or strategy. To model a literacy concept, skill, or strategy, we must show children how it is to be done, using lots of talking about our thinking out loud. Just for a moment, think about a magic show by the renowned magician David Copperfield. You observe his trick of making the Statue of Liberty disappear from New York harbor and wonder to yourself, "How does he do that?" Well, this is not dissimilar to what the struggling reader or writer is thinking when he or she observes other children reading and writing with ease. Struggling readers and writers just don't know the processes or steps behind the trick of reading and writing. Now imagine you were allowed a backstage pass to have David Copperfield show you step by step how he performed the trick of making the Statue of Liberty disappear. You would then exclaim, "Oh, so *that's* how you do it!" Modeling "thinking or talking out loud about our thinking as teachers" helps students get a toehold, as it were, on how to do the thinking in reading or writing that is necessary to acquire the literacy concept or skill, and how to apply the literacy concept, skill, or strategy to read or write effectively (Duffy, 2003). In short, talking aloud about your mental processes when reading or writing helps to make the steps of the reading and writing "magic trick" obvious to children who do not understand these processes through mere exposure alone to models of reading and writing.

Finally, how do we scaffold or support a student to apply the to-be-learned literacy concept, skill, or strategy independently, effectively, and strategically? At first we provide a great deal of support to help students begin to take ownership of the process of applying the literacy concept, skill, or strategy taught by the teacher. Over time, we gradually reduce the amount of assistance we provide to students as they gradually take ownership of the process and become independent, self-regulated readers and writers. Pearson and Gallagher (1983) visually depict this gradual fading of teacher support during the release of a reading or writing concept, strategy, or skill from the teacher to the independent and self-regulated application by the individual learner in Figure 14.1.

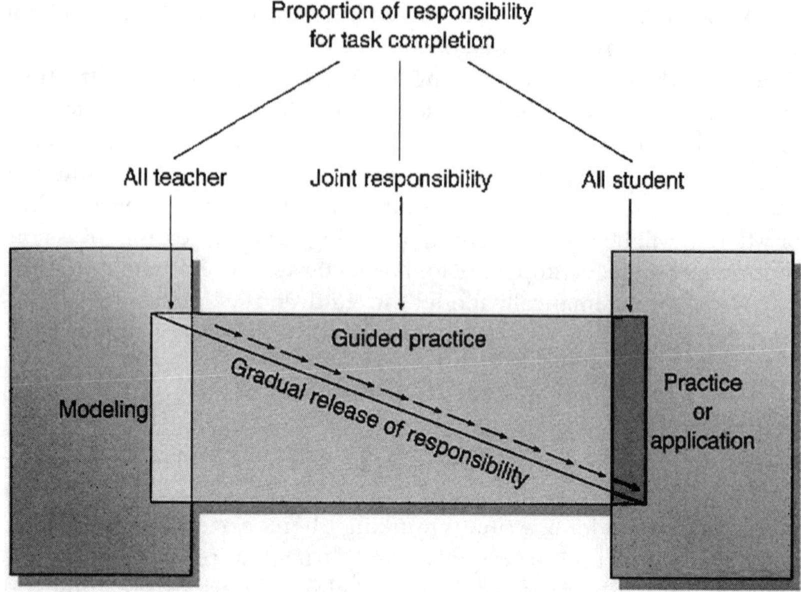

FIGURE 14.1. The Gradual Release of Responsibility model of instruction. From Reutzel and Cooter (2000). Copyright 2000 by Prentice-Hall. Reprinted by permission.

Other effective literacy instructional practices found in the successful literacy teacher's repertoire include the interactive read-aloud, shared reading, guided or small-group differentiated reading, paired reading, and wide and repeated reading opportunities for children, modeled writing, interactive writing, and establishing an effective writer's workshop. Since the constraints of this single chapter do allow sufficient space to discuss each of these effective instructional practices in detail, we provide the following partial list of resources for learning more about each:

Interactive read-aloud—Polette, K. (2005). *Read and write it out loud: Guided oral literacy strategies.* Boston: Allyn & Bacon.

Shared reading—Payne, C. D. (2005). *Shared reading for today's classroom: Lessons and strategies for explicit instruction in comprehension, fluency, word study and genre.* New York: Scholastic.

Small-group differentiated reading—Tyner, B. (2004). *Small-group reading instruction: A differentiated teaching model for beginning and struggling readers.* Newark, DE: International Reading Association.

Small-group guided reading—Fountas, I. C., & Pinnell, G. S. (1996). *Guided reading: Good first teaching for all children.* Portsmouth, NH: Heinemann.

Paired reading—Daley, A. (2005). *Partner reading: A way to help all readers grow.* New York: Scholastic.

Independent reading—Bryan, G., Fawson, P. C., & Reutzel, D. R. (2003). Sustained silent reading: Exploring the value of literature discussion with three non-engaged readers. *Reading Research and Instruction, 43*(1), 47–73.

Modeled and interactive writing—McCarrier, A., Pinnell, G. S., & Fountas, I. C. (2000). *Interactive writing: How language and literacy come together, K–2.* Portsmouth, NH: Heinemann.

Writer's workshop—Widmer, K., & Buxton, S. (2004). *Workshops that work!* New York: Scholastic.

Differentiated Literacy Instruction: Effective Grouping Plans

Organizing classrooms into smaller groups of children fills the moral imperative often felt by teachers to meet diverse individual student needs (Gregory & Chapman, 2002; Tomlinson, 1999, Tyner, 2004). However, somewhere between the meeting of diverse individual needs and managing a classroom filled with children lies an expansive chasm to be bridged, at least in part, by the use of various grouping strategies. Individualized instruction in classrooms filled with 20–30 children, while desirable as the ideal, is also virtually impractical. On the other hand, the exclusive use of whole-class instruction fails to address students as individuals whose needs, skills, performance, and dispositions differ greatly. It is through using a blend of whole-class, small-group, and individual grouping strategies that teachers can begin to effectively address students' needs, skills, and motivations in becoming readers and writers. In this next section, we discuss a variety of grouping strategies that provide classroom teachers workable and effective options in addition to whole-class and homogeneous groups.

Whole-Class Instruction

Whole-class instruction can be used to effectively teach the critical components of the literacy process to an entire classroom of children. In whole-class instruction no attempt is made to subdivide the class of students into smaller or more focused instructional groups along any dimension of learning, interest, need, or skill.

Whole-class instruction is a popular format for providing explicit, direct, and systematic skill and strategy instruction as well as for studying literature using a core-books approach or for shared reading (Reutzel & Cooter, 2003, 2004; Cox & Zarillo, 1993; Fisher & Medvic, 2000). It is an effective means for safety-netting young learners as they develop conventional and increasingly sophisticated literacy learning strategies. Whole-class instruction shields the individual within a community of learners from potentially harsh emotional and psychological consequences that may result from the risks associated with being singled out for *solo reading.* Whole-class instruction can also reduce some of the negative effects of labeling young learners: "below-average," "slow," "special-needs," "at-risk," or "disabled."

Because becoming literate is at least partially a social as well as a cognitive endeavor, whole-class instruction engages teachers and children in a community of socially shared literacy activities and discussions. Shared literacy learning activities generally provided in whole-class instruction need to be a regular and integral part of the daily literacy time block (Flood, Lapp, Flood, & Nagel, 1992; Cunningham, Hall, & Defee, 1998; Wilkinson & Townsend, 2000). Just a few examples of potentially effective literacy learning activities that can be used in connection with whole-class instruction include telling stories; dramatizing; reading books aloud and sharing student-authored stories, poems, songs; reading big books together; reading the enlarged texts of songs, poems, raps, and jingles; participating in an experiment or some other active-learning experience; and creating language experience charts. On the downside, whole-class instruction used exclusively clearly fails to meet the needs of diverse groups of children, especially those with learning disabilities (Schumm, Moody, & Vaughn, 2000). Flexibility in grouping seems to be a key element of successful literacy instruction (Opitz, 1998a; Wilkinson & Townsend, 2000).

Small-Group Alternatives to Whole-Class Instruction

Flexible Groups. Flexible grouping is a partial answer to the looming question for many teachers about how to differentiate reading and writing instruction (Wilkinson & Townsend, 2000; Gregory & Chapman, 2002; Tyner, 2004). In flexible grouping, children are placed into *temporary* groups based on their level of independence as learners and their personal interests that sustain independence. Optiz (1998a) describes flexible grouping as allowing "students to work in differently mixed ability groups depending upon the learning task at hand" (p. 10). There are several key differences between ability grouping strategies and flexible grouping strategies, some of which are summarized in Table 14.1.

Flexible groups are formed and re-formed on the basis of a set of principles. Some of these summarized principles are well articulated by Unsworth (1984, p. 300):

1. There are no permanent groups.
2. Groups are periodically created, modified, or disbanded to meet new needs as they arise.

TABLE 14.1. Comparing Characteristics of Ability and Flexible Grouping Strategies

	Ability grouping	Flexible grouping
Forming groups	Test scores	Ability to manage leveled books
Nature of groups	Static	Dynamic, changing
Instructional tasks	Given low-level tasks	Given high-level tasks
Reading practice	Oral round-robin	Oral guided and silent reading
Reading materials	Basal selections chosen by teacher	Trade and leveled books chosen by teacher and students
Typical assessment	Test scores	Observations, informal checklists, performance of authentic reading tasks

3. At times there is only one group consisting of all pupils.
4. Groups vary in size from 2 or 3 to 9 or 10, depending on the group's purpose.
5. Group membership is not fixed; it varies according to needs and purposes.
6. Student commitment is enhanced when students know how the group's work relates to the overall program or task.
7. Children should be able to evaluate the progress of the group and the teacher's assessment of the group's work.
8. There should be a clear strategy for supervising the group's work.

It is clear from these principles that flexible grouping strategies can be used to accommodate student interests, learning preferences, and social needs such as friendship groups in addition to meeting instructional needs and goals. For flexible grouping to function effectively, the organization, purpose, and tasks must be clearly understood by students.

Concerns such as what is to be accomplished and how it is to be accomplished must be clearly stated and understood by students. The potential for unproductive chaos is high in flexible grouping arrangements if the teacher has not carefully prepared the learning tasks and the environment for success.

For example, a classroom in which flexible grouping is used to provide for participation in multiple learning centers or stations might operate something like the following. This hypothetical classroom has six literacy learning centers, established in various locations around the classroom. The first center is an alphabet and word-building station where children use magnetic letters and word pattern cards (rimes/word families) to build words, sort words, and store words in personalized word banks. A second center houses listening stations where students have multiple copies of a single title to be read with a read-along cassette tape. A third center provides a quiet, comfortable area for reading self-selected books, magazines, comics, etc. A fourth center seats children at a horseshoe-shaped table for guided reading and interactive writing sessions with the teacher. A fifth center is a Writing Workshop, where students can have peer conferences, get and give editing assistance, and prepare student-authored products ranging from greeting cards, recipes, and calendars, to newspaper ads, books, and story murals. Finally, there is a center for individual student conferences that are scheduled in advance with the teacher.

Flexible groups of children are formed to participate in these six designed learning center activities. Each flexible group includes a mix of reading and writing ability levels, called heterogeneous grouping, to avoid the pitfalls associated in the past with static ability grouping. Flexible groups may also have an elected or appointed group leader to oversee cleanup of centers, operation of necessary equipment, management of supplies, and other tasks. In any case, these groups have assigned tasks to complete in each center. Behavioral and instructional guidelines and goals are clearly established and communicated to each group prior to center time. And most importantly, students are helped to know what they may do as follow-up work, should they finish before the others. All of this requires extraordinary instructional planning and management skill on the part of the teacher, but the busy and productive activity and learning that come from the flexible grouping strategy make it well worth the effort!

Literature Circles. In literature circles, teachers and children use trade books or literature books, both narrative and expository, as the core for reading instruction. To form literature circles, the teacher has children look through several selected titles of trade books available for small-group instruction. (This will mean that multiple copies of each book or title will be needed! It is recommended that teachers purchase about eight copies of each book rather than purchasing classroom sets. Opitz [1998b] recommends that books on a common topic or theme called "text sets" be used in literature study groups.) At the conclusion of this exploration period, the teacher reads available book titles aloud and asks how many students would like to read each book. In this way teachers can get a quick idea of which available books seem to interest the students most and which engender no interest. The teacher selects from the high-interest trade books three to four titles, depending on how many literature circles he or she can reasonably manage and how many copies of each book are available. Next, the teacher works up a "book talk" on each of the selected books to present to the students the following day. A book talk is a short, interesting introduction to the topic, setting, and problem of a book. After presenting a book talk on each of the books selected, the teacher asks older children to write down the titles of their first two choices. The teacher asks the younger children to come to the chalkboard and sign their names under the titles of the two books they like best of those presented. Only one literature circle meets each day with the teacher to discuss and respond to a chapter or predetermined number of pages to have been read in a trade book. It is best if the teacher meets with each literature circle after children have indicated their choices to determine how many weeks will be spent reading the book and how many pages per day need to be read to reach that goal. The remaining steps for organizing literature circles are summarized in the following list:

1. Select three or four books children may be interested in reading from the brief interest inventory of literature available in the school or classroom, as described.
2. Introduce each of the books by giving a book talk on each.
3. Invite children to write down the titles of their two top choices.
4. Depending on the number of multiple copies of trade books available, fill each group with those children who have indicated the book as their first choice. Once a group is filled, move the remaining children to their second choice until all children have been invited to attend the group of their first or second choice.
5. Decide how many days or weeks will be spent reading this series of book choices.
6. Meet with each of the literature circles and determine the following:
   a. How many pages per day will need to be read to complete the book in the time allowed.
   b. When the first group meeting will be held. (The teacher meets with only one group per day.)
   c. How children will respond to their reading. This may involve a reading response log, character report cards, or wanted posters.
7. Help children understand when the first or next meeting of their literature-response group will be, how many pages in the book will need to be read, and which type of response to the reading—such as group retellings, wanted posters, a story map, etc.—will need to be completed before the meeting of the literature-response group (Wood & Jones, 1998).

8. Near the completion of the book, the group may discuss possible extensions of the book to drama, music, art, and other projects.

Peterson and Eeds (1990), in their book *Grand Conversations*, suggest a checklist that may be used by teachers to track student preparation for and participation in literature-response groups. I have modified this form to be used with literature circles, as shown in Figure 14.2.

When the literature circle book has been completed, literature circles are disbanded and new groups are formed for selecting and reading a new series of books. Thus, students' interests are engaged by encouraging choice (Raphael et al., 2003), and the problem of static ability-grouping plans can be avoided.

Name ____________________ Date __________

Author ____________________ Title __________

Preparation for Literature Study

• Brought book to the literature circle.	Yes ___	No ___
• Contributed to developing group reading goals.	Yes ___	No ___
• Completed work according to group goals.	Yes ___	No ___
• Read the assigned pages, chapters, etc., for the goals.	Yes ___	No ___
• Noted places to share (ones of interest, ones that were puzzling, etc.)	Yes ___	No ___
• Completed group response assignments before coming to the day's discussion.	Yes ___	No ___

Participation in the Literature Circle Discussion

• Participated in the discussion.	Weak ___	Good ___	Excellent ___
• Gave quality of verbal responses and contributions.	Weak ___	Good ___	Excellent ___
• Used text to support ideas and assertions.	Weak ___	Good ___	Excellent ___
• Listened to others.	Weak ___	Good ___	Excellent ___

FIGURE 14.2. Record of goal completion and participation in literature circles. Adapted from Peterson and Eeds (1990). Copyright 1990 by Scholastic Canada. Adapted by permission.

Cooperative Learning Groups. Another grouping strategy for effective reading and writing instruction is called cooperative learning. This grouping strategy makes use of heterogeneous groups ranging from two to five children working together to accomplish a *team task* (Harp, 1989; Opitz, 1992; Slavin, 1987; Johnson & Johnson, 1999). Harp (1989) indicates four characteristics of cooperative learning groups. First, each lesson begins with teacher instruction and modeling. Second, children in a cooperative learning group work together to accomplish a task as assigned by the teacher. Third, children work on individual assignments related to a group-assigned task. Each student must be willing to complete his or her part of the group-shared assignment. Finally, the team is recognized by averaging each individual grade and assigning one grade to the group.

Much research indicates that children in cooperative learning groups have consistently shown greater achievement than children who participate in traditional grouping schemes (Johnson, Maruyama, Johnson, Nelson, & Skon, 1981; Jongsma, 1990; Opitz, 1992; Radencich, 1995; Slavin, 1988; Stevens, Madden, Slavin, & Farnish, 1987a, 1987b; Topping, 1989; Webb & Schwartz, 1988; Wood, 1987). In a synthesis of research on cooperative learning, Slavin (1991) found that cooperative learning not only increased student achievement but also increased student self-concept and social skills.

Manarino-Leggett and Saloman (1989) and Wood (1987) describe several different grouping alternatives that can be applied in concert with the concept of cooperative learning. A few of these group alternatives are briefly described in Table 14.2.

Assessment Data Grouping. Assessment data groups are determined by using progress-monitoring data teachers collect at regular intervals. Through the use of progress-monitoring assessment strategies like running records, anecdotal records, group participation records, and 1-minute fluency samples, etc., teachers determine individual student learning needs. Assessment data groups are formed when progress-monitoring data indicate several children with similar learning needs, whether these needs be skill-, content-, or strategy-based. Typically, an assessment data group will include as few as two students or as many as half the class, 10–15 students. The purpose of an assessment data group is to teach a temporary group of students a particular literacy skill, concept, or strategy they have yet to learn and apply. The vehicle for instruction within assessment data groups is an explicit concept, skill, or strategy lesson, as previously described in this chapter.

Dynamic Grouping for Small-Group Differentiated Literacy Instruction. Small-group differentiated literacy instruction is an essential part of an

TABLE 14.2. Alternative Grouping Plans for Encouraging Cooperative Learning

Dyads
Wood (1987) assigns roles to each student in a dyad or pair of readers. Each student reads two pages of text silently, or in some cases the two students read orally in unison. After reading these two pages, one student acts as the recaller and verbally recounts what the two have read. The other student acts as listener and clarifier for the recaller. Dyad reading is an effective means for supporting young children's reading development, especially for at-risk readers (Eldredge & Quinn, 1988).
Focus trios
Children may be randomly assigned or may form social groups of three students for the purposes of summarizing what they already know about a reading selection and developing questions to be answered during reading. After reading, the trio discusses answers to the questions and clarifies and summarizes their answers.
Group retellings
Students read different books or selections on the same topic. After reading, each student retells to the other group members what he/she has read. Group members may comment on or add to the retellings of any individual.
Groups of four
Groups of four are randomly assigned task completion groups. Each individual is given a responsibility to complete some phase of a larger task. For example, when writing a letter, one student might be the addresser, another the body writer, another the checker, etc. In this way, all students contribute to the successful completion of the task. Roles should be exchanged regularly to enable students to experience all aspects of task completion.
Jigsaw
Students in a group are each assigned to read a different part of the same selection. After reading, each student retells to the others in the group what he/she has read. A discussion usually ensues in which students may interview or question the reteller to clarify any incomplete ideas or correct misunderstanding. After this discussion concludes, students can be invited to read the rest of the selection to confirm or correct the retellings of other group members.
Metacomprehension pairs
Students alternate reading and orally summarizing paragraphs or pages of a selection. One listens, follows along, and checks the accuracy of the other's comprehension of the selection.

(*continued*)

TABLE 14.2. (*continued*)

Problem-solving/project groups
Having children work together cooperatively in pairs or small groups to solve reading or writing problems is another effective classroom practice involving the collaboration of children to enhance classroom instruction. Small problem-solving groups are initiated by children who wish to work collaboratively on a self-selected reading or writing problem. In project groups, children are encouraged to explore a wide variety of possible reading and writing projects (e.g., plays, puppetry, reader's theater, research, student-authored books, poetry, lyrics to songs, notes, invitations, or cards). The products resulting from project groups are to be of publishable quality. The culmination of a project group is sharing the project or product with an authentic audience.
Think–pair–share
Lyman (1988) recommends that students sit in pairs as the teacher presents a reading minilesson to the class. After the lesson, the teacher presents a problem to the group. The children individually think of an answer; then with their partners they discuss and reach a consensus on the answer. A pair of students can be asked to share their agreed-upon answer with the class.
Turn-to-your-neighbor
After listening to a student read a book aloud, share a book response, or share a piece of published writing, students can be asked to turn to a neighbor and tell one concept or idea they enjoyed about the presentation. They should also share one question they would like to ask the reader or author.

effective literacy program (Tyner, 2004). Children are typically placed into differentiated literacy instruction only after they have had ample opportunities as a class group to listen to stories, poems, songs, etc., and to participate in shared or community-based whole-class literacy experiences. Thus, after teachers have accomplished initial screening assessment of students, built a sense of community, and observed children carefully during the first 4–6 weeks of each new school year, then small-group differentiated literacy instruction can begin in earnest.

Children in differentiated *reading* instructional groups are placed together based upon their assessed word study and text reading levels. This means that teachers have assessed each child's instructional reading levels in connected texts as well as each child's ability to recognize, decode, and write words. In practice, small-group differentiated reading instruction plays out in a five-part lesson structure: (1) *rereading*—repeated reading of a familiar book or selection; (2) *word bank*—sight word and vocabulary word work; (3) *word study*—spelling and decoding work; (4) *writing*—including interactive and dictation writing; and (5) *new read*—applying previously instructed concepts, skills, and strategies in an unfamiliar book.

At first, dynamic grouping for differentiated reading instruction looks somewhat similar to ability or achievement grouping practices used in decades past. Dynamic grouping for differentiated reading instruction is begun by placing children into small homogeneous groups. The most important consideration in creating dynamic differentiated reading instructional groups centers on each child's ability to successfully handle and process word decoding and recognition tasks as well as reading within leveled books (Tyner, 2004). Dynamic differentiated reading instruction groups are composed of five to eight children who work together for a finite period of time under the guidance and with the feedback of the teacher. Unlike the static ability groups of yesteryear, dynamic differentiated reading instructional groups change as children make progress during the year—usually changing by months rather than by weeks or days.

Prior to beginning small-group differentiated reading instruction, great care is taken to match children to a book at their instructional level, meaning that children can enjoy and control the reading of the book on their first reading. Instructional-level texts should present children with a reasonable challenge but also with a high degree of success. Typically, children should be able to read 90–95% of the words correctly in an instructional-level book chosen for use in a differentiated reading instruction group. During small-group differentiated reading instruction, teachers teach short lessons and ask students to engage in various word recognition, decoding, spelling, and writing tasks using the five-step cycle described previously.

As teachers work with children in differentiated reading instruction groups, they lead them to understand and strategically use effective reading and writing strategies. Differentiated reading instructional groups also provide a context for systematic skill instruction related specifically to the critical components of the reading and writing as well as practicing the application of strategies and skills within the context of reading a leveled book. Small-group differentiated reading instruction is a time to focus instruction directly on student reading skill and strategy development rather than focusing on appreciating and discussing high-quality literature. In fact, the use of leveled books in differentiated reading instruction does not always allow for the use of recognized literature of enduring quality, but rather necessitates using books that are written specifically to support individual readers in their development and use of self-extending and self-regulated reading and writing strategies. When reading leveled texts, whether new to or previously read by the children, teachers use questions, prompts, and comments to help children effectively apply decoding and comprehension strategies they have been previously taught in whole-class settings or in their differentiated reading instruction group.

The Daily Literacy Block: Organizing an Effective Instructional Routine

Children develop a sense of security when the events of the school day revolve around a sequence of anticipated activities. Although variety is the spice of life for children, too, they find comfort in familiar instructional routines and schedules in a well-organized classroom (Holdaway, 1984). There are any number of ways to organize the activities and instruction of the school day. However, it is important that children experience a variety of interactive settings in the whole class, in small groups, and individually each day. Groups should be flexible, meet the needs of the students, and involve the "best practices" of literacy instruction. Also, it is important that children receive daily planned, intentional, and explicit instruction in the critical components, strategies, and skills of learning to read and write successfully.

One such approach used to organize the school day is the *Five-Block Schedule* based in part on the recommendations of Shanahan (2004) and also based on the recent work of Mathes et al. (2005) relating to the value of small-group reading instruction. This organizational framework, the Five-Block Schedule, is a functional and flexible instructional scaffolding used by teachers in classrooms to provide interactive, shared, and small-group differentiated reading and writing experiences for children similar to such other organizational plans as the four-block plan by P. M. Cunningham (Cunningham et al., 1998).

The Five-Block Schedule is divided into five clearly defined instructional time and activity blocks: (1) word work, (2) fluency, (3) writing, (4) comprehension strategy instruction, and (5) small-group differentiated reading instruction. The Five-Block Schedule incorporates into its structure the critical components of reading and writing instruction recommended in this chapter and in several recent national reading research reports, including decoding and word recognition instruction, fluency development, writing, vocabulary and comprehension strategy instruction, and guided oral reading (Snow, Burns, & Griffin, 1998; National Reading Panel, 2000). The Five-Block Schedule is designed for 180 minutes of allocated daily instructional time. The structure of the time allocations found in the Five-Block Schedule is outlined in Figure 14.3.

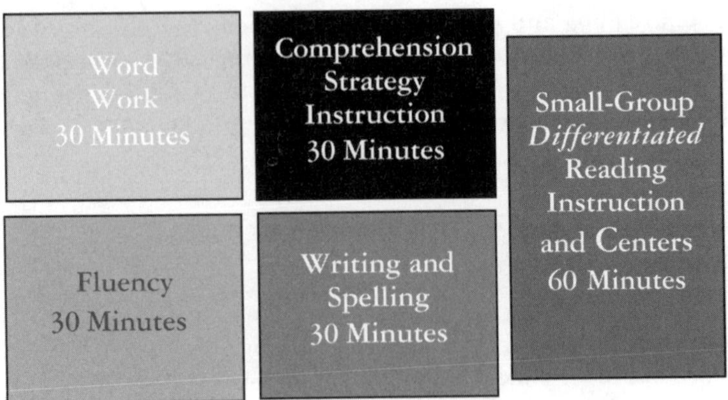

FIGURE 14.3. Five-block schedule for literacy instruction.

Word Work (30 Minutes)

The purpose of the *word work* instructional block is to develop children's (1) phonological and phonemic awareness, (2) concepts about print, (3) letter recognition and production, (4) decoding and word recognition, and (5) spelling concepts, skills, and strategies. Effective instructional practices used within this time allocation include shared reading of enlarged texts, including charts, posters, overhead transparencies, and big books; the co-construction of interactive written sentences and brief stories, making and breaking words using manipulative letters, and choral response techniques used such tools as gel, white dry erase, or magnadoodle boards. I cannot overemphasize the importance of providing the whole class with direct explicit instruction on each of these word-related skills, strategies, and concepts. Children need clear explanations, "think-alouds" coupled with expert modeling of reading and writing behaviors, and guided application of these concepts, skills, and strategies during this time segment as well. I also strongly recommend that daily lessons focus on both decoding and spelling—reading and writing processes that help children better understand the reciprocal nature of all reading and writing processes.

Fluency (30 Minutes)

The daily fluency lesson framework begins with an explicit explanation, description, or definition of the importance of reading fluency and the elements, terms, and metalanguage of fluent oral reading as defined in the research and professional literature: (1) accuracy, (2) rate, and (3) expression. Children need to see and hear models of what one means, as well. So, the next part of the Fluency Development Lesson (FDW) lesson framework involves teacher modeling, think-alouds, and demonstration of the elements of fluent oral reading, including examples and intentional miscues. Teachers select one of the essential elements of oral reading fluency for each lesson (i.e., accuracy). After reading a text aloud to the group of children with accuracy, the teacher reminds the children that accurate oral reading is *reading what is on the page.* Next, the teacher performs an inaccurate oral reading of the same text. Once the inaccurate oral reading of this text is complete, the teacher again reminds the children that accurate oral reading is reading what is on the page. Next, the teacher invites the children, usually amid snickering and giggles, to comment on the accuracy of the "inaccurate" modeling of oral reading. I have noticed that greater discussion and attention flow from the inaccurate reading than from accurate renditions of text.

After explaining, defining, describing, modeling, demonstrating, and discussing fluent reading, the teacher involves the children in repeated group-guided oral rereadings of the text that has been previously modeled. During this part of the daily fluency lesson, teachers use various formats for choral reading, such as echoic (echo chamber), unison (all together), popcorn (hopping up when called upon), antiphonal (one side against another), mumble, line-a-child, and so on. For those who are unfamiliar with these choral reading variations, we recommend reading Opitz and Rasinski's (1998) *Good-Bye Round Robin,* or Raskinski's (2003) *The Fluent Reader.* Next in the daily lesson framework, children are involved in individual guided practice and repeated readings of the text previously modeled. Pairs of readers are either same-age peers or older peers from another age- or grade-level classroom. Each pair of children alternates the roles of reader and listener. After each oral reading by the reader, the listener provides feedback. Guided, oral, repeated reading practice with feedback is one of the practices that produced the largest effect sizes and student gains for fluency practice in the studies analyzed by the National Reading Panel (2000).

Once children sense their emerging fluency, they want to demonstrate it to others. Children love to perform their practiced oral reading for an audience of either parents or other students in the school building. When preparing an oral reading performance, teachers might use one of three well-known oral reading instructional approaches: (1) readers' theater, (2) radio reading, and (3) recitation (Opitz & Rasinski, 1998).

Remember that fluency achieved in just one type of task or text types is insufficient, and that children require instruction and practice with a variety of reading fluency tasks and a variety of text types and levels of challenge. In grades 2–6 we found that we needed to provide new, fresh, or novel short but high-interest texts for fluency practice nearly every day.

In grades K–1, we found that multiple days of fluency practice with the same texts were often needed to move the oral reading of a text to fluency.

Writing Instruction (30 Minutes)

The purpose of the *writing* instructional block is to develop children's (1) composition skills, (2) spelling, (3) mechanics, (4) grammatical understandings, and (5) literary and writing genre concepts, skills, and strategies. Effective instructional practices used within this time allocation include modeled writing by the teacher; a writer's workshop, including drafting, conferencing, revising, editing, publishing, and disseminating; and direct explicit whole-class instruction on each of these writing skills, strategies, and concepts. Children need clear explanations, "think-alouds" coupled with expert modeling of writing behaviors, and guided application of these writing concepts, skills, and strategies during this time segment as well. I also strongly recommend that daily lessons provide a time segment for sharing children's writing in an "author's chair" or using some other method of disseminating and sharing children's writing products.

Comprehension Strategy Instruction (30 Minutes)

The purpose of the *comprehension strategies* instructional block is to develop children's (1) vocabulary and (2) comprehension concepts, skills, and strategies. Effective instructional practices used within this time segment include explicit instruction of vocabulary concepts, using a variety of methods and requiring a variety of responses (Beck, McKeown, & Kucan, 2002; McKenna, 2002); wordplay (Johnson, 2001); and a focus on explicit instruction of comprehension strategies, including: (1) questioning, (2) text structure, (3) graphic organizers, (4) inferences, (5) predicting, (6) visual imaging, (7) monitoring, (8) summarizing, (9) background knowledge activation, etc. Here too, I cannot overemphasize the importance of providing the whole class with direct explicit instruction on each of these vocabulary and comprehension skills, strategies, and concepts. Children need clear explanations, "think-alouds" coupled with expert modeling of comprehension thought processes and behaviors, as well as teacher-guided application of these concepts, skills, and strategies in the reading of many texts at different levels and in many genres. It is also strongly recommend that, at some point in time, teachers strongly consider working toward teaching a set or family of multiple comprehension strategies such as *reciprocal teaching* (Palincsar, 2003), *concept-oriented reading instruction* (Guthrie, 2003; Swan, 2002), and *transactional strategies* (Brown, Pressley, Van Meter, & Shuder, 1996) to be used collectively and strategically while interacting with a variety of texts over long periods of time (National Reading Panel, 2000; Reutzel, Smith, & Fawson, 2006).

Small-Group Differentiated Reading Instruction (60 Minutes)

Small-group differentiated reading instruction time is divided into three blocks of 20 minutes each. The structure of this time is fairly rigid in the beginning as students learn to rotate from center to center, use their time wisely in completing center tasks, and manage themselves so as to minimize off-task behaviors when they are not in the meeting with the teacher for small-group differentiated reading instruction. Within each 20-minute block of time two major types of activities dominate: *small-group differentiated reading group* and *small groups at learning centers.* The teacher is stationed in the small-group differentiated reading area of the classroom prepared to offer differentiated reading instruction. The children, on the other hand, are called to their small reading group (homogeneous group) from an assigned "center rotation" group (mixed-abilities group). *Learning centers* are teacher-selected, - designed, and -provisioned. Learning centers focus on follow-up activities and tasks drawn from previously taught *word work, fluency, comprehension strategy,* and *writing lessons.* Management of learning centers is a central concern for teachers; they must be designed so that the activities and tasks are clearly understood, independent of teacher supervision, and able to be completed within the time allowed. It is also important that tasks completed in learning centers have a component of accountability and performance. We show in Figure 14.4 two possible approaches for managing learning center group rotations.

Managing the small-group differentiated reading instruction time block is a complex effort for most teachers. We caution teachers against the creation of too many learning centers. In the early part of the year, fewer centers are easier for both teachers and students to handle. As the year progresses, adding a few new centers, especially optional centers, can add variety to this time block. We have also found that very little flexibility is desirable in the group rotation schedule early in the year. As time progresses and children acquire more experience with the rotation between learning centers, we have found it better to assign children specific tasks to be completed during this time period rather than a time-controlled rotation through various learning centers.

REFLECTIONS AND FUTURE DIRECTIONS

Teachers want to accommodate individual student needs in literacy instruction. Throughout the history of classroom literacy instruction,

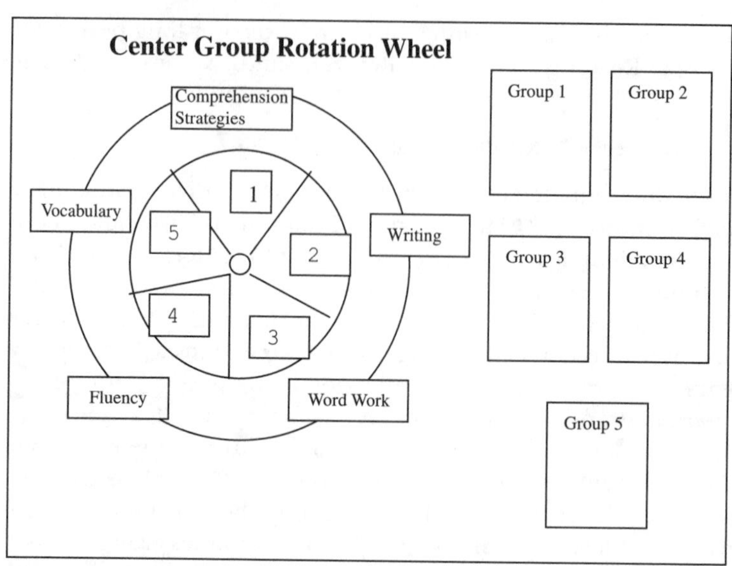

Center Group Management Chart

Working with Comprehension Strategies	Writing	Word Work	Fluency	Vocabulary
1	2	3	4	5
5	1	2	3	4
4	5	1	2	3
3	4	5	1	2
2	3	4	5	1

FIGURE 14.4. Learning center group management/rotation plans.

several variations on ability grouping and whole-class instruction have persisted despite a large body of relevant research pointing to many negative outcomes for students and teachers related to these grouping strategies. In recent years, however, a number of alternative grouping strategies have emerged, including flexible groups, literature circles, co-operative learning groups, assessment data groups, and dynamic small differentiated reading groups. These strategies offer teachers a wide range of possibilities.

CONCLUDING COMMENTS

More research is needed to determine the effects of alternative grouping strategies on students' reading growth, engagement, motivation, and achievement. For example, we do not know how homogeneous grouping for small-group differentiated reading instruction affects students' achievement, motivation, engagement, or reading growth as compared with whole-class or homogeneous or heterogeneous grouping strategies singly or in combination. Also, we need to know more about how flexible grouping strategies interact to ameliorate the effects of homogeneous grouping for students with varying needs and abilities.

ENGAGEMENT ACTIVITIES

1. Discuss why learning-disabled students seem to dislike mixed-ability grouping strategies when the research also seems to point to many negative effects for same-ability grouping on struggling students.
2. Observe several levels of dynamic small differentiated reading groups in classrooms and take field notes. Then, interview four or five children in various levels of these groups about their perceptions. Do the typical issues associated with ability grouping seem to be present in the observations and interview responses of the children in these groups?
3. Given a reading or writing task to perform individually or in a cooperative learning group, what is the result on student's performance? Is quality higher or lower? Do individuals or groups use learning time more efficiently? Is the performance or product given to individuals or cooperative learning groups higher or lower? How do children of varying abilities and skill levels feel about the group processes and products?
4. Discuss whether it is important for teachers to know what children are learning from time spent in learning centers? If it is important, how can teachers require accountability from children for learning activities found in typical independent learning centers—like a listening center, for example?

5. Although children often have rich discussions of trade book literature in literature circles, do these arrangements produce better comprehension abilities, larger vocabularies, and greater motivation to read than do whole-class discussions?

REFERENCES

Beck, I. L., McKeown, M. G., & Kucan, L. (2002). *Bringing words to life: Robust vocabulary instruction.* New York: Guilford Press.

Brown, R., Pressley, M., Van Meter, P., & Schuder, T. (1996). A quasi-experimental validation of transactional strategies instruction with previously low-achieving second-grade readers. *Journal of Educational Psychology, 88,* 18–37.

Chall, J. S. (2000). *The academic achievement challenge: What really works in the classroom?* New York: Guilford Press.

Cox, C., & Zarillo, J. (1993). *Teaching reading with children's literature.* Upper Saddle River, NJ: Merrill/Prentice Hall.

Cunningham, P. M., Hall, D. P., & Defee, M. (1998). Nonability-grouped, multilevel instruction: Eight years later. *The Reading Teacher, 51*(8), 652–664.

Delpit, L. D. (1988). Silenced dialogue: Power and pedagogy in educating other people's children. *Harvard Educational Review, 58,* 280–298.

Duffy, G. G. (2003). *Explaining reading: A resource for teaching concepts, skills, and strategies.* New York: Guilford Press.

Fisher, B., & Medvic, E. F. (2000). *Perspectives on shared reading: Planning and practice.* Portsmouth, NH: Heinemann.

Flood, J., Lapp, D., Flood, S. & Nagel, G. (1992). Am I allowed to group? Using flexible patterns for effective instruction. *The Reading Teacher, 45*(8), 608–616.

Good, R. H., & Kaminski, R. A. (2002). *Dynamic Indicators of Basic Early Literacy Skills (DIBELS), Sixth Edition* [online]. Retrieved from: *dibels.uoregon.edu.*

Goodlad, J. I., & Oakes, J. (1988). We must offer equal access to knowledge. *Educational Leadership, 45*(5), 16–22.

Gregory, G. H., & Chapman, C. (2002). *Differentiated instructional strategies: One size doesn't fit all.* Thousand Oaks, CA: Corwin Press.

Guthrie, J. T. (2003). Concept-oriented reading instruction. In C. E. Snow & A. P. Sweet (Eds.), *Rethinking reading comprehension* (pp. 115–140). New York: Guilford Press.

Harp, B. (1989). What do we know now about ability grouping? *The Reading Teacher, 42*(6), 430–431.

Holdaway, D. (1984). *Stability and change in literacy learning.* Portsmouth, NH: Heinemann.

Johnson, D. D. (2001). *Vocabulary in the elementary and middle school.* Boston: Allyn & Bacon.

Johnson, D. W., & Johnson, R. T. (1999). *Learning together and alone: Cooperative, competitive, and individualistic learning* (5th ed.). Boston: Allyn & Bacon.

Johnson, D. W., Maruyama, G., Johnson, R. T., Nelson, D., & Skon, L. (1981). Effects of cooperative, competitive and individualistic goal structures on achievement: A meta-analysis. *Psychological Bulletin, 89,* 47–62.

Jongsma, K. S. (1990). Collaborative learning (questions and answers). *The Reading Teacher, 43*(4), 346–347.

Manarino-Leggett, P., & Salomon, P. A. (1989, April–May). *Cooperation vs. competition: Techniques for keeping your classroom alive but not endangered.* Paper presented at the Thirty-Fourth Annual Convention of the International Reading Association, New Orleans.

Mathes, P. G., Denton, C. A., Fletcher, J. M., Anthongy, J. L., Francis, D. J., & Schatschneider, C. (2005). The effects of theoretically different instruction and student charactertistics on the skills of struggling readers. *Reading Research Quarterly, 40*(2), 148–183.

McKenna, M. C. (2002). *Help for struggling readers: Strategies for grades 3–8.* New York: Guilford Press.

National Reading Panel. (2000). *Report of the National Reading Panel: Teaching children to read.* Washington, DC: National Institute of Child Health and Human Development.

Oakes, J. (1986). Keeping track: Part 1. The policy and practice of curriculum inequality. *Phi Delta Kappan, 68*(1), 12–17.

Oakes, J. (1988). Beyond tracking. *Educational Horizons, 65*(1), 32–35.

Opitz, M. F. (1992). The cooperative reading activity: An alternative to ability grouping. *The Reading Teacher, 45*(9), 736–738.

Opitz, M. F. (1998a). *Flexible grouping in reading: Practical ways to help all students become better readers.* New York: Scholastic.

Opitz, M. F. (1998b). Text sets: One way to flex your grouping—in first-grade, too! *The Reading Teacher, 51*(7), 622–624.

Opitz, M. F., & Rasinski, T. V. (1998). *Good-bye round robin: 23 effective oral reading strategies.* Portsmouth, NH: Heinemann.

Palincsar, A. S. (2003). Collaborative approaches to comprehension instruction. In C. E. Snow & A. P. Sweet (Eds.), *Rethinking reading comprehension* (pp. 99–114). New York: Guilford Press.

Pearson, P. D., & Gallagher, M. C. (1983). The instruction of reading comprehension. *Contemporary Educational Psychology, 8*(3), 317–344.

Peterson, R., & Eeds, M. (1990). *Grand conversations: Literature groups in action.* New York: Scholastic.

Radencich, M. C. (1995). *Administration and supervision of the reading/writing program.* Boston: Allyn & Bacon.

Raphael, T. E., Florio-Ruane, S., Kehus, M. J., George, M., Hasty, N. L., & Highfield, K. (2003). Constructing curriculum for differentiated instruction: Inquiry in the teachers' learning collaborative, In R. L. McCormick & J. R. Paratore (Eds.), *After early intervention, then what? Teaching struggling readers in grades 3 and beyond* (pp. 94–116). Newark, DE: International Reading Association.

Rasinski, T. V. (2003). *The fluent reader: Oral reading strategies for building word recognition, fluency, and comprehension.* New York: Scholastic.

Rathvon, N. (2004). *Early reading assessment: A practitioner's handbook.* New York: Guilford Press.

Reutzel, D. R., & Cooter, R. B., Jr. (2000). *Teaching children to read: Putting the pieces together* (3rd ed.). Upper Saddle River, NJ: Merrill/Prentice-Hall.

Reutzel, D. R., & Cooter, R. B., Jr. (2003). *Strategies for reading assessment and instruction: Helping All Children Succeed* (2nd ed.). Upper Saddle River, NJ: Merrill/Prentice-Hall.

Reutzel, D. R., & Cooter, R. B., Jr. (2004). *Teaching children to read: Putting the pieces together* (4th ed.). Upper Saddle River, NJ: Merrill-Prentice-Hall.

Reutzel, D. R., Smith, J. A., & Fawson, P. C. (2005). An evaluation of two approaches for teaching reading comprehension strategies in the primary years using science information texts. *Early Childhood Research Quarterly, 20*(3), 276–305.

Schumm, J. S., Moody, S. W., and Vaughn, S. (2000). Grouping for reading instruction: Does one size fit all? *Journal of learning disabilities, 33*(5), 477–488.

Shanahan, T. (2004, November). *How do you raise reading achievement?* Paper presented at the Utah Council of the International Reading Association Meeting, Salt Lake City.

Slavin, R. E. (1987). Ability grouping and student achievement in elementary schools: A best-evidence synthesis. *Review of Educational Research, 57*(3), 293–336.

Slavin, R. E. (1988). Cooperative learning and student achievement. *Educational Leadership, 45*(2), 31–33.

Slavin, R. E. (1991). Are cooperative learning and "untracking" harmful to the gifted? *Educational Leadership, 48*(6), 68–71.

Snow, C. E., Burns, M. S., & Griffin, P. (1998). *Preventing reading failure in young children.* Washington, DC: National Academy Press.

Stevens, R. J., Madden. N. A., Slavin, R. E., & Farnish, A. (1987a). *Cooperative integrated reading and composition: A brief overview of the CIRC program.* Baltimore: Johns Hopkins University, Center for Research on Elementary and Middle Schools.

Stevens, R. J., Madden, N. A., Slavin, R. E., & Farnish, A. M. (1987b). Cooperative integrated reading and composition: Two field experiments. *Reading Research Quarterly, 22*(4), 433–454.

Swan, E. A. (2002). *Concept-oriented reading instruction: Engaging classrooms, lifelong learners.* New York: Guilford Press.

Taylor, B. M., Pearson, P. D., Clark, & Wadpole (1999). *Beating the odds in teaching all children to read* (CIERA Report No. 2-006). Ann Arbor, MI: Center for the Improvement of Early Reading Achievement.

Tomlinson, C. A. (1999). *The differentiated classroom: Responding to the needs of all learners.* Alexandria, VA: Association for Supervision and Curriculum Development.

Tomlinson, C. A. (2001). *How to differentiate instruction in mixed-ability classrooms* (2nd ed.). Alexandria, VA: Association for Supervision and Curriculum Development.

Topping, K. (1989). Peer tutoring and paired reading: Combining two powerful techniques. *The Reading Teacher, 42*(7), 488–494.

Tyner, B. (2004). *Small-group reading instruction: A differentiated teaching model for beginning and struggling readers.* Newark, DE: International Reading Association.

Unsworth, L. (1984). Meeting individual needs through flexible within-class grouping of pupils. *The Reading Teacher, 38*(3), 298–304.

Webb, M., & Schwartz, W. (1988, October). Children teaching children: A good way to learn. *PTA Today,* pp. 16–17.

Wilkinson, I. A., & Townsend, M. A. R. (2000). From Rata to Rimu: Grouping for instruction in best practice New Zealand classrooms. *The Reading Teacher, 53*(6), 460–471.

Wood, K. D. (1987). Fostering cooperative learning in middle and secondary school classrooms. *Journal of Reading, 31*(1), 10–19.

Chapter 15

EFFECTIVE USES OF TECHNOLOGY IN LITERACY INSTRUCTION

Michael C. McKenna
Linda D. Labbo
David Reinking
Tricia A. Zucker

This chapter will:

- Demonstrate the need for a broader definition of literacy, one that includes digital contexts.
- Describe how the instructional use of technology relates to sociocognitive learning theory.
- Investigate how technology can support special populations of readers.
- Examine research-based classroom practice using technology for beginning readers and skilled readers.
- Suggest how teachers, reading specialists, and reading coaches can successfully embrace technology in the reading curriculum.
- Identify activities for self-reflection and planning.

THE EVOLVING CONCEPT OF LITERACY

Traditional notions of literacy, based squarely on the printed word, are rapidly giving way to multiple ideas of what constitutes literate activity. It is now common to use the plural of the term, *literacies*, to refer to a range of concepts, including visual, digital, and others (see Richards & McKenna, 2003). Digital literacy has been defined as being skillfully prepared to use, comprehend, and manipulate computer-related content and processes to meet communicative, personal, academic, social, and cultural goals (Labbo, 2004). But even digital literacy is no longer viewed as singular, and we now speak of the "new literacies" of the Internet and other digital environments (Lankshear & Knobel, 2003).

Where technology is concerned, these are far more than theoretical musings. Literacy use in digital environments varies considerably from its print origins (Gambrell, 2005; Leu, 2000, 2002; Reinking, 1994, 1998; Valmont, 2003). Moreover, because digital applications are increasingly represented both in the workplace and at home, the curricular imperative to prepare children for such applications is clear. We believe that it is essential for schools to assist students in developing the technological skills that will be required of literate citizens in the future. After all, as Brandt (2001) argues, literacy is the energy supply of the information age. Modern-day demands for literacy increasingly require us to be adept users of digital literacies.

A second reason for integrating technology into literacy instruction, even with the youngest children, is its efficacy. Research has shown that digital environments, when properly structured, have extraordinary potential to engage and scaffold students. The advantages of multimedia are considerable and include new and powerful ways of communicating, ways that better reflect developmental realities than a strict diet of print.

For both of these reasons, we explore in this chapter some of the major technology-based classroom applications shown to be effective to date, applications that we believe offer promise to literacy teachers. First we examine overarching principles for successfully integrating technology. Then, while space prevents our describing all possibilities, we hope to exemplify best practices through descriptions of innovative teaching.

SUCCESSFULLY INTEGRATING COMPUTERS INTO THE LITERACY CURRICULUM

We begin by drawing on relevant research and underlying sociocognitive theory (Vygotsky, 1978) to offer suggestions for establishing a classroom environment that promotes demonstration, collaboration, and other forms of social interaction. The evidence is clear that the social environment of the classroom will always play a central role in determining how a computer is used by children in schools (see Kamil, Intrator, & Kim, 2000; Leu, 2000). It is our belief that, if computers are to adequately support both the conventional and electronic literacy development of children, the computer-related activities must be woven into the fabric of daily classroom routines through planned activities in such areas as (1) teacher-interactive demonstration, (2) diverse collaboration among students and teachers, and (3) attention to special needs.

Interactive Demonstration and Discussion

Our research (Labbo, Phillips, & Murray, 1995–1996) suggests that teachers can effectively integrate technology by employing interactive demonstrations of classroom computer applications during whole- and small-group lessons. For example, an LCD projector allows a teacher to demonstrate specific features, such as how to navigate through software. However, the makeup of the demonstration should include more than just a teacher explaning or modeling. Rather, demonstrations should combine teacher modeling with opportunities for child involvement. Teachers might solicit children's input during demonstrations of using the computer for maintaining a class calendar of events, setting alarm reminders for special class appointments, composing and printing notes to parents, writing the morning message, making class lists of things to do, and creating signs for classroom events. In the middle grades, teachers might demonstrate using PowerPoint to craft multimedia reports and presentations. Likewise, a high school math teacher might use a digital tablet to project notes and examples, storing them after class for students to retrieve if they wish.

By socially negotiating the form, content, and context of the demonstration, teachers can help children create a rich schema for employing technology in ways that quite naturally involve many literacy-related activities. Moreover, this schema will, over time, become more sophisticated as teachers present new applications that students assimilate. Thus, the perspective we advocate implies much more than perfunctory uses of technology. Computers should be placed as seamlessly as possible into the mainstream of the literacy activities in the classroom. The first step in doing so is an interactive, shared viewing of the computer application using an LCD projector or large monitor. The following steps prepare students to use the software or website effectively:

- First, introduce the title and general purpose of the computer application and demonstrate procedures to open the application. Then, state a specific purpose for interacting with the program. Comparing the objectives of different software reveals distinct software functions, such as reading for pleasure, practicing decoding, or playing a game to learn a stated objective.

- Next, model how to navigate through the program. For example, when modeling how to use an electronic text, guide students in how and when to click on words to hear the pronunciation.
- During this modeling, children may be invited to take turns operating the software as a check for understanding. This provides an opportunity for students to offer opinions about the software and develop strategies for making decisions when using the software independently.
- Add procedural reminders during the demonstration, such as how to take turns with computer partners. This helps avoid "mouse wars" that can detract from cooperative learning at the computer (see Labbo, 2000).
- After a shared viewing, encourage the children to critically discuss the information, presentation of the content, and the operation of the program itself. This activity helps students develop the ability to critically analyze software and digital material, just as we hope they will critically examine conventional printed materials.

Adult modeling of literacy activities is a major factor in children's acquisition of conventional literacy. Such modeling is no less powerful in the acquisition of digital literacy. As Papert (1980) suggested during the infancy of technology applications, children will use a computer in ways they see the adults in their lives use computers. When children dictate personal news to the morning message and watch their words appear on the screen, they have an opportunity to become aware of letter–sound relationships, to be sure, but they also gain a new perspective on what it means to write. Likewise, when children receive an individual printout of the morning message and are invited to circle words, letters, or letter-sounds they recognize, it represents an opportunity not only to enrich or refine their conventional literacy knowledge but also to appreciate the interconnectedness of print and digital literacies. Similar benefits of social, interactive digital processes are evident for older children as well. For example, when adults model how to compose emails with proper Internet etiquette (netiquette) or how to evaluate in practical terms the veracity of a website, students' digital literacy knowledge may increase. But through such modeling, teachers also afford their students platforms for productive social interaction within the literate community they are joining.

Diverse Opportunities for Collaboration

Weaving computer-related activities into the classroom culture requires collaboration among students and teachers. From a sociocognitive perspective, we believe that children who observe and interact with teachers and peers during technology demonstrations will internalize relevant vocabulary, develop approaches to problem solving, and encounter action schemes—all of which enable them to use the computer as a tool for thinking, learning, and communicating. Collaborative computer activities are also beneficial because children who collaborate at the computer can simultaneously construct both conventional and digital literacy knowledge. In this section we examine various worthwhile collaborative computer-based applications.

Collaborative writing processes employing paper-and-pencil tools are enhanced by the malleability possible on a computer screen (e.g., cut and paste). Other effective collaborations involve digital pen pals, now called keypals. Garner and Gillingham (1998) explain how students use email to communicate effectively with students in various geographic regions. Beach and Lundell (1998) report that shy students become more interactive and even develop online personalities when they exchange messages through digital communication systems.

Another computer-based collaboration is paired keyboarding. This occurs when a child with knowledge about computer operations and the Internet is paired with another who is less knowledgeable about accessing information from the Internet. Peters (1996) suggests that such interaction can extend the less-knowledgeable partner's zone of proximal development, enabling the child to internalize strategies for successful explorations. Lewis and Fabos (2005) suggest using instant messaging and other socially mediated technologies, such as blogging, to heighten students' analytical thinking skills, which are crucial for critically navigating the vast assortment of online materials. Leu and Leu (2000) argued for a project approach to Internet use because it is naturally collaborative and because students can share their expertise. In the middle grades teachers can use projects with highly motivating possibilities (Miller, 2003), and linking projects to technology appears especially promising.

Teachers should be aware that empowering students to use technology cooperatively can be a demanding task that requires persistence. Yang & Liu (2005) found that it took considerable time and effort for collaborative learning to move beyond the simple skills of technological proficiency to higher-level skills such as synthesizing information. We suggest that teachers remain diligent in training their students to work cooperatively with technology by modeling strategies and cooperative learning procedures, mentoring children's use of strategies, and managing strategy use and computer procedures (see Labbo, 2000, for a detailed description). Purposeful and goal-directed computer tasks encourage better collaboration. This approach helps minimize interpersonal struggles such as "mouse wars" (see Labbo, Sprague, Montero, & Font, 2000, for computer center management tips). Carroll (2004) describes how concluding computer projects by asking students to rate their collaborative efforts with a "Collaboration Rubric" helped students work more effectively (p. 119).

Digital Applications for Special Populations

Technology can support the learning needs of diverse learners. Students at all grade levels who struggle with reading and writing may benefit from particular computer applications. We define special populations broadly to include readers who are not fluent in decoding, reluctant readers, children for whom English is a second language, or students who struggle with a particular area of reading and writing. Software applications can make age-appropriate text comprehensible to these learners through a system of built-in supports. Dalton and Strangman (2006) describe this notion in terms of "universal access," the architectural concept that has led to barrier-free construction to permit easy access by the handicapped.

Children who struggle with learning to read may benefit from various types of support available in electronic texts, supports that make the texts accessible. Rather than a traditional instructional or tutorial approach for struggling readers, one that may slow down the pace of instruction (Walmsley & Allington, 1995), supported texts can allow these readers to maintain a pace similar to that of the regular classroom. How readers use supported text will vary with their developmental level. Struggling emergent readers can access the full listening version of a text, whereas readers at later developmental levels who are learning to decode may gain more from resources such as digitized pronunciations of difficult words. More advanced readers who are approaching fluency will have greater recourse to glossary entries, prose simplifications, digitized video clips, and the like as they endeavor to acquire content from expository text (Anderson-Inman & Horney, 1998). At this stage, their comprehension will also benefit from accessing linked resources, such as graphic organizers, databases, or electronic encyclopedias. Because the efficacy of these resources is based on aligning software with a child's stage of reading development, it is essential that assessment be aimed at precisely determining that stage. This alignment allows teachers to guide the child to the most appropriate use of electronic resources (McKenna, Reinking, Labbo, & Kieffer, 1999; Reinking, Labbo, & McKenna, 2000).

Technology for struggling readers must offer resources that meet the needs of the individual learner. Dalton and Strangman (2006) argue that technology should not be approached from the standpoint of one size fits all. They review promising research on hypertext enhanced with learning supports to create a "scaffolded learning environment." Dalton and Strangman's work with a program called *Thinking Reader* supports a range of learners by offering a text-to-speech function, a multimedia glossary, background knowledge links, and embedded strategy instruction. The software aims to develop metacognitive strategies and increase comprehension by prompting children to "stop and think" or to use a comprehension strategy such as predicting, clarifying, questioning, summarizing, making connections, or visualizing. Their research with middle-school students reading at or below the 25th percentile rank showed significantly better gains in reading achievement when using *Thinking Reader* and reciprocal teaching as compared with the control group. Dalton and Strangman's (2006) work suggests that digitized, flexible, leveled supports in a hypertext environment can improve students' comprehension skill.

Many young readers and a small percentage of middle-grade readers require extensive decoding support to read successfully. When using electronic texts, children find they can "read" material that far exceeds their decoding ability because of the support the computer offers. When beginning readers click on unfamiliar words and hear them pronounced, they make substantial gains in sight word acquisition, provided they can already name letters and recognize word boundaries (Reinking, Labbo, & McKenna, 2000). We have obtained the same results with older struggling readers (McKenna, Cowart, & Watkins, 1997; McKenna & Shaffield, 2002). Hasselbring (1999) provided *Start-to-Finish* (Don Johnston, Inc.) electronic books to struggling middle-grade readers and reported significantly improved comprehension and motivation. Similarly, McKenna and Shaffield (2002) used *WriteOutLoud* to create tailored texts (including scanned textbook passages) for a similar sample of students, and observed increased confidence and success as a result of the support received. Another example of effective electronic decoding instruction is the work of Hanlon & Cantrell (1999), who used software called *WordSort* to compare and contrast spelling patterns in conjunction with additional tutoring to help a 31-year-old male experiencing severe problems learning to read make notable strides in learning to read and spell.

A future abundance of supported text will mean both advantages and drawbacks for the struggling reader. Surely, one of the challenges of electronic literacy is the need to develop the ability to navigate strategically through hypermedia environments. Even when these environments are limited to a few helpful sources, the appearance of so many choices can seem like a labyrinth to a struggling reader. On the positive side, students will be able to read text independently that would have frustrated them without the built-in support that McKenna (1998) has called "electronic scaffolding" (p. 47). Indeed, the notion of the instructional reading level will have to be reexamined in electronic environments, because many struggling readers will be able to read at or near their listening levels (McKenna, Reinking, & Labbo, 1997).

Burns (1996) and Kamil, Intrator, and Kim (2000) note that multimedia technology can be used to facilitate the English-language acquisition of nonnative speakers. Multimedia resources accommodate the needs of English-language learners as they progress in second-language proficiency and gain content-area knowledge. Some electronic books have the option of listening to the story in Spanish or another language. After using CD-ROM storybooks with children who were inexperienced with the mainstream school language, Bus, de Jong, and Verhallen (2006) reported promising results for scaffolding these children's understanding of the story through supportive animations. They concluded that hearing the text in combination with animations bolsters children's ability to derive the meaning of unknown words and sentences. They describe this as an "interactive cycle." Specifically, "when children understand more of the story, they will understand more of the text. When language is better understood this will stimulate their understanding of the story" (Bus et al., 2006, p. 137). More research about the effectiveness of such programs on children's acquisition of a second language, and their understanding of specific reading passage content, is needed.

Notably, speech synthesizer software offers some promising directions for supporting spelling development of English-language learners and native-speaking nonfluent writers. Shilling (1997) introduced the use of a basic word processing program and an external speech synthesis unit that gave children a choice of listening to a word they had attempted to spell on the screen, listening to the entire text they had typed on the screen, or not using speech synthesis at all. Findings suggest that before children consistently benefit from synthesizer software they need to have acquired some basic concepts about print, phonemic awareness, and a notion of the alphabetic principle. As the capabilities of speech synthesizer software improve, continued research is warranted.

For struggling and proficient readers alike, technology often increases student motivation and can boost confidence when children use technology successfully. Our work with Digital Language Experience Approach activities (D-LEA; Labbo, Eakle, & Montero, 2002) provided a unique opportunity for a struggling reader to envision herself as a literate being, capable of writing and reading. When adding text to a digital photograph of her writing, she exclaimed, "Say, "I'm writing! I'm [verbal emphasis and a pause] writing! I'm a writer!" (Labbo et al., 2002). It is worth noting that this new self-awareness appeared to foster an elevated level of confidence that resulted in her willingness to participate more actively in literacy activities in the classroom. Kamil et al. (2000) also described consistent findings that computer use in classrooms leads to increased intrinsic motivation, especially when technology gives opportunities to "customize one's work and increase the control, curiosity, and challenge of a task" (p. 778). Gambrell (2006) noted that the Internet in particular holds great capabilities for motivating and engaging students because students can self-select their reading materials and explore others' opinions about texts.

EVIDENCE-BASED BEST PRACTICES

In the following sections we describe the classroom applications of actual teachers who recognize the potential of technology to enhance their literacy instruction. We turn first to effective computer applications with children in primary classrooms. These students are all learning to read and can be classified as emergent or beginning readers. Several of the scenarios occur at the classroom computer center, which is centrally located and adjoins other areas of high activity, thereby making the computer part of the classroom culture (Haughland, 1992). We will use a series of vignettes from Ms. Martin's kindergarten unit, "Creatures That Fly in the Night Sky," to demonstrate how this teacher puts the classroom computer to good use. Then we will consider a variety of other computer applications useful with beginning readers.

Thematic Integration and Innovation: Ms. Martin's Kindergarten Class

It is 9:20 A.M. on a cold October morning in Ms. Martin's kindergarten class, and the room is filled with the sounds of children working at various centers. Ms. Martin provides her students with choices (within limits) at the computer center so that children learn how to select an activity that they find interesting and meaningful. Patrick and Dartrell chose a software application called *My First Incredible Amazing Dictionary* (1995). Because Ms. Martin already introduced the class to this software with an interactive demonstration, Patrick and Dartrell are equipped to seek out new information about bats and other nocturnal creatures by using the electronic dictionary. They adeptly locate a definition of *bat* and hear the text on the color monitor read aloud to them (see Figure 15.1). Next, they decide to click on the illustration that produces the sound of a feeding bat.

Digitally innovative teachers like Ms. Martin often discover natural connections between curricular themes, learning objectives, and innovative uses of technology. Ms. Martin's unit, "Creatures That Fly in the Night Sky," brings together a variety of children's books and software related to the theme, computer-based learning center activities connected

FIGURE 15.1. Patrick and Dartrell learn about bats.

to the theme, and occasions for celebrating children's computer experiences and products. Collecting, displaying, and demonstrating themed books and software is the first step to a successful technology-related unit. After reading aloud a favorite children's book, *Stella Luna* (Cannon, 1993), and discussing the plot, characters, and author's purpose, Ms. Martin extends the learning at the classroom computer center with activities like the ones Patrick and Dartell chose. She carefully introduces additional software applications related to the theme, such as an electronic book version of *Stella Luna.*

At 9:50 A.M., Arial and Jasmine sit side by side at the computer center and compare a storybook version to the electronic book version of *Stella Luna*—a technique we have called a "screen and book read-along" (Labbo & Ash, 1998). The children connect the audio, text, and animation on the screen with the print and illustrations of the book by turning the virtual pages on the screen and the real pages in the book simultaneously. Children can point to the words in the book as they are read on the screen. Our research suggests that listening to an electronic book, echo reading, or chorally reading all can help children develop a sense of story, extend their vocabulary, increase knowledge of words, and enrich concepts about print (McKenna, 1998).

Arial and Jasmine delight in clicking on screen illustrations and watching animation of the mother bat flying over trees, calling, and looking for her baby, who is lost but safely snuggled in a nest of baby birds. Soon after, the girls move to the sociodramatic play center and use a *Stella Luna* bat puppet and a bird puppet to retell the story they just read in the electronic book. They invite three peers to serve as an audience to their innovative retelling, which is filled with plot twists, melancholy dialogue, humorous events, and voices that sound a great deal like the characters from the electronic book.

Notice how Arial and Jasmine's sociodramatic or dramatic play is related to the unit theme and to the use of technology. In Ms. Martin's classroom, the sociodramatic play center was transformed into a puppet theater equipped with puppets related to the characters in the books and the software. Reenacting and often extending the story through dramatic puppet play gives children additional occasions for trying out characterizations, reinforcing story structure, and reliving story plots.

Later in the day, JaMaris has decided to contribute to the class book of collected stories on nocturnal creatures by drawing and writing something about bats using *KidPix*. When JaMaris visits the computer during afternoon center time, he brings an informational book about bats and the *Stella Luna* puppet from Ms. Martin's unit display area with him. He props the book up beside the computer monitor and holds the puppet in his lap as he prepares to begin his composition. When children bring objects with them to the computer center, they may use the objects to inspire stories and illustrations, to focus them on the topic, and to help them acquire information from a different source. As Schwartz (1985) has pointed out, three-dimensional objects such as stuffed animals or books may help children connect to a similar two-dimensional object they see on the computer screen.

As JaMaris begins he is joined for a few minutes by his teacher, who crouches by his side and offers gentle scaffolding.

MS. MARTIN: So, what's your story going to be about?

JAMARIS: It's going to be a story about a really cool bat named Spidey and his super powers.

MS. MARTIN: Okay. So how do you want to begin? With "Once upon a time"?

JAMARIS: No . . . my name first (*selects the keyboard function and types in the letters of his name using the hunt-and-peck method*) . . . and I want to draw Spidey.

MS. MARTIN: That's not a bad idea. If you draw that bat, you might get some good story ideas. So, what does this old bat look like—like Stella Luna?

JAMARIS: Sorta like this one but with big green eyes (*pointing to the photograph of a bat on the book cover*). How do I get green?

Ms. Martin: Remember how I showed you the other day, during rug time? (*Ms. Martin demonstrates how to access the color option from the program's menu before leaving the computer center.*)

JaMaris uses electronic artist tools to draw a bat with big green eyes, large fangs, and a crooked "B" on his chest (see Figure 15.2). He then writes a two-line story that consists of strings of letters and a word copied from the book cover. He makes two printouts. One is placed in a folder of children's stories that will be bound into a class book, and the other goes into his backpack, so he can show his mother.

These scenarios provide concrete instances of four guidelines that have proved to be instrumental in designing technology-related units, such as Ms. Martin's "Creatures That Fly in the Night Sky":

1. Collect, display, and demonstrate how to use themed children's books and software related to the unit.
2. Design computer-based learning center activities connected to the theme.
3. Enhance sociodramatic play that connects the theme and computer-based activities.
4. Provide occasions for celebrating children's computer experiences and products.

The fourth step, celebrating children's computer experiences and work, is crucial in making technology a central element of the classroom culture and in increasing student motivation. Collections of students' computer-related work may be bound into a class book, exhibited as artwork, or displayed in a computer presentation, such as an electronic slide show.

FIGURE 15.2. JaMaris's bat story.

When children learn how to use a computer to accomplish their communicative tasks, teachers can invite them to demonstrate and explain their newfound knowledge to their classmates.

A useful technique for supporting and celebrating children's development of conventional and digital literacy is to provide a physical space to share and discuss computer activities at the Author's Computer Chair (Labbo, 2004). Our research suggests that that, although many of the goals and procedures of the Author's Computer Chair are similar to the traditional Author's Chair that was conceived during the 1980s (see Calkins, 1983; Graves, 1983; Graves & Hansen, 1983), the key difference is that children discuss computer-mediated meaning making. The Author's Computer Chair is a time of social peer collaboration in which children request feedback and support from peers and teachers during any phase of a computer task. This routinely scheduled time period benefits students as they seek out advice, share knowledge and pointers, and celebrate the completion of a computer activity (see Labbo, 2004, for guidelines to successfully implement Author's Computer Chair).

A classroom visitor witnessing the children's computer work in Ms. Martin's room might assume that all the students are remarkably gifted or that they come from affluent homes where they have daily access to computers. However, quite the reverse is true. None of the five children mentioned in these vignettes has a computer at home; all qualify for free or reduced-price lunches and have average or below-average literacy ability. The primary reason the children are adept at using technology is because their teacher consistently plans inviting, enriching, and appropriate computer-related experiences. In Ms. Martin's classroom, computer-related learning is meaningful and purposeful.

Exploring Other Computer Applications with Beginning Readers

Thematic integration and innovation is a powerful tool for promoting digital literacies with young readers. We now turn to other effective computer applications for beginning readers. For instance, we used case studies to explore the use of Digital Language Experience Approach activities in Ms. Maggie's kindergarten classroom (see Labbo et al., 2002). Like the traditional Language Experience Approach (LEA), this digital version utilizes the same powerful strategy of providing students a unique contextualized occasion for literacy development through dictation of a story that is usually related to a specific stimulating experience (Stauffer, 1970). However, it is enhanced by digital photography and creativity software. Ms. Maggie created partnerships with her local community to bring in adults who could work one-on-one with children of different ability levels to take digital photos of an experience and record students' D-LEA stories on the computer. The adult and child collaborate to create a digital presentation enhanced with multimedia features of word-processing and creativity software such as *KidPix* (Hickman, 1994). D-LEA allows students to compose stories with drawing tools, imported video animations, sounds, speech synthesis, and writing (see also Turbill, 2003; Turbill & Murray, 2006).

D-LEAs offer endless possibilities for Ms. Maggie's students to see their oral words transformed into digital texts. Each child utilized their D-LEA compositions to distinguish themselves as readers and writers. For example, after reading an ABC book with her adult facilitator, one of Ms. Maggie's students created her own digital version of an alphabet book. She used the creativity software to embellish a close-up picture of herself as a clown to represent the letter *c*. Another student used the voice-recording feature on the *KidPix* software to create an interactive text for her peers to explore. Authoring digital LEA stories is an authentic literacy experience, because the stories are shared with admiring peers. Purcell-Gates (2004) suggests that technology is best used to facilitate authentic literacy tasks, or tasks that replicate or reflect reading and writing events that occur in the world outside of a schooling context.

Recall how Ms. Martin enhanced sociodramatic play that was connected to the unit theme and to computer-based activities. This is an effective use of technology, because when sociodramatic play centers are enriched with literacy props, including a computer center or even a cardboard model of a computer, children gain insights into the role of technology and literacy in various cultural and workplace settings (see Labbo & Ash, 1998; Neuman & Roskos, 1992). For example, if a unit theme focuses on various ways to travel, the sociodramatic play center may be transformed into an imaginary travel agency. After the teacher demonstrates ways to plan travel online and learn about possible destinations using the Internet, children can transfer this knowledge to the computer center, where they make tickets, timetables, maps, travel posters, destination booklets, and passports to use in their dramatic play scenarios. As an extension, a field trip or a virtual field trip (using videoconferencing) to a travel agency will help children understand how the office works, the role of print and digital literacies in the workplace, and what types of conversational discourse are appropriate in that setting. By creating and playing at the computer and dramatic play centers, children have opportunities to enrich their schemata about the forms and functions of workplace literacy.

Another digitally innovative teacher, Mr. Saunders, uses software and electronic texts effectively in his first-grade computer centers. He makes use of well-designed decoding software, such as *Reading Mansion,* that embodies research underlying effective instructional practice (see Fox & Mitchell, 2000; Kuhn & Stahl, 2006; McKenna, 2002).

Computer centers are an ideal location for engaging students with electronic texts. Electronic texts include commercially available electronic texts such as the *Living Books* software developed by Broderbund and Internet texts such as the electronic books available at websites such as *www.Starfall.com* free of charge. Students can click on words to hear them read aloud, and they can interact with hidden seek-and-find features within the illustrations. Caution is suggested, because these hidden animations or sound effects can be both engaging and distracting for children (see Labbo & Kuhn, 2000). Mr. Saunders managed this by allowing students to first explore the book in a spirit of play and later return to the book in a "read-only" manner. Teachers recognize that they cannot rely on the computer to produce positive literacy results. Therefore, clear expectations must be communicated, and careful monitoring must follow (Labbo et al., 2000). Brief postreading discussions and comprehension checks lead children to critical and inferential questioning.

Another promising technology for beginning readers is teacher-created electronic texts, which have become simple to produce. Teachers can compose passages and use a text-to-speech program such as *WriteOutLoud*, produced by Don Johnston, Inc. The software automatically provides pronunciations for any of the words typed into the program. Even programs with widespread use such as Microsoft's PowerPoint contain tools to record voice narration of text. Teachers can tailor texts to focus on specific words or word study features.

In a meta-analysis of 42 computer-assisted instruction (CAI) studies with children in first through third grade, Blok, Oostdam, Otter, and Overman (2002) concluded that these programs have a small but positive effect size ($d = 0.19$) on beginning readers. Their analysis included a range of CAI programs in six categories: phonological awareness, word reading with speech feedback, flashed word reading, text reading with speech feedback, reading/listening, and mixed-methods software. Their review also noted an interesting finding—that English-speaking students benefited more from CAI programs than speakers of other languages. Blok et al. (2002) suggested that this finding could be explained by the fact that English orthographic rules require more practice to master than those of the other languages employed in their sample. They caution that the poor quality of many studies may have negatively influenced their findings for effect size and that more research with better research designs are needed.

These applications by resourceful teachers are representative of a wide variety of effective strategies for integrating technology in classroom-based literacy centers (for others, see Labbo, 2000). For a list of additional ideas for integrating technology into beginning readers' literacy curricula, see Figure 15.3.

FIGURE 15.3. Suggested applications that integrate technology into literacy instruction. This list presents examples, organized by instructional area.

Instructional Area	Suggested Application
Phonological Awareness	• Use well-designed phonological awareness software such as *DaisyQuest* or *Daisy's Castle* by Blue Wave Software (Pressley, 2006) at the computer center. • Students can use talking electronic books for phonological awareness tasks such as identifying rhyming words and checking by clicking the computer pronunciation (see Labbo, 2000).
Phonics and Spelling	• Teachers can type daily Morning Message or student stories using an LCD projector (see Labbo, 2005a) and smart boards to highlight word features and spelling patterns. • Well-designed decoding software such as *Reading Mansion* can supplement students developing phonics skills (see McKenna, 2002, for guidelines to select phonics software aligned with research-based practices.) • Tutors, paraprofessionals, volunteers, or teachers can create individual student word banks for beginning readers (Bear, Invernizzi, Templeton, & Johnston, 2004) but store the words electronically using Microsoft PowerPoint. This is a growing bank of words the child can read automatically in isolation. • Students dictate digital language-experience stories (D-LEA). Print individual copies for isolating words and phonics lessons (see Labbo, Eakle, & Montero, 2002; Turbill, 2003).
Vocabulary	• Extend themes and concepts with Internet content, electronic encyclopedias, video streaming, and other multimedia (see Labbo, 2005c, for ideas to support young learners). • Virtual field trips can build vocabulary (Blachowicz & Obrochta, 2005) related to units of study. Use the Internet, electronic encyclopedias, and other media to build prior knowledge and vocabulary that can be saved digitally (see Doe, 2003, for more on virtual field trips). • Use digital photography combined with text to document class field trips and build rich vocabulary in class-authored books (Turbill & Murray, 2006). • Build a collection of useful and important vocabulary in a class database. This resource can include a reference to the text or place where the vocabulary word was first encountered (see Doe, 2003). • Students can build their vocabulary and prior knowledge by going on a virtual scavenger hunt. See

(*continued*)

FIGURE 15.3. (*continued*).

	Valmont (2003) for a step-by-step guide to creating an HTML document to guide your students to specific websites during a virtual scavenger hunt.
Fluency	• Students can build fluency by using electronic texts with computer pronunciations of speech as a model for fluent reading. Speech recognition software can record and track students' fluency progress (see Adams, 2006). • Repeated readings and echo readings of electronic texts are beneficial for students who need practice reading aloud in a risk-free environment (see Labbo, 2000). • Students can use talking books for Readers Theater practice (see Labbo, 2000) and then share their performance with an online webcast or podcast of their dramatic reading. • Students can practice repeated readings of literature, record themselves reading the book on tape, then donate the books and student-authored tapes to kids in hospitals. Using a class webpage to spread the word about this community service brings in an authentic audience (see Sangiuliano, 2005).
Comprehension	• Electronic texts at the computer learning center can include response activities or retellings at the sociodramatic play center to foster comprehension (see Labbo, 2000). • Children can benefit from the meaning making that occurs when they respond to read-alouds or literature using desktop publishing software such as *KidPix* or *Inspiration* (see Labbo, 1996). • Internet links to author websites (see Valmont, 2000) can enhance author studies by sharing more information about the author and his or her writing process and by encouraging communication via email with the author. • Students evaluate and take a critical stance toward digital material, including considerations relating to the credibility of the source and potential bias (see Leu, 2000; Morrell, 2002). • Internet, instant messaging, and email provide opportunities for socially constructed learning (see Lewis & Fabos, 2005).
Writing	• Written responses to stories or process-writing techniques such as Writing Workshop can include computer-based work that constructs knowledge through a variety of symbol systems (see Labbo, 1996, 2003).

- Student's poetry creations using the computer can be enriched with symbols, including unique font type, colors, stamps/clip art, layout templates, animated graphics, and embedded music (see Carroll, 2004).
- A variety of open-ended tools for digital publishing facilitate process writing. See Wood (2004, p. 23) for a description of publishing tools, including PowerPoint (Microsoft), Microsoft Publisher (Microsoft), EasyBook Deluxe (Sunburst Communications), HyperStudio (Knowledge Adventure), Inspiration (Inspiration, Inc.), Amazing Writing Machine (Broderbund, The Learning Company).
- Electronic pen pals, via email or instant messaging, can link students and classrooms around the globe. Topics can include literature discussions or common units of study (see Leu, 2002; Wood, 2004)
- Teacher- and student-authored classroom websites or blogs (electronic journals) can display student work and communicate classroom events (see Chamberlain, 2005; Leu, 2002)
- Students conduct research projects using the Internet and present their findings in a multimedia PowerPoint presentation (see Kinzer, 2005). See Morrell (2002) for ideas on critically evaluating pop culture using the Internet and other sources.
- Collaborative Internet projects may be based on traveling stuffed animals (see Leu, 2002) or the Flat Stanley Project, which generate online reading and writing experiences (see Hubert, 2005).

Recommended Practices with Older Children

More sophisticated applications are possible as children's print literacy improves. Collaborations now result in products that reflect higher-order decision making. These students are now reading to learn and can be described as skilled or independent readers who have a firm grasp of decoding and recognize many words automatically. We will discuss how creating multimedia book reviews can increase the amount and diversity of students' independent reading. We then consider a variety of other potentially effective computer practices with skilled readers. Together these examples provide insights into classroom communities where students are as comfortable with reading and writing on a computer screen as they are with reading and writing on paper. As with younger students, teachers must aim for applications in which the technology becomes transparent, merely a platform for communicating.

Multimedia Book Reviews

It is 1:45 P.M. and the computer lab is bustling with the sounds of Ms. Broward's fourth graders developing their multimedia book reviews by means of PowerPoint. One student is adding a digital movie to a slide, capturing the thoughts of a classmate. Another student links a slide to an audio file containing her best voice impressions of celebrities speaking about books. The slide contains pictures of those celebrities captured from the Internet. Another student is coaching a peer who is preparing to submit her book review to the school database of PowerPoints so that others can access it. They discover a misspelled word and quickly address it, because they know others will be using these reviews. You would hardly know that many of these students struggle with reading, because they exude confidence as they enter sophisticated critiques of books they read during independent reading time into a school database. In our work with students and teachers in upper elementary school grades, creating multimedia book reviews on the computer benefited students' reading and writing in ways unlikely to be achieved with conventional book reports and produced results that exceeded the widely used Accelerated Reader program (Reinking & Watkins, 2000).

Students were much more engaged in creating the multimedia book reviews, and we found their use of technology to respond to independent reading provided them a much richer socially interactive process (Reinking & Watkins, 2000). These benefits were derived partly from the fact that, unlike conventional book reports, the multimedia book reviews were stored in a searchable database that was easily accessible to other students looking for books to read and to parents who visited the school at various times (including a technology fair). Students' interactions about the books they were reading often took place incidentally outside of the classroom, because they were celebrating their accomplishments in mastering the technology. For example, when one student eagerly explained to another, who was avidly listening, how he had added sound effects to his book review, the latter student incidentally discovered an interest in the book that was the subject of the sound-enhanced review. Note that this example illustrates how celebrating accomplishments in one medium can enhance involvement in another medium. Likewise, we found that some teachers' outlooks, approaches to instruction, and patterns of social interaction in the classroom changed through the process of creating and celebrating multimedia book reviews with their students.

Additional Computer Applications with Skilled Readers

Technology supplies skilled readers with myriad tools to conceptualize the knowledge they gain from reading and to chronicle their developing understanding of reading and writing. Jonassen (2006) suggests that the best way to use computers is to use technology-based modeling tools, which he calls "Mindtools" (p. 12). Modeling tools help learners build alternative representations of ideas or experiences. For instance, Jonassen describes how using semantic organizers, concept mapping, or databases helps students construct representations of processes and relationships. After reading an expository text, a student could use the computer to develop a concept map to reconstruct the most important concepts from the text. Alternatively, students could collect an index of texts read in a database. Then, students can use this as a reference for solving problems and answering questions based on ideas they have documented. As these examples illustrate, technology provides enriching methods for students to acquire and manage ideas gained in content-area reading.

A process-writing approach to composition, such as Writing Workshop, can be enhanced by computer-based collaborations. When children brainstorm, write drafts, revise, edit, and publish with a word processing program, they can focus more on managing and organizing ideas and less on tedious or mechanical aspects of writing (Jones, 1994). Creating high-quality final drafts is also facilitated by desktop publishing capabilities such as formatting text, incorporating graphics, and selecting fonts. Wild and Braid (1996) noted that collaborative or cooperative computer-related word processing experiences foster children's cognitively oriented talk related to the task of writing.

We believe that it is important for teachers to provide enough time for children to be able to compose on the computer and not just retype a handwritten draft to be printed. To reap the benefits of technology, and, indeed, to prepare children to use the tools of contemporary writing, word processing must be integrated into all phases of the writing process. The computer can function as a digital writing folder or portfolio by storing text files such as reflective journals, topic ideas, responses to books, works in the early draft stage, works to be edited or spell-checked, or works to be read by and responded to by peers. However, unlike a conventional portfolio, the digital version reinforces the idea that electronic writing is never a final product. Each electronic file awaits future modification. Valmont (2003) described teachers who have successfully used technology to encourage older students to write. He illustrates how e-cards (electronic greeting cards) and e-zines (electronic magazines) are motivating opportunities for students to compose. Guzzetti and Gamboa (2004) also studied how adolescent girls use e-zine writing to develop and express their individual identities.

For teachers who are interested in improving their students' fluency, and thereby enhancing comprehension, Adams's (2006) work sheds light on a new technology that has the potential to boost reading while tracking fluency progress: a speech recognition program called *Reading Assistant.* This promising technology best supports novice and intermediate readers. These levels of readers already know how to decode but lack automaticity, vocabulary, or comprehension skills. When the child mispronounces a word, the *Reading Assistant* pronounces it correctly and marks the difficult word. When using the read-and-record feature, the speech recognition layer of the software listens to the student as she or he reads aloud. If the computer detects that the student has stumbled or gotten stuck on a word, it provides assistance. Simultaneously, the computer records the reading and builds an ongoing record of what the student has read and reread, the difficulties the student had, and the progress made. A teacher can access fluency reports and various data that parallel the types of notes taken during a traditional running record. Adams's (2006) initial findings suggested that students who used the speech recognition program made fluency gains that were significantly greater than children who did not. Furthermore, many students were motivated to use the program because it kept them engaged during rereadings and they could chart their improvements.

As with the research on beginning readers, how to use technology appropriately with skilled readers is an area where more research is needed. Unfortunately, much of the research in this area is broad but shallow (Labbo & Reinking, 1999). For additional suggestions and strategies for integrating technology and literacy with skilled readers, see Figure 15.3.

EDUCATOR COLLABORATION TO ENVISION NEW DIGITAL REALITIES

How do you envision the model classroom that successfully integrates technology into literacy instruction? McKenna (2006) described a model primary-level classroom as including "computer-guided word study, electronic storybooks with decoding scaffolds, social interaction guided by software applications, graphics packages to assist children as they illustrate their work, and software designed to reinforce concepts about print" (p. xi). How many of these model classrooms have you visited recently? Despite what is known about effective uses of technology in literacy instruction, it appears that schools are slow to change and model classrooms are hard to come by. For instance, Turbill and Murray (2006) observed the disinclination of many Australian teachers to integrate technology and commented, "It is our belief that currently most teachers of early literacy view technology as something that their students can 'play' with during 'free time' or as a 'reward' after the real 'work' has been completed" (p. 93). Further, many websites claim to be technological resources for educators but only contribute to the problem by offering little more than drill-and-skill activities or printable blackline images (Turbill & Murray, 2006).

How do you achieve your vision of new digital realities? When integrating technology into the reading curriculum, there is no prescription for how it should occur. Each classroom and school must negotiate the multiple realities that shape their own practice (Labbo & Reinking, 1999). An initial step in the change process may be locating or creating assessments like Turbill and Murray's (2006) "Concepts of Screen" that measures children's basic skill level in using the computer (e.g., use of the mouse, matching cursor and mouse, understanding the function of icons, etc.). Assessment data can guide starting points for instruction.

Safe first steps might include adding digital innovations that emulate established effective literacy practices that lend themselves to computer innovation (see Labbo, 2005a, for ideas on Digital Morning Message or Digital K–W–L charts). Generally, teachers who succeed at making the cutting edge a comfortable place to be are constantly becoming technologically literate and keeping up with technological innovations through activities such as taking educational technology courses, participating in professional development either online or in real time, attending professional conferences, and reading professional articles (Labbo, 2005b, pp. 167–168). These professional development activities can be a starting point for conceiving new digital realities in one's classroom.

Yet, new digital technologies will not transform classrooms if teachers are not interested in and comfortable using them. Coiro (2005) describes teachers' lack of enthusiasm for large-group workshop-style presentations about technology, in part because this format does not allow teachers to voice their own needs and their agendas for professional development. In contrast, she reports teachers' active engagement when they direct literacy learning Internet projects that are supported by various constituents including the library media specialist, the principal, and a university researcher. Small-group or online professional development is adaptable to teachers' specific needs and to technological realities. Collaboration can enhance technology-based professional development (see Kinzer, Cammack, Labbo, Teale, & Sanny, 2006), just as collaboration can enrich the process of reflecting on one's practice.

ENGAGEMENT ACTIVITIES

Before reflecting on your next steps to implement technology in your classroom, school, or district, consider these overarching goals for integrating technology into literacy curricula:

1. New digital technologies should be available for literacy instruction.
2. New digital technologies should be used to enhance the goals of conventional literacy instruction.
3. New technologies should be used to positively transform literacy instruction.
4. New technologies should be used to prepare students for the literacy of the future.
5. New technologies should be used to empower students. (Labbo & Reinking, 1999, p. 481)

Your school or district may have similar technology goals and standards in place. With these general goals in mind, narrow your focus to your particular role and educational context as you address the following reflection questions.

Teachers

1. What resources can I take advantage of to integrate literacy and technology? Consider the computers and digital tools that are available, the professional development opportunities, and which people have a previous background in technology (e.g., reading specialists, technology coordinators, older students, parent volunteers, university partnerships).
2. What tools (hardware or software) do I need to achieve my literacy and technology goals, how can I get these things, and how much time will be needed?
   - Hardware/software: digital cameras, LCD projectors, flash drives, literacy software, etc.
   - Time: time to explore software and available resources, time to plan, and time to collaborate with others.
3. Do I need to seek additional funding through grant writing or donations from local businesses?
4. How will I celebrate and showcase my students' digital work (e.g., organizing technology open houses, writing articles for professional journals, creating classroom websites, blogs, or podcasts)?
5. What is my action plan for implementing technology this year? What steps will I take first? What is my major goal, and how do I need to collaborate to achieve this goal? How will I expand these goals next year?

Reading Coaches and Administrators

1. How can I support teachers as they explore new technologies, trade ideas, and gain mastery of digital innovations?
2. How can I create environments where teachers can experiment with technology together, collaborate, and develop action plans for implementing technology?

Authors' Note

Although this chapter contains references to commercial materials, none of the authors has a financial interest in them.

REFERENCES

Adams, M. J. (2006). The promise of automatic speech recognition for fostering literacy growth in children and adults. In M. C. McKenna, L. D. Labbo, R. D. Kieffer, & D. Reinking (Eds.), *International handbook of literacy and technology* (Vol 2, pp. 109–128). Mahwah, NJ: Erlbaum.

Anderson-Inman, L., & Horney, M. A. (1998). Transforming text for at-risk readers. In D. Reinking, M. C. McKenna, L. D. Labbo, & R. D. Kieffer (Eds.), *Handbook of literacy and technology: Transformations in a post-typographic world* (pp. 15–43). Mahwah, NJ: Erlbaum.

Beach, R., & Lundell, D. (1998). Early adolescents' use of computer-mediated communication in writing and reading. In D. Reinking, M. C. McKenna, L. D. Labbo, & R. D. Kieffer (Eds.), *Handbook of literacy and technology: Transformations in a post-typographic world* (pp. 93–112). Mahwah, NJ: Erlbaum.

Bear, D. R., Invernizzi, M., Templeton, S., & Johnston, F. (2004). *Words their way: Word study for phonics, vocabulary, and spelling instruction.* Upper Saddle River, NJ: Pearson Education.

Blachowicz, C. L., & Obrochta, C. (2005). Vocabulary visits: Virtual field trips for content vocabulary development. *The Reading Teacher,* 59, 262–268.

Blok, H., Oostdam, R., Otter, M. E., & Overmaat, M. (2002). Computer-assisted instruction in support of beginning reading instruction: A review. *Review of Educational Research, 72,* 101–130.

Brandt, D. (2001). *Literacy in American lives.* Cambridge, UK: Cambridge University Press.

Burns, D. (1996, March). Technology in the ESL classroom. *Technology and Learning, 16*(8), 50–52.

Bus, A. G., de Jong, M. T., & Verhallen, M. (2006). CD-ROM talking books: A way to enhance early literacy? In M. C. McKenna, L. D. Labbo, R. D. Kieffer, & D. Reinking (Eds.), *International Handbook of Literacy and Technology* (Vol 2, pp. 129–142). Mahwah, NJ: Erlbaum.

Calkins, L. M. (1983). *Lessons from a child.* Portsmouth, NH: Heinemann.

Cannon, J. (1993). *Stella Luna.* New York: Harcourt Brace.

Carroll, M. (2004). *Cartwheels on the keyboard.* Newark, DE: International Reading Association.

Chamberlain, C. J. (2005). Literacy and technology: A world of ideas. In R. A. Karchmar, M. H. Mallette, J. Kara-Soteriou, & D. J. Leu (Eds.), *Innovative approaches to literacy education: Using the Internet to support new literacies* (pp. 44–64). Newark, DE: International Reading Association.

Coiro, J. (2005). Every teacher a Mrs. Rumphis: Empowering teachers with effective professional development. In R. A. Karchmar, M. H. Mallette, J. Kara-

Soteriou, & D. J. Leu (Eds.), *Innovative approaches to literacy education: Using the Internet to support new literacies.* (pp. 199–219). Newark, DE: International Reading Association.

Dalton, B., & Strangman, N. (2006). Improving struggling readers' comprehension through scaffolded hypertexts and other computer-based literacy programs. In M. C. McKenna, L. D. Labbo, R. D. Kieffer, & D. Reinking (Eds.), *International handbook of literacy and technology* (Vol. 2, pp. 75–92). Mahwah, NJ: Erlbaum.

Doe, H. M. (2003). *Technology through children's literature: Grades K–5.* Portsmouth, NH: Teacher Ideas Press.

Fox, B. J., & Mitchell, M. J. (2000). Using technology to support word recognition, spelling, and vocabulary acquisition. In S. B. Wepner, W. J. Valmont, & R. Thurlow (Eds.), *Linking literacy and technology: A guide for K–8 classrooms* (pp. 42–75). Newark, DE: International Reading Association.

Gambrell, L. B. (2005). Reading literature, reading text, reading the Internet: The times are a' changing. *The Reading Teacher, 58,* 588–591.

Gambrell, L. B. (2006). Technology and the engaged literacy learner. In M. C. McKenna, L. D. Labbo, R. D. Kieffer, & D. Reinking (Eds.), *International Handbook of Literacy and Technology* (Vol. 2, pp. 289–294). Mahwah, NJ: Erlbaum.

Garner, R., & Gillingham, M. G. (1998). The Internet in the classroom: Is it the end of transmission-oriented pedagogy? In D. Reinking, M. C. McKenna, L. D. Labbo, R. D. Kieffer (Eds.), *Handbook of literacy and technology: Transformations in a post-typographic world* (pp. 221–231). Mahwah, NJ: Erlbaum.

Graves, D. (1983). *Writing: Teachers and children at work.* Exeter, NH: Heinemann.

Graves, D., & Hansen, J. (1983). The Author's Chair. *Language Arts, 60,* 176–183.

Guzzetti, B. J., & Gamboa, M. (2004). Zines for social justice: Adolescent girls writing on their own. *Reading Research Quarterly, 39,* 406–436.

Hanlon, M. M., & Cantrell, J. (1999). Teaching a learning disabled adult to spell: Is it ever too late? *Journal of Adolescent and Adult Literacy, 43,* 4–11.

Hasselbring, T. (1999, May). *The computer doesn't embarrass me.* Paper presented at the meeting of the International Reading Association, San Diego, CA.

Haughland, S. W. (1992). The effect of computer software on preschool children's developmental gains. *Journal of Computing in Childhood Education, 3,* 15–29.

Hickman, C. (1994). *KidPix, Version 2.* Novato, CA: Broderbund Software.

Hubert, D. (2005). The Flat Stanley Project and other authentic applications of technology in the classroom. In R. A. Karchmar, M. H. Mallette, J. Kara-Soteriou, & D. J. Leu (Eds.), *Innovative approaches to literacy education: Using the Internet to support new literacies* (pp. 121–137). Newark, DE: International Reading Association.

Jonassen, D. H. (2006). *Modeling with technology: Mindtools for conceptual change.* Upper Saddle River, NJ: Pearson Education.

Jones, I. (1994). The effect of a word processor on the written composition of second-grade pupils. *Computers in Schools, 11*(2), 43–54.

Kamil, M. L., Intrator, S., & Kim, H. S. (2000). Effects of other technologies on literacy and learning. In M. L. Kamil, P. B. Mosenthal, P. D. Pearson, &

R. Barr (Eds.), *Handbook of reading research* (Vol. 3, pp. 771–788). Mahwah, NJ: Erlbaum.

Kinzer, C. K., (2005). The intersection of schools, communities, and technology: Recognizing children's use of new literacies. In R. A. Karchmar, M. H. Mallette, J. Kara-Soteriou, & D. J. Leu (Eds.), *Innovative approaches to literacy education: Using the Internet to support new literacies* (pp. 65–82). Newark, DE: International Reading Association.

Kinzer, C. K., Cammack, D. W., Labbo, L. D., Teale, W. H., & Sanny, R. (2006). Using technology to (re)conceptualize pre-service literacy teacher education: Considerations of design, pedagogy, and research. In M. C. McKenna, L. D. Labbo, R. D. Kieffer, & D. Reinking (Eds.), *International handbook of literacy and technology* (Vol. 2, pp. 211–233). Mahwah, NJ: Erlbaum.

Kuhn, M. R., & Stahl, S. A. (2006). More than skill and drill: Exploring the potential of computers in decoding and fluency instruction. In M. C. McKenna, L. D. Labbo, R. Kieffer, & D. Reinking (Eds.), *International handbook of literacy and technology* (Vol. 2, pp. 295–301). Mahwah, NJ: Erlbaum.

Labbo, L. D. (1996). A semiotic analysis of young children's symbol making in a classroom computer center. *Reading Research Quarterly, 31*, 356–385.

Labbo, L. D. (2000). 12 things young children can do with a talking book in a classroom computer center. *The Reading Teacher, 53*(7), 542–546.

Labbo, L. D. (2003). The symbol-making machine: Examining the role of electronic symbol making in children's literacy development. In J. C. Richards & M. C. McKenna (Eds.), *Integrating multiple literacies in K–8 classrooms: Cases, commentaries, and practical applications* (pp. 10–17). Mahwah, NJ: Erlbaum.

Labbo, L. D. (2004, April). Author's computer chair [Technology in Literacy department]. *The Reading Teacher, 57*(7), 688–691. Available at *www.readingonline.org/electronic/elec_index.asp?HREF=/electronic/RT/4-04_column/index.html*.

Labbo, L. D. (2005a). Moving from the tried and true to the new: Digital Morning Message. *The Reading Teacher, 58*(8), 782–785.

Labbo, L. D. (2005b). Fundamental qualities of effective Internet literacy instruction: An exploration of worthwhile classroom practices. In R. A. Karchmar, M. H. Mallette, J. Kara-Soteriou, & D. J. Leu (Eds.), *Innovative approaches to literacy education: Using the Internet to support new literacies* (pp. 165–179). Newark, DE: International Reading Association.

Labbo, L. D. (2005c). Books and computer response activities that support literacy development. *The Reading Teacher, 59*(3), 288–292.

Labbo, L. D., & Ash, G. E. (1998). Supporting young children's computer-related literacy development in classroom centers. In S. Neuman & K. Roskos (Eds.), *Children achieving: Instructional practices in early literacy* (pp. 180–197). Newark, DE: International Reading Association.

Labbo, L. D., Eakle, A. J., & Montero, K. M. (2002, May). Digital language experience approach: Using digital photographs and creativity software as a language experience approach innovation. *Reading Online, 5*(8). Available at *www.readingonline.org/electronic/elec_index.asp?HREF=labbo2/index.html*.

Labbo, L. D., & Kuhn, M. R. (2000). Weaving chains of affect and cognition: A young child's understanding of CD-ROM talking books. *Journal of Literacy Research, 32*, 187–210.

Labbo, L. D., Phillips, M., & Murray, B. (1995–1996). "Writing to read": From inheritance to innovation and invitation. *The Reading Teacher, 49*(4), 314–321.

Labbo, L. D., & Reinking, D. (1999). Negotiating the multiple realities of technology in literacy research and instruction. *Reading Research Quarterly, 34*, 478–492.

Labbo, L. D., Sprague, L., with Montero, M. K. & Font, G. (2000, July). Connecting a computer center to themes, literature and kindergarteners' literacy needs. *Reading Online, 4*(1). Available at *www.readingonline.org/electronic/elec_index.asp?HREF=labbo/index.html.*

Lankshear, C., & Knobel, M. (2003). *New literacies: Changing knowledge and classroom learning.* Philadelphia: Open University Press.

Leu, D. J. (2000). Literacy and technology: Deictic consequences for literacy education in an information age. In M. L. Kamil, P. B. Mosenthal, P. D. Pearson, & R. Barr (Eds.), *Handbook of reading research* (Vol. 3, pp. 745–772). Mahwah, NJ: Erlbaum.

Leu, D. J. (2002). The new literacies: Research on reading instruction with the Internet. In A. E. Farstrup & S. J. Samuels (Eds.), *What research has to say about reading instruction.* (pp. 310–336). Newark, DE: International Reading Association.

Leu, D. J., & Leu, D. D. (2000). *Teaching with the Internet: Lessons from the classroom* (3rd ed.). Norwood, MA: Christopher-Gordon.

Lewis, C., & Fabos, B. (2005). Instant messaging, literacies, and social identities. *Reading Research Quarterly, 40*, 470–501.

McKenna, M. C. (1998). Electronic texts and the transformation of beginning reading. In D. Reinking, M. C. McKenna, L. D. Labbo, R. D. Kieffer (Eds.), *Handbook of literacy and technology: Transformations in a post-typographic world* (pp. 45–59). Mahwah, NJ: Erlbaum.

McKenna, M. C. (2002). Phonics software for a new millennium. *Reading and Writing Quarterly, 18*, 93–96.

McKenna, M. C. (2006). Introduction: Trends and trajectories of literacy and technology in the new millennium. In M. C. McKenna, L. D. Labbo, R. D. Kieffer, & D. Reinking (Eds.), *International handbook of literacy and technology* (Vol 2. pp. 1–18). Mahwah, NJ: Erlbaum.

McKenna, M. C., Cowart, E., & Watkins, J. W. (1997, December). *Effects of talking books on the reading growth of problem readers in second grade.* Paper presented at the meeting of the National Reading Conference, Scottsdale, AZ.

McKenna, M. C., Reinking, D., & Labbo, L. D. (1997). Using talking books with reading-disabled students. *Reading and Writing Quarterly, 13*, 185–190.

McKenna, M. C., Reinking, D., Labbo, L. D., & Kieffer, R. D. (1999). The electronic transformation of literacy and its implications for the struggling reader. *Reading and Writing Quarterly, 15*, 111–126.

McKenna, M. C., & Shaffield, M. L. (2002, May). *Creating electronic books and documents for poor decoders.* Paper presented at the meeting of the International Reading Association, San Francisco, CA.

Miller, S. D. (2003). How high- and low-challenge tasks affect motivation and learning: Implications for struggling learners. *Reading and Writing Quarterly, 19*, 39–57.

Morrell, E. (2002). Toward a critical pedagogy of popular culture: Literacy development among urban youth. *Journal of Adolescent and Adult Literacy, 46*, 72–77.

My first incredible amazing dictionary (CD-ROM). (1995). New York: Dorling Kindersley Multimedia.

Neuman, S. B., & Roskos, K. (1992). Literacy objects as cultural tools: Effects on children's literacy behaviors in play. *Reading Research Quarterly, 27*, 202–225.

Papert, S. (1980). *Mindstorms*. New York: Basic Books.

Peters, J. M. (1996). Paired keyboards as a tool of Internet exploration of 3rd grade students. *Journal of Educational Computing Research, 14*, 229–242.

Pressley, M. (2006). *Reading instruction that works: The case for balanced teaching.* (3rd ed.). New York: Guilford Press.

Purcell-Gates, V. (2004). Foreword. In J. M. Wood *Literacy online: New tools for struggling readers and writers.* (pp. v–viii). Portsmouth, NH: Heinemann.

Reinking, D. (1994). *Electronic literacy.* (Perspectives in Reading Research No. 4, National Reading Research Center). Athens: University of Georgia Press.

Reinking, D. (1998). Introduction: Synthesizing technological transformations of literacy in a post-typographic world. In D. Reinking, M. C. McKenna, L. D. Labbo, & R. Kieffer (Eds.), *Handbook of literacy and technology: Transformations in a post-typographic world* (pp. xi–xx). Mahwah, NJ: Erlbaum.

Reinking, D., Labbo, L. D., & McKenna, M. C. (2000). From assimilation to accommodation: A developmental framework for integrating digital technologies into literacy research and instruction. *Journal of Reading Research, 23*, 110–122.

Reinking, D., & Watkins, J. (2000). A formative experiment investigating the use of multimedia book reviews to increase elementary students' independent reading. *Reading Research Quarterly, 35*, 384–419.

Richards, J. C., & McKenna, M. C. (Eds.). (2003). *Teaching for multiple literacies: Cases and commentaries from K–6 classrooms.* Hillsdale, NJ: Erlbaum.

Sangiuliano, G., (2005). Books on tapes for kids: A language arts-based service-learning project. In R. A. Karchmar, M. H. Mallette, J. Kara-Soteriou, & D. J. Leu (Eds.), *Innovative approaches to literacy education: Using the Internet to support new literacies.* (pp. 13–27). Newark, DE: International Reading Association.

Schwartz, S. (1985). Microcomputers and young children: An exploratory study. In *Issues for educators: A monograph series.* Flushing, NY: School of Education, Queens College, City College of New York.

Shilling, W. (1997). Young children using computers to make discoveries about written language. *Early Childhood Education Journal, 24*, 253–259.

Stauffer, R. G. (1970). *The language-experience approach to the teaching of reading.* New York: Harper & Row.

Turbill, J. (2003, March). Exploring the potential of the digital language experience approach in Australian classrooms. *Reading Online, 6*(7). Available at *www.readingonline.org/international/inter_index.asp?HREF=turbill7.*

Turbill, J., & Murray, J. (2006). Early literacy and new technologies in Australian schools: Policy, research, and practice. In M. C. McKenna, L. D. Labbo, R. D. Kieffer, & D. Reinking, (Eds.), *International handbook of literacy and technology* (Vol. 2, pp. 93–108). Mahwah, NJ: Erlbaum.

Valmont, W. J. (2000). What do teachers do in technology-rich classrooms? In S. B. Wepner, W. J. Valmont, & R. Thurlow (Eds.), *Linking literacy and technology*. Newark, DE: International Reading Association.

Valmont, W. J. (2003). *Technology for literacy teaching and learning*. Boston: Houghton Mifflin.

Vygotsky, L. (1978). *Mind in society: The development of higher psychological processes*. Cambridge, MA: Harvard University Press.

Walmsley, S. A., & Allington, R. L. (1995). Redefining and reforming instructional support programs for at-risk students. In R. L. Allington & S. A. Walmsley (Eds.), *No quick fix: Rethinking literacy programs in America's elementary schools* (pp. 19–44). Newark: DE/New York: International Reading Association and Teachers College Press.

Wild, M., & Braid, P. (1996). Children's talk in cooperative groups. *Journal of Computer Assisted Learning, 12,* 216–321.

Wood, J. M. (2004). *Literacy online: New tools for struggling readers and writers*. Portsmouth, NH: Heinemann.

Yang, S. C., & Liu, S. F. (2005). The study of interactions and attitudes of third-grade students learning information technology via a cooperative approach. *Computers in Human Behavior, 21,* 45–72.

Chapter 16

BEST PRACTICES IN PROFESSIONAL DEVELOPMENT FOR IMPROVING LITERACY INSTRUCTION

Rita M. Bean
Aimee Morewood

> Professional development is not about workshops and courses; rather, it is at its heart the development of habits of learning that are far more likely to be powerful if they present themselves day after day.
>
> —FULLAN (2001, p. 253)

This chapter will:

- Provide background about professional development efforts.
- Describe and synthesize the available research and literature about professional development.
- Discuss several promising approaches to professional development and what they mean for teachers and schools.

Over the years, there have been varying views about what matters in terms of improving student achievement in reading. Researchers have studied the effect of various factors, including programs, materials, group size, and teacher quality. Overwhelmingly, there is evidence that teacher quality matters. In the 1980s, the often cited report *Becoming a Nation of Readers* (National Institute of Education, 1984), called for an emphasis on continuing professional development for teachers. Again, in this millennium, policy makers, educators, and researchers stress the importance of the highly qualified teacher in promoting student success in reading. There tends to be agreement that, even with the most rigorous and comprehensive teacher preparation program, there is a need for ongoing professional development that enables teachers to build on what they know. Just as a physician needs to be current about new treatments or approaches for improving medical care, so too does the teacher, responsible for students' reading performance, need to be knowledgeable about effective reading practices. Concern about the achievement gap that exists between the "haves and have-nots," white students and those of color, those whose primary language is English and those whose primary language is not English, has also generated an interest in how we prepare teachers to teach effectively the neediest of our students.

In this chapter, as mentioned previously, we discuss professional development for improving literacy instruction in schools. We address the following issues and topics:

- *Issues and concerns about professional development.* We begin the chapter with a section that provides necessary background for understanding professional development and the problems that have arisen in development and implementation.
- *Evidence-based Best Practices.* In this section, we discuss what is known about effective professional development, describing and synthesizing the available research and literature. We focus on professional development at the school level rather than activities or experiences that individuals might select for their own personal growth, given what is known about the importance of a well-organized, thoughtful plan for total school improvement. In summarizing this section, we provide a rubric that can be used for thinking about a comprehensive professional development program for literacy instruction.
- *Best practices in action.* We describe more fully several promising approaches and the research that supports them. We also provide examples of some of the initiatives in which these professional development approaches have been used to improve literacy instruction.
- *Reflections and future directions.*

ISSUES AND CONCERNS ABOUT PROFESSIONAL DEVELOPMENT

Guskey (2000) defines professional development as "those processes and activities designed to enhance the professional knowledge, skills, and attitudes of educators so that they might, in turn, improve the learning of students" (p. 16). This definition provides for much variation in how one might envision professional development, e.g., professional reading by individual teachers or groups of teachers, enrollment in university coursework, stand-alone workshop sessions organized by schools or professional organizations, or a mentoring or coaching approach in which teachers receive support and guidance from another educator in implementing literacy instruction, and so forth. The focus on student learning is an important aspect of Guskey's definition, since it emphasizes student outcomes as a key component for evaluating professional development. Too often, however, the evaluation focus has been on the "happiness" or "satisfaction" of participants. At best, those implementing professional development have looked for changes in teacher knowledge, teacher beliefs, or teacher practices.

Criticisms of professional development are many and include concerns about the quality of the ideas or program, partial or incomplete implementation efforts, the unavailability of necessary resources, or the lack of sufficient feedback and follow-up. Too often, there are multiple efforts at one time, and professional development seems fragmented and contradictory to participating teachers. As Fullan (2001) indicates, problems can occur at the initiation, implementation, or institutionalization stages of any new initiative. In other words, there may be difficulties because of the way in which decisions about a specific program or a set of teaching strategies are made, e.g., a specific program mandated by central administration without teacher involvement, or buy-in. Likewise, implementation, if poorly constructed, can be problematic. Finally, even if a thoughtful implementation plan is undertaken, many initiatives are discontinued once the funding is gone or the administrator supporting that initiative has left; in other words, the initiative may not become institutionalized.

The amount of time and resources given to professional development have also been problematic. According to the National Center for Education Statistics (Choy & Ross, 1998), districts have a great deal of control in planning professional development for teachers and, indeed, are responsible for providing much of the professional development that teachers receive; but most of these programs are of a short duration. Yet, according to Learning First Alliance (2000), professional development in literacy can include 80 or more hours per year. Moreover, districts do not spend much on staff development. Killeen, Monk, and Plecki (2002) found that, from 1992 to 1998, districts devoted only 3% of their total yearly expenditures to professional development.

At the same time, even though there is much concern about high-quality teaching in literacy, professional development research has not been a top priority for researchers in the literacy area. Anders, Hoffman, and Duffy (2000) in their extensive review of what they call "inservice" education found that studies on this topic represented less than 1% of the total number of studies reported for reading education. Moreover, in research about classroom practices the primary focus of the experimental studies was the effect of specific programs on students. There was little discussion of teacher practices or beliefs. Nevertheless, there is research on the topic of professional development that is critical for those interested in improving literacy instruction in the schools. In the following section, we discuss those findings.

EVIDENCE-BASED BEST PRACTICES

Anders et al. (2000) identified six salient features that characterized quality inservice: intensive/extensive commitments, monitoring/coaching support, reflection and deliberation, dialogue and negotiation, voluntary participation or choice, and collaboration (p. 730).

The National Reading Panel (2000) also analyzed research about professional development related to reading. Again, because of the limited number of research studies that met their criteria for inclusion in the report, there were only a few conclusions that could be drawn. However, the writers did find that teachers' attitudes and practices did change as a result of professional development, and there was also improvement in student outcomes in several studies. They also concluded that professional development required extensive support and extended periods of training. Their major conclusion was that there is a need for more research in this area, especially research in which the nature of the intervention is described fully.

Research conducted in other subject fields (e.g., math and science) and by those interested in school change have also contributed to the knowledge base about professional development (Desimone, Porter, Garet, Yoon, & Birman, 2002; Sparks & Loucks-Horsley, 1990; Richardson & Placier, 2001; Garet, Porter, Desimone, Birman, & Yoon, 2001). Researchers have addressed questions about content, processes, context, and possible effects on teacher knowledge, teacher practices, and student outcomes.

Results of these various efforts have enabled researchers to tentatively identify "best practices" in professional development. The characteristics that are often cited as important are an emphasis on content (teachers need to know the subject that they are teaching and how students learn it); the importance of active in-depth learning opportunities that occur over time; teacher leadership in schools; and the collective participation of teachers from the same schools, grades, or departments (Desimone et al., 2002). These are similar to the six features identified by Anders et al. (2000), except for the emphasis on content.

In a recent document published by American Educational Research Association (2005, p. 4), four points were made about critical elements to include in any professional development effort; they are:

1. Professional development should focus on the subject matter teachers will be teaching.
2. Teachers' learning opportunities should be aligned with real work experiences, using actual curriculum materials and assessments.
3. Adequate time for professional development should be provided: there should be extended opportunities to learn, with an emphasis on observing and analyzing students' understanding of the subject matter.
4. School districts should have reliable systems for evaluating the impact of professional development on teachers' practices and student learning.

Taylor, Pearson, Peterson, and Rodriguez (2005) discussed a large-scale study in which they examined a professional development program based on the CIERA School Change Framework as a means of improving reading instruction in 13 schools over the course of 2 years. The authors focused on two important bodies of scholarship to build their school reform initiative: knowledge about curriculum and pedagogy in literacy (what should be taught and how) and research about how to improve schools in general (e.g., effective processes for professional development). These researchers found that when more elements of their CIERA School Change Framework were implemented, the greater the growth in students' reading achievement. Also, there was a larger effect size when data were examined across 2 years rather than 1 year. These findings highlight the necessity of sustained and long-term efforts. As Taylor et al. (2005) state: "Growth in students' reading scores as well as change in classroom teaching practices came in small increments from one year to the next. There were no quick fixes and no magic bullets in these schools —only hard work, persistence, and professional commitment" (p. 64). Taylor et al. (2005) also addressed the importance of sustained collaborative work with colleagues that includes reflection and a commitment to collective problem solving, facilitation and support for teachers (both internal and external), and strong curricular leadership. They also highlighted the importance of refocused classroom instruction based on data about student achievement.

The evidence is clear: schools need to think about content, context, and process factors when developing professional development programs (National Staff Development Council [NSDC], 2001). They need to recognize that professional development is hard work; it takes time; and it requires a total school commitment if it is to ultimately improve teacher practices and student achievement. In the paragraphs below, we expand upon each of the elements identified by the NSDC (2001).

Content

As mentioned previously, a focus on content is an important variable in an effective professional development program. In other words, professional development must be built on a well-conceptualized in-depth framework of just what teachers need to know about what they are required to teach *and* how students learn this content. In the literacy area, there are many resources that school district personnel can consult in developing their notions of what content to consider in any professional development program. Research in the field of literacy provides excellent information about both curricular and instructional elements. Those responsible for professional development can consult work from the *National Reading Panel* (2000), the *Report of the National Academy of Education on Preventing Reading Difficulties in Young Children* (Snow, Burns, & Griffin, 1998), *Handbook of Reading Research* (Kamil, Mosenthal, Pearson, & Barr, 2000); *Handbook of Early Literacy Research* (Neuman & Dickinson, 2001), *Handbook of Research on Teaching the English Language Arts* (Flood, Lapp, Squire, & Jensen, 2003); and *Reading Next: A Vision for Action and Research in Middle and High School Literacy* (Biancaros & Snow, 2004). A set of well-articulated, consistent, and systematic standards of content about literacy curriculum and instruction that teachers need to know and understand in order to provide instruction for all students in their schools is essential.

Context

Fullan (2001) has written extensively about the importance of context considerations. What works for one school may not work for another. Factors such as teacher experiences and abilities, their receptivity and attitude toward change, needs of the students, and the resources that are available in the school must be taken into consideration when planning professional development programs. Moreover, successful staff development programs must emphasize the importance of teacher buy-in, that is, teachers must understand and value the need for a specific focus. The leadership that exists in the school is indeed important and provides the foundation for change (Marzano, 2003).

Lieberman and Miller (1986) indicate that there is a need for both a top-down and bottom-up approach. In other words, there is a need for the district or school to set the general direction or vision for the literacy program and to communicate expectations to the teachers. At the same time, effective programs must involve teachers in establishing specific goals and in designing the staff development activities that lead toward achieving the goals.

This is an important proposition: both the needs of the school and the needs of individual teachers need to be taken into consideration in planning for effective professional development. According to Odden and Anderson (1986), "When instructional strategies, which aim to improve the skills of individuals, were successful, they had significant effects on schools as organizations. When school strategies, which aim to improve schools as organizations were successful, they had significant impacts on individuals" (p. 585). This proposition requires that structural support, such as scheduling, effective and supportive leadership, resources, and recognition for participants, be taken into consideration when building and implementing programs.

Processes

Researchers are consistent in their recommendations that the best professional development is job-embedded; that is, it is closely related to the classroom work of the teacher. There is a need for collegial work that requires programs of some duration and opportunities for feedback in which teachers can think about and reflect on what they are learning and implementing in their classrooms. The importance of using student data to determine priorities and to monitor progress is another essential element.

As mentioned previously, there are many approaches or processes that can be used. However, seldom is one used in isolation. Teachers may attend workshops to learn about a specific set of literacy strategies and the theory and research underlying these "best practices." However, in a well-developed program, other forms of support are provided. Joyce and Showers (2002), in their classic work, indicated that, in addition to becoming knowledgeable about a specific educational endeavor and understanding the rationale or theory for it, the following types of support strengthen learning and the potential for transfer of what is learned into classroom practice. These components include:

- Demonstration—Teachers get to see the strategies, appropriately implemented, either by watching videotapes or actual teaching in classrooms.
- Practice—Teachers practice what they are learning, with their peers, or with small groups of students. Such opportunities enable them to experience what it means to use specific strategies or approaches, problems that may arise, etc. Such practice should be accompanied with feedback that enables teachers to get answers to their questions about actual implementation and assistance in how to implement a specific skill or strategy.
- Coaching—Teachers receive in-classroom support from their peers that enables them to solve problems or answer questions that arise when they are teaching in their own classrooms. (pp. 73–74)

Joyce and Showers (2002) estimate that, when a combination of components is employed, especially peer coaching, there is likely to be a real and strong transfer to classroom practice by 95% of the participants (p. 78).

We used the results of research about professional development to develop a rubric that can be used to think about a school's current professional development program for improving literacy and as a means of making modifications or adaptations in that program (see Figure 16.1). The major categories in this rubric are Content, Collaboration and Sense of Community in the School, Duration and Amount of Time, Active Learning, and Application and Feedback Opportunities.

CURRENT PRACTICES IN PROFESSIONAL DEVELOPMENT

We now discuss four approaches to professional development that seem to show promise in terms of improving classroom instruction in literacy and ultimately in enhancing student achievement. We choose these four, given their potential and the emerging research that supports efforts using these approaches. Each of them would fit effectively into a comprehensive school professional development program, although none is sufficient in itself. The four approaches are literacy coaching, communities of learners, teacher research, and technology (i.e., online courses or experiences).

Literacy Coaching

Coaching is a growing phenomenon in schools today. The concept of coaching, however, is not a new one. As early as the 1980s, Joyce and Showers were studying the power of coaching, specifically peer coaching,

FIGURE 16.1. Professional development for promoting school change in literacy.

Rating Scale

3	High implementation
2	Partial implementation
1	Not an established part of the comprehensive professional development program or plan

Content

Score	Description
	School has a coherent set of literacy goals and standards across grade levels that can be used as a framework to guide professional development. (Standards for literacy performance at each grade level have been identified, e.g., what should students know and be able to do?)
	Curriculum and instructional practices are evidence-based.
	Curriculum and instructional practices set high expectations for all students.
	Curriculum and instructional practices to be emphasized relate to the needs of students as determined by multiple sources of data.
	Opportunities enable teachers to gain in-depth understanding of the theory and research underlying practices (why something is important).

____/15 Total

Collaboration and Sense of Community in the School

Score	Description
	Teachers have a decision-making role in how they learn what is necessary to achieve the goals set by the school.
	Teachers in school are given opportunities to work together, interact, network, learn from one another (in grade-level meetings, study groups, etc.) in a collegial manner.
	There is a focus on the value of parents and their role as members of the community.
	Teachers are recognized for the work that they do.
	Teachers have opportunities to serve as leaders in planning and implementing professional development activities.

____/15 Total

(*continued*)

FIGURE 16.1. (*continued*).

Duration and Amount of Time

Score	Description
	Professional development programs are ongoing (over time) and give teachers opportunities to develop in-depth understanding of the content to be learned.
	Teachers have ample contact hours related to the professional development topic.

_____/6 Total

Active Learning

Score	Description
	School makes use of new technologies in helping teachers achieve their professional goals.
	Teachers use information from their classrooms and students in their professional development work (e.g., they use data, review student work samples, do lesson study).
	Activities are differentiated according to teacher needs and styles of learning.
	Teachers have opportunities to participate in inquiry-based activities that necessitate critical thinking, application, and reflection.
	Teachers have opportunities to practice what they are learning with their peers or in small groups.

_____/15 Total

Application and Feedback Opportunities

Score	Description
	Teachers have opportunities to apply what they are learning in their classrooms.
	Teachers interact with their peers about their experiences in a risk-free environment and reflect on what they are doing.
	Feedback is geared toward supporting and guiding teacher practices (it is not evaluative).
	Teachers are recognized for what they know and do.
	Teachers have opportunities to self-evaluate and reflect on their work (video, reviewing student work, discussing observations, etc.)

_____/15 Total

as a means of improving the quality of professional development. At the present time, we find coaches at all levels, K–12, in various subjects (math, science, reading), and indeed there seem to be various models or approaches as to how coaches should function. Some coaching models (e.g., Cognitive Coaching; Costa & Garmston, 2002) stress the importance of the processes used. The emphasis is on reflection, helping teachers to move from where they are to where they want to be. Others, such as Content-Focused Coaching (Staub & West, 2003), define the coach as one who has a deep understanding of the content and knows how to plan lessons in collaboration with teachers to assist them in becoming more proficient in their instructional practices and to assure that all students achieve the planned goals. Some writers have a broader view of the coaches' role—that is, coaches, in collaboration with the principal and others, must build instructional capacity in the school. These coaches, called "change" or "capacity" coaches (Neufield & Roper, 2003), work with principals and teachers in creating a culture or climate that promotes total school reform. Also, coaches can be internal to the school or come from an external partner or resource. Some school-level reform projects, such as Success for All or the aforementioned CIERA School Change Framework, incorporate a facilitator or coach to support teachers' efforts. In LEADERS (Literacy Educators Assessing and Developing Early Reading Success) Bean (2004) discusses a reading initiative that, in addition to regularly scheduled workshops held over a year's time, included "coaches" or facilitators from the university assigned to schools to assist teachers in their implementation efforts. These facilitators helped with assessment, modeled, co-taught, observed, and provided feedback. They communicated with principals about the program and discussed ways in which they and the university could facilitate program implementation. Because the instructional practices were consistent with those of the school district, the coaches were readily accepted by teachers as an important source of support.

Although coaching can be viewed in several different ways, most educators who write about coaching agree on several key points. One is that the coach does not serve in an evaluative role; rather, the coach is there to support the work of the teacher in a collaborative manner. Second, the role of the literacy coach is to provide the job-embedded professional development that will enhance literacy instruction in the schools and ultimately improve student achievement. The belief is that the presence of a coach will enable teachers to apply more successfully "best" practices in their classrooms. Third, coaches must have the interpersonal and communication skills that enable them to work effectively with other adults. They must have an understanding of adult learning and its relevance to their work (Position Statement, International Reading Association, 2004).

One well-known coaching program is the Collaborative Coaching and Learning Initiative (CCL) in the Boston public schools. In this initiative, small groups of teachers work together to gain a better understanding of literacy strategies. The initiative runs on an 8-week cycle in which a group of teachers is involved with strategies that incorporate Readers Workshop and Writers Workshop. During these cycles, coaches model the strategies, teachers practice and conference about the strategies, and support is given throughout teacher implementation. Involvement in the initiative is expected, and leadership opportunities are ample (Boston Plan for Excellence, 2002–2003). One of the major initiatives in which literacy coaching is designated as an important aspect of professional development is Reading First, the instructional component of No Child Left Behind. Given that this federally funded program is being implemented nationwide, there is much attention given to literacy coaching, what it is, and how it should function in the schools.

At the present time, there is little evidence that coaching will have the impact on practice and student achievement that those investing in it expect. It certainly exemplifies many important elements of effective professional development: it is job-embedded, provides modeling and feedback to teachers, and assists them in implementing effective practices in their classroom. At the same time, coaching presents many challenges, some of which are related to the culture of isolation that exists in schools (e.g., teachers do not understand the role of coaches or their own role as learners). Likewise, coaches may be asked to assume duties that reduce their effectiveness; that is, they may be required to evaluate teachers or serve as quasi-administrators. However, any professional development plan has obstacles to address. The coaching model, if implemented effectively, may enable a school to become a community of learners.

Given the emphasis on and the extent to which coaching is being implemented in schools, there should be much information forthcoming as to what constitutes effective coaching. Moreover, there should be more empirical evidence about whether coaching does make a difference in teacher practices and in student achievement.

Communities of Learners

As mentioned previously, researchers who study professional development mention, time and time again, the importance of teachers working collegially as an effective means of effecting change in schools. Hord (2004) organized the characteristics of professional learning communities into five themes or dimensions: "supportive and shared leadership, shared values and vision, collective learning and application of learning, supportive conditions, and shared practice" (p. 7). Indeed, in the National Board of Professional Teachers Standards (NBPTS; 1993), one of the major propositions is that teachers are members of learning communities. That is, they work collaboratively with others in the school, evaluating school programs and the allocation of school resources; they are knowledgeable about resources, school, and community, and work with their peers and with parents.

What is important is that collegiality, or a sense of community, be established in an authentic manner. Fullan and Hargreaves (1996) indicate, for example, that when certain activities are imposed on teachers (e.g., engaging in coaching, planning, or consulting), the result may not be a positive one. Such contrivance may be necessary in initial phases, but generally administrators need to foster and facilitate a collegial atmosphere over time. Building a community of learners requires establishing a culture where teachers are involved in decision making and problem solving and where norms of conduct are established by teachers and administrators together (Marzano, 2003). In other words, when teachers, with support from school administration, meet on a regular basis to share and network, there is the opportunity to build a community in which there is an atmosphere of trust, respect, and the commitment to providing the best possible educational program for students. Indeed, Little (1990) indicates that the best form of collaboration is what she calls "joint work" (planning together, team teaching, action research, sustained mentoring or peer coaching). Teachers are committed to achieving a specific set of goals and to a vision of what effective literacy instruction is. Professional development, if planned effectively, can contribute to this sense of collegiality. Such professional development must be coherent (related to the goals and curriculum) and sustained. Processes by which such coherent professional development can be established include curriculum study and development, study groups or book clubs, and effective use of grade-level or content focus groups. Communities of learners can also be established in partnership with universities, for example, the establishment of professional development schools where preservice teachers, experienced teachers, administrators, and university faculty work together to develop a strong literacy program (Darling-Hammond, Bullmaster, & Cobb, 1995; Jett-Simpson, 1992). Although any of the aforementioned approaches can assist in building a community of learners, we describe the use of curriculum development and study groups or book clubs in greater detail below.

Curriculum Development Efforts

Certainly, when teachers work together with administrators to set goals, build curriculum, and develop evaluative tools that measure the effects of various curricula, they can develop a strong sense of community and caring for the organization. Such work must be focused on the ultimate outcomes expected—that is, student achievement. Au (2002) describes a process that she uses when working in schools to develop effective elementary school reading programs. First, as the leader of the proposed work, she seeks input from teachers about their current thinking about literacy instruction. She then asks teachers to generate descriptions of skilled readers at the various grade levels. Based on the descriptions, teachers, with student input, set goals and determine activities and experiences to achieve those goals. An assessment system, with benchmarks, is developed, and teachers are asked to establish conditions to support instruction. Finally, teachers summarize and evaluate student learning. Assessment is an important aspect of the process model; teachers analyze student results frequently and use them to reflect on the curriculum and necessary changes.

Teacher Study Groups

Cramer, Hurst, and Wilson (1996) provide the following definition of a study group: "a collaborative group organized and sustained by teachers to help them strengthen their professional development in areas of common interest. In these groups, teachers remain in charge of their own independent learning but seek to reach personal goals through interaction with others" (Cramer et al., 1996, p. 7). One of the important aspects of study groups is that teachers are to devise their own learning path. In other words, once the group identifies a topic or problem it wishes to investigate, each teacher may select a personal learning goal related to the broad topic chosen, thus becoming a specialist in that particular area. At times, members of these study groups get together during school hours, but often they meet after school in more informal settings.

Raphael, Florio-Ruane, Kehus,George, Hasty, and Highfield (2001) describe the Teacher Learning Collaboration (TLC), a network that encompasses three teacher study groups—Literacy Circle, Book Club *Plus*, and the Literacy Circle Study Group. According to Raphael et al. (2001), these study groups consisted of volunteer teachers who assumed different roles and responsibilities based on their experiences and interests. The framework, based on a student book club, was then applied to a Master's level course and was continued after completion of the course because of the members' sustained interest in the area of struggling readers.

Although school personnel can decide upon the questions and topics to be studied and the material to be read, various materials are available to assist schools in their efforts. For example, the International Reading Association has published modules on a variety of topics (e.g., struggling readers, beginning reading, comprehension, adolescent literacy, English-language learners) that can be used to facilitate study group efforts. Although each module contains materials that are specific to the topic, all modules include a facilitator's guide and a reading reflection journal.

A variation on the study group, book clubs are organized by teachers as a means of increasing their knowledge about current trends and an opportunity to discuss this information and how to use it in their own classrooms. According to a survey conducted by the National Reading Research Center (Commeyras & DeGroff, 1998), teachers read research journals anywhere from one to five times a year; they also read books; however, the most commonly read materials were magazines such as *Instructor*, *Mailbox*, and *Teaching K–8*. Book clubs help extend teachers' reading habits into journals and books that contain current research in their field.

The advantages of study groups or book clubs are several: they allow teachers to focus on individual goals while interacting on a larger scale with professional colleagues; they reduce the sense of isolation so common in schools; they increase the opportunity for problem solving, inquiry, and reflection; and they acknowledge the teacher as a learner (Flood & Lapp, 1994; Lefever-Davis, Wilson, Moore, Kent, & Hopkins, 2003). Swan (2002), in a presentation at the West Virginia Reading Assocation, shared this comment from a study group participant: "The casual sharing during study group has increased my confidence, and this has been reflected in my willingness to try out new ideas in the classroom."

Establishing a community of learners, although strongly supported by research and the literature on school change, can be problematic because of the current structure and schedule in schools: there is little time available for professional development. Schools, however, have come up with creative ways to find time for professional development. For example, some schools have hired substitutes, during which time teachers meet or observe other teachers; others have established days on which there is an early-release for students, giving teachers an opportunity to meet. Teachers in other schools have given up their daily planning period, accumulating the time so that it can be used later for an extended period of professional development.

Teacher Research

The term *teacher research* has several different meanings, but it does serve as an umbrella term to describe a wide range of activities that can be traced to the "action" research notion of the 1950s and 1960s (Cochran-Smith and Lytle, 1990, p. 3). According to Cochran-Smith & Lytle (1990), teacher research is "systematic, intentional inquiry by teachers" (p. 2). Often teachers become involved in such research because of their work in a graduate program at a college or university. But teacher research can be school-initiated and -sustained also, especially if teachers and university-based faculty are working together. Richardson and Anders (2005) indicate that "many teachers appear to enjoy and value action research and inquiry as a means of examining their practice" (p. 207). The potential of teacher research has led several organizations to support and sanction teacher research through direct funding. For example, both the National Council of Teachers of English and the International Reading Association provide grants for teachers wishing to undertake action research.

A strength of this approach to professional development is that it allows for teachers to feel a sense of empowerment, given their active involvement. It further increases the opportunity for teachers to become decision makers, problem solvers, and school leaders. What is truly exciting is that research gives teachers opportunities to interact with ideas or data that promote reflection and thinking. Most importantly, it can have an immediate impact on teaching practices and perspectives (Lytle, 2000; Van Tassell, 2002). Further, if done collaboratively, such research can have great impact on the school as a whole.

Teacher research, however, can be problematic. Often the results are limited to local context, and therefore its professional quality may be difficult to ascertain (Lytle, 2000). Also, if conducted solely by individuals acting alone, the results may have limited usefulness; that is, they may not provide the type of coherent, systematic conclusions needed to achieve long-range organizational goals. Finally, teacher research is time-consuming and costly, and therefore its implementation by larger groups may be difficult. Nevertheless, for those individuals who undertake such efforts, teacher research has the potential to increase their sense of self-efficacy and professionalism.

Online Courses or Experiences

The growing potential and the spreading use of online computer experiences for increasing teacher knowledge and enhancing teacher practices oblige us to include a discussion of it in this chapter. As explained by the Web-Based Education Commission (2000):

> The Internet is making it possible to connect teachers to each other, giving opportunities for mentoring, collaboration, and formal and informal on-line learning. Traditional one-size-fits-all professional development workshops are giving way to a new, more teacher-centered, self-directed model of teacher learning. Through the Internet, teachers have access to high quality on-line professional development opportunities beyond what the local school or district is able to offer." (p. 60)

In addition to the use of online or distance-education courses at universities, such experiences are being incorporated into the professional development plans of various states as a means of improving literacy instruction in schools. Florida, for example, offers a series of online experiences that is designed to help teachers improve reading instruction for learners in grades pre-K through 12 (Zygouris-Coe, Yao, Tao, Hahs-Vaughn, & Baumbach, 2004). The online program, which has been developed with the support of literacy and technology experts, school districts, professional organizations, and teacher educators across Florida, functions as a primary statewide delivery mechanism for improving teaching methods in reading instruction and enables the state to monitor teachers' experiences. The Department of Education in Pennsylvania is studying the potential of using online experiences in its Reading First schools for teachers and administrators as a means of providing consistent, systematic professional development about literacy instruction.

The advantages of providing professional development through technology include the opportunity for teachers to engage in activities at convenient times, at their own pace; as mentioned, it also provides for consistency in content and emphasis. The access to information and flexibility are considered to be the main advantages of online learning. As Owston (1997) observes, "What the Web can offer that traditional media cannot is information that is instantly available, often very up-to-date, worldwide in scope" (p. 31).

At the same time, these online courses have limitations. Edwards, Cordray, and Dorbolo (2000) point out that "the development of distance-education teaching tools . . . requires even greater attention to detail because students are asked to learn on their own" (p. 388). Brown and Green (2003) also indicate that the lack of modeling may be a problem. If the online experiences do not include opportunities for teachers to "see" something and then discuss their understandings, misinterpretations and incomplete learning may be the result. Online efforts are not created equal. Just as some materials or approaches may be better in some contexts than others, so too, are online experiences. Requiring all teachers to participate in the same experiences, regardless of their knowledge base or experience, flies in the face of what is known about effective learning. Further, unless these online experiences include elements of good instruction and adult learning, such as opportunities for questioning, reflection, feedback, and application to classroom practice, they may not live up to the expectations of those who see them as a primary means of improving teacher practices. The use of technology, although a promising practice, must be studied carefully, since the evidence for such professional development is somewhat thin. Ongoing research efforts must be undertaken, especially given the new emphasis on this approach to learning.

REFLECTIONS AND FUTURE DIRECTIONS

Although we have learned a great deal about professional development in the past 10 years, there is still much more to learn, especially about professional development as it relates to literacy instruction. Much of what we know has been gained from the work of researchers who study school change and reform. These theorists and researchers have provided solid evidence about the importance of school culture and collaboration in effecting teacher growth. Indeed, Garmston (2005) states: "Teachers' thoughts, feelings, decisions, and behaviors are influenced more by the culture of the workplace than by their skills, knowledge, and prior or current training. As the work culture of schools changes, so do the schools themselves" (p. x). This powerful statement recognizes the importance of school leadership in professional development. Individual teachers may seek to increase their knowledge and skills through readings, coursework, book clubs, involvement in special initiatives or projects. But if the achievement of all students in a school is to improve, there must be a concerted effort to provide a strong, comprehensive professional development program that is based on a vision of what literacy instruction means for the students in a specific school, and opportunities for teacher choice in how to achieve that vision. This means that many factors need to be in place: strong leadership; a culture in which teachers see themselves as learners working together to improve the literacy of all students in a specific school; and the creation of a professional development program that addresses content, process, and context variables—that is, the program must be tailored to meet the needs of students and teachers in a specific school and yet focused on long-term efforts to improve reading achievement.

We also need to continue research efforts to study professional development. Given the many factors that affect successful professional development, such research will be complex and will require collaborative efforts of researchers interested in the content of literacy curriculum and instruction and those interested in school change and reform.

CONCLUDING COMMENTS

Professional development is an essential element in any school improvement plan. Effective professional development requires schools to attend to content, context, and process variables. It requires a commitment from all involved in the schools. Effective professional development can and should be structured so that it addresses the identified needs of students in a school, that is, it should be based on the available data about student performance. At the same time, it must be responsive to the teachers in the school and their knowledge about literacy instruction and curriculum. The best professional development is that in which schools function in a collaborative, collegial fashion, in which all personnel strive to achieve the set goals for promoting literacy achievement.

ENGAGEMENT ACTIVITIES

1. Using a T-chart, list the most effective professional development you have experienced (on one side) and the least effective professional development you have experienced. With a group of colleagues, compare your charts. Are there similarities? differences?
2. Using the rubric in Figure 16.1, think about the professional development in your school and how it compares to the criteria identified as important for professional development.
3. Interview a principal of a school, using the rubric (of Figure 16.1) and discuss the professional development in his or her school. Write a short summary of how the professional development in that school compares to the criteria identified in the rubric.

REFERENCES

American Educational Research Association. (2005). Research Points. *Teaching teachers: Professional development to improve student achievement* (Vol. 3, Issue 1) [brochure]. Washington, DC: American Educational Research Association.

Anders, P., Hoffman, J., & Duffy, G. (2000). Teaching teachers to teach reading: Paradigm shifts, persistent problems, and challenges. In M. L. Kamil, P. B. Mosenthal, P. D. Pearson, & R. Barr (Eds.), *Handbook of reading research* (Vol. 3, pp. 719–742). Mahwah, NJ: Erlbaum.

Au, K. H. (2002). Elementary programs: Guiding change in a time of standards. In S. B. Wepner, D. S. Strickland, & J. T. Feeley (Eds.), *The administration and supervision of reading programs* (Vol. 3, pp. 42–58). New York: Teachers College Press.

Bean, R. M. (2004). *Reading specialist: Leadership for the classroom, school, and community.* New York: Guilford Press.

Biancarosa, G., & Snow, C. E. (2004). *Reading next: A vision for action and research in middle and high school literacy: A report to Carnegie Corporation of New York.* Washington, D.C.: Alliance for Excellent Education.

Boston Plan for Excellence. (2002–2003). Collaborative Coaching and Learning (CCL). Retrieved November 4, 2005, from *www.bpe.org/text/workwithschools.aspx.*

Brown, A., & Green, T. (2003). Showing up to class in pajamas (or less!): The fantasies and realities of on-line professional development courses for teachers. *The Clearing House, 76*(3), 148–151.

Choy, S. P., & Ross, M. (1998). *Toward better teaching: Professional development in*

1993–94 (NCES No. 98-230). Washington, DC: National Center for Educational Statistics.

Cochran-Smith, M., & Lytle, S. L. (1990). Research on teaching and teacher research: The issues that divide. *Educational Researcher, 19*(2), 2–11.

Commeyras, M., & DeGroff, L. (1998). Literacy professionals' perspectives on professional development and pedagogy: A United States survey. *Reading Research Quarterly, 33*(4), 434–472.

Costa, A. L., & Garmston, R. J. (2002). *Cognitive coaching: A foundation for renaissance schools* (2nd ed.) Norwood, MA: Christopher-Gordon.

Cramer, G., Hurst, B., & Wilson, C. (1996). *Teacher study groups for professional development.* Bloomington, IN: Phi Delta Kappa Educational Foundation. (ERIC Document Reproduction Service No. ED 406371).

Darling-Hammond, L., Bullmaster, M. L., & Cobb, V. L. (1995). Rethinking teacher leadership through professional development schools. *The Elementary School Journal, 96*(1), 87–106.

Desimone, L. M., Porter, A. C., Garet, Yoon, K. S., & Birman, B. F. (2002). Effects of professional development on teachers' instruction: Results from a three-year longitudinal study. *Educational Evaluation and Policy Analysis, 24*(2), 81–112.

Edwards, M. E., Cordray, S., & Dorbolo J. (2000). Unintended benefits of distance-learning technology for traditional classroom teaching. *Teaching Sociology, 28*(4), 386–391.

Flood, J., & Lapp, D. (1994). Teacher book clubs: Establishing literature discussion groups for teachers. *The Reading Teacher, 47*(7), 574–576.

Flood, J., Lapp, D., Squire, J., & Jensen, J. (2003). *Handbook of research on teaching the English language arts,* (Vol. 2). Mahwah, NJ: Erlbaum.

Fullan, M. (2001). *The new meaning of educational change* (3rd ed.). New York: Teachers College Press.

Fullan, M., & Hargreaves, A. (1996). *What's worth fighting for in your school.* New York: Teachers College Press.

Garet, M. S., Porter, A. C., Desimone, L., Birman, B. F., & Yoon, K. S. (2001). What makes professional development effective? Results from a national sample of teachers. *American Educational Research Journal, 38*(4), 915–945.

Garmston, R. (2005). *The presenter's fieldbook: A practical guide* (2nd ed.). Norwood, MA: Chistopher-Gordon.

Guskey, T. (2000). *Evaluating professional development.* Thousand Oaks, CA: Corwin Press.

Hord, S. (Ed.). (2004). *Learning together, leading together: Changing schools through professional communities.* New York: Teachers College Press.

International Reading Association. (2004). *The role and qualifications of the reading coach in the United States* [brochure]. Newark, DE: Author.

Jett-Simpson, M. (1992). *Portrait of an urban professional development school.* San Francisco, CA: American Educational Research Association. (ERIC Document Reproduction Service No. ED351285).

Joyce, B., & Showers, B. (2002). *Student achievement through staff development: Fundamentals of school renewal.* White Plains, NY: Longman.

Kamil, M. L., Mosenthal, P. B., Pearson, P. D., & Barr, R. (Eds.). (2000). *Handbook of reading research* (Vol. 3). Mahwah, NJ: Erlbaum.

Killeen, K. M., Monk, D. H., & Plecki, M. L. (2002). School district spending on professional development: Insights available from national data (1992–1998). *Journal of Education Finance, 28*(1), 25–50.

Learning First Alliance. (2000). *Every child reading: A professional development guide.* Baltimore, MD: Author.

Lefever-Davis, S., Wilson, C., Moore, E., Kent, A., & Hopkins, S. (2003). Teacher study groups: A strategic approach to promoting students' literacy development. *The Reading Teacher, 56*(8), 782–784.

Lieberman, A., & Miller, L. (1986). School improvement: Themes and variations. In A. Lieberman (Ed.), *Rethinking school improvement: Research craft, and concept.* New York: Teachers College Press.

Little, J. (1990). The persistence of privacy: Autonomy and initiative in teachers' professional relations, *Teachers College Record, 91*(4), 509–536.

Lytle, S. L. (2000). Teacher research in the contact zone. In M. L. Kamil, P. B. Mosenthal, P. D. Pearson, & R. Barr (Eds.), *Handbook of reading research* (Vol. 3, pp. 691–718). Mahwah, NJ: Erlbaum.

Marzano, R. J. (2003). *What works in schools: Translating research into action.* Alexandria, VA: Association for Supervision and Curriculum Development.

National Board for Professsional Teaching Standards. (1993). *What should teachers know and be able to do?* Detroit: Author.

National Institute of Education. (1984). *Becoming a nation of readers.* Washington, DC: Author.

National Reading Panel (2000). *Teaching children to read: An evidence-based assessment of the scientific research literature on reading and its implications for reading instruction.* Rockville, MD: National Institute of Child Health and Human Development.

National Staff Development Council. (2001). *Standards for Staff Development, Revised.* Retrieved September 1, 2005, from *www.nsdc.org.*

Neufeld, B., & Roper, D. (2003, June). *Coaching: A strategy for development instructional capacity.* Providence, RI: Annenberg Institute for School Reform.

Neuman, S. B., & Dickinson, D. K. (Eds.). (2001). *Handbook of early literacy research* (Vol. 1). New York: Guilford Press.

Odden, A., & Anderson, B. (1986). How successful state education improvement programs work. *Phi Delta Kappan, 67*(8), 582–585.

Owston, R. D. (1997). The World Wide Web: A technology to enhance teaching and learning? *Educational Researcher, 26*(2), 27–33.

Raphael, T. E., Florio-Ruane S., Kehus M. J., George, M., Hasty, N. L., & Highfield, K. (2001). Thinking for ourselves: Literacy learning in a diverse teacher inquiry network. *The Reading Teacher, 54*(6), 339–350.

Richardson, V., & Anders, P. L. (2005). Professional preparation and development of teachers in literacy instruction for urban settings. In J. Flood and P. L. Anders (Eds.), *Literacy development of students in urban schools* (pp. 205–230) Newark, DE: International Reading Association.

Richardson, V., & Placier, P. (2001). Teachers change. In V. Richardson (Ed.),

Handbook of research on teaching (4th ed., pp. 905–947). Washington, DC: American Educational Research Association.

Snow, C., Burns, S., & Griffin, P. (Eds.). (1998). *Preventing reading difficulties in young children.* Washington, DC: National Academy Press.

Sparks, D., & Loucks-Horsley, S. (1990). Models of Staff Development. In R. Houston (Ed.), *Handbook of research on teacher education* (pp. 234–250). New York: Macmillan.

Staub, F., & West, L. (2003). *Content-focused coaching: Transforming mathematics lessons*: Portsmouth, NH: Heinemann.

Swan, A. L. (2002, November). *Literature study groups: Professional learning, Communities of Learners and Chocolate Cake.* Presentation at the West Virginia Reading Association.

Taylor, B. M., Pearson, P. D., Peterson, D. S., & Rodriguez, M. C. (2005). The CIERA school change framework: An evidence-based approach to professional development and school reading improvement. *Reading Research Quarterly, 40*(1), 40–69.

Van Tassell, M. A. (2002). Getting started on teacher research. In J. M. Irwin (Eds.), *Facilitator's guide* (pp. 20–21). Newark, DE: International Reading Association.

Web-Based Education Commission. (2000, December 19). *The power of the Internet for learning: Moving from promise to practice.* Retrieved October 31, 2005, from *www.ed.gov/offices/AC/WBEC/FinalReport/WBECReport.pdf.*

Zygouris-Coe, V., Yao, Y., Tao, Y., Hahs-Vaughn, D., & Baumbach, D. (2004). Qualitative evaluation on facilitator's contributions to online professional development. Chicago: Association for Educational Communications and Technology. (ERIC Document Reproduction Service No. ED 485072).

Part V

FUTURE DIRECTIONS

Chapter 17

ACHIEVING BEST PRACTICES

Michael Pressley

Readers leave books with generalized understandings of what was read rather than remembering the many details that led to those understandings. So, with this commentary, I share with you my general understandings after reading the contributions to this volume. Of course, these conclusions are not just the product of the content of the book but reflect as well my prior knowledge of reading research and practice (Anderson & Pearson, 1984; Rosenblatt, 1978). These understandings also are not simply cold cognition but rather also represent my interpretation of what I have read, my critical understanding and appreciation of it. So, I anticipate that readers will differ with respect to points of agreement and disagreement with me.

DIVERSE BEST PRACTICES

This is a book filled with commentary by leading researchers about what they regard as the current best practices in reading education. The contributors are diverse in their expertise and interest, with the result that the volume reviews practices that are appropriate for preschoolers but also ones that are intended for high schoolers. There's discussion of early language learning, English second-language reading, alphabetics, phonemic awareness, phonics, development of fluency, vocabulary instruction, comprehension strategies, writing, teacher professional development and teacher education, technology, and assessment issues. That is, conceptually, the book hits many of the major research topics in literacy. I have to stop short of claiming that it covers all of the topics as extensively as they should be covered. For example, while children's literature is highlighted in a number of chapters in this book, there is no chapter that is devoted exclusively to the topic. Given the No Child Left Behind (NCLB) legislation (2002), which completely ignores children's literature, it is especially important that we recognize the critical role of children's literature in reading instruction. After all, this volume is intended for professional development in the United States, with much of professional development currently impacted by the legislation. The topics represented in the volume are the ones that come up often in professional development that teachers are expected to be knowledgeable about, as conceived in the federal law.

This is also true for the substantial commentaries on assessment in this volume, for NCLB demands much more assessment of students than has ever occurred before. The volume touches on many aspects of contemporary thinking about assessment but, as it does so, certainly does not project the message that reading assessment is a settled issue. The challenges and frustrations about assessment come through clearly. That comments about the issue are spread over so many chapters addressing so many areas of reading makes clear that reading assessment is going to require many different reading assessments rather than just one or a few. A strength of much of the thinking in this volume was that assessment was placed in the context of instructional decision making, making clear that reading assessments should tap the literacy tasks students are taught to do, and, in turn, the assessments should inform teaching.

RECENT RESEARCH

Although there were occasional references to research in the first half of the 20th century, most of the research informing this volume was conducted in the past quarter-century. This reflects the recent explosion of research on reading and reading education.

Readers should recognize, however, that some topics and some best practices have been explored much more extensively than others. In fact, there are quite a few practices in this volume that have been explored in only one or a very few studies. Of course, this is inevitable when so much of the work is recent. It takes a while for research studies to accumulate, even in the case of a "hot topic." There are also quite a few practices highlighted in this volume that have never been explored in fully randomized true experiments, which groups such as the National Reading Panel (2000) consider a gold standard with respect to evaluating educational intervention research. Evidence-based best practices in this volume are drawn from professional wisdom integrated with the best available empirical evidence (Allington, 2005). Given this state of affairs, readers should recognize that few of the conclusions offered in the volume are written in stone. Rather, they represent the state of the art and science in 2006, when the chapters were written, and undoubtedly some of the ideas in this volume will enjoy additional support in future studies and some will not.

AUTHORIAL INTERPRETATIONS

In addition to being limited temporally, the findings are limited by the authors who were invited to contribute. These authors definitely came to their task with strong perspectives on the field of literacy, and they did not hesitate to let their perspectives show. Other equally distinguished authors might have offered very different thinking about the topics represented here. What this means is that this volume is an introduction to best practices. If your goal is to improve your teaching of phonics or vocabulary or comprehension instruction or any of the other dimensions of reading considered here, the relevant chapter in this volume can serve as a good start in getting informed. Use it and its references as an entrée to the relevant literature. As you do so, you will encounter many leads to other literature you should read. This is not meant as a criticism of this volume: it would be impossible for a single volume to represent comprehensively what is known about any of the dimensions of reading and reading instruction covered in this survey book. There are a variety of entire books available with respect to virtually every chapter topic covered in this volume. The teacher who wants to improve his or her literacy instruction has a wealth of resources to tap.

MORE THAN ISOLATED PRACTICES

One of the strengths of this volume is that it does not focus simply on isolated best practices but rather provides many portraits of teachers using the practices as part of multidimensional instruction. The many portraits of practice make very clear just how much is involved in teaching literacy. As I reflect on the complexity of excellent reading practice, I find myself asking how it will be possible to produce many more teachers such as the ones depicted in this volume. That wondering comes from an understanding that when a teacher attempts even to improve one dimension of practice, for example, phonics or comprehension strategies instruction, it is often very challenging for the teacher to do so. Although there is attention in this volume to professional development and teacher education, I am not confident at all that it is currently known how to develop teachers who are like the excellent teachers offered as examples in this volume. As researchers are doing more work on individual reading practices, they also need to be working very hard to understand how to develop teachers who can do it all in their classroom. I urge readers of this volume never to lose sight of the fact that teachers of whole reading curricula and whole readers must be developed, that being an excellent teacher of any or a few of the components of reading (e.g., phonics, vocabulary) would never make for excellent reading instruction or stimulate the development of readers who are all they could be. For example, the goal in developing first-grade teachers should be to develop teachers who can stimulate phonemic awareness in students who need it while also beginning to teach comprehension strategies to students who arrive in September already reading chapter books.

DIFFERENTIATED INSTRUCTION

Some attention was devoted to differentiation of instruction in this volume, but my sense is that virtually every topic in the book could be approached from that perspective. I cannot imagine any aspect of reading instruction for which one-size-fits-all instruction would make sense in a classroom. Walk into any elementary classroom, and you will find that students differ vastly in their knowledge and skill of virtually every aspect of reading. To the extent that the issue has been examined carefully, the indications are that learning for all students is likely to be maximized by matching instruction to their capabilities (e.g., Connor, Morrison, & Katch, 2004; Juel & Minden-Cupp, 2000).

Certainly, that is the assumption underlying an instructional model that received considerable support in this volume. There was much urging in this volume for teachers to begin teaching skills by modeling and explaining them, followed by teacher scaffolding of student efforts to use the skill (Duffy, 2003). When teachers scaffold, they monitor carefully how the students are doing, and they adjust their teaching to student needs (i.e., they differentiate instruction). Thus, if a student is struggling, the teacher may reteach the skill entirely. If the student is doing fine, the teacher might encourage the student to stretch the skill—for example, as the student practices using quotations in writing, the teacher might also urge the student to diversify the vocabulary in the text by employing the many synonyms for *said.*

Although many of the authors explicitly or implicitly endorsed this model of skills instruction, what they did not acknowledge was just how challenging it is to become a teacher who models, explains, and scaffolds skillfully (e.g., Pressley & El-Dinary, 1997). Consider that, in order to teach phonics within this model, the teacher must know a great deal about phonics, including alternative ways for teaching a phonics skill when a child does not get it the first time. In fact, the skilled first-grade phonics teacher knows many ways to teach just about every type of phonics understanding. If the teacher is a generally good reading teacher, he or she knows as well many ways to teach the many aspects of all the skills that occur in the first grade. All indications are that to become a very good reading teacher—one who can model, explain, and scaffold in an articulated way the many skills that constitute reading—requires years of practice doing it with diverse students (see Pressley et al., 2003).

One "best practice" that did not get its own chapter but was referenced repeatedly was the commitment to children and teachers learning together. Many of the contributors to this volume believe deeply in cooperative learning and the associated concept of communities of learners. In contrast, there was not a hint in the volume that any good comes from encouraging competition among students. Thus, the motivational positions expressed in the volume were ones consistent with enhancing students' achievement (see Brophy, 2004). Consistent with the Vygotskian framework and the foundational idea of scaffolding, the commitments by chapter authors in this volume focused on figuring out where students are at present and encouraging them to improve from that point. Such motivational stances, completely consistent with the principles of differentiated instruction, also are associated with positive and engaging classrooms. Thus, a consistent instructional message in this volume was that being positive and supportive of children is critical, with the positiveness and support required varying from child to child. Certainly there was not a single showcased teacher who was anything but exceptionally positive in his or her interactions with students, as far as I could tell from reading the many teaching vignettes in this book.

That said, struggling readers received much more attention in this volume than average or superior readers. This, of course, reflects the state of the art and science of reading instruction, which has been much more concerned with students who struggle than those who thrive. Excellent teachers must serve all students well, however, and thus I hope the readers of this volume will think deeply about how the ideas presented here can inform instruction of students who are already doing well, ones who have sailed or are sailing through beginning reading instruction. I make this urging very aware that the NCLB policy has focused attention on the primary-grade years, beginning reading, and struggling beginning readers, in particular, to the exclusion of the rest of elementary and secondary students. Moreover, there has been disproportionate reading research on beginning reading. Given increases in awareness of the literacy education crisis during the secondary years (see Biancarosa & Snow, 2004),

I am hopeful that future editions of this volume will have more to say about developing literacy in older students.

MORE THAN ABOUT READING OF SINGLE PRINTED TEXTS

Although this volume provided some commentary on new literacies that are products of technological advances, I am certain that future editions of this volume are going to have to go much further. With every passing school year, more and more children are spending more and more time with electronic documents of various sorts. The children now in school must learn to be adept in working with such documents but also must be equally competent in working with conventional documents as well. I regularly watch elementary students preparing reports that are informed both by informational texts found in the school library and web-based texts, using the computer to create yet a new document, one that can import elements such as pictures found on the Web or music clips. Across a number of chapters, this volume prompts readers to think about issues of technology and multiple texts, recognizing that at present little is known about how best to develop readers who are technologically savvy and skilled at using multiple texts, each of which has very different characteristics.

THE CLASSROOM TEACHER AS ONE OF A GROUP OF EDUCATORS

There are reminders at several junctures in the volume that the teacher principally responsible for literacy instruction does not work alone or only in the area of literacy. Thus, there are now technology specialists. The role of librarians was touched upon briefly, as was the role of the family. Literacy instruction in the content areas, sometimes offered by a teacher other than the instructor teaching reading and writing, received some discussion. To be an excellent literacy teacher, it is imperative that he or she learn how to interact with a variety of other educators, working with them to promote literacy across the school day and after school. As the roles of libraries, families, technology, and content instruction were touched upon in this volume, it was apparent that these are arenas in which very little really is known at present. More positively, the current literature emphasis in reading instruction certainly is causing more research on how students and teachers interacting with libraries as well as families can boost achievement. Also, that literacy is demanding increasingly more of the school day is requiring that there be harder thinking about how literacy instruction and content-area instruction can be blended and coordinated. For the present, however, all that a volume such as this one can do is alert the readership that these directions are on the radar screen of the literacy research and practice community. What practices will be the best practices with respect to libraries, families, technologies, and learning in the content areas has yet to be worked out. Future editions of this volume will include much more on these critical topics, with likely more emphasis on the homeroom teacher who interacts with multiple other players to accomplish all that needs to be accomplished to craft a complete literacy education for students.

CLOSING COMMENTS

Volumes such as this one are very important. If excellent research is to find its way into classrooms, it is imperative that the literacy research community continue to develop resources such as this one as a means of disseminating researchers' thinking and evidence-based insights. Early in this commentary, I made the point that many best practices have been studied in relatively few investigations. That is the way it is, and I am certain that is the way it will remain, with just a few exceptions. Because of the theoretical interest in phonemic awareness, there have been a dozen experimental studies of that construct in the past quarter-century. Typically, however, researchers, educators, and policy makers are going to have to make decisions on the basis of much less research. The scholar who succeeds in informing well is going to be one who understands research and the practice as investigated but who also understands curricula and instruction as it occurs in actual schools. Such a researcher is capable of crafting new and informative research and reporting it well to all the constituencies who need to know about it, from other scholars reading scholarly journals to educators reading methods texts to policy makers reading briefing reports. The teacher who is excellent and evidence-based also needs to understand the research, at least as depicted in volumes such as this, as well as the curricula and instruction in his or her school. I am confident that there are many teachers determined to be so broadly informed. Ideally, policy makers also would be so broadly informed, with one of the greatest challenges being the preparation of documents that provide clear insight about the full range of evidence-defensible practices (Pressley, Duke, & Boling, 2004) as well as enhanced understanding about the reality of schooling. A book like this one can provide insight; to experience the reality, policy makers must spend more time in schools, thinking about the ideas in volumes such as this one in light of the instruction they find in schools that they believe need improvement. There is hard work ahead as we strive to improve reading education and provide comprehensive literacy instruction for all our students.

REFERENCES

Allington, R. L. (2005). What counts as evidence in evidence-based education. *Reading Today, 3*(3), 16.

Anderson, R. C., & Pearson, P. D. (1984). A schema-theoretic view of basic processes in reading. In P. D. Pearson (Ed.), *Handbook of reading research* (pp. 255–291). New York: Longman.

Biancarosa, G., & Snow, C. E. (2004). *Reading Next: A Vision for action and research in middle and high school literacy: A report to Carnegie Corporation of New York.* Washington, DC: Alliance for Excellent Education.

Brophy, J. (2004). *Motivating students to learn* (2nd ed.). Mahwah, NJ: Erlbaum.

Connor, C. D., Morrison, F. J., & Katch, L. E. (2004). Beyond the reading wars: Exploring the effect of child-instruction interactions on growth in early reading. *Scientific Studies of Reading, 8*, 305–336.

Duffy, G. G. (2003). *Explaining reading: A resource for teaching concepts, skills, and strategies.* New York: Guilford Press.

Juel, C., & Minden-Cupp, C. (2000). Learning to read words: Linguistic units and instructional strategies. *Reading Research Quarterly, 35*, 458–492.

National Reading Panel. (2000). *Teaching children to read: An evidence-based assessment of the scientific research literature in reading and its implications for reading instruction.* (NIH Publication NO. 00-4769). Washington, DC: National Institute of Child Health and Human Development.

No Child Left Behind Act, Public Law No. 107-110, 115 Stat. 1425. (2002). Codified at 20 USCA §§6301 *et seq.*

Pressley, M., Duke, N. K., & Boling, E. (2004). The educational science and scientifically based instruction we need: Lessons from reading research and policymaking. *Harvard Educational Review, 74*(1), 30–61.

Pressley, M., & El-Dinary, P. B. (1997). What we know about translating comprehension strategies instruction research into practice. *Journal of Learning Disabilities, 30*, 486–488.

Pressley, M., Roehrig, A., Raphael, L., Dolezal, S., Bohn, K., Mohan, L., et al. (2003). Teaching processes in elementary and secondary education. In W. M. Reynolds & G. E. Miller (Eds.), *Handbook of psychology: Vol. 7. Educational psychology* (pp. 153–175). New York: Wiley.

Rosenblatt, L. M. (1978). *The reader, the text, the poem: The transactional theory of the literary work.* Carbondale, IL: Southern Illinois University Press.

INDEX

("f" indicates a figure, "t" indicates a table)

Accountability, assessment and, 272, 276–277
Achievement gap, 34–35, 34*f*
Achievement, research on
  balance in literacy curriculum and, 34–35, 34*f*
  literacy development and, 64
Adaptive knowledge, 17
Adequate Yearly Progress (ATP), 11–12
Adolescent students
  engagement activities, 152
  evidence-based best literacy practices and, 129–132, 133*t*–134*t*, 134–135, 135*f*, 136*f*–137*f*, 137, 138*f*, 139–144, 140*f*, 141*f*, 401–402
  example of exemplary instruction with, 145–149
  overview, 127–129, 149–152
  text selection and, 142–143
Alliance for Excellent Education, 151
Alphabet knowledge, English-language learners and, 112–113
Alphabetic code
  English-language learners and, 108–117
  literacy development and, 64
Annotation rubric, 139–142, 141*f*
Art center, 69. see also Centers, classroom
Assessment
  balancing formative and summative reading assessments, 273–274
  of depth and breadth of word knowledge, 193–195
  differentiated instruction and, 316–318
  engagement activities, 279–280
  evidence-based best literacy practices, 18, 23–24, 265–278
  example of in a kindergarten classroom, 70–71
  of fluency, 213–214, 213*t*, 214*f*
  grouping plans using data from, 329
  imbalance in, 265, 269–277, 278
  overview, 264–265, 277–279
  writing instruction and, 254–255, 256*f*, 257, 257*f*, 258*f*, 259–260
Assessment data grouping, 329
Assessments, state, 11–12
Audiobooks, reading-while-listening strategy and, 208
Auditory discrimination, 61
Authentic literacy activities
  overview, 20
  writing instruction and, 247–248
Authentic repeated readings strategy, 210–211
Authenticity, balance in literacy curriculum and, 36–38
Author's chair activity, 336
Automatic knowledge, 246. *see also* Knowledge

Automaticity in reading
  comprehension and, 224–225
  fluency instruction and, 206

B

Background knowledge. *see also* Knowledge
  comprehensive literacy instruction and, 15, 336
  evidence-based best literacy practices, 18, 22
Balance in literacy curriculum. *see also* Literacy curriculum
  comprehensive literacy instruction and, 15
  early-childhood education and, 62
  engagement activities, 50–51
  evidence-based best literacy practices and, 22–23, 36–47, 37*f*, 39*f*, 40*f*
  overview, 30–36, 34*f*, 47
  rethinking, 47–50, 48*f*, 49*f*, 50*f*
Best literacy practices. *see* Evidence-based best literacy practices
Blending skills, 164, 165
Block center, 69. *see also* Centers, classroom
Blogging, 348
Book clubs
  overview, 47
  professional development and, 386–387
  text difficulty and, 42
Bookmark activity, 231–232
Breadth of vocabulary knowledge. *see also* Knowledge
  assessing, 193
  overview, 192

C

Centers, classroom. *see also* Classroom environment
  differentiated instruction and, 319–320
  example of in a kindergarten classroom, 68–70, 74–75
  flexible groups and, 325–326
  technologies and, 358
Choices, student, 253–254
Choral reading, 335
"Classic" Inspiration Project, 255, 256*f*
Classroom discourse, 38
Classroom environment. *see also* Centers, classroom; Explicit instruction
  evidence-based best literacy practices, 18, 19, 22
  example of in a kindergarten classroom, 68–70
  qualities that determine effectiveness of teachers and, 16
  vocabulary instruction and, 183–184
  writing instruction and, 248–250
Classroom instruction
  examples of with struggling readers and writers, 87–99
  struggling readers and, 84–85, 99–100
  supplemental support and, 86–87
Coaching
  professional development and, 380, 383–384
  teachers and, 16
Code emphasis in curriculum. *see also* Decoding skills
  balance in literacy curriculum and, 31
  "Reading Wars" and, 32
Cognate-recognition strategies, 116, 121–122
Cognitive development, 272–273
Collaborative Coaching and Learning Initiative (CCL), 384
Collaborative learning. *see also* Communities of learners
  evidence-based best literacy practices, 22–23
  integrating technologies into curriculum and, 347–349, 364–365
Communication skills, 61–62
Communities of learners. *see also* Collaborative learning
  evidence-based best literacy practices, 401
  professional development and, 384–387
Composition, 47–50, 48*f*, 49*f*, 50*f*
Comprehension. see also Comprehension instruction
  assessing, 271–272

balance in literacy curriculum and, 35, 47–50, 48*f*, 49*f*, 50*f*
comprehensive literacy instruction and, 15
evidence-based best literacy practices, 18, 19, 20
integrating technologies into curriculum and, 363–364
literacy assessment and, 267
National Reading Panel Report (2000) on, 63
preschool language and literacy programs, 65–66
processes involved in, 227*t*
resources for, 360*f*
time for reading in class and, 21
word recognition and, 205
Comprehension instruction. *see also* Comprehension
engagement activities, 237
evidence-based best literacy practices, 226, 227*t*, 228–235, 231*f*, 232*f*
Five-Block Schedule and, 336–337
informational texts, 233–235
overview, 220–221, 235–237
research regarding, 221–226
strategies to include in, 225–226, 230–232, 232*f*, 233*f*
Comprehension Strategy Instruction, 316
Comprehensive framework of literacy instruction
early-childhood education and, 62
overview, 12–13, 14–15
Computers. *see* Technologies
Computers in the classroom. *see* Technologies
Concept knowledge, 35. *see also* Knowledge
Concept-oriented reading instruction, 336–337
Conditional knowledge, 17. *see also* Knowledge
Confidence, technologies and, 351–352
Construction of meaning. *see* Meaning construction
Constructivism, 224
Content-Focused Coaching, 383
Content in professional development programs, 378
Content of curriculum, 40–47, 40*f*. *see also* Curriculum, literacy
Context for assessment, 265–267
Context for writing, 248–250
Context in professional development programs, 378–379
Contextual analysis, 185
balance in literacy curriculum and, 46–47
comprehension and, 222
Control of learning
vocabulary instruction and, 184–185
writing instruction and, 253–254
Cooperative learning opportunities
adolescent students and, 143–144
evidence-based best literacy practices, 401
group instruction and, 329, 330*t*–331*t*
Critical thinking, 15
Culture
adolescent students and, 144
writing instruction and, 247
Curricular control, 39–40
Curriculum, literacy. *see also* Literacy curriculum, balance in
content of, 40–47, 40*f*
fluency instruction and, 206–207
integrating technologies into, 345–352
professional development and, 385–386

D

Daily routines
differentiated instruction and, 333–337, 334*f*
example of in a kindergarten classroom, 71–78
preschool language and literacy programs, 66
Daily schedule
differentiated instruction and, 332–337, 334*f*
time allocated for literacy and, 315–316
Decision making, 15–16
Declarative knowledge, 17
Decoding skills
comprehension and, 222
evidence-based best literacy practices, 160–162

Decoding skills (*continued*)
Five-Block Schedule and, 334
literacy assessment and, 266
Using Words You Know activity, 171–174
word recognition and, 205
Definition map, 190, 191*f*
Demonstration
integrating technologies into curriculum and, 346–347
in professional development, 380
writing theory and, 244–245
Depth of vocabulary knowledge. *see also* Knowledge
assessing, 193–195
overview, 192–193
Descriptive Writing Checklist, 257*f*
Descriptive Writing Rubric, 258f
Development, cognitive, 272–273
Development, literacy
assessing, 272–273
differentiated instruction and, 314–315
early-childhood education and, 57–64
in preschool-age children, 63–64
preschool language and literacy programs, 65–67
Development, oral language
early literacy education and, 63
English-language learners and, 116–117
literacy development and, 64
preschool language and literacy programs, 65–67
writing theory and, 245
Dewey, John, 59–60
Diagnostic assessments, 317
Dialogic reading, 181–182
Dictionary use, 186–187
Differentiated instruction
assessment and, 316–318
comprehensive literacy instruction and, 15
engagement activities, 339–340
evidence-based best literacy practices, 314–318, 400–402
grouping plans, 323–329, 325*t*, 328*f*, 330*t*–331*t*, 331–333, 338*f*
instructional practices, 319–323
overview, 314–315, 337, 339
routine and, 333–337, 334*f*
Digital Language Experience Approach activities (D-LEA)
examples of classroom applications of, 356–357
overview, 351–352
Direct instruction, 222–223, 224
Dramatic play center, 69. *see also* Centers, classroom
Dynamic grouping, 329, 331–333

E

Early-childhood education, 57–64. *see also* Early literacy instruction
Early literacy instruction
early-childhood education and, 57–64
engagement activities, 80
evidence-based best literacy practices, 64–67
example of in a kindergarten classroom, 67–78
historical influences on, 59–61
literacy development and, 63–64
overview, 57–64, 78–80
Editing in writing, 251
Effective literacy instruction, balance in literacy curriculum and, 34–35
Emergent literacy
fluency instruction and, 206
phonemic awareness and, 160
research regarding early-childhood education and, 61–62
vocabulary instruction and, 180–182
Engagement
assessing, 272–273
writing theory and, 244–245
English-language learners
alphabetics instruction and, 108–117
balance in literacy curriculum and, 35
comprehension instruction and, 236
demographics of, 105–106
engagement activities, 123
evidence-based best literacy practices, 117–119, 120*f*, 121–122
learning to read in a second language, 106–108
letter naming instruction and, 112–113
overview, 104–106, 122–123

phonological awareness instruction and, 109–112
policy regarding, 106, 108
technologies and, 349–352
vocabulary instruction and, 114–117, 185, 186–187, 200
word recognition instruction and, 113–114
Environment, classroom. *see also* Centers, classroom
evidence-based best literacy practices, 18, 19, 22
example of in a kindergarten classroom, 68–70
qualities that determine effectiveness of teachers and, 16
vocabulary instruction and, 183–184
writing instruction and, 248–250
Environment, family
preschool language and literacy programs, 66–67
vocabulary and, 180–182
Environment, literacy development and, 58–59
Environment, school
assessment and, 276–277
qualities that determine effectiveness of teachers and, 16
Ethnicity, 247
Evidence-based best literacy practices
achieving, 397–404
adolescent students and, 129–132, 133*t*–134*t*, 134–135, 135*f*, 136*f*–137*f*, 137, 138*f*, 139–144, 140*f*, 141*f*, 144
assessment, 265–278
balance in literacy curriculum and, 36–47, 37*f*, 39*f*, 40*f*
comprehension instruction, 226, 228–235, 231*f*, 232*f*
comprehensive literacy instruction and, 15
decoding skills and, 160–162
differentiated instruction, 314–318
diversity among, 397–398
early-childhood education and, 57–64
engagement activities, 24–25
English-language learners and, 117–119, 120*f*, 121–122
overview, 12–13, 13–14, 17–18
in preschool programs, 64–67
professional development, 376–380
recent research regarding, 398–399
struggling readers and, 83–87, 99–100
teachers and, 15–16
ten best practices, 18–24
vocabulary instruction, 178–195, 184*f*, 187*f*, 189*f*, 191*f*
writing instruction and, 244–248
Explaining in explicit instruction
evidence-based best literacy practices, 400–401
fluency instruction and, 334
overview, 321
Explicit instruction. *see also* Classroom instruction
balance in literacy curriculum and, 38–39, 39*f*
comprehension instruction and, 336
differentiated instruction and, 320
English-language learners, 117–119, 120f, 121–122
explaining in, 321, 334, 400–401
research regarding early-childhood education and, 61
supplemental support and, 86–87
vocabulary instruction and, 179, 190–192, 191f
whole-class instruction and, 323
Expository writing, 252–253

F

Facilitating, 38–39, 39*f*
Family environment
preschool language and literacy programs, 66–67
vocabulary and, 180–182
Family involvement in education
example of in a kindergarten classroom, 78
preschool language and literacy programs, 66–67
Fast Start strategy, 212–213
First grade, 57–64. *see also* Early literacy instruction
Five-Block Schedule, 333–337, 334*f*, 338*f*

Flexible groups, 324–326, 325*f*
Fluency. *see also* Fluency instruction
  assessing, 213–214, 213*t*, 214*f*
  balance in literacy curriculum and, 35
  comprehension and, 221–223
  engagement activities, 216
  evidence-based best literacy practices, 18, 19, 20
  integrating technologies into curriculum and, 363–364
  National Reading Panel Report (2000) on, 63
  overview, 214–216
  research regarding, 214–215
  resources for, 360f
  time for reading in class and, 21
Fluency Development Lesson strategy
  Five-Block Schedule and, 335
  overview, 212–213
Fluency instruction. *see also* Fluency
  evidence-based best literacy practices, 204–214, 213*t*
  literacy curriculum and, 206–207
  principles of, 207–214, 213t
  time allocated for, 316, 334–336
Fluency Oriented Oral Reading, 211–212
Formative reading assessment, 273–274
Funding issues, struggling readers and, 84–85

G

Gender differences, writing instruction and, 247
Genre study activity, 252
GO! Chart activity, 230–231, 231*f*
Goals 2000 Project, 131
Gradual-release model, 20, 321, 322*f*
Grammar instruction, 245–247, 251
Graphic organizers
  adolescent students and, 132
  comprehension instruction and, 230–232, 336
  example of, 135*f*
  overview, 132
  vocabulary instruction and, 186–187, 187*f*
  writing instruction and, 253
Group reading instruction. *see* Small-group reading instruction
Guided Discovery, 165–171
Guided practice, 321

H

High school students
  engagement activities, 152
  evidence-based best literacy practices, 129–132, 133*t*–134*t*, 134–135, 135*f*, 136*f*–137*f*, 137, 138*f*, 139–144, 140*f*, 141*f*, 401–402
  example of exemplary instruction with, 145–149
  overview, 127–129, 149–152
  text selection and, 142–143
High-stakes testing
  assessment and, 272
  English-language learners, 108
  instruction and, 316–318
  writing instruction and, 243–244
Holistic approaches, 32

I

Immersion, writing theory and, 244–245
Implicit instruction, 118
In situ assessments, 273–274
Independent reading
  evidence-based best literacy practices, 18, 20
  text difficulty and, 42–43
  time for in class, 20–21
Individuals with Disabilities Education Act (IDEA), 84–85
Infancy, 57–64
Inferences, 336
Informational texts, 233–235
INSERT notemaking system, 139, 140*f*
Instant messaging, 348
Instruction, classroom. *see also* Explicit instruction
  examples of with struggling readers and writers, 87–99
  struggling readers and, 84–85, 99–100
  supplemental support and, 86–87

Instruction, differentiated
assessment and, 316–318
comprehensive literacy instruction and, 15
engagement activities, 339–340
evidence-based best literacy practices, 314–318, 400–402
grouping plans, 323–329, 325*t*, 328*f*, 330*t*–331*t*, 331–333, 338*f*
instructional practices, 319–323
overview, 314–315, 337, 339
routine and, 333–337, 334*f*
Instruction, early literacy
engagement activities, 80
example of in a kindergarten classroom, 67–78
historical influences on, 59–61
overview, 57–64, 78–80
Instruction, explicit. *see also* Classroom instruction
balance in literacy curriculum and, 38–39, 39*f*
comprehension instruction and, 336
differentiated instruction and, 320
English-language learners, 117–119, 120f, 121–122
explaining in, 321, 334, 400–401
research regarding early-childhood education and, 61
supplemental support and, 86–87
vocabulary instruction and, 179, 190–192, 191f
whole-class instruction and, 323
Instruction, multisource. *see* Multisource instruction
Instruction, reading. *see also* Small-group reading instruction
balance in literacy curriculum and, 40*f*, 45
learning to read in a second language, 106–108
Instruction, whole-class
consequences of, 314
differentiated instruction and, 323–324, 325*t*
integrating technologies into, 346–7
Instructional focus
assessment and, 316–318
"Reading Wars" and, 33
Instructional scaffolding. *see* Scaffolding
Intentional writing instruction, 250–254
International Reading Association, 151, 386–387
Internet. *see* Technologies
Interpretive variability, 224
Intervention, 85
Intonation in reading out loud, 205–206
Invented spelling, 160, 165

K

Keypals, 348
Keyword method, 189, 189*f*
Kindergarten. *see also* Early literacy instruction
comprehension instruction and, 229, 230
early-childhood education and, 57–64
example of literacy-rich instruction in, 67–78
Knowledge
adolescent students and, 133*t*
background, 15, 18, 22, 336
comprehension and, 227t
depth and breadth of, 192–195
evidence-based best literacy practices, 17
Knowledge, background
comprehensive literacy instruction and, 15, 336
evidence-based best literacy practices, 18, 22

L

Langer's Partnership for Literacy, 131
Language arts, balance within, 40*f*, 45
Language conventions, 47–50, 48*f*, 49*f*, 50*f*
Large-motor skills, 61
LEADERS, coaching and, 383
Learning communities. *see also* Collaborative learning
evidence-based best literacy practices, 401
professional development and, 384–387
Learning disabilities, 247
Letter knowledge, 334

Letter naming
English-language learners and, 112–113
literacy development and, 64
preschool language and literacy programs, 65
Literacy block
daily schedule and, 333–337, 334*f*, 338*f*
time allocated for, 315–316
Literacy center, 68–69. *see also* Centers, classroom
Literacy curriculum. *see also* Literacy curriculum, balance in
content of, 40–47, 40*f*
fluency instruction and, 206–207
integrating technologies into, 345–352
professional development and, 385–386
Literacy curriculum, balance in. *see also* Literacy curriculum
comprehensive literacy instruction and, 15
early-childhood education and, 62
engagement activities, 50–51
evidence-based best literacy practices and, 22–23, 36–47, 37*f*, 39*f*, 40*f*
overview, 30–36, 34*f*, 47
rethinking, 47–50, 48*f*, 49*f*, 50*f*
Literacy, defining, 344–345
Literacy, development
assessing, 272–273
differentiated instruction and, 314–315
early-childhood education and, 57–64
in preschool-age children, 63–64
preschool language and literacy programs, 65–67
Literacy, emergent
fluency instruction and, 206
phonemic awareness and, 160
research regarding early-childhood education and, 61–62
vocabulary instruction and, 180–182
Literacy practices, best. *see* Evidence-based best literacy practices
Literacy strategies
adolescent students and, 131–132, 133*t*4*t*, 134, 135*f*, 136*f*–137*f*, 137
assessing, 271–272
comprehension instruction and, 15, 336
evidence-based best literacy practices, 18
metacognition and, 137, 139
Literacy Team, example of, 145–149
Literary aspects, 47–50, 48*f*, 49*f*, 50*f*
Literary coaching, 380, 383–384
Literature Chart, 289–290, 291, 292*f*–293*f*, 294*f*–296*f*, 298*f*–299*f*, 303*f*–308*f*
Literature, children's, 397–398. *see also* Text selection
Literature circles, 326–328, 328*f*
Living Books program, 358
Look–say approach, 32

M

Making Words activity, 165–171, 173–174
Math center, 69. *see also* Centers, classroom
Meaning construction
adolescent students and, 133*t*
comprehensive literacy instruction and, 15
evidence-based best literacy practices, 18, 19–20
fluency instruction and, 206
learning to read in a second language and, 107
Meaning emphasis in curriculum, 32
Metacognition
adolescent students and, 137, 139–142
comprehension and, 222, 223–224
comprehension instruction and, 237
spelling skills and, 246
Middle school students. *see also* Adolescent students
evidence-based best literacy practices, 401–402
overview, 127–129, 149–152
text selection and, 142–143
Mindtools, technologies and, 363
Mnemonic strategies, 188–193, 189*f*, 191*f*
Modeling
balance in literacy curriculum and, 38–39, 39*f*
comprehension instruction and, 228

evidence-based best literacy practices, 400–401
fluency instruction and, 334–335
integrating technologies into curriculum and, 347, 363
overview, 321
strategy instruction and, 134
technologies and, 363
vocabulary instruction and, 182–183, 190
Monitoring, comprehension instruction and, 336
Montessori, Marie, 60
Morphology, 186
Motivation
assessing, 272–273
technologies and, 351–352
Multisource instruction
engagement activities, 309
examples of, 288–290, 291, 292*f*–293*f*, 294*f*–296*f*, 297, 298*f*–299*f*, 300–302, 303*f*–308*f*
overview, 286–288, 302, 309
Multisyllabic word decoding, 162

N

National Assessment of Educational Progress's (NAEP) Oral Reading Fluency Scale, 213–214, 214*f*
National Governors Association, 151
National Reading Panel Report (2000)
on early literacy instruction, 63
evidence-based best literacy practices, 398
National Reading Research Council's on Preventing Reading Difficulties in Young Children, 108
New read strategy, 332
No Child Left Behind Act (NCLB)
assessment and, 278
balance in literacy curriculum and, 44–45
children's literature and, 398
coaching and, 384
funding issues and, 84
overview, 12
Note taking, 234
Number naming, 64

O

Objective data, 13
Office of Educational Research and Improvement (OERI), 150
Online courses, 388–389
Oral language development
early literacy education and, 63
English-language learners and, 116–117
literacy development and, 64
preschool language and literacy programs, 65–67
writing theory and, 245
Oral Reading Fluency (ORF) Target Rate Norms, 213–214, 213*t*
Oral reading strategies, 211–212, 335
Orthographic patterns, 119
Outcomes assessments, 318

P

Paired keyboarding, 348
Paired repeated reading strategy, 208–210
Paraprofessionals, 86–87
Participating role of teachers, 38–39, 39*f*
Pen pals, digital, 348
Performance assessment, 271–272
Performance in repeated readings
fluency instruction and, 335
overview, 210–211
Personnel funding, 85
Philosophy, 59–60
Phonemic awareness
activities to develop, 162–176
balance in literacy curriculum and, 35, 45–46
blending and segmenting and, 164
engagement activities, 176–177
English-language learners and, 109–112
evidence-based best literacy practices, 18, 20, 160–161
Five-Block Schedule and, 334
Making Words activity, 165–171, 173–174
National Reading Panel Report (2000) on, 63

Phonemic awareness (*continued*)
overview, 159–160, 176
rhymes and, 163–164
Using Words You Know activity, 171–174
vocabulary instruction and, 183–184
Word Detectives activity, 174–176
writing and invented spelling and, 165
Phonics. *see also* Phonics instruction
activities designed to aid in understanding, 162–176
balance in literacy curriculum and, 35, 46–47
engagement activities, 176–177
evidence-based best literacy practices, 18, 20, 161–162
literacy assessment and, 266–267
National Reading Panel Report (2000) on, 63
overview, 159–160, 176
resources for, 359*f*
Phonics instruction. *see also* Phonics
evidence-based best literacy practices, 401
"Reading Wars" and, 32
Phonological awareness
English-language learners and, 109–112
Five-Block Schedule and, 334
overview, 109, 159–160
resources for, 359*f*
Phrasing in reading out loud, 205–206
Piaget, Jean, 60–61
Picture aids, 118–119, 120*f*
Picture walks activity, 118
Pleasure, reading for, 19–20
Policy, educational
evidence-based best literacy practices, 403
regarding English-language learners, 106, 108
Positioned skills, 32
Post-it note activity, 231, 232*f*
Practice, in professional development, 380
Predicting strategy
comprehension instruction and, 229, 230–232, 336
informational texts, 234–235
Preschool. *see also* Early literacy instruction
early-childhood education and, 57–64
evidence-based best literacy practices, 64–67
literacy development and, 63–64
overview, 78–80
Preschool, universal
literacy development and, 59
reasons for, 64
Previewing strategy
comprehension instruction and, 230–232
instruction in, 134–135
Print knowledge
Five-Block Schedule and, 334
literacy development and, 64
preschool language and literacy programs, 65
Prior knowledge. *see also* Knowledge
comprehensive literacy instruction and, 15, 336
evidence-based best literacy practices, 18, 22
Problem-solving strategy instruction
balance in literacy curriculum and, 62
contextual analysis and, 185
Procedural knowledge, 17. *see also* Knowledge
Process-oriented reading assessment, 269–271
Processes in professional development programs, 379–380
Product-oriented reading assessment, 270
Professional development
assessment and, 276–277, 278
current practices in, 380, 383–389
engagement activities, 391
evidence-based best literacy practices, 376–380
funding issues and, 84–85
issues and concerns regarding, 375–376, 381*f*–382*f*
overview, 373–374, 390–391
for paraprofessionals, 87
qualities that determine effectiveness of teachers and, 16
Progress-monitoring assessments, 317–318

Project CRISS
  adolescent students and, 151
  overview, 131
Prosody in reading out loud, 205–206

Q

Questioning strategy
  comprehension instruction and, 230–232, 336
  informational texts, 234
Questioning, teacher, 273–274

R

Read-alouds
  comprehension instruction and, 229
  differentiated instruction and, 322
  example of in a kindergarten classroom, 78
  vocabulary and, 181–182
Readers Workshop, 384
Reading Assistant program, 364
Reading First Initiative
  balance in literacy curriculum and, 44–45
  coaching and, 384
  overview, 12
Reading instruction. *see also* Small-group reading instruction
  balance in literacy curriculum and, 40*f*, 45
  learning to read in a second language, 106–108
Reading process
  adolescent students and, 130–131, 133*t*–134*t*
  assessing, 269–271
Reading readiness, 61
Reading skills, assessing, 271–272
"Reading Wars", 31, 32
Reading-while-listening strategy, 207–208
Reciprocal process of reading and writing, 15
Reciprocal teaching
  comprehension instruction and, 232–233, 336–337
  technologies and, 350
Reflective knowledge, 17
Reliable data, 13
Repeated readings strategy
  authentic, 210–211
  fluency instruction and, 335
  overview, 208–209
  paired, 208–210
Rereading strategy, 331–332
Research, literacy, 61–62
Response to literature, 40*f*, 43
Rhymes
  phonemic awareness and, 163–164, 165
  Using Words You Know activity, 171–174
Routines, daily
  differentiated instruction and, 333–337, 334*f*
  example of in a kindergarten classroom, 71–78
  preschool language and literacy programs, 66

S

Scaffolding
  balance in literacy curriculum and, 38–39, 39*f*
  comprehension and, 224
  evidence-based best literacy practices, 18, 20, 400–401
  fluency instruction and, 211–212
  meaning emphasis in curriculum, 32
  overview, 321, 322f
  picture aids as, 118
  read-alouds and, 181–182
Schedule, daily
  differentiated instruction and, 333–337, 334*f*
  time allocated for literacy and, 315–316
School environment
  assessment and, 276–277
  qualities that determine effectiveness of teachers and, 16
Science center, 69. *see also* Centers, classroom
Screening assessments, 317
Secondary School Principals Association, 151

Secondary students
  engagement activities, 152
  evidence-based best literacy practices, 129–132, 133*t*–134*t*, 134–135, 135*f*, 136*f*–137*f*, 137, 138*f*, 139–144, 140*f*, 141*f*, 401–402
  example of exemplary instruction with, 145–149
  overview, 127–129, 149–152
  text selection and, 142–143
Segmenting skills, 164, 165
Self-evaluation
  overview, 274–276
  writing instruction and, 249
Self-talk, 245
Shared storybook reading. *see* Read-alouds
Sight word reading
  balance in literacy curriculum and, 46–47
  English-language learners and, 119
  picture aids and, 119
Silent reading, 229–230
Skill-based instruction, 40*f*, 41, 62
Small-group reading instruction
  comprehension instruction and, 232–233
  consequences of, 314
  differentiated instruction and, 324–326, 325*t*
  example of in a kindergarten classroom, 71, 75–76
  Five-Block Schedule and, 337
  integrating technologies into, 346–347
Social-constructivism, 22–23
Social contexts for learning, 144
Social interactions, 245
Sociocognitive theory, 345–346
Sociodramatic play, 357
Socioeconomic status, 180–182
Sound discrimination, 110–112
Speech development, 245
Speech recognition software, 364
Speech synthesizer software, 351
Spelling instruction
  Five-Block Schedule and, 334
  resources for, 359*f*
  technologies and, 351
  writing instruction and, 245–247
Standards, state
  examples of, 303*f*–308*f*
  instruction and, 316–318
  pressure that goes along with, 11–12
  writing instruction and, 243–244
www.Starfall.com, 358
Strategic Literacy Initiative, 131
Strategic Reading Initiative, 151
Strategies, literacy
  adolescent students and, 131–132, 133*t*4*t*, 134, 135*f*, 136*f*–137*f*, 137
  assessing, 271–272
  comprehension instruction and, 15, 336
  evidence-based best literacy practices, 18
  metacognition and, 137, 139
Stress in reading out loud, 205–206
Striving Readers Grant Program, 151
Struggling readers
  engagement activities, 101
  evidence-based best literacy practices, 83–87, 99–100, 401–402
  examples of exemplary instruction with, 87–99
  technologies and, 349–352
  time for reading in class and, 21
Study groups, 386–387
Subject-matter emphasis, 40*f*, 43–45
Summarizing, 336
Summative reading assessments, 273–274
Supplemental support, 86–87
Sustained silent reading, 229–230, 236
Systematic data, 14

T

Teacher Learning Collaboration (TLC), 386
Teacher-reader groups, 233
Teacher research, 387–388
Teachers
  as decision makers, 15–16
  evidence-based best literacy practices, 402–403
  qualities that determine effectiveness of, 16
  questioning by, 273–274
  struggling readers and, 84–85
  writing instruction and, 248

Teachers' roles, 38–39, 39*f*
Teaching, reciprocal
comprehension instruction and, 232–233, 336–337
technologies and, 350
Technologies
comprehension instruction and, 232–233
defining literacy and, 344–345
engagement activities, 365–366
evidence-based best literacy practices, 18, 19, 23, 402
examples of classroom applications of, 352–358, 353*f*, 355*f*, 359*f*–361*f*, 361–364
integrating into the literacy curriculum, 345–352
overview, 364–365
professional development and, 388–389
resources for, 359*f*–361*f*
for special populations, 349–352
text genres and, 41–42
writing instruction and, 246, 254, 260
Tempo in reading out loud, 205–206
Testing, high-stakes
assessment and, 272
English-language learners and, 108
instruction and, 316–318
writing instruction and, 243–244
Text difficulty, 40*f*, 42–43
Text genres
adolescent students and, 128
balance in literacy curriculum and, 40*f*, 41–42
writing instruction and, 252
Text selection
adolescent students and, 129, 142–143
evidence-based best literacy practices, 18, 19, 21–22
literature circles and, 326–327
multisource instruction and, 289
Text structure, 230–232, 336
The Hungry Thing (Slepian and Seidler, 1967), 163–164
Thematic integration, 356
There's a Wocket in My Pocket (Seuss, 1974), 163
Think-alouds
comprehension instruction and, 229
writing instruction and, 336
Thinking Reader Program, 349–350
Time for reading in school, 20–21
Transactional strategies, 224, 336–337
overview, 139

U

Using Words You Know activity, 171–174

V

Valid data, 13
Visual memory, 64
Visual skills, 61, 64, 130–131, 336
Vocab-O-Gram activity, 197, 197*f*
Vocabulary. *see also* Vocabulary instruction
balance in literacy curriculum and, 35
comprehension instruction and, 221–223, 230–232, 336
English-language learners and, 107, 114–117
evidence-based best literacy practices, 18, 19, 20, 21–22
informational texts, 234
National Reading Panel Report (2000) on, 63
resources for, 359*f*–360*f*
writing instruction and, 246–247
Vocabulary instruction. *see also* Vocabulary
comprehension and, 222–223
contextual analysis, 185, 188–193, 189*f*, 191*f*
control of learning and, 184–185
dictionary use and, 186–187
emergent literacy and, 180–182
engagement activities, 198
evidence-based best literacy practices, 178–195, 184*f*, 187*f*, 189*f*, 191*f*
example of exemplary instruction in, 195–197, 196*f*, 197*f*
graphic organizers and, 187–188, 187*f*

Vocabulary instruction (*continued*)
- guidelines for, 179
- overview, 197–198
- phonemic awareness and, 183–184
- resources for, 198–200

Voice-onset timing (VOT)
- English-language learners and, 110
- overview, 110–111

Vygotsky, Lev, 245

W

Whole-class literacy instruction
- consequences of, 314
- differentiated instruction and, 323–324, 325*t*
- integrating technologies into, 346–347

Whole language approach
- balance in literacy curriculum and, 31
- "Reading Wars" and, 32

Wide Reading strategy
- fluency instruction and, 211–212
- overview, 182, 185

Word bank activity, 332
Word Detectives activity, 174–176
Word-level processing, 221–223
Word meaning, 114

Word recognition
- comprehension and, 205, 221–223
- English-language learners and, 113–114
- evidence-based best literacy practices, 18
- Five-Block Schedule and, 334
- time for reading in class and, 21

Word study strategy, 332
Word Walls, 194
Word Work instruction, 316, 334
Word Writing CAFÉ, 259–260
Wordplay, 183–184
WriteOutLoud program, 358

Writing instruction
- assessment and, 254–255, 256*f*, 257*f*, 258, 258*f*, 259–260
- context for writing and, 248–250
- differentiated instruction and, 332
- engagement activities, 261
- evidence-based best literacy practices, 244–248, 248–255, 256*f*, 257, 257*f*, 258*f*, 259–260
- examples of, 76–77, 87–99
- Five-Block Schedule and, 336
- integrating technologies into curriculum and, 348, 363
- intentional, 250–254
- overview, 243–244, 260
- phonemic awareness and, 165
- preschool language and literacy programs, 66
- resources for, 360*f*–361*f*
- time allocated for, 316

Writing theory, 244–245

Writing workshop
- coaching and, 384
- example of, 251
- examples of with struggling readers and writers, 88, 92
- group instruction and, 326
- technologies and, 363

Z

Zone of proximal development, 22